W9-DJJ-376

LITERARY HISTORY
OF THE
UNITED STATES

CONTRIBUTORS

RANDOLPH G. ADAMS
CARLOS BAKER
RICHARD P. BLACKMUR
BRAND BLANSHARD
HAROLD BLODGETT
DAVID BOWERS
SCULLEY BRADLEY
HENRY SEIDEL CANBY
WILLIAM CHARVAT
GILBERT CHINARD
HENRY STEELE COMMAGER
ALEXANDER COWIE
MALCOLM COWLEY
MERLE CURTI
RALPH H. GABRIEL
MAXWELL GEISMAR
ERIC F. GOLDMAN
GORDON S. HAIGHT
HAROLD F. HARDING
ARTHUR PALMER HUDSON
EVERETT L. HUNT
THOMAS H. JOHNSON
HOWARD MUMFORD JONES
ADRIENNE KOCH
JOSEPH WOOD KRUTCH
LEWIS LEARY
HARRY T. LEVIN
TREMAINE MC DOWELL
LUTHER S. MANSFIELD
F. O. MATTHIESSEN
H. L. MENCKEN
JOHN C. MILLER
KENNETH B. MURDOCK
ALLAN NEVINS
HENRY A. POCHMANN
J. H. POWELL
CARL SANDBURG
TOWNSEND SCUDDER
ODELL SHEPARD
HENRY NASH SMITH
ROBERT E. SPILLER
WALLACE STEGNER
GEORGE R. STEWART
WALTER F. TAYLOR
HAROLD W. THOMPSON
STITH THOMPSON
WILLARD THORP
FREDERICK B. TOLLES
CARL VAN DOREN
JOHN D. WADE
DIXON WECTER
GEORGE F. WHICHER
STANLEY T. WILLIAMS
LOUIS B. WRIGHT
MORTON D. ZABEL

LITERARY HISTORY OF THE UNITED STATES

Editors

ROBERT E. SPILLER · WILLARD THORP

THOMAS H. JOHNSON · HENRY SEIDEL CANBY

Associates

HOWARD MUMFORD JONES · DIXON WECTER

STANLEY T. WILLIAMS

REVISED EDITION IN ONE VOLUME

1959

THE MACMILLAN COMPANY · NEW YORK

Revised Edition, 1953

PRINTED IN THE UNITED STATES OF AMERICA

FOURTH PRINTING, 1959

ACKNOWLEDGMENT

PERMISSION to quote copyrighted material is acknowledged to publishers and authors as follows: Albert & Charles Boni, Inc.—*Collected Works of Ambrose Bierce*, 1909–1912; Doubleday & Company, Inc.—*The Octopus,* by Frank Norris, copyright, 1901, by Doubleday & Company, Inc., and *The Responsibilities of the Novelist,* by Frank Norris, copyright, 1901, 1902, 1903, by Doubleday & Company, Inc.; Harcourt, Brace & Company, Inc.—*Collected Poems 1909–1935,* by T. S. Eliot, copyright, 1936, by Harcourt, Brace & Company, Inc.; *Essays Ancient and Modern,* by T. S. Eliot, copyright, 1936, by Harcourt, Brace & Company, Inc., *The People, Yes,* by Carl Sandburg, copyright, 1936, by Harcourt, Brace & Company, Inc., and *Criticism in America: Its Function and Status,* by Joel E. Spingarn, copyright, 1924, by Harcourt, Brace & Company, Inc.; Harper & Bros.—*Mark Twain: A Biography,* by Albert Bigelow Paine (1929), and *The Mysterious Stranger,* by Mark Twain (1916); Harper & Brothers and Edward C. Aswell as Executor—*The Web and the Rock,* by Thomas Wolfe (1937, 1938, 1939); Harvard University Press—*Literary Pioneers: Early American Explorers of European Culture,* by Orie W. Long (1935); Henry Holt & Company, Inc.—*Collected Poems of Robert Frost,* copyright, 1930, 1939, by Henry Holt & Company, Inc., copyright, 1936, by Robert Frost, and *Chicago Poems* by Carl Sandburg, copyright, 1916, by Henry Holt and Company, Inc., copyright, 1943, by Carl Sandburg; Houghton Mifflin Company—*Mont Saint Michel and Chartres,* by Henry Adams, copyright, 1905, by Henry Adams, *The Education of Henry Adams,* by Henry Adams, copyright, 1918, by the Massachusetts Historical Society, *Letters of Henry Adams,* ed. Worthington C. Ford, copyright, 1930, 1938, by Worthington C. Ford, *The Life of George Cabot Lodge,* by Henry Adams, copyright, 1911, by Houghton Mifflin Company, *Journals of Ralph Waldo Emerson,* ed. Edward W. Emerson and Waldo Emerson Forbes, *Outlines of Cosmic Philosophy,* by John Fiske, and *Some Imagist Poets,* by Amy Lowell; International Publishers, Inc.—the introduction to *Proletarian Literature in the United States,* by Joseph Freeman, 1935; Alfred A. Knopf, Inc.—*Not Under Forty,* by Willa Cather, copyright, 1936, by Willa Cather, *Imaginary Interviews,* by André Gide, 1944, and *Prejudices:*

Fourth Series, by H. L. Mencken, 1924; Little, Brown & Company—*The Complete Poems of Emily Dickinson,* ed. Martha Dickinson Bianchi and Alfred Leete Hampson, 1924, 1929, 1930, 1936, 1937; The Macmillan Company—*Collected Poems,* by Vachel Lindsay, 1925, *Collected Poems,* by Edwin Arlington Robinson, 1937, and *The Autobiography of William Allen White,* 1946; The *Nation*—"Individualism and the American Writer," by Newton Arvin, Oct. 14, 1931; *Poetry,* Chicago—the article "Private Experience and Public Philosophy," by Philip Rahv and William Phillips, *Poetry,* May, 1936; Princeton University Press—*The Poetical Works of Edward Taylor,* ed. Thomas H. Johnson, copyright, 1939, Rockland Editions, copyright, 1943, Princeton University Press; *Publishers' Weekly* and Lovat Dickson—"The American Novel in England," *Publishers' Weekly,* Oct. 29, 1938; Charles Scribner's Sons—*Gondola Days,* by F. Hopkinson Smith, 1897, and *This Was a Poet: Emily Dickinson,* by George F. Whicher, 1937; University of California Press—*Singing for Power,* by Ruth M. Underhill, copyright, 1938, by the Regents of the University of California; The Viking Press, Inc.—*A Story Teller's Story,* by Sherwood Anderson, 1924; Yale University Press—*Collected Essays,* by William Graham Sumner, 1934, *Notes While Preparing Sketch Book, etc., by Washington Irving,* ed. Stanley T. Williams, 1927.

Also acknowledgment is made to Mrs. Millicent Todd Bingham for permission to quote brief passages from *Letters to Emily Dickinson,* ed. Mabel Loomis Todd, 1931; to John Dos Passos to quote from *The Big Money!,* copyright, 1933, 1934, 1935, 1936, by John Dos Passos; to the editors of *Fortune* magazine to quote from the article on Thoreau, in the May, 1944, issue; to the Ralph Waldo Emerson Memorial Association and the Widener Library of Harvard University for the use of manuscripts of Ralph Waldo Emerson; to the Committee on Higher Degrees in the History of American Civilization, Harvard University, to quote brief passages from the MS *Billy Budd,* by Herman Melville; to the Library of Harvard University to quote from the Howells papers, Jan. 31, 1902, and from the Ticknor Letter Books, May 10, 1851; also to the Henry E. Huntington Library and Art Gallery to quote from the letters of Harriet Beecher Stowe; to The Executive Council of the Modern Language Association of America to quote from *The English Language in America,* by George Philip Krapp, 1935; to Mrs. Dorothy Pound and Yale University Press to quote from *Make It New,* by Ezra Pound, 1935; and to G. P. Putnam's Sons for "Herman Melville: Adventurer," preprinted by them with permission of the editors in *A Man's Reach,* ed. Thomas H. Johnson, copyright, 1947, by G. P. Putnam's Sons.

PREFACE

Each generation should produce at least one literary history of the United States, for each generation must define the past in its own terms. A redefinition of our literary past was needed at the time of the First World War, when the *Cambridge History of American Literature* was produced by a group of scholars. It is now needed again; and it will be needed still again.

At mid-point, the twentieth century may properly establish its own criteria of literary judgment; indeed, the values as well as the facts of modern civilization must be examined if man is to escape self-destruction. We must know and understand better the recorders of our experience. Scholars can no longer be content to write for scholars; they must make their knowledge meaningful and applicable to humanity. As our part of that task, the editors, associates, and contributors have undertaken and completed this work.

Such a history could be the work of one or a few hands, or it could be a collaboration of many. But the United States, in its life of less than two centuries, has produced too much literature for any one man to read and digest. Its literary history can therefore be best written by a group of collaborators, whatever the risk of differences of perspective or opinion.

Those who have joined in this undertaking are historians and critics rather than specialists in a narrow sense. Their contributions are related to one another within a frame rather than separately composed essays. Each member of our company has a proportional share in the whole enterprise rather than an exclusive interest in his part of it.

The drawing of the design and the assignment of chapters took a year of conferences in which every point was discussed to a satisfactory conclusion. Seven men took part in this planning: the four editors and the three associates. Each of the additional forty-eight contributors had at hand a detailed outline of the entire work and a statement of basic principles before he agreed to write. Upon his acceptance, he was asked to meet, either individually or in group conferences, with the editors and associates and with the authors of allied chapters, and discuss the problems presented by his assignment. Three years were given to the writing; two more, to the editing and publishing. During this period each of the three editors who had undertaken major tasks of detail was granted a year of freedom from professional duties in order to give full time to the work, and in some instances contributors received grants-in-aid. All the bibliographical essays were written by one editor in close collaboration with the authors of relevant chapters.

A genuine collaboration requires some sacrifice of the individual in the interest of the group. The authorship of each chapter is given on pp. 1403–1406, but the chapters are unsigned in the text. Many of them have been substantially revised in order to fit them into the larger plan, and parts of some have been lifted and incorporated elsewhere. The editors have themselves written many chapters and have supplied necessary links; but individual opinions and styles have not been altered in substance. The result is, they believe, a coherent narrative, with valuable differences on individual points. Principles of orthography in quotations have been left to the judgment of the respective contributors.

The almost ideal conditions which made this procedure possible were created by The Macmillan Company and the Rockefeller Foundation, with supplementary aid from the American Council of Learned Societies, the American Philosophical Society, and the institutions with which several of the editors were connected—Swarthmore College, Princeton University, the University of Pennsylvania, and the Lawrenceville School. The disruptions of the war and postwar eras, far from presenting handicaps, have stimulated interest by emphasizing the need for cultural redefinition.

It would be impossible to make specific acknowledgment of indebtedness to the scholars who indirectly contributed to this work. In some instances, the debt was immediate and personal, but more often it took the form of dependence upon the great body of critical, historical, and analytical studies that the past quarter of a century has produced. The mere listing of names and books here or in footnotes would be meaningless. The bibliographical essays, which attempt to be critical both in their selection and in their arrangement of entries, must serve as confession of obligation on almost every point. There would be little reason for attempting again the task which the *Cambridge History* undertook for its generation were it not for the pioneering work of such historians as F. L. Pattee, A. H. Quinn, W. B. Cairns, P. H. Boynton, and V. L. Parrington; the stimulation of scholarship by these and other such teachers as Norman Foerster, J. B. Hubbell, R. L. Rusk, and H. H. Clark; the bibliographical work of E. E. Leisy, Gregory Paine, and their associates; the invigorating perceptions of such critics as W. C. Brownell, John Macy, Stuart P. Sherman, Van Wyck Brooks, and Edmund Wilson; and the specific investigations of a host of careful scholars.

The entire text of this book was prepared specifically for it under individual contracts with contributors for their respective parts of a single overall plan.

THE SECOND EDITION

A NEW edition of *Literary History of the United States* after five years and ten thousand copies suggests a few comments and reflections. As the possibility of reducing the text from two volumes to one was anticipated when the work was first planned, the form and pagination of the first edition have not been altered except in the correction of errors of fact or detail where they have been detected. For most such alterations, the editors are gratefully indebted to their readers.

The original plan of the book, including omissions for which the editors have been admonished and critical opinions for which they have been challenged, has therefore been kept intact. LHUS is the creative work of a group of scholars who will never be assembled again. Any extensive revision would have to be total, and the time has not yet come for that. Most of the critics who read it consecutively have found that, whatever other faults it may have, it is a solid whole. More than perhaps in any similar undertaking, the collaborators in LHUS really collaborated. The book they have written tells a single and unified story.

A few changes have been made in format and some new material has been added. In the listing of chapters, the titles of those which were designed to supply information about the history of thought and of the instruments of culture have now been distinguished from those which deal more directly with literature by being set in italics. The master plan of the work may thus be seen more clearly, it is hoped, as a literary history of the United States rather than as a history of American literature. The view of literature as the aesthetic expression of the general culture of a people in a given time and place was, from the start, an axiom in the thinking of the editors and their associates. Rejecting the theory that history of any kind is merely a chronological record of objective facts, they adopted an organic view of literature as the record of human experience and of its history as the portrait of a people, designed from the curves of its cultural cycles and the colors of its rich and unique life. LHUS is one kind of history of the United States.

The brief "Postscript" chapter has been added, not to provide a full literary history of the period 1945–1953 as a thing apart, but to carry some of the themes and motives of the larger story, already developed in the earlier chapters, forward past the century's mid-point and in this way to round out the account of the second literary "renaissance."

The new bibliographical essay has been designed for the general reader rather than for the scholar. It does not attempt, even in part, what the separate bibliographical volume does thoroughly. Some time in the future that volume too may be carried forward in time by the use of supplementary essays, but it also is too much of a single work to lend itself readily to partial revision. The two parts of LHUS, text and bibliography, still belong together.

May, 1953

CONTENTS

VOLUME I

ADDRESS TO THE READER

THE literary history of this nation began when the first settler from abroad of sensitive mind paused in his adventure long enough to feel that he was under a different sky, breathing new air, and that a New World was all before him with only his strength and Providence for guides. With him began a different emphasis upon an old theme in literature, the theme of cutting loose and faring forth, renewed under the powerful influence of a fresh continent for civilized man. It has provided, ever since those first days, an element in our native literature, whose other theme has come from a nostalgia for the rich culture of Europe, so much of which was perforce left behind.

It is not surprising that our own writers in the first three centuries of New World history were more often purveyors of this nostalgia than recorders of the warmth of the American imagination kindling in novel scenes. They believed that their mission was to be importers and middlemen for America of this European culture. They encouraged nostalgia, even while spreading civilization, and they were often insensitive to the effect upon the imagination of the novel experiences developing upon this continent with extraordinary rapidity and force.

Yet the literature of the new country was to be shaped more by a hope for the future than by a clinging to the past. Observers from across the seas have noted from the beginning the buoyancy of our writing, its richness in spiritual conflicts, carried in such great writers as Poe and Melville, and in such moderns as William Faulkner, Ernest Hemingway, and Thomas Wolfe, to the bounds, and sometimes beyond the bounds, of neuroticism. They have been impressed by the vigorous self-assertion, expressed in the lesser men as naïve pride. The slow emergence of an articulate racial mixture—a race of races, as Whitman called it—had deeply interested them, for this was an experience not known in Europe since the Roman Empire; and they have seen that the remark of Michel Guillaume Jean de Crèvecœur, one of our most sympathetic immigrants, was true: English dogs after two or three generations in the new land became in habits and experience American; and so it was with men and with literature.

The first historians of American literature wrote of it as if they were describing transplanted English flowers and trees. A later school of historians discovered its democratic, psychological, and economic differentiations; but in their zeal for argument and their eagerness to establish our originality, they often left unemphasized the timeless values in our writing. The Emersons, the Mark Twains, the Whitmans emerged from the criticism of these historians with new depths of national significance; the Poes, the Hawthornes, and all writers who were primarily artists, and whose merits often did not depend upon the peculiar circumstances of American history, were less adequately estimated.

The time has now come, and the materials of research and criticism are available, to strike a balance between those who protested against European dominance and those who did not. To draw a new and truer picture of our literary tradition is the intention of the chapters that follow.

2

It is quite possible, and indeed necessary, to write of American literature in terms of its European, and especially its British, sources. That was the way in which Longfellow viewed our literature, the way in which Howells seems to have felt that it could be best understood. It was the approach of teachers, critics, and historians in general until the 1920's. From the academic point of view, American literature was simply a hoped-for extension of the great literature of the English-speaking peoples. And so it is; and such a history, as far as it goes, is entirely valid. Even the radical Walt Whitman insisted that in this new continent we should absorb, not discard, our European past. We could not discard it, if we willed to do so. The progenitors of our literature are in a European and usually in an Anglo-Saxon past. Chaucer, Shakespeare, the folk ballads, the great religious literature of the English seventeenth century, are as deep in our ancestral strain as in the genealogy of modern British writing. The English eighteenth century, English romanticism, the English novel of character, and all later and vital English literature, have a family resemblance to ours, and a family influence, with which any other source for the American imagination outside our own terrain is by comparison weak indeed. A history of American literature exclusively in terms of democracy or the frontier is no less false than a history of American writing regarded as a colonial extension. There is a blending of elements in our culture which is inevitable in a newspaper editorial or in *John Brown's Body* or the *Song of Myself*.

Obviously, our literature is a *transported* European culture, bringing with it the richness of its sources in the classical world, the Middle Ages, and the

Renaissance. Obviously, the roots of our literary culture reach down into British literature which itself has absorbed so long and so much. Yet it is equally true that our literature is a *transformed* culture. It has been written in a new continent, and under conditions definitely and impressively different in the vast majority of instances from the circumstances of Great Britain, or of Europe in general. Slowly, yet inevitably, it has found its own accent, as has American speech. But the divergence has been much greater than that between American and British habits in the use of the English language, because literature is speech made expressive of values, and from the very beginning the values, the expectations, the experience of life in America have been different, with a difference that would continue to increase were it not for the influence of America upon Europe, now making itself strongly felt.

Progress, for example, as a concept may have little general validity; but whether we call it progress, or change, or development, increasing power and vitality are extraordinarily characteristic of the American nineteenth century with which so much of this book is concerned. Never has nature been so rapidly and so extensively altered by the efforts of man in so brief a time. Never has conquest resulted in a more vigorous development of initiative, individualism, self-reliance, and demands for freedom. Never have the defeats which preceded and accompanied this conquest of nature led to more surprising frustration, decadence, sterility, and dull standardization. All this is in American literature, and the causes of both our successes and our failures are implicit, and often explicit, in our early national books. James Fenimore Cooper, for us, is more significant than Sir Walter Scott, although he only rarely equals Scott as a novelist. Melville and Whitman mean more to an American, and are more revealing for our own times, than Thackeray and Wordsworth.

The mobility of the Americans throughout their history has been another transforming factor in their life, and therefore in their literature. They moved across a continent, and continue to move, from habit as much as necessity. And although their speech is English and their political and social organization largely Anglo-Saxon they have assimilated millions whose cultural background was not English at all. Tradition in America is not the same as tradition in Europe. Our national tradition has been acquired by study and by imitation as often as by childhood inheritance of an environment. Thus the relation of what is called the American way of life—which really means the American way of thinking and feeling—to the national unity is extremely important. Our national unity does not and cannot depend upon blood or upon inherited tendencies. Thus very naturally our literature, which is a record of our experience, has been deeply, often subconsciously, aware of its responsibility in the making of a nation from a complex of peoples in voluntary union. It has been an inquiring, an exploratory, literature from the beginning—asking questions of the New World, challenging the effects of sudden release and expansion upon the spiritual nature, delighting in adventure, whether along the Indian borders or on the Mississippi or in the trek across the continent, easily elated in a Whitman, easily depressed in a Hawthorne or Poe. It has been a literature profoundly influenced by ideals and by practices developed in democratic living. It has been intensely conscious of the needs of the common man, and equally conscious of the aspirations of the individual in such a democracy as we have known here. It has been humanitarian. It has been, on the whole, an optimistic literature, made virile by criticism of the actual in comparison with the ideal.

All this has been transforming, and has given to American writing, even to American style, qualities which no Aristotelian criticism, no study of literary influences from abroad, can explain. Our contemporary literature, which from comic strip to satiric novel is really the adult education of most Americans, can be rightly understod only by readers who have followed the history of this American tradition.

3

Such readers of this book as are neither critics nor specialists in scholarship are probably more interested in the literature itself than in the vast historical changes which it reflects. Fortunately for them American literature is not merely in a state of becoming. Our national history is already long enough to have had its periods of maturing and fruition. We do not have to leave our readers confused and bored by writing in which imagination is only half formed and half worded. We are not dependent upon the topical and the timely, the imitative or the unconsciously intuitive, upon the half-gods of journalism, or the sprawlings or conventions of experimental or commercialized fiction. These are all in the background, but we have had a sufficiency of great writers representative of whatever in our history could in their time and by them be put into the forms of art. In this book the approach will be through the varied and extensive experience of a national culture on its way, but the objective of the history will be to record and explain the great men and women who have made this culture speak to the imagination. Literature as they have written it, and as the term is used in the title of this book, is any writing in which aesthetic, emotional, or intellectual values are made articulate by excellent expression. It is the record of man made enduring by the right words in the right order. It is a feeling or thought which by some inner necessity has created for itself a form. Literature can be used, and has been magnificently used by Americans, in the service of history, of science, of religion, or of political propaganda. It has no sharp boundaries, though it passes through broad margins from art into instruction or argument. The writing or speech of a culture such as ours which has been so closely bound to the needs of a rapidly growing, democratic nation, moves quickly into the utilitarian, where it informs without lifting the imagination, or records without attempting to reach the emotions. History as it is written in this book will be a history of literature within the margins of art but crossing them to follow our writers into the actualities of American life. It will be a history of the books of the great and the near-great writers in a literature which is most revealing when studied as a by-product of American experience.

Inside these margins are so many notable writers that the emphasis in the following chapters will inevitably fall upon men rather than upon movements and institutions, although these will not be neglected. There is available for discussion the enlightened common sense of Franklin, the first to make a modernizing Europe feel that there was a still more modern America. There are the astonishing intellects of a Hamilton and a Jefferson arguing great causes in documents and letters which became the political classics of their times. We have the communicable fire of Thomas Paine, the most effective propagandist of modern times before Hitler, and the antithesis of Hitler in the history of human liberty. In the youth of the nation the art of style was mastered by Irving, suave in a tumultuous commonwealth. In the same decades the equally great art of story-telling was enriched by Cooper, who added to the sagas of the world the heroic myth of Red Indian and pioneer. There is the somber beauty of Hawthorne, the moral romancer as Milton was the heroic poet of Puritanism; the fierce humor of Thoreau's individualism; the shrewd saintliness of Emerson, who spiritualized expansion; the soul-plunging adventures of Melville's imagination; the prophecy of Whitman, seeking and finding new rhythms in which to sing democracy and the future of the common man. We have had historians who were also men of letters, and statesmen like Lincoln who could say the word which makes aspiration articulate. There was Henry James, looking both ways across the sea from an Atlantis of his own creating; and Emily Dickinson who saw eternity through the windows of Amherst; and Mark Twain, tasting the bitterness of uncharted freedom while he told tall tales of an expanding America. There are the modernists of our twentieth century. Both in prose and in poetry they have pushed through the mists and illusions of romance and idealism and given us pictures of psychological oppression and moral divergence in a vast society transformed by industrialism. These and subtler strides of spiritual change have enlarged the boundaries of literary truth. The chapters that follow will be an account of such writers and their background and their associates and of a literature which must be known more fully in order to estimate their contribution to the country and to the world.

4

It may enlighten the reader of these introductory remarks to think of American literature as the record and analysis of a series of cultural waves beating in from across the Atlantic to our shores in a continuous series and changing their form and nature and sometimes their direction as they sweep over the New World.

The first waves that came with the explorers and the settlers of the seventeenth century retained their European characteristics with only slight modifications from circumstance. When the wilderness became new towns and organized communities, and immigration swelled into the floods of the eighteenth century, the waves became more numerous and more complex. For nearly two centuries they were dammed by the long walls of the Appalachians, yet their contour and content were subject to changes only less extensive than the novelties in the actual experience of millions of settlers now committed to a life in which opportunity, hardship, and danger were in equal proportions.

After the Revolutionary War and the establishing of independence, itself a modifying influence of tremendous force, the wall of the mountains was breached in a dozen places, and waves from the seaboard pool and new waves from across the sea swept into the Mississippi Valley and on toward the Western mountains and the Pacific. Here in this vast frontier the colonial culture of the East, and later the powerful literature of what was now an old New England and a mature East and South, were fertilized by pioneer experience, dynamized by the sense of a continent in unity, and transformed by the needs and new imagination of a people no longer European. Sectional literature became national literature. And while new ideas from abroad were continually absorbed, currents typically American in their influences began to roll back toward Europe and the rest of the world, a reversal that had begun with Cooper and Emerson in the early nineteenth century.

By the twentieth century and especially after the First World War, the United States was no longer a New World. Culture was now not immigrant here except on a basis of equal exchange, and the complex interactions of democracy and industrialism and the new struggle for economic democracy outweighed in importance any pressures from abroad. By the mid-century American fiction and the American drama of the screen were beginning to dominate the imagination of the masses throughout the world, although of this striking fact the American intellectual was as yet scarcely aware.

To write a simple account of these complex developments is not easy; and a chronology of writers and their books is obviously insufficient. But if a historian will view in perspective a century of this nation's history from any one place and time he will discover a logical pattern in its literary growth. He will see the raw and objective records of the explorers and settlers, usually our earliest writing, developing into documents of politics and religion. Gradually the sense of art awakes as primary needs become more certain of fulfillment; but art in this stage is either primitive or imitative. Not until the settler or his descendant is thoroughly at home in his new world can he create an art which is an organic expression of his experience. A century is not too long for the full cycle of this process, whether the place be New England, Virginia, Ohio, or California. Because this cycle unrolled in all regions, and because there was no single time schedule for the various parts of the continent, nor even a consistent tempo of westward movement, the historical account must be complex, however simple and oft repeated this formula of literary evolution.

Yet the imagination often discovers truths where complications of fact obscure it; and the imagination responds to two great movements in our literary history: the era of Emerson, Melville, and Whitman; and the age in which we are living today. The first epoch is evidently the climax of a long growth from colonial beginnings to a self-conscious and organized nation, but a nation on the brink of a destructive Civil War and a westward expansion transforming in its character. The other, the era of complete national fulfillment, shows its beginnings in the earliest hints of a country that was to be continental in scope and cosmopolitan in population, but that would not realize itself completely and make its voice heard and its power felt in the world at large until the twentieth century. These two main cycles of growth overlap and intervene, and one American author, Whitman, is clearly a pivot upon which sectional America swings into its continental phase. Yet they afford a pattern for marshaling facts and for tracing developments, and thus provide a ground plan for this book. The details will range far but find their organization in this view, which we believe to be an accurate view, of American literary history.

5

We shall tell in the following chapters the story of the importation into our New World of European ideas and shapes for the imagination. We shall show that American literature differs from all the modern literatures of Europe in that it depends both upon an imported culture and upon the circumstances of a New World radically different in human experience from the Old, and thus has a quality which will presumably be characteristic of the literature of the future in a world society more mobile and yet more integrated than our own. We shall discuss the instruments of our national culture as they existed and developed. We shall set in order the progress from colonies to republic, from republic to democracy, from East to West, from sections and regions to a national unity. We shall treat at length these regions and sections, and discuss the rise and fall of literary dominations, the schools and coteries, the prophets and mythmakers, the interactions of politics, economics, and religion with literary expression, and those strong impulses toward escape and refinement and toward revolt and the needs of the common man, so characteristic of the United States. We shall correlate American literature with the successive swings of this country, which sometimes have been toward an ideal of leadership in all human progress, and sometimes have been away from the world we have helped to make smaller by our own energy and into an isolationism where we hoped vainly to solve our own peculiar problems. And we shall pause where genius emerges; for this is a history of literature, and literature, unlike politics, can never be measured by quantity, but only by the crystallization of strong imagination in words.

THE COLONIES

--- importation and adaptation

1. THE EUROPEAN BACKGROUND

THE world in which the mainland colonies in North America were founded and out of which American letters were to grow was a world at once incredibly remote from modern man and strangely like his own. In the sixteenth century "Europe" was a tiny island in a dim, gray universe. To all intents, "Europe" was Great Britain, the Low Countries, the Iberian Peninsula, France, Italy, and "Austria," with a few adjacent territories. The Scandinavias and Germany existed, one had commercial relations with them, but they existed as remote and savage parts of the world—travelers describing German inns, for example, as if they were writing about nineteenth century Siberia. Distant in the East, "Muscovy," a part of mankind even less known to western man than is Soviet Russia, loomed darkly; southward from it, the Turks pressed into Hungary and besieged Vienna in 1529. As late as 1602 Captain John Smith's travels in Wallachia had a remote, fantastic air.

Little vessels kept to the northern half of the Mediterranean to reach the Levant, avoiding, their masters hoped, the Moslem pirates of Tripoli. Southward from the Mediterranean stretched something huge and unknown called "Africa," where dwelt the anthropophagi and men whose heads do grow beneath their shoulders. Somewhere beyond was the flashing splendor, the brilliance intermittently revealed, of "Asia," where Prester John, Cipango, Kambalu, and the Spice Islands were all jumbled together. As for the western outlook, there was for Englishmen the savage and inhospitable land of Ireland, beyond which lay the gray Atlantic main and such legendary islands as O Brasil. Past these cloudy archipelagoes—and it was difficult to distinguish actual Iceland from mythical Cibola—there was perhaps something called America. Writing *A New Interlude and a mery of the nature of the .iiij. elementes* about 1519, John Rastell said that "westwarde be founde new landes," and thought they were "muche lenger than all christendome," but Englishmen were not overly eager to find them out.

Small groups of educated men labored throughout the century to inform themselves and their countrymen more accurately about the globe. But the efforts of Thorne, Barlow, Eden, Hacket, Dee, Hakluyt, and others to improve the knowledge of geography scarcely touched the general mind. We do not know the rate of illiteracy in the kingdom of Gloriana, but we know that the vast majority of Englishmen could not read. The art and mystery of chart reading was even more severely restricted by the regulations of the guilds, governmental policy, and the profit motive of merchants and mariners; in the next century, when John Donne was writing about the round earth's imagined corners and Milton could not make up his mind whether to be a Ptolemaist or a Copernican, it is probable they were picturing the general confusion of the English imagination. Most of the great library of travel literature available to middle-class readers, moreover, was not published until either very late in the sixteenth century or in the seventeeth.

In the art of landscape painting Tudor England lagged woefully behind the continent; and though New World flora and fauna began to appear on canvases painted in sixteenth century Italy or Spain, England had no comparable pictures. What was worse, the technique of landscape description in literature, by which the small reading public might have been familiarized with America was, even as late as Hakluyt's *Principal Navigations* (1598, 1600), still struggling to pass beyond the medieval stereotypes which had satisfied literary workmen from Chaucer through Spenser. The consequence was that only a few visualized America. When Jamestown was at last founded, the world was certainly wider and better known than it had been to Sebastian Cabot; but, so far as the average literate middle-class Englishman was concerned, it was a world still vague in outline, still filled with inexplicable miracles and stupefying terrors, an inhospitable world, in which only a dogged determination not to be swallowed up by Spain drove the English out of the bastions of their island fortress set in a silver sea. This determination explains why, for many decades, the West Indies seemed to Tudor statesmen far more important than the mainland. You could raid the Spanish silver fleet with vessels based on Barbados; the James River and the Charles were much too far north.

The four million Englishmen who inhabited the southern portion of Great Britain when Elizabeth came to the throne seemed to themselves to be greatly crowded together. The suppression of the monasteries, which ended the obligations of celibacy for about ninety thousand persons; the weakening of the guild system, a social pattern which had postponed marriage for apprentices; the prosperity of the towns and the contrasting poverty of the countryside—these and other causes had increased the number of inhabitants from an estimated two and one-half million in the fifteenth century to a probable four million in 1558. This increase in population had two important effects upon the image of America. The first was to increase the confidence of Englishmen in themselves, to make them feel that along with Spain,

Portugal, and France, England deserved a place in the New World sun. If the Queen was, indeed, the "Great Ladie of the greatest isle," that isle should be the center of an empire of her majesty's subjects

through the speciall assistance, and blessing of God . . . searching the most opposite corners and quarters of the world, and . . . compassing the vaste globe of the earth.

Hakluyt continued with Miltonic majesty:

For, which of the kings of this land before her Majesty, had theyr banners ever seene in the Caspian sea? which of them hath ever dealt with the Emperor of Persia, as her Majesty hath done, and obteined for her merchants large and loving privileges? who ever saw before this regiment, an English Ligier in the stately porch of the Grand Signor at Constantinople? who ever found English Consuls and Agents at Tripolis in Syria, at Aleppo, at Babylon, at Balsara, and which is more, who ever heard of Englishman at Goa before now? what English shippes did heeretofore ever anker in the mighty river of Plate? passe and repasse the . . . straigth of Magellan, range along the coast of Chili, Peru, and all the backside of Nova Hispania, further than any Christian ever passed?

These achievements were, however, principally the work of a dedicated few.

The second effect of the increase in population, together with the new economic forces at work in Europe, was to demand relief from poverty through emigration. The enclosure movement had followed upon the Wars of the Roses. When Henry VII put down livery and maintenance, he ended the necessity for great lords to maintain bands of followers through their connection with the land. And as mines in the New World poured gold and silver into Europe, coinage, agricultural prices, rents, and wages were thrown into confusion. The slow emergence of a spending economy led to the rise of a race of *novi homines* replacing the ancient nobility, whose ranks had been depleted by civil war and sectarian strife. The wool market boomed while new trade arrangements led to the growth of towns. The old common lands were obviously in better use for sheep grazing than for "strip" farming or the pasturage of occasional cows; and, moreover, sheep required fewer attendants. Said Latimer: "Where there have been many householders and inhabitants, there is now but a shepherd and a dog." The *novi homines,* wanting estates, got them by enclosure; and the villeins, no longer permitted their old pasture and farm lands, owning no acreage, unable to pay rent, and unhired as plow hands, were thrown upon the roads or crowded into the evil-smelling cities. They formed the race of sturdy beggars against whom statutes were passed, and for whom the Elizabethan poor law was written.

Some of these landless men were lured into the unprofitable enterprise of colonizing Ireland, and others were enlisted for service in the Low Countries. But in the opening years of the seventeenth century propaganda pictured a New World paradise where farms could be acquired by mere manual labor; and relieving the pressures of superfluous population became a standard theme in colonial promotion. Those who could not read listened to sermons.

Thus it was that the attractions of empire and the pressures of poverty operated to overcome the vagueness, the indifference, the parochialism, the prejudice, and the terrors of the Tudor world. Thus England eventually entered the colonial race to compete with the Latins. If the delay seems to many Americans inexplicable, we who are children of the colonial fathers must remember that we read into the records of their random enterprises a sense of importance subsequent to the event. The English did not consciously create the United States. If it is not flattering to think of Jamestown and Boston as being founded in fits of absence of mind, they were founded at least in fits of absence of plan, for the sufficient reason that neither Tudor government nor Tudor theory had any clear notion of "plantations." The astonishing thing is not that English discoveries were made at random or that colonies were nourished by neglect; the astonishing thing is that out of the social confusion of the Tudor world there emerged any colonial enterprises at all.

2

The social confusion of Tudor England was, then, great; great also was its cultural disharmony. Three opposed systems of life fought for supremacy over the Tudor mind and, in some degree, for supremacy in the New World—medievalism, the Renaissance, and the Reformation. Despite the brilliance of Spenser and Shakespeare, the massive structure of the medieval world order did not crumble at the discovery of America; on the contrary, even Marlowe's *Dr. Faustus,* with its immortal passage on the pagan Helen, contains the Seven Deadly Sins and a description of hell as vivid as that in Jonathan Edwards' famous sermon.

Tudor Englishmen in truth still looked upon the visible world as a bridge between two bottomless eternities. In relation to these the earth was but a fretful midge; but because the age of the world was less than seven thousand years the story of mankind was essentially without historic change, Troy being a town like London, and the relation of sinful poets to Christ being very like those of medieval vassals to their lord. As mankind marched across this narrow span, the chief concern of each individual was still that relation—in other words, the salvation of the soul. Catholicism may have been altered to the Church of England; Christian eschatology in the days of Ben Jonson was what it had been to St. Augustine.

History began when God, fulfilling an ancient purpose, called the visible universe into being and created Adam and Eve for his glory. These twain disobeyed him of their own free will; wherefore God placed the curse of travail and death upon their descendants from Cain and Abel to Sir Walter Raleigh, who, though he imagined he saw the grave where Laura lay, saw also heaven as a place where Christ, as an unfeed king's attorney, got his clients off. For God was not merely just, he was also kind, and offered to save some part of mankind, first through a succession of symbolic events like the preservation of Noah, and afterwards through the birth, ministry, crucifixion, and resurrection of Christ. History would come to a fitting end at the Day of Judgment, when the souls of the saved were to rejoice in the presence of God. If this be Christian orthodoxy in the modern Bible belt, we forget that it is a medieval inheritance.

Crossing the bridge of life, sinful man was surrounded by various supernatural beings of superhuman power. A great angel had instigated the original fall. This angel had evil companions, driven with him out of heaven. He was Satan or the Devil, whose chief purpose was to prevent as many human souls as possible from attaining salvation; he, with his confederates, therefore delighted to work mischief, both grotesque and terrifying. Though his power was less than God's, his followers were enabled to do magical things. These followers might be witches and wizards—human souls gone wrong; or they might be human beings who never had opportunity to go right. Such were, for example, the American Indians, whose origin could best be explained by supposing they were the offspring of Satan. Human history was (as conducted by Divine Providence) an enormous campaign between Satan and Christ; therefore colonial historians like Bradford and Winthrop anxiously examined and recorded special providences revealing the cosmic significance of striking events. Even a hard-boiled character like John Smith wrote that Lord De La Warr's coming to Virginia showed "how God inclineth all casuall events to worke the necessary helpe of his Saints."

Had the medieval world persisted unchanged in Europe, the governing concepts of a single church, a single state, and a single ordering of knowledge might have been transferred to the colonies there to shape a culture comparable to the culture of the Latin-American colonies south of the Rio Grande. In fact, nationalism, sectarianism, and the New Learning had already arisen to wreck the old unity. Yet elements descending from the medieval unity persisted, notably in New England. That human reason unaided by divine revelation could go but a partial way toward understanding the causes of things was a proposition no more unsympathetic to the New England minister than to his remote scholastic progenitor. The logic of Peter Ramus of Paris replaced Aristotelian traditionalism in the search for a lost accord; and, with the entrance into the United States of Roman Catholic education, the old scholasticism was in a sense reborn. So likewise the American colonial, though he hated the Pope, could think of the realm of the spirit as a *civitas Dei* or polity of God, as Augustine had taught, and differed chiefly from his Catholic contemporary by considering that Rome was in schism, not New England. Finally, the shadowy concept of unity in Christian society was not lost in crossing the Atlantic. All that Rome had to do was to turn Protestant.

In the feudal system man had status. Status consisted of the place he occupied in the social hierarchy, together with the rights and duties appropriate to his social function. This was his "calling." Status extended beyond military and political duties; it included the economic order, or that "practical life" which existed in order that man might fulfill his chief obligation, to glorify God and serve him. "Business" was therefore also a part of the great drama of time and eternity. Buying and selling were not something done by individuals for private personal gain, but occupations to be directed toward the great religious purpose set for mankind. This control emanated from the church, the feudal order, and various professional and occupational associations. The church, for instance, long frowned upon interest ("usury") as a violation of Christian charity, and church and state likewise denounced such forms of individual profit as "engrossing," or cornering the market. Economic life was supposed to conform to an ideal order; and since a part of this ideal was the assumption that everything had its just price or ideal value (fixed partly by custom and partly by the relation of the cost of production to the selling price) law and custom demanded and frequently secured a stabilization of price and wage. Guilds, furthermore, were organized to guard particular occupations; and as the guild (together with the town) might properly seek to fix the just price of anything, so it might also properly regulate the number of apprentices admitted to a calling. Fundamental to this system, so far as trade is concerned, was the tacit assumption that the town or community is the true economic unit. In Jamestown, in Plymouth, and in other early colonies, these assumptions had considerable vitality, and the communal idea of economic activity was for a time accepted as a matter of course.

The medieval notion of a community of goods cannot be pushed too far inasmuch as men have fallen from that state of innocence which alone would make possible a holy communism. The individual's desire for wealth is the result of man's imperfection since the Fall. But God so manages history that in commanding Adam to earn his living by the sweat of his brow and so sanctioning both private property and profit, he had still in mind his own glory. Only through property can the individual keep that status in society to which God has called him; only through the love of wealth can human industry increase the amount of private riches sufficiently to make charity possible. Only, in fact, through property can God's church be maintained from the gifts of the faithful. Communism was, indeed, the original ideal, reflected in the practice of the primitive church and in such institutions as the monastery, but over the institution of private property medieval doctors managed to throw a sacred veil; and private property thus indirectly received from the medieval world a sanction which in America it has not lost.

3

The most striking, influential, and permanent influence of medieval thought upon American development was, then, the concept that the primary values of life are theological. But the British colonies were founded after the European Renaissance and the Protestant Reformation, which obliterated some parts of the medieval inheritance, altered others, and added to that inheritance elements of their own. The gifts of the Renaissance to American development were manifold; here there is space to particularize only a few: scientific curiosity; a particular kind of individualism; and the concept of the commonwealth as an autonomous structure.

John Addington Symonds' haunting definition of the Renaissance as the rediscovery of the world and of man, despite repeated attempts to point out its inadequacy, will not down, because it contains a living truth. Doubtless Roger Bacon was not the only man of a scientific turn of mind in the Middle Ages. Doubtless if the New World had been discovered in the twelfth century, men's curiosity would have been as great as it was later, things would have had to be named, and despite metaphysical realism there would have been a pragmatic approach to problems arising from the discovery. But the New World was a Renaissance invention; and it was unnecessary to consult the schoolmen about its prodigious natural wonders. It was possible to catalogue its phenomena with a certain innocence of the eye, to describe things as they really were and not as they appeared in bestiaries—to begin, in other words, founding natural science in the United States. The reports of voyagers and settlers are strewn with specific observations, with lists of words, with careful documentation about river and cape, thunderstorm and iceberg, the increase of plants, the habits of animals, the life of Indians, manifestations of natural wealth, the operation of religion, anthropology, and much else to which we give our modern names. Medieval travelers could report, and report vividly; the Renaissance voyager was nevertheless by comparison of a more scientific habit of mind. The *Ymago Mundi* of Pierre d'Ailly, the excellent geographical compilation from the fifteenth century which fascinated the imagination of Columbus, begins by postulating nine spheres "according to the opinions of the astrologers," though Aristotle "admits of eight only." The heavens do not share in the four elements and possess none of their qualities; therefore they are neither generative nor corruptible. If we contrast this appeal to authority and dogma with Winthrop's experimental study of Atlantic weather as he went his way to Massachusetts, we see the immense distance men had come, even though Winthrop's contemporaries frequently appealed to authority and even though Pierre d'Ailly himself is capable of experimental observation.

If we turn from the thing observed to the observer, we are face to face with Renaissance man. The man of the Renaissance has been often and variously described, but always in terms of eminence, superiority, *virtù,* the conscious development of extraordinary capacities. This emphasis upon superiority and leadership is an important clue to understanding the history of the discovery and settlement of British North America, since, at least in its earlier phases, the history was to a surprising degree determined by men of *virtù.* The great names in this history—Lok, Frobisher, Gilbert, Raleigh, Drake, Smith are representative—share in greater or less degree the quality of *noblesse oblige,* even if they are of the middle class. Expeditions to the New World are, as it were, each a *posse comitatus*; one almost expects the giving out of gold rings as in *Beowulf,* so immediately does the personal capacity of the man in charge as statesman, mariner, economist, writer, and general fill the imagination. One forgets the humbler joint-stock enterprises that sent them forth. Products of a culture in which the old, rigid class structure was yearly less evident, these men, violent, capable, headstrong, command only by the sheer weight of personality; at that immense distance from England the authority of king or queen, parliament or city company, is meaningless, and they stand alone, confronting their mutinous and headstrong crews. What drove them forth? They thirsted for an immortality of fame which for them eclipsed a promised immortality of soul. The works of Captain John Smith open with complimentary verses comparing him to Moses, Caesar, Monluc, and Homer:

> Like *Caesar* now thou writ'st what thou hast done,
> These acts, this Booke will live while ther's a Sunne.

Shakespeare cannot promise more to the mysterious W. H. But these verses merely say what Hakluyt and Purchas have said, what Drayton repeated:

> Thy voyages attend
> Industrious Hakluÿt,
> Whose reading shall enflame
> Men to seek fame.

This individualism is, furthermore, a completely masculine individualism A few like Raleigh, when in England, were aware of the softer side of Renaissance culture, wrote sonnets to their mistress's eyebrow or capered to the lascivious pleasing of a lute; but for the most part elegance and scholarship did not cross the ocean main until the second third of the seventeenth century. The explorers, the founders, were men brought up in the turbulence of Tudor England, of a Europe torn by civil strife and religious warfare. They scarcely knew the humanitarian virtues, rationalizing the slaughter of Indians or papists with the sublime indifference they brought to the slaughter of the wild Irish. Their careers were under the guardianship of Fortuna, that survivor from the Middle Ages, who, after presiding over the destinies of Wolsey, Cromwell, and Lady Jane Grey, came as it were to preside over the destinies of Edward Maria Wingfield, Captain John Smith, the "Lost Colony" at Roanoke, or any other strange bit of early American history. In such a situation the Platonic Academy, Petrarchan amorousness, or nice differences about meter or prose style were meaningless; fortitude and statesmanship, a bravura recklessness, the kind of unlicensed egoism that fascinated Marlowe and Shakespeare, were the qualities needed for success. If these men read, their libraries were those of Captain Myles Standish: Plutarch, "Bariffe's Artillery Guide and the Commentaries of Caesar," and somebody on the art of war were more to the point, not Ovid.

But the personal qualities that will lead unlettered men into the wilderness are not necessarily the same as those that will create settlements; the fishing post yields to the plantation; the marauder is replaced by the statesman; and a colony is born. The most striking fact about these colonies is that they are states in little, autonomous commonwealths, miniature nations, not those dependent invertebrate settlements which to this day helplessly dot the African coast line. An older generation of historians traced the ancestry of the Mayflower Compact to the traditional liberties of the German *Volk;* it is more historical to note that Jamestown, Plymouth, Massachusetts Bay, Providence, Hartford, each of these little settlements is conceived in the spirit of *respublica,* even when (as in the instance of Maryland) one is studying a proprietary colony. The commonwealth may be tiny, but it is a commonwealth, a single state usually with its single church, in the best manner of Renaissance theorizing. If, as Louis Le Roy wrote only thirty years before Jamestown was founded, Providence guides the transition of prosperity from state to state, the colonial founders were conscious of an historic mission; the course of empire took its way westward in men's minds long before Berkeley wrote.

These little states followed current Renaissance theory. In them as in Europe the emphasis was long upon subordination, hierarchy, and order. It was assumed as a fact in nature that there must be a ruling class, the "people" being subordinate. Government was necessarily by a minority. Citizenship was not a right but a privilege; and the dwellers in a given community did not *ipso facto* become citizens of the state. Government was something divinely sanctioned, the necessity for order arising from the spiritual corruption of mankind whether in France or in Virginia, on the coast of Maine or in Italy. The contract theory, so far as it operated, was not as with Rousseau a compact of individuals mystically conscious of their natural rights; on the contrary, "contract" was characteristically a covenant between the ruling classes and Deity, to which such minor matters as royal charters or the directives of a trading company were but codicils. We misunderstand the early years of the American colonies if we read their history through the eyes of Locke, Samuel Adams, Freeman, or Theodore Roosevelt. They grew up, not in anticipation of the Glorious Revolution, the Declaration of Independence, or the "Germanic" theory of liberty; they were creations, imperfect, tiny, obscure, but typical, of Renaissance speculation about the nature of government and the commonwealth; and the transition from these postulates to nineteenth century liberalism was as painful in the New World as it has been in the Old.

4

To remark that the Reformation was also a basic factor conditioning American cultural development is surely a work of supererogation. The rest of this history is lengthy proof of the fact that the spirit of American letters is predominantly Protestant. To the disentangling of the many threads of this Protestant influence whole subsequent chapters are given. It would be idle here to argue such vexing questions as whether Lutheranism or Calvinism was the more democratic faith; whether there was a distinctive and unique American Puritanism; or whether the protest of Protestantism and the dissidence of dissent appearing in such nineteenth century faiths as Mormonism and Christian Science are lineal descendants of the European Reformation. It is a commonplace that colonial clergymen were learned men who continued the traditions of humanism, and who sought to found Christian utopias (strictly limited to godly of the right sort) up and down the Atlantic coast. Latterly, ink has been spilled to show that Puritanism had an aesthetic, that the Pilgrims liked strong liquors and were lusty fellows. For intellectual history these questions are not so important as is the realization that in northern Europe Protestantism conquered humanism in the degree that Calvin was no Pico della Mirandola and Luther was no Erasmus. The American colonies were the children of north European Protestantism.

If humanism was the rediscovery of a literature, Protestantism was the rediscovery of a book. American colonials, even in Virginia, became the people of that book. Displacing ancient Israel as the chosen of God, the founders of American plantations regarded themselves as divinely appointed to increase the kingdom of a Protestant Christ and to further the cause revealed by Deity in the Old Testament and continued in the New World. Bibliolatry took shape as an attempt to legalize in the wilderness the Mosaic code and to learn from the cloudy pages of the prophets the American signs of the times. A kind of *sortes Biblicae* aided the magistrate; whether at Geneva or at Salem, orthodoxy became the primary test of citizenship. One has only to study, as Otto Benesch has done, the Renaissance art in northern Europe to see how profoundly Protestantism alters values; out of this alteration of values America was born. Contrast portraits by Dürer, Cranach, and Holbein with canvases by Raphael, Titian, and Tintoretto. The difference is not that the Puritan is opposed to art and the Catholic embraces it, nor that the Teutonic world distrusted paganism and the Latin culture went out to meet paganism with open arms; the difference is that in the one culture life is the education of a character, in the other it is the cultivation of a personality. The grave faces which look out at us from the pictures of the northern masters are the faces of men of affairs, men whose integrity is a credit-making virtue, who do not deny that recreation has its place in life, but to whom pleasure is never spontaneous because they have read in the Book that there is an appointed time for everything. Theirs is, in sum, a Biblical culture, not, as in the Mediterranean world, a spontaneous one.

For such men, belief is an inner experience; seeking to evaluate that experience, they are filled alternately with enthusiasm and melancholy—not the sensuous melancholy of Da Vinci's portraits, but that melancholy which transcends all wit in Dürer's most celebrated engraving. Translate this melancholia into New England theology, it becomes the inwardness, the perpetual dubiety and concern for the symbolical significance of trifles that make the diary of a man like Cotton Mather so curious and remote. A world whose deepest significance lies within is not a world of pictorial splendor, architectural magnificence, colorful theater, or sensuous verse. In America baroque architecture appears only in the Latin colonies; the spare, geometrical lines of our seventeenth century houses are boundaries about a life within, not, as in the case of Spanish-American cathedrals, a reaching outward into the air and the sky. The Spaniards and the Portuguese found theaters, give concerts, produce architects, painters, poets who really rival Camoëns; in North America there are sermons, domestic architecture, the handicraft arts, political controversy, and the most erudite colonial literature the world has ever seen. But the erudition is principally theological and looks within. Life is not an artistic affair, it is sober duty; thrift, industry, carefulness, the qualities of Poor Richard, the economic virtues do not conceal this inwardness. The most characteristic production in stone of New England culture is the tombstone, on which the local cutter engraved an hourglass, a skeleton, or a winged head.

In sixteenth century Europe Protestantism was a fighting faith. In an either-or world there was no room for the tolerant grays of modern latitudinarianism; the century which saw the Massacre of St. Bartholomew was understandably suspicious of mere toleration. To modern readers the harsh, bounding line of any religious faith in the period is repellent and strange. It was, however, as necessary to be clearly and definitely an Anabaptist, a Quaker, a Lutheran, a Calvinist in that epoch as it is today to be definitely a Communist, a Fascist, or a democrat. He who was not for you was against you, and he who was against you was also against God and therefore capable of any wickedness. Elizabethan gentlemen undoubtedly treated Spanish grandees with the courtesies due to class and breeding, and there are records of the polite reception of even Jesuits in seventeenth century New England. We are, however, so bemused by the historical fame of Mrs. Hutchinson, Roger Williams, and other victims or examples of intolerance in an intolerant time that we overlook the darkest heritage of the Reformation in American history—the hatred of the Catholic faith. Not merely were Tudor voyages directed toward defeating Spain; not merely did Elizabeth encourage legends about Catholic plots against her life; but this prejudice also landed at Jamestown, at Plymouth, swarmed up the Shenandoah Valley, ended the well meant experiment of Baltimore in Maryland, and, save for a brief period during and after the American Revolution, still conditions the folkways of "old Americans" in dealing with their newer fellow citizens. It is also an unexpressed assumption of American literary history that Protestantism is intellectually more important than Catholicism, and that, for example, Jonathan Edwards or Emerson is of greater cultural importance than Bishop England of Charleston or Cardinal Gibbons of Baltimore. The United States derives from the Protestant Reformation a *Kulturkampf* like in kind, though not in present intensity, to that of sixteenth and seventeenth century Europe. It is one of the longest-lived and one of the most baffling inheritances to reach us from the sixteenth century world.

It has been already here remarked that the world which brought the first English colonies into being was a strongly masculine world. But among the most important legacies of the Reformation to the United States was the position of women. In the annals of Latin America women figure as poets, as religious mystics, as great ladies in colonial courts; but they figure always within the confines of customs that are both Catholic and Mediterranean. The

Protestant world being both mercantile and middle-class, women were primarily wives and daughters. In American legend Priscilla Alden is seated at her spinning wheel, and the heroic pioneer women engage in domestic economy. In a world without nunneries, without viceregal courts like those in Lima or Mexico, the Virgin was replaced by the mother; and the curious and singular purity of the history of womanhood in the United States is no less a product of the Protestant Reformation than is Woolman's *Journal* or Emerson's Divinity School Address. American culture produced no *belle dame sans merci* (until Hollywood); and it is characteristic of its mores that the first cabinet crisis of its first frontier President, Andrew Jackson, concerned a chivalric defense of Peggy Eaton. In the United States female wickedness comes from France—from, in other words, a Latin and Catholic culture. Classic American literature is without sexuality, but has domesticity; its most serious description of passion is *The Scarlet Letter,* a book taught in the public schools; and when the Protestant imagination of Longfellow finished with anthropological lore, Minnehaha was as properly a bride of Hiawatha as ever Mrs. Lapham was of Silas the paint king. Doubtless the domestic virtues are the middle-class virtues; but in the New World the middle class was originally Protestant, and when we seek the origin of their codes of conduct we are led backward to the world of the Reformation, which, in the name of domestic morality, attacked indulgences and replaced celibacy by the marriage of its prelates. From the point of view of the influence of feminine taste upon culture, the place of women in Protestant domesticity is one of the most important facts in our inheritance from sixteenth century Europe.

By the end of the seventeenth century the English mainland colonies, absorbing every other racial stock settling from Maine to Florida, were launched upon an autonomous cultural life. To the north and west the Catholic French were unabashed and defiant; from Florida and Alabama to the river Plate His Most Catholic Majesty of Spain held sway. Any map of the New World for 1700 shows only a ribbon of coast belonging to the English. If they were later to absorb most of the continent, the long delay allowed them time to adjust to new conditions, to put down roots, to adapt their heterogeneous Old World inheritance to a new environment. They developed colonial education, colonial books, colonial publishing, colonial literary art. Out of this came in time a national culture. The chronicle of this development now follows. It is the history of a complex European inheritance, by slow degrees and ceaseless experimentations becoming so unique a phenomenon that modern transatlantic observers have difficulty in recognizing its Old World roots.

2. COLONIAL LITERARY CULTURE

THE Protestant communities which sprang up in Virginia, New England, and elsewhere in America were much like country towns and villages of England. The people for the most part were hard-working, simple folk without much acquaintance with belles-lettres, and it would have been a miracle indeed if polite literature had suddenly bloomed in the American woods. The truth is that the majority of settlers had little or no literary background. They were a plain people faced with the task of subduing a wilderness.

Though some of the stricter Puritans and Quakers were actively prejudiced against many forms of imaginative literature, which they conceived to be idle and frivolous, they nevertheless placed a high value on certain forms of learning. The Puritans emphasized Biblical and theological learning; the Quakers stressed practical studies which served for the relief of man's estate. The significant fact is that colonial Americans cherished learning even when they did not share it, and in spite of great difficulties they fashioned instruments of culture which made possible a literary development in the eighteenth century.

Frontier conditions are rarely conducive to literary production, and the frontier of the seventeenth and early eighteenth centuries was particularly unfavorable. Some colonies, notably in the South, lacked the means of printing until well along in the eighteenth century. The lack of towns was also a serious deterrent in the South to the development of literary activity. Inspiration may come from vernal woods, but sustained literary production is a characteristic of urban rather than rural environment. Until the colonies along the Atlantic seaboard achieved settled towns, citizens with a modicum of leisure, and the paraphernalia of urbane life—such as schools, libraries, booksellers, lecture platforms, printing presses, and discussion clubs—literature was in abeyance.

But, from the very first, American colonists showed a deep concern lest their children grow up barbarous in the wilderness. This concern was equally great in New England and in Virginia, though the methods of meeting the danger varied with differing conditions. In New England villagers quickly set up schools for their children, and the Puritan fathers in 1636 established Harvard College to insure a learned ministry and provide a nursery of learning for their sons. In Virginia the wealthier planters hired tutors, and the less well-to-do organized plantation schools and shared the expense of a teacher; those who were able sent their sons, and sometimes their daughters, to England for more advanced education. In 1693 Virginians established the College of William and Mary from the same motives that had prompted the founders of Harvard.

By 1760 some cities, particularly Boston and Philadelphia, had excellent grammar schools, and throughout the colonies public-spirited citizens were laboring to increase educational opportunities. Stern Calvinists were convinced that education was necessary to combat the devil, and easy-going deists were equally certain that education was needed to bring about man's perfection. The doctrine of universal educational opportunity, which Thomas Jefferson was to advocate near the turn of the century, was already incipient, and movements were on foot which would transform the ideal of education into something akin to a religious fervor for Americans in the nineteenth century. Before 1760 the colonies could take pride in six colleges which freed them from dependence for higher learning upon the Old World. In addition to Harvard, and William and Mary, these institutions were Yale (1701), the College of New Jersey (1746—later Princeton), King's (1754—later Columbia), and the Charity School in Philadelphia (1740—later the Academy and College of Philadelphia, and eventually the University of Pennsylvania). Vernacular belles-lettres, it is true, had small place in formal education in this period; but classical rhetoric and the prose and poetry of Greece and Rome exerted a profound influence in the development of a literary consciousness.

2

Despite the laborious tasks faced by the earliest settlers, both North and South, they did not entirely neglect the benefits of letters. Indeed, the books which they brought with them were remarkable for their variety and significance, and the importance of little household libraries in the transmission of the literary tradition can scarcely be overemphasized. Seventeenth century inventories show a wide dispersion of books throughout the colonies. Before the end of the seventeenth century Boston had a half-dozen or more booksellers. One of the earliest of these was Hezekiah Usher, who at his death in 1676 left a comfortable fortune made in the book trade. Peddlers often carried books and pamphlets in their packs. Cotton Mather proposed to induce an itinerant hawker to "fill this Countrey with devout and useful

Books"—from Mather's own pen—but complained, years later, that peddlers were corrupting good manners by disseminating ballads and foolish poems. In the tobacco colonies, where local booksellers were virtually unknown, English factors supplied the literary needs of planters. Letters from Virginia and Maryland to merchants in London or Bristol contain frequent requests for specific books, though the planters sometimes asked their factors to send the latest things in the booksellers' stalls and left the choice of titles to the agents' discretion.

The subject matter of the books imported in the seventeenth and eighteenth centuries is indicative of the serious purpose of the colonists. In the broadest sense, their selections were utilitarian, and books designed merely for entertainment or amusement found small place in their household libraries. Picaresque narratives, jest books, ballads, and other literary frivolities were not unknown, it is true; but little money was squandered upon idle reading. This concentration upon "useful" books was as characteristic of Virginia planters as it was of New England Puritans.

Although the New England and the Southern colonists showed differences of emphasis in literary taste, they showed more striking—and perhaps more significant—similarities. The books having the widest circulation before 1760 can be broadly classified as religious and pious. Many of the same religious books were read by Calvinists in the North and Anglicans in the South. Though preachers and some laymen bought and read strictly theological works, the majority of readers preferred less controversial handbooks of piety. Books which had pleased middle-class Tudor and Stuart Englishmen remained standard reading in the colonies for generations. Lewis Bayly's *Practice of Piety* and the sermons of the Reverend William Perkins edified alike merchants and apprentices in Boston and Philadelphia and gentlemen in the region of Chesapeake Bay. Households possessing no other book might have a well thumbed copy of the King James Version of the Bible; a remarkable number had Foxe's *Acts and Monuments*. The appetite of the seventeenth and early eighteenth centuries for pious reading should not be discounted too cavalierly in appraising the cultural development of Americans. Many books of piety were written with a conscious effort at simplicity and clarity to appeal to the understanding of plain men. In such works colonial readers found not only lessons in ethics and good morality but patterns and forms of expression.

Historical works, both classical and modern, were second only to religious literature in the favor of colonial Americans. From Greek and Roman historians, they drew lessons of statecraft as well as facts about the ancient world. Tacitus was a favorite author, for example, and Thomas Jefferson, who read him in his youth, declared later in life that he was the wisest of all writers. Raleigh's *History of the World,* Bishop Gilbert Burnet's *History of the*

Reformation in England, and many another English work entertained and instructed colonial readers.

Books of conduct, instructions in domestic relations, political treatises, legal discussions and handbooks for the amateur as well as the professional lawyer, medical books, and sundry guides to farming, navigation, surveying, and other practical pursuits were among the useful books which colonists bought and treasured.

The most influential writers in the eighteenth century were probably Joseph Addison and Richard Steele. Countless Americans who bought and read the *Tatler* and the *Spectator* could not entirely escape the moral and social lessons which the authors intended. Neither could they avoid being affected by the style. Benjamin Franklin was not the only colonial writer who deliberately imitated the *Spectator* essays.

By the end of the seventeenth century, poetry and drama had come to have a larger place in colonial reading, and the appetite for belles-lettres gradually increased. A few men and women of advanced literary taste dipped into Spenser's *Faerie Queene* and Milton's *Paradise Lost*; considerably more read the poetical works of George Herbert, Francis Quarles, and Abraham Cowley. By the mid-eighteenth century, Shakespeare's plays were frequently found in gentlemen's libraries. By the same period, booksellers had discovered a considerable market for chapbooks, fiction something less than edifying, and other trifling works which serious folk still regarded as frivolous and perhaps iniquitous.

During the seventeenth century most libraries were gathered for the immediate utility to their owners; but by the end of the century book collecting in almost a professional sense had begun. Cotton Mather in Massachusetts and William Byrd in Virginia during the early years of the eighteenth century gathered substantial libraries; and at death each had nearly four thousand volumes divided among the various branches of learning. By 1751 James Logan had gathered in Philadelphia a library of approximately three thousand volumes, which he bequeathed to the city for public use. To the collecting instinct of the Reverend Thomas Prince of Boston, we are indebted for the preservation of many rare books and manuscripts of the period. Many other private libraries of substantial proportions were gathered during the colonial period and helped in the dissemination of learning. Records of book borrowing show that the influence of the private libraries extended far beyond the households of the owners.

Institutional libraries date from the founding of the first colleges. John Harvard's bequest of his books to the college at Cambridge established a library that continued to grow in importance and usefulness. By the middle of the eighteenth century Yale also had a respectable library, and the other colleges had working collections of learned books.

A systematic effort to foster piety and learning by the circulation of books was started near the end of the seventeenth century by the Reverend Thomas Bray, moving spirit in the founding of the Society for the Propagation of the Gospel in Foreign Parts. He devised a plan for sending parish libraries to the colonies for the use of the Anglican clergy and their parishioners. By his efforts it is estimated that approximately thirty-four thousand volumes reached America and were widely distributed, chiefly in regions where Anglicans were most numerous. In 1700 the provincial legislature at Charleston, South Carolina, made Dr. Bray's parochial library a public institution.

Public and semipublic libraries began to develop in the seventeenth century and by 1760 were fairly numerous. A merchant, Robert Keayne, by his will in 1653, established a public library in Boston which in some degree served the needs of the populace for several generations. In 1700 the Reverend John Sharpe, chaplain to the governor, bequeathed his books to found a public library in New York; although this benefaction was augmented somewhat, it made little impression until a group of citizens in 1754 took up a subscription, bought about seven hundred additional volumes, and rejuvenated an institution which eventually grew into the New York Society Library, a proprietary institution. Benjamin Franklin was instrumental in founding the Library Company of Philadelphia, incorporated in 1742 but actually started by subscription some time before. A few years later, in 1747, a merchant, Abraham Redwood, provided funds for the Redwood Library in Newport, Rhode Island; and a year afterward "seventeen young gentlemen" founded the Charleston Library Society in South Carolina. All of these institutions, which still exist, exerted an important influence. Benjamin Franklin, in his pride over the Philadelphia Library Company, wrote in his *Autobiography* that such libraries had made common tradesmen and farmers as intelligent as gentlemen elsewhere and had contributed to the ability of Americans to defend their privileges.

3

Before an indigenous literature could develop in the colonies, an adequate means of printing was essential. Massachusetts led all the other colonies in this endeavor with the press established at Cambridge in 1639 and operated by Stephen Day for the widow Glover. From this press came the Bay Psalm Book, the earliest laws of Massachusetts, and many religious and learned works. Day was succeeded by Samuel Green, whose descendants later carried the art of printing to several other colonies. Before the end of the century the Cambridge press had competitors in Boston, which soon became an important center for New England publishing. There James Franklin had his shop, and there his half-brother Ben learned the craft. After Boston, Philadelphia became the most important printing center, and by the middle of the eighteenth century it had equaled if not surpassed its northern rival. William Bradford, the first printer in Philadelphia, was also responsible for the establishment of a press in New York in 1693.

Printing got under way more slowly in the South, where royal governors took a sour view of printing presses and at first sought to suppress them (if Massachusetts Bay had not been virtually independent of royal interference for most of the seventeenth century, it is certain that the press there would have enjoyed much less freedom). In 1682 William Nuthead attempted to establish a press at Jamestown, Virginia; but he soon became involved with the authorities, and his efforts were suppressed by order of the governor. In 1685 he transferred his activities to the proprietary colony of Maryland. Thereafter no press was attempted in Virginia until 1730, when William Parks came over from Maryland to Williamsburg and set up a print shop. In 1731 three printers working separately tried to start presses at Charleston, South Carolina; but it remained for Lewis Timothy, a partner of Benjamin Franklin, in 1733 to become the first successful printer there.

By 1763 printing was firmly established in each of the thirteen colonies. Although censorship varied from colony to colony and from time to time, printers had achieved considerable freedom by the mid-eighteenth century, and had become potent influences in shaping public opinion. After the beginning of the eighteenth century nearly every printer aspired to be the proprietor of a newspaper, for newspaper publishing—along with the printing of official documents—was regarded as essential to a printer's prosperity.

A writer in the *Gentleman's Magazine,* in November 1796, observed that "the newspapers of Massachusetts, Connecticut, Rhode Island, Pennsylvania, and Maryland are unequaled whether considered with respect to wit and humour, entertainment or instruction." And he added that "every capital town on the [American] Continent prints a weekly paper; and several of them have one or more daily papers." The journalism that excited the admiration of this writer had not suddenly flowered after the Revolution, but had developed over a long period of years. Indeed, newspapers from the mid-eighteenth century onward provided a means of expression which had a far-reaching influence upon the literary, as well as the political, development of the country.

The first newspaper was Benjamin Harris' *Publick Occurrences,* which appeared on September 25, 1690, in Boston and expired four days later when the governor and council "disallowed" its further publication because Harris had presumed to make his venture without permission. The next endeavor of this kind was made in the same city by a cautious Scot, John Campbell, who, in 1704, founded the *News-Letter,* which lasted until the Revolution.

By 1735 Boston alone had five newspapers, and other cities of the Atlantic seaboard were not far behind. By 1750 the colonies were well provided with newspapers, published weekly and in some cases oftener.

Many of the early papers were partly literary in content. James Franklin, for example, mingled poems and humorous pieces with the news items in the *New-England Courant.* The stated purpose of this journal was to be entertaining, amusing, and instructive. Benjamin Franklin contributed anonymously his first literary efforts to his brother's paper. Many another American achieved a brief literary life in the columns of newspapers. Among the more literary papers were the Boston *Evening-Post,* the *Virginia Gazette,* and the *South Carolina Gazette.* The last-named paper published extensive selections from contemporary English authors as well as from the pens of local writers.

Benjamin Franklin and Andrew Bradford founded rival monthly magazines in Philadelphia in 1741, but both periodicals soon collapsed for lack of support. Magazines were to be a later development in American letters. Even earlier, Samuel Keimer, a visionary printer of Philadelphia, had endeavored to give a literary quality to the weekly paper which he founded in 1728 under the title of *The Universal Instructor in all Arts and Sciences: and Pennsylvania Gazette.* Besides attempting to reprint a contemporary encyclopedia, he started the serial publication of Daniel Defoe's *Religious Courtship.* The heavy instructional and literary quality of the paper was too much for Philadelphia, and Franklin bought it for a song the year after its establishment. The new publisher made the *Pennsylvania Gazette* more lively—if less consciously "literary"—and the publication flourished.

Of several attempts to establish foreign-language newspapers during this period, only two achieved success. Christopher Sower and Heinrich Miller published German-language papers, religious in sentiment, at Germantown and Philadelphia respectively.

An event of vast import for the freedom of expression in the colonies was the fight made in 1734–1735 by John Peter Zenger, publisher of the New York *Weekly Journal,* against the persecution by the governor's party. His imprisonment and trial for libel, and his vindication by the jury, made a great stir, not only in New York but in all the colonies, and quickened men's zeal to defend the liberty of speech and press.

4

The tradition of public discussion in the colonies was a strong influence in the training of men's intellects. Long before newspapers gave an outlet for written thoughts, colonial citizens were practiced in self-expression. In the legislative assemblies, political debate was not the exclusive monopoly of the rich and well born. An occasional speech or state paper, preserved in the records of the popular assemblies, is written in vivid and sinewy prose. The town meetings of New England and the political gatherings in the Southern colonies are more famous for their effect upon the development of democratic institutions, but their influence upon literary expression should not be overlooked.

The pulpit, particularly in the seventeenth century, was a forum for learned exposition on religion, ethics, sociology, science, politics, and almost any phase of the life of man. Puritan sermons are amazing in the variety of subjects treated directly or incidentally. Here and there preachers succeeded in putting their thoughts into moving prose; and even though the literary qualities of the clergy have been exaggerated by later historians they at least furnished a pattern of logical reasoning and taught their audiences useful lessons in formal expression. The Puritan clergy of New England were far more influential than ministers elsewhere, but an occasional Anglican clergyman in the middle and Southern colonies furnished intellectual stimulation in his region.

Informal clubs and discussion groups helped to foster literary as well as scientific interest. Most famous was Franklin's Junto in Philadelphia, the later American Philosophical Society, but nearly every town of importance had some sort of discussion club by the mid-eighteenth century.

Religious opposition to theatrical performances was widespread throughout the seventeenth century. Besides a prejudice against plays on moral grounds, a lingering belief among middle-class folk that stage productions were frivolous and wasteful of precious time helped retard theatrical progress. The first professional actors to perform in the colonies presented a play in Charleston in 1703. Within a year of production in London, George Lillo's sentimental drama *George Barnwell* (1731) was published serially in the *New-England Weekly Journal,* which recommended it to readers on the ground that it tended to promote virtue and piety, though Boston censorship forbade dramatic activity in the city for many years to come. Professional companies appeared in New York after 1732, and Philadelphia and Williamsburg witnessed mid-century performances, often written or acted by college students. But on the whole the theater was late in development, and its influence was relatively unimportant in this period.

During the first century and a half of settlement and development, the colonists spent their main energies in practical and utilitarian pursuits, as would be expected in a raw and unexploited continent. Although the colonial contribution to literature was small, these busy settlers salvaged time for intellectual interests and attached great importance to schools, books, libraries, and other influences above and beyond material considerations. The foundation for a later manifestation of remarkable intellectual and literary capacity was laid in the period before 1760.

3. REPORTS AND CHRONICLES

The earliest writing to come from the New World can be called literature only by stretching the meaning of the word. Before the English had settled their strip of coast, men of many nations had explored the continent from Newfoundland to Mexico and from the Atlantic to the Pacific. The records of their adventures, many of them crude and utilitarian, are our first literature. They are letters home, diaries written in the midst of dangerous actions, chronicles compiled while the memory of the actions was still warm. They were written in the languages of the explorers—Spanish, French, Dutch, and the Scandinavian—some were written in or translated into Latin, others English. Some were published at the time, some were excerpted for collections of voyages, some remained in manuscript for centuries. Together they form a body of documents recording one of the great adventures of man, the opening and settling of the western hemisphere. In them, American literature made a cosmopolitan beginning which was narrowed to the Anglo-Saxon cultural tradition only after two centuries. The story of these reports and chronicles is vast and complex; only its main outlines and principal documents can be noted. But unless it is told, our literature would seem more provincial in its origins than it was. The British colonial period was but an episode—a major episode to be sure—in our cultural history.

2

Suppose that one Leif Ericsson did sail west from Greenland about A.D. 1000, and suppose that ten years later one Thorfinn Karlsefne did the same thing—what reports of their adventures exist?

Three manuscripts, the *Flateyjarbók, Hauksbók,* and a document known as A[rna]-M[agnean] 557, which contains the story of Eric the Red, are in the Royal Library at Copenhagen. Written in the thirteenth or fourteenth century, these tell of events which had occurred about four hundred years earlier. They are the oldest extant writings containing traces of the reports on "Vineland"—which may have been anywhere between Labrador and Long Island. What these "sagas" have to tell did not get into print until Adam of

Bremen's "Ecclesiastical History" was published in 1595—more than a century after Christopher Columbus got his story into type. These sources have been often republished, translated and reproduced in facsimile, while critical works about them multiply, and authorities continue to agree vaguely, or disagree openly as to what they mean. It may be, indeed it has been said, that the history of America would be precisely the same if no Norseman had ever steered his Viking ship west from Greenland. As reports these manuscripts are not contemporary, and as chronicles they are not trustworthy. They are merely parts of that Scandinavian literature which has occasionally inspired American writers from Longfellow to the present.

3

Spain got a head start with respect to "voyages" to and through the "Newe Worlde." "It is therefore apparent that the heroical facts of the Spaniards of these days deserve so great praise that the author of this book (being no Spaniard) doth worthily extoll their doings." Thus Richard Eden, in his *Decades of the Newe Worlde* (1555), introduced the first collection of "voyages" to the English reading public in its own language. His magnanimity to Spain may have owed something to the fact that the English sovereign was the Catholic Mary who had temporarily forged a bond with Spain's Philip. More than sixty years had elapsed since the first printing of Columbus' own "Epistola" in 1493. Of that book, in which the discoverer published his own story, there were at least seventeen "incunabula editions"—but not one in English.

So let the literary history of the United States begin in Texas. Between 1528 and 1536, Alvar Núñez Cabeza de Vaca, Spaniard, walked across the present area of Texas, New Mexico, and Arizona and wrote a book about his wanderings. His *Relación* appeared in print in 1542, has been translated into many languages, and reprinted in every century since. Colored by the religious zeal of his time, it is not altogether the work of a mere superstitious observer though he lived in a day when impossible wonders found their way into the literature of travel. De Vaca's inaccuracies are gratifyingly few, and he provided the first report on two animals without which American literature would be the poorer: his opossum was to become a character in the writings of Joel Chandler Harris, and what would be the literature of the trans-Mississippi West without the buffalo?

The next "overland narrative" tells of Hernando de Soto, who between 1539 and 1542 marched his Spanish expedition from Florida to North Carolina, thence west to the Mississippi. There his death and dramatic burial in the Father of Waters ended his career. The chronicler of this exploit lives only as "The Gentleman of Elvas," an unknown Portuguese who accompanied De Soto and whose *Relaçam verdadeira* was published in 1557. His work was introduced to the English reading public by Richard Hakluyt (of whom, more, later) as *Virginia richly valued* (1609). Said Hakluyt, quite correctly: "This work . . . though small in show, yet great in substance, doth yeeld much light" upon the immensity of the area and resources of what was to become the United States.

In 1540 Francisco Vásquez Coronado started from Mexico into our Southwest. Searching for the "seven cities of Cibola," Coronado certainly got as far north as the present state of Kansas. His chronicler was Pedro Castañeda, who did not write the full and fascinating "Relación de la jórnada de Cibola" until twenty years after the expedition's return to Mexico. It lay in manuscript (occasionally transcribed by men who had no share in the original work) for more than three hundred and fifty years. Not until 1896 were the Spanish text and a translation into English printed for the first time. Partly because the region explored was sparsely settled (discoveries are still being made there), partly because of the ever-changing place names, and partly because the Southwest was not much exploited by European colonization at the time, the Coronado-Castañeda story has only recently assumed its proper place in the literature of the United States. The expedition was one of the last of those swashbuckling and panoplied raids for God, glory, and gold, wherein Cortez and Pizarro succeeded in Mexico and Peru, but Coronado failed because the gold was not found. The "Conquistador" has persisted in national legend.

Less well known than Coronado is Antonio de Espejo, who roamed the Southwest in 1582 and 1583. His work produced a book in English, the authorship of which is credited to him: *New Mexico: otherwise the voiage of Anthony of Espeio . . . translated out of the Spanish copie printed first at Madreel [Madrid], 1586, and afterward at Paris, in the same yeare* (London, 1587). The modern reader will find the elaboration in Hakluyt's *Voyages,* as these early Spanish and French editions are hard to come by and the English edition survives in a single copy in the Huntington Library; but translations and successive reprintings are some measure of the significance of a book.

4

The first Frenchman who wrote satisfactory reports on what is now the United States was Samuel de Champlain, soldier, explorer, and "Father of New France." He knew how to make bold decisions and to act with dispatch, suggesting a clearheadedness which, in turn, reveals itself in clarity of style. What he saw, he described vividly and in detail. In the 1613 edition of his

Voyages he first reports upon his mapping of New England and his celebrated "battle" with the Iroquois, which had far-reaching effects since it allied the French with the enemies of that all-powerful league. Champlain's powers of description are well illustrated by his reports on such matters as the effects of scurvy and by word pictures (often with engraved maps) such as that of Port St. Louis (Plymouth, Massachusetts). Despite the many printings of his works, it was 1922 before a complete and satisfactory edition in English began to appear; yet many a traveler has followed Champlain's routes, text in hand, and been able to check and verify the accuracy of his observations. The reader of Champlain's *Voyages* may be reminded of Caesar's "Commentaries." Both captains were dealing with a disorganized and semibarbarous foe. As Caesar played off the Gauls against one another, so Champlain allied himself with Algonquins against Iroquois. Both were able to view and to describe their enemies objectively, admiring their meritorious qualities while pointing out less desirable characteristics. Champlain's description of his attack on the Iroquois fort is a miniature of Caesar's siege of Alesia. Both writers seem fascinated by mechanical details, and enjoy describing them. At times a reader is apt to feel that Champlain had a more genuine sympathy for, and understanding of, the American Indians than Caesar ever had toward the Gauls. It is entirely possible, if anything may be inferred from such a comparison of their writings, that Champlain was more deeply and sincerely concerned with the glory of France than Caesar ever was with that of Rome. On the whole, a critic might well conclude that Champlain was the greater of the two. His report of wandering in upper New York State in 1615 appears in the 1627 edition of the *Voyages et decouvertures*. His personal explorations ended in 1616, and the final summing up of all his work appears in his longest and last book *Les Voyages de la Nouvelle France* (1632).

Promotion writing is sometimes literature. The annual reports of a commercial corporation, a government bureau, or a missionary society may be literature if they are well written, and if they are widely read throughout the years for more reasons than the original reporter anticipated. Such is that series which has come to be known as the "Jesuit Relations." They were originally prepared to tell the superiors of the Order what the Jesuit missionaries were doing in New France, to secure financial support, and to inform the pious of the great work "ad majorem Dei gloriam." The Jesuits covered the world, but the expression "Jesuit Relations" has come to designate the group of reports which came from the area of the Great Lakes in the seventeenth century, more particularly between 1632 and 1673 when they were being published by Sébastien Cramoisy in Paris. A substantial part of them recount what was going on in the areas of the present states of New York, Michigan, Illinois, Wisconsin, and Minnesota. The "Relations" tell of the folklore, the mores, the economic condition, and the daily life of an Indian people now practically vanished. They were written by men who combined the physical endurance of the athlete with the scholar's academic training, for these Jesuits had to be, and were, rigidly educated in rhetoric, the humanities, and what would today be called psychology. Although the driving force back of this writing was religious zeal, the intellectual curiosity of these missionary reporters led them to record all sorts of phenomena so that generations of readers have found the "Relations" a source of information in many fields. After enjoying a considerable and significant popularity, the "Jesuit Relations" sank into relative obscurity for two centuries, to be revived in the latter half of the nineteenth century, possibly because of their republication by the Canadian government (1858), the popularity of Francis Parkman's *The Jesuits in North America* (1867), and the publication of the series with translation into English by R. G. Thwaites in seventy-three volumes. The expression "Jesuit Relations" should not be permitted to obscure the fact that these volumes were written by individual authors, many of whom became martyrs to their faith at the hands of the Indians. Any consideration of them should record the names of Paul Le Jeune, Barthélemy Vimont, Jérôme Lalament, Paul Ragueneau, Claude Allouez, Claude Dablon, Jean de Brébeuf—and Jacques Marquette. They were trained men with a thirst for adventure, a zeal for Catholicism, and an unusual ability to express themselves.

A by-product of these writings was the "War of the Orders," the rivalry between the Jesuits and Franciscans (Recollects, in this case). The administrators, explorers, and traders of New France were inclined to favor the Franciscans because they were more tolerant than the Jesuits, particularly with respect to using brandy as legal tender to the Indians. Foremost among these Franciscans is Brother Gabriel Sagard, historian of the Hurons, whose first book appeared in 1632 with a dictionary of the Huron language. His *Histoire du Canada* (1636) sums up his previous works and first accounts for the arrival in the present area of the United States of one Etienne Brulé who probably reached Mackinac and the Sault a year before any Pilgrim got to Plymouth. Father Chrétien le Clercq's *Premier etablissement de la foy dans la Nouvelle France* (1691) is a compilation of original accounts of La Salle's voyages, especially that down the Mississippi, and particularly the writings of Father Zenobius Membré. But the most widely read of these Recollects was Father Louis Hennepin, whose *Description de la Louisiane* (1683) is a more reliable account of his work, particularly in the upper Mississippi Valley, than his subsequent *Nouveau Voyage* (1696)—story of a journey he probably never made but plagiarized from Membré's account in Le Clercq. Although Hennepin's writing is marked by the literary egotism characteristic of his day, his geographical observations and his comments on men and manners are excellent. It may be that something has been lost in the continued reliance upon the seventeenth century English translation. Does "This Calumet is the most mysterious Thing in the world among the Savages" express quite the same thought as "Il faut avouer, que le Calumet est quelque chose de fort mysterieux parmi les Sauvages du Grand Continent de l'Amerique Septentrionale"? Hennepin's books ran to thirty-five variant editions in five languages.

Among these Frenchmen was the charming Baron Louis-Armand Lahontan. While the Jesuits and Recollects were minutely describing the American Indian, Lahontan philosophized about him. The fifty-two editions of Lahontan's *Nouveaux Voyages* (1703), which appeared in five different languages, provide some quantitative measure of his work. A more subtle evaluation of his influence is suggested by a modern critic who has pointed out the significance of Lahontan's "noble savage" Adario. That imaginary Indian describes "man in a state of nature" in a manner which is a perfectly logical outcome of many descriptive writings by the Jesuits and the Recollects in the previous decades. French critics have been the first to point out that Montesquieu and Rousseau drew their inspiration from these French reporters and chroniclers of the Indian in New France, and have suggested that the French Revolution actually takes its origin in Huronia

5

In that seventeenth century when the Thirty Years' War eliminated Central Europe from the colonial game, the maritime nations played for high stakes—overseas. In America, two lost out. Both were Protestant, both apparently had the resources and energy for expansion. Both favored the region between New England and Virginia. But, while failing in North America, the Dutch succeeded in the other hemisphere, whereas the Swedes elected to attack Russia and lost out in the east as well as the west. England displaced both in the river valleys of the east coast of North America.

A Florentine, Giovanni da Verrazano, in the service of France, probably looked in at New York harbor in 1524. But from then until 1609 that water was relatively undisturbed by the white man. Emanuel van Meteren published the first account of Henry Hudson and his *Half-Moon,* which bore the flag of the Dutch West India Company. Said Meteren in 1610: "They reached 40° 45′ where they found a good entrance, between two headlands and entered on the 12th of September into as fine a river as can be found." With this, the Hudson River gets into American literature; but Meteren never came to America—he wrote that simply as a part of his story of the Netherlands. More important is the account given by Robert Juet, an English sailor on the *Half-Moon* whose story appears in 1625 in Purchas' *Pilgrimes*. Better than either is a book published in that year by Johann de Laet. He was himself a director of the West India Company, a learned business man, and an associate of the great publishing house of the Elzevirs with whom, under Abraham of that name, he published his *Nieuwe Wereldt* (1625), the first work devoted solely to these Dutch colonies of which New Amsterdam was only one.

So much for the "North," or "Hudson," River. A reporter of the "South," or "Delaware," River is David Pieterszoon de Vries whose *Korte historiael,* published in 1655, recounts his travels in the "four quarters of the globe"—which seem based on some sort of contemporary journals or notes. He went out to the previously abandoned Dutch settlement at Swanendael (near the present Lewes, Delaware), did a bit of trading, then went to the more promising settlement at New Amsterdam, where his descriptions cover the years 1633 to 1643. As a patroon he displays a natural prejudice in favor of that system and is often critical of the administration of the West India Company. His observations show him to have been a person of energy and ability, with a style that is both quaint and vivid. His book is illustrated by exceedingly well executed etchings on copper (including a portrait of the author), which like the narrative sometimes betray a naïve plagiarism.

A somewhat more reliable volume is Adriaen van der Donck's *Beschryvinge van Nieuw Nederlant* (1655). The author was a Dutch lawyer who, as a young man, was brought out to manage the finances, particularly to collect the rents, on the patroonship of the great Kiliaen van Rensselaer. He got into difficulties with that worthy because he seemed to understand the point of view of the tenants who could not always meet their obligations. This led to his preparation of the *Vertoogh van Nieu-Neder-Land* (1650), one of the first of a long line of "remonstrances" stating the grievances of the tenant farmers in the Hudson Valley, a line which did not end (if indeed it is yet ended) until the days of the Anti-Rent War in the mid-nineteenth century. Although this book was begun under the approval of Governor Petrus Stuyvesant, van der Donck quarreled with that worthy, and when writing the *Beschryvinge* was refused access to the official records. His work is less a narrative than a description—and a very satisfactory description at that.

The short-lived colony of "New Sweden" follows the usual literary pattern—some books published at the time, and at least one important report which was not fully published until two centuries afterward, yet was drawn upon by later writers. Peter Mårtensson Lindeström, engineer, visited these Swedish settlements on the Delaware, 1653–1654, then returned home and spent the last years of his life compiling his *Geographia Americae* (published 1925). The first detailed chronicle was *Kort beskrifning om provincien Nya Swerige* (1702), by Tomas Campanius Holm. This author never came to America but composed his work from the journals left by his grandfather, Pastor Campanius Holm. The latter was for six years minister to the colony and made a translation of Luther's catechism into the Lenape Indian language that was printed in 1696. Possibly the best of these Swedish chroniclers was Israel Acrelius who was pastor of the church at Christina (Wilmington, Delaware) 1749–1756. His *Beskrifning om . . . Nya Swerige* (1759) is somewhat ecclesiastical but contains a good description of the land and people. Mention should also be made of a curious series of "theses" on America published at the University of Upsala in the eighteenth century, one of which, by Tobias Erick Biörck, may be accounted the first such "dissertation" about Pennsylvania by a native Pennsylvanian (1731).

6

The literature of the British conquest of America owes an inestimable debt to Richard Hakluyt. This scholar, collector, and editor introduced the English-speaking public to the American discoveries by the Cabots, Verrazano, and Ribaut in his slender volume *Divers Voyages* in 1582. Although he has been variously called a geographer and historian, Hakluyt was, above all, a collector of narratives in the time when it was most important to rescue them. In 1589 appeared *The principal navigations, voiages, traffiques and discoveries of the English nation,* a folio volume which through subsequent editions down to 1600 trebled in size. For America the work is supremely important as gathering the then known narratives of what the explorers were finding, and making these first-hand accounts available to posterity. Stylistically the sections are uneven, varying with their authors; but the value of the source material transcends any consideration of literary quality. At his death Hakluyt had a mass of unused material. By good fortune it was bequeathed to one with similar tastes, Samuel Purchas, who carried on the work by publication of his *Hakluytus posthumus; or, Purchas his Pilgrimes* (1625). Purchas used much material that he had himself gathered as well as what Hakluyt had left him. On the whole his editorial work is far less satisfactory than Hakluyt's, but even so posterity is grateful for it.

The first English book on the first English colony in what is now the United States was *A briefe and true report of the new found land of Virginia* (1588) by Thomas Hariot, professor of mathematics at Oxford. He was especially selected by Raleigh to go with the expedition of 1585 to observe and to report. The result was a slim volume which must ever be "Number One" in the literary history of the British colonies which form the present United States. It is an excellent illustration of the fact that a clear and precise thinker can produce an accurate and readable statement. The economic resources of the North Carolina coast, the manners and customs of the Indian inhabitants, and the possibilities for colonization are succinctly set forth. The book was promptly translated into Latin, French, and German and republished. But its pre-eminence in the literature of history lies also in the fact that Raleigh, besides sending out so expert an observer, sent with him an artist, John White, who painted scores of water-color drawings of what he saw. At the same time Theodore De Bry, publisher in Frankfurt-am-Main, conceived the idea of combining the text of discoveries currently being made with illustrations in full-page engravings made from the drawings the explorers were bringing back to Europe. These De Bry produced periodically, somewhat in the manner of the modern *Illustrated London News* or *Life*. The first "part" combined the text of Hariot and the pictures of John White (1590)—and it had to be reprinted at least nineteen times before 1625. The extent to which the Hariot text was borrowed and the White and De Bry pictures were plagiarized by subsequent writers and artists for the next two hundred years is evidence of the widespread influence of the volume. No other English colony in America ever produced anything comparable to it. De Bry did the same thing with René Goulaine de Laudonnière's *L'histoire notable de la Floride* (1586), the tragic history of the Huguenot colony in Florida, conceived by Admiral Coligny, and planted by Jean Ribaut, which ended in a general massacre by the Spaniards. Laudonnière was also accompanied by an artist, Jacques Le Moyne, whose paintings got back to France and were used by De Bry to provide illustrations for his edition of *La Floride* (1592).

Here let a distinction be made between "adventurers" and "planters." The former "adventured" (invested) their money, not their lives, wives, and labor. The latter "planted" homes as well as seed in the soil. The word "plantation" did not connote a lush growth of tobacco, sugar cane, or rice, but was used to characterize so agriculturally unpromising a place as "Providence Plantation." Thus advertising literature, designed to sell an idea to an absentee "adventurer," had to precede such a book as *Advertisements for the unexperienced planters of New England, or anywhere* (London, 1631), the author of which now enters the story.

For the Old Dominion of Virginia, there is, instead of the careful Hariot, that cheerful romancer and valiant soldier, Captain John Smith. The fact that he was "Governour in Virginia" has, rightly or wrongly, overshadowed the fact that he was also "Admirall of New England," and strove for most of the last years of his life to plant a colony farther north than Chesapeake Bay. The puzzle of his writings is well illustrated by the story of Joseph Sabin's *Dictionary of Books Relating to America*. That great work began publication in 1868, and foundered in 1892 when it reached "Smith, John." "Sabin" stayed on the rocks for twenty-six years before a combination of scholars, foundations, and book collectors pulled it off and arranged the works of John Smith in order. Critics and bibliographers alike have spent three hundred years trying to ascertain exactly what John Smith did write, and did publish—and, worse than that, just what he meant. In those Jacobean days writers did not always observe the canons of scholarship current in the twentieth century. If a traveler writing of what he has seen departs from accuracy, he is apt to be checked up and contradicted by some other member of his expedition. Cortez told his own story of the conquest of Mexico and provoked his companion Bernál Díaz to correct him with yet another book. But the curious thing about John Smith is the manner in which his contemporaries ignored rather than contradicted his yarns. Consider the Pocahontas story—and one cannot well avoid it. Smith's own account in 1608 is matter-of-fact. When he retold it in 1624, the story had become gorgeously and glamorously enlarged. Perhaps the 1608 text is history and the 1624 version is literature. Mark Twain characterized this kind of wisdom after the event in a single word: "embroidery." John Smith may have had that adventure with the comely Indian girl, but he does not mention it in his first account, and his companions, Edward Wingfield, Ralph Hamor, and Christopher Newport, did not record it. Then there is the story of the first Church of England service in America. It is told by others besides Smith, but Smith alone gives us a word picture of that rude first Episcopal church, in his *Advertisements for the unexperienced planters,* published in 1631 nearly a quarter-century after the event. One will never know whether his description is correct, but no artist, sculptor, or even dioramist would dare reproduce that memorable scene without putting in the hewn-log seats and the roof of "sayle" cloth, for the existence of which John Smith is the sole authority. Three of his books are "musts": *A True relation of . . . occurrences in Virginia* (1608); *The Generall historie of Virginia* (1624); and *New Englands trials* (1620). His descriptions of what he saw, what happened to him, his narrow escapes, his bad luck, his triumphs, and his unappreciated greatness give us a picture of an egoist who must have been thoroughly delightful if not always reliable.

7

During the seventeenth century a change came over the temper of the pioneers to the New World, and with it a change in their reports and chronicles. After 1607 the attempted settlements of the Atlantic coast began to succeed. The letters and diaries of the seventeenth and eighteenth centuries are records of hardships encountered and overcome, of plans for living that finally worked. Still contemporaneous in their interest, the stories of these permanent settlements—most of them British—become a more immediate part of our literature. They constitute the first step in our cultural tradition in its specific and dominant Anglo-Saxon phase.

Although Champlain described the harbor of Plymouth, it was Captain John Smith who, in 1614, put "Plimouth" on the map in the position it still occupies. Not until six years later came that band of English Separatists who produced and provoked some notable specimens of literature of their own. The first book about the "Pilgrim" colony seems to have been compiled from memoranda sent back by William Bradford and Edward Winslow in the returning *Mayflower*. But because the volume was seen through the press by one George Morton, of the original Scrooby congregation, he was credited with the authorship of *A relation or journall of the beginning and proceedings of the English plantation settled at Plimoth in New England* (1622)—a title so long that the book was at once dubbed "Mourt's Relation." Its importance lies in the facts that, unlike Bradford's own Journal, it was written at the time the events took place, that it contains the only contemporary account of the voyage of the *Mayflower,* and that it tells of what happened in the first few months of the life of the Plymouth colony.

Far better known are two journals: that of William Bradford, perennial governor of Plymouth, and that of John Winthrop, Sr., who was similarly persistent governor of Massachusetts Bay. Both journals remained in manuscript for a long time, Bradford's until 1856 and Winthrop's until 1790. None can deny the simplicity and sincerity of Bradford's literary style, nor the fact that he reveals the Puritan at his best. Winthrop's character was slightly more complex, and he did not always display the Christian charity of his contemporary at Plymouth.

These articulate founders of New England, and others who will be mentioned below, not only were educated gentlemen, but were well educated. Within certain narrowing limits of their religious beliefs, they were able to discern and to think clearly. They were "planting" as well as "adventuring" in a new country in which they proposed to make permanent homes. It was inevitable that they should want to write about what they were doing. To select the more significant of these men and generalize about them and their writings, would betray a lack of understanding. They were individuals and individualists—that is why they came to America in the first place. They displayed in common the pietism of their sect, and they thought in terms of their own consequent concept of the Deity. But it must be remembered that if occasionally they displayed intolerance, they had been the victims of intolerance; if they seemed inhospitable to other emigrants such as Quakers and Catholics, whose views were at variance with their own, this may well have been because the Puritans felt that America was big enough for all and that the dissidents ought to go elsewhere. The heterodox should find other open spaces even if the Puritans had to whip them or imprison them to make that point clear. True, they made a fetish of hard work; but that was not only because these people had work to do in making new homes in a comparatively unfertile land with a chilly climate, it was also because they genuinely enjoyed hard work.

The language in which they expressed themselves was the language of their day, contemporaneous with the publication of the King James Version of the Bible, and all that that implies with respect to the standardization of literary expression and form. Because the King James Version is still readable, so are these Puritan books.

Although the literature of New England in this period is more fully treated in later chapters, mention should here be made of those reporters and historians whose works first chronicled the process of settlement. A thorn in the side of the serious people at Plymouth was Thomas Morton, "Gent.," who persisted in conducting a rum-and-gun-running house (even worse) at "Merrymount" between Boston and Plymouth. The Plymouth people threw him out bodily twice, whereupon he wrote *New English Canaan* (1637), which had to be printed in Amsterdam. In it he "reports" what was going on from a point of view quite different from that of the patient Governor Bradford who had to handle him. There was not likely to be any agreement with an author who always referred to Myles Standish as "Captain Shrimp."

A very different Morton was Nathaniel of that name, actually one of the original "pilgrim fathers," and a minor politician at Plymouth. He used the unpublished works of Bradford and Winslow in the preparation of his *New-England's memoriall* (1669), and reported from his own knowledge the painstaking character of the life of his region. More readable is *New Englands prospect* (1634), wherein William Wood describes the natural features of the country with an easy grace and intersperses really meritorious verse in his prose. In contrast is Edward Johnson's *History of New England* (1654), which covers the period 1628–1652, and which he wanted known by its ponderous subtitle "Wonder-working providence of Sion's saviour in New England." This is a homely record of workaday facts to which other chroniclers are apt to be superior. But to provide such facts was not Johnson's purpose in writing it. His design was to prove that the Deity in person ordained the success of the Bay Colony and that he took a personal interest in such matters as the price of cattle and the accuracy of Myles Standish's aim when shooting at an Indian. The book is revivalistic in style, and the text is garnished with original verse of questionable merit. Better balanced is John Josselyn, who hovered on the border line between herbalist and botanist, and whose *New Englands rarities discovered* (1672) was noticed by the Royal Society. This encouraged him to write *An account of two voyages to New-*

England (1674), which combines scientific lore with hints to settlers and sly digs at the Puritans.

Toward the close of the seventeenth century the colonies had become so firmly established that they had histories to be written. Among the historians whom New England produced, three—William Hubbard, Thomas Prince, and Thomas Hutchinson—wrote about their own day as well as of earlier times. Hubbard was a clergyman, and his *A Narrative of the troubles with the Indians in New England* (1677) is a graphic account of those wars which later came to be associated with the name of the Indian King Philip. Hubbard lived through those struggles, and though one feels that sometimes he agreed with General Sheridan that the only good Indian was a dead Indian he did interpret his own times. A more ambitious work was his *A general history of New-England from the discovery to MDCLXXX,* based on the previous works of Morton and Winthrop. It was not published until 1815, but the manuscript was drawn upon heavily by subsequent historians, notably Cotton Mather and Thomas Prince. Unlike Hubbard—an historian who happened to be a clergyman—Prince was a clergyman who made an historian of himself. He must have been a precocious youngster. He got into print by issuing sermons, which led to his writing an introduction to a life of Cotton Mather, thence to a deep collector's interest in Matheriana and the planning of his ambitious *A chronological history of New-England,* the first volume of which appeared in 1736. In this noteworthy work Prince seems to have outgrown his earlier subject-matter limitations and developed a style which was both lively and fairly objective. But his praiseworthy love for verifying details bogged down his history.

Thomas Hutchinson was a chronicler of a different and far broader experience than these clergymen. He was a cultivated gentleman, a merchant, a lawyer, a man of the world, and Governor of Massachusetts. The first volume of his *The History of the Colony of Massachusetts Bay* appeared in 1764, and although it is rather dull reading today, its reception encouraged him to continue work so as to bring his story down to 1750. His conservative position in the Stamp Act troubles led to disorders wherein his house was invaded by a Boston mob and his papers scattered. Rescuing them the next day from the mud (which may still be seen on the manuscripts) and undeterred by the ill manners of his fellow townsmen, he pushed his second volume to conclusion and wrote with facility and grace on happenings of which he himself had been a witness. On the losing side in the Revolution, he colored his third volume with his prejudices and displayed a failure to appreciate that his world was changing.

When the Dutch yielded New York to the British, two little books appeared which, because of their extreme rarity, are probably less known than they should be. Daniel Denton, a native Long Islander, published in 1670 *A brief description of New York: formerly called New Netherlands.* Since this is the first separate publication in English describing New York, it is noteworthy that the author insists he has "writ nothing, but what I have been an eye witness to all or the greatest part of it" and deliberately cries down the extravagant claims of both the Indians and the Dutch as to the possibilities of the real estate—yet he concludes with a not-too-subtle statement that the poor of the Old World will find haven here. In the next year appeared a tiny volume by the first American minister to have a charge in New York, Charles Wolley. His *A two years journal in New-York* (1701) is worth while if only for his anecdote on how he reconciled the pugnacious Lutheran and Calvinist ministers whom the Dutch had left behind. These two, says Wolley, "behav'd themselves one toward another so shily and uncharitably as if *Luther* and *Calvin* had bequeathed and entailed their virulent and bigotted Spirits upon them and their heirs forever."

Of the many published writings of William Penn, few deal with his great colony. His *Some account of the province of Pennsylvania* (1681) was written before he set sail—yet gives us this phrase: "Colonies are the seeds of nations." His *Frame of Government* (1682) suggests, "Any government is free to the people under it where the laws rule and the people are a party to the laws." This antedates by a century John Adams' adaptation from Jean Bodin, "to the end that it shall be a government of laws and not of men." After Penn reached Philadelphia, he reported to the "Free Society of Traders" in London, by *A letter from William Penn* (1683), a document which is largely descriptive but contains a priceless introductory paragraph in which he gently corrects the reports by his enemies in London about him, and explains that he is not dead and is not a Jesuit. Upon his return to London he published his *Further Account* (1685), wherein he sums up by saying to prospective emigrants, "Be moderate in Expectation, count on Labour before a Crop, and Cost before Gain"—than which no entrepreneur ever gave better advice.

As what Penn had to say about Pennsylvania was the least of his literary output, the investigator must turn to Thomas Budd's *Good order established in Pennsylvania & New Jersey* (1685), a delightful seventeenth century imprint wherein the author tries to summarize the entire book on the title page. Few specimens of colonial promotional literature state so succinctly that the capitalist system will do Christian work and produce 7 per cent:

> Taking into consideration the distressed Condition that many Thousand Families lie under in my Native Country, by reason of the deadness of Trade, and want of work, and believing that many that have great Store of Money, that lies by them unimploy'd, would be willing and ready to assist and encourage those

poor distressed People, by supplying them with Monies, in order to bring them out of Slavery and Poverty they groan under, if they might do it with safety to themselves, these Considerations put me on writing this small Treatise, wherein I hope . . . that the Rich may help relieve the Poor, and yet reap great Profit and Advantage to themselves by their so doing.

The practical tone of Budd's advice was predominant in all the reports and chronicles, as well as the other literature, of the Southern colonies discussed in the next chapter. Even indentured servants like John Hammond and George Alsop praised the pioneer life in a gay and worldly spirit reflected, in more serious vein, in the histories of Robert Beverley and William Stith. Characteristic of these writers are John Lederer and Thomas Ash.

Tourists of the future will become more and more familiar with the "skyline" drive along the Blue Ridge, Shenandoah Valley, and the Great Smokies, in the back country of Virginia and North Carolina. The earliest reporter of this country was one of whom little is known save his book, *The Discoveries of John Lederer in three several marches from Virginia to the west of Carolina* (1672). Lederer introduced the geology, botany, and native inhabitants to the English-reading world. Of German origin, he wrote in Latin, whence his book was rescued by a member of the Virginia "Council" and translated into English because the author was "a modest ingenious person, and a pretty scholar." There is reason to think that Lederer was first to climb the Appalachian Divide and look over into what was to become the Middle West.

For writing that is picturesque one turns to Thomas Ash who, as "T. A." in *Carolina* (1682), describes the synthesis of the elements of the social history of the region. Noteworthy among these are two derivatives of corn: hominy and a beverage wherein the corn is treated "by Maceration, and when duly feremented, a strong spirit like *Brandy* may be drawn off from it, by the help of an *Alembick*." Both Ash and Governor John Archdale, whose *A new description . . . of Carolina* appeared in 1707, are careful writers within the limits of the scientific knowledge of their day. Archdale betrays the fact of his previous residence in the Bible commonwealths to the north when he suggests that it "pleased Almighty God to send unusual sicknesses amongst" the Indians since, in order to make room for the white man, "there seemed a Necessity of thining the barbarous *Indian* Nations." Yet he has misgivings and comforts himself with the assurance that the English colonists "in comparison to the Spaniard, have but little *Indian* Blood to answer for."

Thus the discovery, opening, and settlement of the continent was recorded by those who took part in the adventure. There is the charm of the primitive, not only in the expression but in the format of these old books. But their principal appeal lies in the fact that they present the feelings of the man who was there at the time the event took place and not what some later interpreter, however learned, may have felt. If the "end of all scribblement is to amuse," there are those who are entertained by these efforts at expression on the part of many a stout Cortez who was not content to remain silent upon a peak in Darien.

4. WRITERS OF THE SOUTH

THE earliest literature of the permanent English settlements came from the Southern colonies and was, for the most part, descriptive and factual, concerned in some fashion with the land itself. Less introspective than the Puritans of New England, the writers of the agrarian South turned their attention to the world outside their doors. Though verse writers frequently were imitators of conventional themes in poetry, a few devoted their efforts to describing their own milieu, sometimes satirically, but with attention to external life in the colonies. Southern writers of prose and poetry rarely, if ever, wrestled with their souls in the manner of Cotton Mather; to most of them, the exposure of one's innermost thoughts and feelings would have seemed indecent. Even when, like William Byrd of Westover, they kept diaries, they were more reticent about their thoughts than about their behavior; and their meditations were more often upon politics and social relations than upon metaphysics.

To its London readers the Reverend Alexander Whitaker's *Good News from Virginia* (1613) described an earthly paradise. In Virginia men might live in ease supported by the fruitfulness of the soil and take their pleasure in sport which the Creator provided, for the woods abounded in wild turkeys, swift as greyhounds, and with pigeons, ducks, geese, partridges, and other game birds, and the rivers teemed with the finest fish: "Shads of a great bigness, and rockfish . . . trouts, bass, flounders, and other dainty fish . . . [and] multitudes of great sturgeons, whereof we catch many." The author vouches for the abundance of the fish which he himself had caught—"with mine angle." Therefore, he advises his readers, "since God hath filled the elements of earth, air and waters with his creatures, good for our food and nourishment, let not the fear of starving hereafter, or any great want, dishearten your valiant minds from coming to a place of so great plenty." If Whitaker's book stirred the hopeful imaginations of Englishmen to contemplate the virtues of the New World, that was his intention. And that, indeed, was the purpose in one way or another of much of the writing in the colonial South.

The first strictly literary work, however, was an exception to this most characteristic type of colonial writing, for it linked the New World with the great cultural past and was prophetic of that interest in the classics which the educated groups in the colonies retained and fostered for many generations. The work was Ovid's *Metamorphoses,* translated into English verse by George Sandys, son of the Archbishop of York and brother of Sir Edwin Sandys, the noble-spirited secretary of the Virginia Company of London. Sandys came to Virginia in 1621 and remained seven years, taking an active part in the colony's administration and defense.

The more cultivated members of the colonial ruling class inherited something of Sandys' zeal for the classics. This tradition, a legacy of the Renaissance more evident in the reading and in the oratory of Southerners than in their literary productions, helped to modify and transmute some of the materialism which frontier conditions induced. Generations later, colonial gentlemen read Sandys' Ovid as they read another of his works, *A Paraphrase upon the Psalms of David* (1636), and they approved of both.

The contrast between the classical interests of Sandys and the literal record of Whitaker provides a revealing introduction to the study of Southern colonial writers. The same contrast is to be found in the person of the master of Westover, William Byrd the younger, most representative Southern colonial writer. A man of means and learning, he collected perhaps the finest private library of colonial times; but his own writing is a record of his life on his plantation and on his surveying expeditions into the interior. The Southern books that have come down to us from these early days are concerned with the things of this world rather than of the next. Behind Thomas Jefferson's *Notes on Virginia* (1784) there is a tradition of scientific, descriptive, and promotional literature unequaled in the colonies to the north.

2

To defend both Virginia and Maryland from traducers, John Hammond in 1656 published in London a little tract entitled *Leah and Rachel, or, the Two Fruitful Sisters, Virginia and Maryland: Their Present Condition, Impartially Stated and Related.* Hammond had lived for nineteen years in Virginia, he tells us, and for two years in Maryland, until dissensions during the Cromwellian period forced him to flee to England. This pamphlet, written after his arrival, describes nostalgically the goodness of the land in the Chesapeake region, where men and women can live in ease and plenty. By contrast England is an abode of misery. "And therefore I cannot but admire," Hammond declares, "and indeed much pity the dull stupidity of people necessitated in England, who rather than they will remove themselves, live here a base, slavish, penurious life, . . . choosing rather than they will forsake England to stuff Newgate, Bridewell, and other jails with their carcasses, nay cleave to Tyburn itself." Like Crèvecœur more than a century later, Hammond vividly emphasizes the opportunities of the new life in America, where everything is inviting, a country "not only plentiful but pleasant and profitable, . . . pleasant in . . . the brightness of the weather, . . . pleasant in their building, . . . pleasant in observing their stocks and flocks of cattle, hogs, and poultry, grazing, whisking, and skipping in their sights, pleasant in having all things of their own, growing or breeding without drawing the penny to send for this and that, without which, in England, they cannot be supplied."

A few serpents had invaded that Eden, notably Maryland, and Hammond is emphatic in his distaste for troublemakers, particularly one of the leaders of a turbulent faction, Will Claiborne, "whom ye all know to be a villain." The earlier tract, *Hammond versus Heamans, or, An Answer to an Audacious Pamphlet, Published by an Impudent and Ridiculous Fellow Named Roger Heamans* (1655), was a vigorous but less literary diatribe against the ship captain who had espoused the cause of rebels against the government and had helped to drive Hammond himself out of Maryland.

The most vigorous and original work of the middle decades of the seventeenth century was George Alsop's *A Character of the Province of Maryland,* printed in London in 1666. The author, who had served four years as an indentured servant in Maryland, wrote in stout defense of life in that colony, even the life of a servant, which he found far pleasanter and more promising than the drudgery and the hopeless poverty of England.

Alsop's descriptions, written in colorful and idiomatic prose, have the rhythms of the Elizabethans and their zest for the world about them. His style is not unlike that of Thomas Dekker's pamphlets. With a boisterous humor that is sometimes coarse but never dull, he tells about the country and its customs, the Susquehannock Indians, and the mutual benefits of trade between England and Maryland. At the end of the book are several letters written to friends and kinsmen about his voyage to the New World and his experiences there. Occasionally Alsop inserts a poem, displaying an ease of versifying and a quality not often encountered among early writers in the colony.

That Alsop is a man of some cultivation appears from his literary allusions. He has read the prose of Dr. John Donne, and, when ill and threatened with death, he quotes from a sermon by the learned dean and includes a philosophic observation: "We are only sent by God of an errand into this world, and the time that's allotted to us for to stay is only for an answer. When God, my great Master, shall in good earnest call me home, which these warnings tell me I have not long to stay, I hope then I shall be able to give him a good account of my message."

Like certain Cavalier poets, Alsop's muse requires no theme of vast importance. When someone sends him a purple cap he lets his imagination range on the possible uses of this piece of velvet headgear. Perhaps it once graced Oliver Cromwell's head, which, Alsop is pleased to note, has lately been hoisted on Westminster's roof:

> Say, didst thou cover Noll's old brazen head,
> Which on top of Westminster'[s] high lead
> Stands on a pole, erected to the sky,
> As a grand trophy to his memory?
> From his perfidious skull didst thou fall down,
> In disdain to honour such a crown
> With three-pile velvet? Tell me, hadst thou thy fall
> From the high top of that cathedral?

Elsewhere in prose and verse, he is equally disdainful of Puritans and their kind. For example, he attributes the ready market of Maryland's pork with ship captains of New England to the stiff Calvinists' need for some kind of softening, "because their bodies being fast bound up with the cords of restrigent zeal, they are fain to make use of the liniments of this non-Canaanite creature physically to loosen them."

Alsop's little book reads less like a promotional tract than most of the descriptive works written in the colonies. He gives the impression of sincerity and truth in his descriptions, as in the passage defending the system of indentured servitude. Those who cannot pay their passage to Maryland, he writes, "may for the debarment of a four years' sordid liberty go over to this province and live there plenteously well. And what's four years' servitude to advantage a man all the remainder of his days, making his predecessors happy in his sufficient abilities, which he attained to partly by the restrainment of so small a time?"

Most of the descriptive prose of the early eighteenth century was less boisterous than Alsop's. Typical of a long series of such works was *The Present State of Virginia and the College* (1727), prepared by a committee of Virginians consisting of Henry Hartwell, James Blair, and Edward Chilton, who presented their report to the Board of Trade in London on October 20, 1697. The author of the portion describing the College of William and Mary was that institution's founder, the Reverend James Blair, an irascible Scot, who as "commissary" of the Church of England was the Bishop of London's personal representative in Virginia. He labored unceasingly to make the College of William and Mary a nursery of Anglican clergymen, and he was the author of a popular series of homilies entitled *Our Savior's Divine Sermon on the Mount,* five volumes, published in London in 1722. A second edition was called for before the author died in 1743, and the work attracted so much attention that it was translated into Danish and published in Denmark in 1761.

By the end of the seventeenth century, settlers in the oldest English colony were beginning to feel a maturity not yet manifest in the newer colonies. Writers began to display an incipient nationalism, a loyalty to the new land as their native region. An anonymous Virginian published in London *An Essay upon the Government of the English Plantations on the Continent of America* (1701) and in place of his name proudly subscribed on the title page the words "By an American." Some evidence suggests that the writer was Robert Beverley, or perhaps his father-in-law, William Byrd the elder. Certainly it was some member of the Beverley-Byrd group of planters. The tract is an earnest and clearly written plea for more intelligent understanding and administration by the colonial authorities in England, and it makes one of the earliest proposals of a plan of union for the English colonies.

Robert Beverley exhibited an originality and self-conscious pride in his Virginia origins that sometimes irritated his contemporaries, especially his socially ambitious brother-in-law, William Byrd the younger, who was pleased to hang the walls of his house at Westover with portraits of English noblemen. In 1705, a London bookseller brought out *The History and Present State of Virginia . . . by a Native of the Place.* On a handsomely engraved frontispiece, Beverley acknowledged the authorship with his initials. Writing with humor, and occasionally with biting sarcasm, he did not spare the feelings of his contemporaries. He was sharply critical of various royal governors, particularly Francis Nicholson, and he ridiculed the lack of enterprise of his fellow planters who had become utterly dependent upon tobacco and the English market. He also suggested somewhat satirically that his fellow Virginians would have been better off if they had followed John Rolfe's example and had intermarried with the Indians. Although the historical narrative for the early years is largely derivative from Captain John Smith and other chroniclers, the sections dealing with the Indians and with contemporary observations are an important contribution to history.

In 1722, the year of his death, Beverley finished and published a revision of the *History* which omitted the acerbities of the earlier version. The second edition, reprinted in the nineteenth century, is less colorful but more charitable. The *History* was translated into French and had four printings on the Continent by 1718. Beverley had written his book with one eye on prospective immigrants, especially French Huguenots, and he must have been pleased at its popularity abroad. It is an early instance of how the patronizing tone of British writers on the colonies could stir the "native" pride to reply.

3

The writer from the Southern colonies best known today is William Byrd the younger, author of the *History of the Dividing Line,* and of an extensive diary lately discovered and published. The son of one of the wealthiest planters in Virginia, Byrd received an English education and while a student of law at the Middle Temple cultivated the acquaintance of literary and social lions. A familiar friend of Wycherley and Congreve, he played with the idea of being a man of letters and wrote dainty or satirical verses, some of which found their way into an English miscellany. Since scientific speculation at the turn of the seventeenth century was both fashionable and appealing, Byrd determined to make himself a man of learning and a virtuoso in science. Flattered by an invitation to join the Royal Society, he submitted a paper describing an albino Negro and for the rest of his life prized his status as a corresponding member of the Society. Although Byrd was called back to Virginia in 1704 on the death of his father, he later spent considerable time in England as agent for the colony, and until the day of his death in 1744 he corresponded with titled and learned friends in the mother country.

His diary indicates a methodical devotion to classical learning; he is careful to record the daily reading of Greek, Latin, or Hebrew, interspersed with an occasional effort at literary translation. A free rendering of the tale of the Matron of Ephesus from the *Satyricon* survives. He also continued to write verses, a few of which are in existence, and he turned his hand to science and mathematics. Fancying himself something of an amateur in medicine, he dosed his household and neighbors when opportunity offered, and wrote *A Discourse Concerning the Plague with Some Preservatives Against It* (London, 1721). This forty-page pamphlet is the only complete work from Byrd's pen known to have been published in his lifetime.

Byrd's diary, kept in shorthand, probably through most of his adult life, is a significant and revealing document with occasional glints of humor. Three portions are known, two of which are now in print. The Virginia Historical Society, which owns a section covering the years 1717–1721, has declined to permit its publication. In this suppressed part Byrd describes with Pepysian frankness his amatory adventures in London, where he pursued without discrimination whores, chambermaids, and great ladies. Most of his diary, however, concerns the matter-of-fact and fairly decorous existence of a man intent upon maintaining his classical learning, managing his estates successfully, and fulfilling his responsibilities to the commonwealth.

Byrd's most important literary contribution is the *History of the Dividing Line Run in the Year 1728,* a narrative of the boundary survey between Virginia and North Carolina in which he commanded the party of Virginians. Although he was clearly ambitious to be regarded as a man of letters, he preferred to pursue his avocation in the genteel manner, without rushing precipitately into print. From a journal kept during the survey, Byrd made a draft of his well known narrative which he called *The Secret History of the Line.* This version, which contained fictitious names of the participants, the author revised, expanded, and polished; but he never brought himself to publish the finished text. Not until 1841 was any version of the narrative printed, though manuscript copies had circulated among Byrd's friends and had attracted their favorable attention, as did two shorter works, *A Journey to the Land of Eden, Anno 1733* and *A Progress to the Mines in the Year, 1732.*

These are all spirited narratives. Writing with the zest of youth and the maturity of a man of the world, Byrd conveys to the reader some of his own adventurousness and commands attention with his shrewd observation and commentary. He spices his story with humor, as in the passage describing the laziness of North Carolinians encountered in the back country:

> They make their wives rise out of their beds early in the morning, at the same time that they lie and snore, till the sun has risen one-third of his course, and dispersed all the unwholesome damps. Then, after stretching and yawning for half an hour, they light their pipes, and, under the protection of a cloud of smoke, venture out into the open air; though, if it happens to be never so little cold, they quickly return shivering into the chimney corner. When the weather is mild, they stand leaning with both their arms upon the cornfield fence, and gravely consider whether they had best go and take a small heat at the hoe: but generally find reasons to put it off till another time. Thus they loiter away their lives, like Solomon's sluggard, with their arms across, and at the winding up of the year scarcely have bread to eat. To speak the truth, it is a thorough aversion to labor that makes people file off to North Carolina, where plenty and a warm sun confirm them in their disposition to laziness for their whole lives.

4

The defense of North Carolina, its products and its native people, was undertaken by John Lawson, a Scottish adventurer who landed at Charleston in 1700 and became surveyor-general of the colony. First published in London in 1709 as *A New Voyage to Carolina,* it is generally referred to as *The History of Carolina* from the title given to the second edition of 1714. Lawson's book, a brisk and readable account from first-hand observation, achieved considerable popularity. A third English edition appeared in 1718, and it was translated into German and published in Hamburg in 1712 and

1722. Like Beverley's *History,* it served as propaganda for immigration to the Southern colonies. "'Tis a great misfortune," Lawson observes in the preface, "that most of our travellers who go to this vast continent in America are persons of the meaner sort, and generally of a very slender education . . . uncapable of giving any reasonable account of what they met withal in these remote parts, tho' the country abounds with curiosities worthy a nice observation. In this point, I think, the French outstrip us." To correct the balance, Lawson expanded the journal of his travels; but he warns the reader that he has aimed at truth and accuracy instead of entertainment, "which is, indeed, the duty of every author and preferable to a smooth style accompanied with falsities and hyperboles."

The most readable part of his narrative is the description of the Indians and their customs, which attributes to them, particularly the women, many attractive qualities, albeit a lack of inhibitions shocking to a Puritan but not to John Lawson. Of a companion of his travels whose fair comrade of the night made off with her lover's shoes and personal possessions, Lawson remarks, "Thus early did our spark already repent his new bargain, walking barefoot in his penitentials like some poor pilgrim to Loretto."

Lawson's earthly and literary career was cut short in 1711 by these selfsame Indians. In company with the Baron de Graffenried, a Swiss promoter of colonization, he made another journey into the hinterland and was captured by the savages, who put him to death. De Graffenried escaped to tell the tale and blame Lawson's rashness for the catastrophe.

The chief literary monuments during the remainder of the colonial period were descriptive histories or narratives. The Reverend Hugh Jones, professor of mathematics at the College of William and Mary, the author of the first American grammar of the English language, published in 1724 *The Present State of Virginia,* a brief factual account, which announced on the title page that the book was designed "for the service of such as are engaged in the propagation of the gospel and advancement of learning, and for the use of all persons concerned in the Virginia trade and plantation." Jones' book is simple and clear without any effort at rhetorical adornment.

The most voluminous historical work in the Southern colonies up to its time was William Stith's *The History of the First Discovery and Settlement of Virginia: Being an Essay towards a General History of this Colony* (Williamsburg, 1747). Stith's 331 pages of small type brought the narrative of Virginia down only as far as 1624. Though his detailed account of Virginia's early history proved tedious to the busy master of Monticello, the work exemplifies a new ideal of historical investigation and a zeal for accurate research hitherto unknown in the American colonies. His preface is a readable and significant landmark in the story of American scholarship, and the main body of the text is far from deserving Jefferson's censure. Like more recent historians, Stith found much to commend in Captain John Smith's own observations, but lamented the confusion of his work and deplored the inattention to documentary evidence displayed by Smith's successors. "And I can further declare with great truth," he says, "that had anything of great consequence been done in our history, I could most willingly have saved myself the trouble of conning over our old musty records, and of studying, connecting, and reconciling the jarring and disjointed writings and relations of different men and different parties."

Stith's uncle, Sir John Randolph, had contemplated an account of the development of the government of Virginia, and had collected many records and public documents which at his death he left still unused. Furthermore, William Byrd, who had procured a manuscript copy of the records of the Virginia Company, made this document available and encouraged Stith to pursue his research. "Neither could I well excuse myself," Stith comments, "if I did not likewise acknowledge with what humanity and politeness that well-bred gentleman and scholar not only communicated those manuscripts to me, but also threw open his library (the best and most copious collection of books in our part of America) and was himself ever studious and solicitous to search out and give me whatever might be useful to my undertaking." Stith's history, which he intended to continue to a later period, was an example of the newly awakened American point of view. For example, his interpretation of King James' interference with the Virginia Company as the machinations of a hostile tyrant—a view which grew ever more congenial under the mistakes of the Georges—became the traditional explanation until our own time.

Somewhat akin to the historical and descriptive narratives was a brilliant satire and an exposé of conditions in Georgia by a group of disgruntled enemies of the founder, General James Oglethorpe. Their tract, *A True and Historical Narrative of the Colony of Georgia* (1741), was published in Charleston, South Carolina. The authors—who announced themselves on the title page as Patrick Tailfer, M.D., Hugh Anderson, M.A., David Dougles, "and others"—had taken refuge there after antagonizing Oglethorpe's agent in Georgia. Prefaced by a dedication of mock deference to Oglethorpe, the book calmly and devastatingly ridicules the vanities and weaknesses of the philanthropist. Jonathan Swift himself need not have been ashamed of the satirical skill demonstrated in the dedication. After referring to the generous governments of certain colonies and the prosperity which commerce had brought, the authors comment that "your Excellency's concern for our perpetual welfare could never permit you to propose such transitory advantages for us. . . . You have afforded us the opportunity of arriving at the integrity of the primitive times by entailing a more than primitive poverty on us. The toil that is necessary to our bare subsistence must effectually defend us from the anxieties of any further ambition. . . . The valuable virtue of humility is secured to us by your care."

Among the grudges which the authors held against Oglethorpe were his injunctions against Negro slavery and the importation of rum. Although promotional tracts had lavished hyperboles on the wholesomeness of the air and water in the colony, they thought a little rum would be a benefit to health, for "the experience of all the inhabitants of America will prove the necessity of qualifying water with some spirit." They were particularly hostile toward John Wesley, whose residence in the colony had encouraged such "attendances upon prayers, meetings, and sermons" as to "propagate a spirit of indolence and of hypocrisy amongst the most abandoned" who by a show of religion managed to live in ease from the public stores.

Although the tract is plainly partisan, its authors display an urbane cultivation, a familiarity with contemporary literature, and a detachment unusual in eighteenth century controversial writings. That its barbs went home is evident from a solemn defense made by the Reverend William Best in a sermon before the trustees for the colony of Georgia, entitled *The Merit and Reward of a Good Intention* (London, 1742)

5

The muse of poetry inspired few Southerners in the colonial period to write from their hearts about their own world. When they wrote verse, the most formalized type of composition, they became self-conscious and imitative. Rarely could they escape the diction, the manner, the style, or the themes of the reigning dictators of poetry in England. Dryden and Pope had their slavish and uninspired disciples on the banks of the James, as well as the Thames. Even incipient democracy was sung in formal measures in the Southern colonies.

The verse with which George Alsop decorated his prose account of seventeenth century Maryland demonstrates that indentured servants were often men of considerable schooling. It is possible that another indentured servant was the author of one of the noblest poems of this period. The rebellion in 1676 of Nathaniel Bacon against Sir William Berkeley, governor of Virginia, inspired both a narrative tribute and a poetic one, which are preserved in a manuscript usually called the Burwell Papers (published 1814). The unknown prose narrator, clearly no partisan of Bacon's, inserted the poem at the conclusion of a passage recounting the rebel's death. The elegy ends:

Mars and Minerva both in him concurred
For arts, for arms, whose pen and sword alike
As Cato's did, may admiration strike
Into his foes; while they confess withal
It was their guilt styl'd him a criminal.
Only this difference does from truth proceed:
They in the guilt, he in the name must bleed.
While none shall dare his obsequies to sing
In deserv'd measures until time shall bring
Truth crown'd with freedom, and from danger free
To sound his praises to posterity.
Here let him rest; while we this truth report;
He's gone from hence unto a higher court
To plead his cause, where he by this doth know
Whether to Caesar he was friend or foe.

Such praise was certain to bring forth an answer, and another unknown writer replied with a poem beginning:

Whether to Caesar he was friend or foe?
Pox take such ignorance, do you not know?
Can he be friend to Caesar that shall bring
The arms of Hell to fight against the King?

Thus in the midst of civil war and Indian forays, men of action could take time to express their emotions in verse that had a depth of feeling and sometimes a grace and ease of diction. Clearly the wilderness of Virginia was far from destitute of literary talent, though few examples have survived.

More in the realistic tradition of Southern colonial writing is a boisterous satire, *The Sot-Weed Factor* (London, 1708), which took for its subject of ridicule the contemporary scene in Maryland. Unfortunately for American literature, its author, who signed himself Ebenezer Cook, declared that he was an Englishman.

Condemn'd by Fate to wayward curse
Of friends unkind and empty purse,

he had been obliged to make a dismal voyage to a rude and ribald land. Twenty-one quarto pages of couplets relate the poet's unhappy adventures in Maryland, where he tried to set up as a tobacco merchant but was roundly cheated by the inhabitants. With his last lines he curses the country:

May wrath divine then lay those regions waste
Where no man's faithful nor a woman chaste.

Belles-lettres in Maryland and Virginia found a fresh stimulation after the arrival of William Parks, the printer, who by the spring of 1726 had established a press at Annapolis, and by 1730 had opened a printing shop in Williamsburg. Parks was more than a printer. He had literary taste and a flair for journalism. In 1736 he established the *Virginia Gazette,* which opened its columns to ambitious poets and essayists. They responded with an assortment of occasional verse and miscellaneous commentary.

The most important poetical work to issue from Parks' Annapolis press was *The Mouse-Trap, or the Battle of the Cambrians and Mice* (1728), a translation by Richard Lewis of Edward Holdsworth's Latin poem *Muscipula,* satirizing the Welsh. Lewis, who served as a schoolmaster in Annapolis, displayed a genuine talent for versification, and a learning which would have been a credit to Augustan London. His verse dedication to Governor Benedict Calvert concludes:

> Yet—hear me!—while I beg you to excuse
> This bold intrusion of an unknown muse;
> And if her faults too manifest appear
> And her rude numbers should offend your ear,
> Then, if you please with your forgiving breath,
> Which can reprieve the wretch condemn'd from death,
> To speak a pardon for her errors past,
> This first poetic crime shall prove her last.

Governor Calvert encouraged the translator by heading a list of one hundred and fifty Marylanders who subscribed for one or more copies of the book. Lewis was the author of a few later poems, but the translation was his most ambitious undertaking. His preface in prose to that work is an urbane, polished, and learned bit of literary criticism, worthy of an Elizabethan courtly scholar.

Two years after the publication of *The Mouse-Trap,* the Annapolis press issued *Sotweed Redivivus, or the Planter's Looking-Glass,* by E. C. Gent. [Ebenezer Cook?] (1730), written in obvious imitation of the earlier satire, *The Sot-Weed Factor,* which had proved popular; but the new work lacked the vigor and the robust humor of the original. The following year Parks brought out a volume bearing the hopeful title of *The Maryland Muse,* which, in addition to a versified account of Bacon's Rebellion, included a third edition of *The Sot-Weed Factor.*

Fittingly William Parks chose to publish as one of his first labors at Williamsburg, J. Markland's *Typographia, an Ode on Printing* (1730). With a panoply of classical allusion, Markland praises King George and Governor Gooch, and then pays tribute to Parks, the printer:

From whom Virginia's laws, that lay
In blotted manuscripts obscur'd,
By vulgar eyes unread,
Which whilom scarce the light endur'd,
Begin to view again the day,
As rising from the dead.
For this the careful artist wakes,
And o'er his countless brood he stands,
His numerous hoards
Of speechless letters, unform'd words,
Unjointed questions, and unmeaning breaks,
Which into order rise, and form, at his command.

If Markland's ode has no great originality it at least displays able craftsmanship in a genre popular in the age of Pope.

Governor Gooch, to whom Markland dedicated his ode, was himself a man of no mean skill in letters. To popularize a new law regulating the inspection of tobacco, he wrote in spirited prose and had Parks publish *A Dialogue Between Thomas Sweet-Scented, William Oronoco, Planters, and Justice Love-Country, Who Can Speak for Himself* (1732). For lightness of touch and humor, Gooch's piece of propaganda surpassed the usual work of this type.

The Williamsburg press brought out in 1736 *Poems on Several Occasions,* by "a Gentleman of Virginia." The unnamed author was William Dawson, a graduate of Queen's College, Oxford, and professor of moral philosophy at the College of William and Mary who later became its president. Dawson's statement in his preface that "the following pieces are the casual productions of youth" is confirmed by the quality of the poems. No verse in the volume shows the slightest glimmer of inspiration from the New World. Though Dawson's poems are not without skill, they can hardly be described as contributions to American literature, for they were most certainly written before he took up residence in Virginia.

A somewhat better claim for a small niche in the annals of American letters can be made for James Sterling, Anglican rector of St. Paul's Parish, in Kent County, Maryland. An Irishman who had already achieved a modest reputation in Dublin as a playwright and poet, Sterling is believed to be the author of an anonymous poem, *An Epistle to the Hon. Arthur Dobbs, Esq. in Europe, From a Clergyman in America* (London, 1752). This work in sixteen hundred lines is a display of patriotic verbosity glorifying the promoter of a voyage in search of the Northwest Passage. Other poems attributed to Sterling appeared in the *American Magazine* between October, 1757, and October, 1758. These ranged from "A Poem, On the Invention of

Letters and the Art of Printing" to "The Royal Comet," praising the King of Prussia as the champion of Protestantism. Sterling's muse inspired him to fluency rather than depths of feeling.

6

By the mid-eighteenth century, the Southern colonies had developed a considerable literary activity, thanks largely to the establishment of local printing presses and newspapers which gave an outlet. Much of the writing was far removed from belles-lettres, but it illustrated the needs and interests of the people. The argument over inoculation for smallpox, for example, precipitated a controversy in 1739 between James Killpatrick and Dr. Thomas Dale, which Lewis Timothy chronicled in pamphlets from his press in Charleston, South Carolina. Doctors in Virginia and Maryland likewise published their observations on various diseases in books which are of considerable interest for the history of American medicine, if not for literary history. Religious disputes often resulted in the publication of controversial sermons. George Whitefield's evangelical tour of South Carolina aroused the ire of Dr. Alexander Garden, rector of St. Philip's in Charleston, and called forth an exchange of letters between the two which Peter Timothy duly published in 1740. Three years before, Lewis Timothy had advertised an edition of hymns and psalms by John Wesley, earlier by nearly a year than Wesley's first London edition. Some of the most interesting bits of writing are to be found in old private letters, which now and then exemplify literary skill. Though they usually wrote about business, an occasional letter of William Fitzhugh or Robert Carter of Corotoman in Virginia, or of Eliza Lucas Pinckney of South Carolina, reads like a little essay on some theme of intrinsic interest.

The growth of an interest in belles-lettres was diverted after the middle of the century by the gathering storm of controversy over the colonies' relation to the mother country. From 1750 onward there was an increasing flood of political writing, and by 1760 literary effort was already being translated into the kind of oratory, satirical verse, and polemics which would occupy such a large place in the intellectual activities of the Southern colonies in the Revolutionary period. For those activities, the substantial and circumstantial accounts of such men as Byrd, Beverley, and Stith provided a solid background in the realities of life in the New World.

5. WRITERS OF NEW ENGLAND

WITH different motives for colonization from their Southern neighbors, the early settlers of New England wrote in order to guide in daily living, to educate and to edify, rather than merely to describe. It is extraordinary that colonists preoccupied with the great task of building a durable state in a new land found time to write so much and so well. But they did so because they were convinced that effective writing was a necessity for a healthy commonwealth. Books were useful tools for teaching. If they gave pleasure, well and good; but to write merely to please would have seemed to the northern colonists usually a dangerous waste of time. They left us no novels, no drama, and very little that can be classified as belles-lettres, not because they were aesthetically blind but because they were sure that there were better uses for their talents. Most of their work was designed to convey religious truth or to give sound instruction on immediate practical issues, political, social, or economic, because they were confident that such work was essential for the building of a vigorous and virtuous state.

If the modern reader is to appreciate colonial New England literature, he must have some familiarity with the state of mind loosely called "Puritanism." In general, the early writers of New England shared that state of mind, and although attitudes shifted quickly after 1700, many of the old ideas and the literary habits fixed by them persisted. Even the work of the few non-Puritan writers in colonial New England was affected by the prevailing intellectual tastes of the community.

The Puritan author, ever striving to make his books useful, recognized that they could be so only when they presented truth understandably and attractively. He chose his methods from those which seemed to have proved useful in practice and also to be in accord with God's laws. Art was a means, not an end; but the New Englander's realization that some degree of artistry was required if his writing was to be effective made him a careful workman and led him to develop a definite, although limited, theory of style.

The theory was shaped by his religious beliefs. He was an extreme Protestant, and saw the Reformation as a great victory of true Christianity over the man-made tenets of the Church of Rome. He was sure that the universe centered not on man, but on God, and that all man's energies must be devoted to God's service. God absolutely controlled all creation. Man was his creature, inherently sinful, and could be freed from evil only by the arbitrary gift of divine grace. Neither his own deeds nor the intercession of a church could help him—although he might do something to escape the fear of damnation by proving that he could persistently do God's will. That will he could best comprehend from the Bible, the precepts of which might be supplemented, but never challenged, by a patient study of God's operations in creating and controlling the world. To claim knowledge of the divine will by direct inspiration was arrogant and "enthusiastic" heresy. God did not speak directly in man's heart, but through the Bible and through the orderly plan of the universe. Those to whom he vouchsafed his grace could and should use their reason to learn what the Bible and God's creations meant; logic, metaphysics, science—any conceptions with which the mind could deal—were serviceable only because God had benevolently granted to some of his fallen children the power to reason. The would-be righteous must hope that God's grace was in them so that their reason might bring them knowledge of his truth. In this hope they must struggle to inform themselves, with all the aids of logic and philosophy, as to God's will and the means of carrying it out on earth. Inevitably they revered scholarship: to be good in any real sense they must learn; they needed both knowledge and faith. As John Cotton, a pioneer Boston divine, put it: "Knowledge is no knowledge without zeal"—that is, without religious conviction—but "zeale is but a wildefire without knowledge." The classics, the heathen philosophers, the teachings of Renaissance humanism were all grist to the Puritan's mill, all helps in his effort to use his reason for the carrying out of divine law.

Such thinking, in its essentials, was common to most Protestants in the sixteenth and seventeenth centuries. The elements in it which affected literary standards are therefore reflected in the writings of Anglicans and Puritans alike, in the religious artists of the Old World as well as the New. But the latter differ markedly from the former in content and style, because Puritanism, of the variety prevalent in early New England, gave special emphasis to certain tenets of Protestantism and developed accordingly some special points of view toward literature.

Starting from the idea that the Bible is God's word, to be believed even when its validity could not be demonstrated by human processes, Puritan and Anglican agreed that reason furnished arguments for the infallibility of Holy Writ. But the Anglican tended to supplement the Bible with other authorities, holding that it stated the fundamental Christian principles but need not be looked upon as a complete guide for every detail of life. Those details were regulated by reason, by the rules of a church taught by experience, and by the judgment of devout men. The Bible was not to be taken so literally as to leave no place for men to act freely when no essential Scriptural precept forbade. But the extreme Protestant—the Puritan—was more strict. If the Bible was God's word, and God was infinite, why suppose its authority to be less than infinite? Why was not its authority complete and binding, regardless of changing human conditions and aspirations, all of which were, after all, decreed by God? The Puritan took his Bible literally as a manual of instruction for every phase of conduct. In it he thought he found precise rules for the structure and polity of the true church, and he was sure that there should be nothing in worship or church government not specifically authorized by it. Inevitably he rejected many elements of the Catholic and Anglican service and polity because he could find no warrant for them in the sacred text. Thus he seemed to conservatives to be a rebel, not because of any basic theological unorthodoxy, but because his conception of a true church was unlike that of English ecclesiastics.

The New England Puritan's difference from the Anglican or Catholic in worship and polity dictated differences in literary theory. His literal attitude toward the Bible left little excuse for any religious art not somehow justified by its text; and the ardor of his Protestantism led him to reject anything traditionally associated with the Church of Rome. Organ music, stained-glass windows, incense, rich vestments, ornate altars, religious images—these were all adjuncts to Catholic, and to some extent to Anglican, worship. Their "Papist" associations were enough to make them anathema to the Puritan. Catholics commonly held that things which appealed to the senses could be fittingly used in the service of religion. The Puritan could not agree. He distrusted sensuous appeals in worship because they usually involved objects and practices not specifically endorsed by Holy Writ, because they smacked of Rome, and because he believed that "fallen man" was likely to become the prey of his senses, subject to the tyranny of passion rather than the dictates of right reason and faith.

This meant that the Puritan writer could not use, as his Catholic and Anglican contemporaries did, a body of material and a set of devices calculated to charm sensuously and to "adorn" his work—such charming and adornment seemed to him dangerous. He wanted to reach men's reason and to convince them of truth, not to lull them to acceptance by drugging their minds with potions all too likely to stir the carnal passions so powerful in the descendants of fallen Adam. The Puritan usually rejected imagery which served merely to delight, accepting only that which seemed to him to make the truth more easily understood, and preferring that which he could find in the Bible. He would rather talk of plain glass, letting in all the light, than of stained-glass windows, which seemed to him empty adornment symbolizing man's aptness to dim the light of truth. Anything which appealed to the senses so strongly as to endanger concentration on what must be grasped by reason, was dangerous. Good writing was to teach; its method must make directly and clearly comprehensible what man most needed to know.

Naturally, early New England writers of prose concentrated on sound and logical structure, and on clarity. The logic and rhetoric of Peter Ramus, the great French anti-Aristotelian logician of the sixteenth century, were adopted by Puritan pundits partly because they seemed to offer useful rules for good expository prose. But more immediately important than such rules was the Puritan's consciousness of the nature of his audience. It comprised men who were neither trained critics nor expert writers, but were, usually, earnest Christians, eager to learn. They were humanly fallible, and if a page, however clear, seemed dull, their thoughts strayed. Therefore the Puritan preacher and writer, although he advocated the "plain style" and objected to adornment for adornment's sake, seasoned his prose with imagery and used whatever literary devices seemed to him legitimate and necessary to make his instruction palatable. Anything in words which might rouse evil passions was forbidden, but picturesque phrasing and evocative images were allowable if their associations were innocent or if they had Biblical precedent.

The last point is important. The Bible had for the Puritan supreme literary value. It was the work of an omnipotent God, who used language perfectly because all that he did was perfect. Allegory, figures of speech—even frankly sexual imagery—crop up often in Puritan writing, sometimes in ways that are startling if we forget that its authors knew that men's "affections" must be charmed if their attention was to be held, and were sure that any literary method used in the Bible had divine sanction. New England authors avoided the rapturous expression of Catholic or Anglican mystics as too sensuous and too redolent of "enthusiasm"; they closed their eyes to much in the great religious literature of seventeenth century England because they did not want to tempt their readers' passions or to cloud their understanding of the truth by too elaborate rhetoric. Moreover, symbols and images, linked with the Mass and with ritualistic forms of worship, were suspect to the Puritan, and, in general, he looked coldly upon the ingenuities of style, the extended similes, the complicated metaphors (often sensuous or even sensual in suggestion), the elaborate prose music, and the rhetorical decoration, which characterized much of the best English writing in the late Renaissance. The Puritan was thus cut off from many sources of literary effect; but mercifully the Bible gave him others. He had no qualms about using its imagery, its rhythms, and its stylistic devices for his own pious purposes.

Part of his success with his audience depended on what he learned from Biblical style; he profited also by his understanding of other means by which he could hold his audience's attention without concessions to its baser appetites. He spoke and wrote principally for fishermen, farmers, woodsmen, shopkeepers, and artisans. However little they knew about classical literature or about rhetorical niceties in English prose and verse, they knew a great deal about the sea, gardens, village life, and the concrete concerns of pioneers busily establishing prosperous colonies in a wilderness. They enjoyed seeing an author drive home his point with a simile or a metaphor that touched their familiar experience; and their experience was rich with homely material. When Thomas Shepard wrote in his *Sincere Convert* (1655 edition), "Jesus Christ is not got with a wet finger," he meant, "Salvation cannot be had by mere study of books"; but his metaphor made a commonplace statement expressive and vivid for his readers by calling up the picture of an earnest student wetting his finger whenever he had to turn a page. Such metaphors and similes abound in Puritan writing. Their purpose is obvious; their effect is to give to pages which might otherwise be abstract and dull the taste of life.

Some New England writers broke away from the usual Puritan conventions of style. They were all to some extent influenced by non-Puritan ways of writing; many of them were English university men, well trained in literary traditions; and those whose work has merit enough to deserve mention today were individuals never completely subjugated by rigid convention. But the variations from orthodox Puritan practice are usually minor, and, so far as the work of any group can be summed up in a formula, the Puritans' can be. The formula called for clarity, order, and logic as supreme stylistic virtues. It admitted some concessions to the reader's liking for sensuous appeal, but limited that appeal to what was unlikely to stimulate man's baser nature and distract his mind from truth.

2

Nathaniel Ward, who came from England and preached at Ipswich, Massachusetts, in the early days of its settlement, is a useful example both of the Puritans' literary theory and of the permissible deviations from it. His *The Simple Cobler of Aggawamm in America,* a vigorously intolerant plea for Puritan orthodoxy, which was first printed in London in 1647 and ran through four editions in a few months, is full of word coinages, jingling phrases, and other forms of verbal display, and its style is certainly far less "plain" than that prescribed by strict Puritan theory. But Ward knew what he was doing. He defended himself against the charge of "levity" by writing:

> To speak to light heads with heavy words, were to break their necks; to clothe Summer matter, with Winter Rugge, would make the Reader sweat.

In other words, he was trying to make his style fit his material—and his audience. He virtually admits that he has now and then adorned his prose too much:

> I honour them with my heart, that can expresse more than ordinary matter in ordinary words: it is a pleasing eloquence; [I honour] them more that study wisely and soberly to inhance their native language. . . . Affected termes are unaffecting things to solid hearers; yet I hold him prudent that . . . will help disedged appetites with convenient condiments.

Ward wrote to teach, and he chose what seemed to him to be an effective method for his audience. If he offended against the strictest Puritan standard in using too many stylistic "condiments," he observed it in his reliance on homely imagery and in his exclusion of anything likely to stir sinful passions.

As for Cotton Mather who, in most of his work, departed from the plainest Puritan "plain style" by peppering his pages with allusions, quotations, and pedantic playings upon words, he knew quite well that he followed a fashion not universally approved in New England. He did so deliberately. He had thought a little about style, knew what he wanted to accomplish, and believed there were good ends to be served by varying from stylistic plainness. But even Mather, although he wrote his ecclesiastical history of New England, the *Magnalia Christi Americana* (1702) in the full tide of an enthusiasm for a prose encrusted with rhetorical eccentricities and learned allusions, in many another book used a style as simple and direct as the most conventional Puritan's. He could ape the new prose writers of the Restoration and the early eighteenth century in England, as well as the rhetoricians of 1630 or 1640. His *Political Fables* (about 1692) are in impeccably lucid prose; his *Christian Philosopher* (1721), an exposition of the arguments for Christianity to be found in the study of the natural world, has its flowery passages and is loaded with quotations and allusions, but the stylistic core is simple expository prose; his *Bonifacius* or *Essays to Do Good* (1710), beloved of Benjamin Franklin, was aimed at plain folk and is appropriately homespun in texture. So in all his voluminous writing—some four hundred and fifty books and pamphlets—Mather chose the kind of prose which seemed to him best suited to his purpose, without ever lapsing into a style so sensuously appealing as to be dangerous for fallen man. The *Magnalia,* he hoped, might reach the erudite abroad, and for such a book a style "richly trimmed" with learned trappings was appropriate. For less pretentious offerings he chose a simpler style, because he understood his audience and, like other good Puritans, held that his first task was to make truth intelligible to it.

The main stream of early New England literary practice is best shown in the chronicles and histories treated elsewhere in this volume, and in the sermons and other religious prose of Cotton Mather's generation and before. His own father Increase, for example, wrote numerous works chiefly striking for their typical Puritan emphasis on clarity and order; so did hosts of other New Englanders before 1700. Their zeal for ordered simplicity and their distrust of the sensuous too often makes their work seem to us cool and thin, colorless, and imaginatively tame. But with the faults went virtues—an effect of patterned dignity and, often, skillful use of homely realism.

This realism appears everywhere. Samuel Sewall, a Puritan layman, writes a paragraph about New England in *Phaenomena quaedam Apocalyptica,* a pamphlet on the Book of Revelation, and we hear of "the hectoring Words and hard Blows of the proud and boisterous Ocean," beating against Plum Island, of the salmon and sturgeon in the Merrimac, and of the "free and harmless Doves" perching in the "White Oak." And Sewall's famous diary is full of vividly realistic phrasing. How could the behavior of an angry man be more sharply pictured in a single phrase than in the diarist's account of the minister, who "with extraordinary Vehemency said, (capering with his feet)"? Even in the pages of a scholar as formidable as the Reverend John Norton, Augustine's "A good life is requisite in respect of ourselves, but a good name is requisite in respect of others" is pointed up by the observation "The gratefulness of the most excellent liquor unto the stomach depends in part upon the quality of the vessel." And elsewhere Norton remarks: "The hen, which brings not forth without uncessant sitting night and day, is an apt emblem of students." Roger Williams, although his advanced democratic ideas and his championship of complete religious toleration made him seem to many New Englanders a dangerous heretic, wrote with the authentic Puritan ring. He tells us of "the day of our last farewell, the day of the splitting of this vessel, the breaking of this bubble, the quenching of this candle." He reminds us that we are mere sojourners on earth, "strangers in an inn," "passengers in a ship," who "dream of long summer days." We "dwell in strange houses" and "lodge in strange beds," and pass like "smoke on the chimney's top" when the time comes for "the weighing of our last anchors." We are "poor grasshoppers hopping and skipping from branch to twig in this vale of tears."

The literary virtue stemming from the Puritans' insistence on order and logical structure as essential for conveying truth appears in a passage from

Samuel Willard's election sermon, *The Character of a Good Ruler* (Boston, 1694):

A People are not made for Rulers, But Rulers for a People. It is indeed an Honour which God puts upon some above others, when he takes them from among the People, and sets them up to Rule over them, but it is for the Peoples sake, and the Civil felicity of them is the next end of Civil Policy; and the happiness of Rulers is bound up with theirs in it. Nor can any wise men in authority think themselves happy in the Misery of their Subjects, to whom they either are or should be as Children are to their Fathers: We have the Benefit of Government expressed, 1. *Tim.* 2:2. *a quiet Life and a peaceable, in all Godliness and honesty,* and it lies especialy with Rulers, under God, to make a People Happy or Miserable. When men can injoy their Liberties and Rights without molestation or oppression; when they can live without fear of being born down by their more Potent Neighbours; when they are secured against Violence, and may be Righted against them that offer them any injury, without fraud; and are encouraged to serve God in their own way, with freedom, and without being imposed upon contrary to the Gospel precepts; now are they an happy People.

Or, to take a more complicated example, here is Thomas Hooker, in *The Application of Redemption* (London, 1659), expounding a point important both theologically and in its implications for literature:

It is by the Spiritual Operations and Actions of our minds that we meet with the Lord, and have a kind of intercourse with the Almighty, who is a Spirit. For al outward things are for the body, the body for the soul, the soul is nextly for God, and therefore meets as really with him in the Actions of Understanding, as the Eye meets with the Light in Seeing; which no other Creature can do, nor no action of a bodily Creature doth. Our Sences in their sinful and inordinate swervings, when they become means and in-lets of evil from their objects, they meet with the Creature firstly, and there make the jar: It's the beauty of the Object that stirs up to lust by the Eye, the daintiness of the Diet that provokes to intemperance by the tast, the harsh and unkind language that provokes to wrath and impatience by the Ear: But the Mind and Understanding toucheth the Lord directly, meets with his Rule, and with God acting in the way of his Government there, and when it goes off from the Rule as before, and attends its own vanity and folly, it justles with the Almighty, stands in open defyance and resistance against him.

In this the effect comes both from the structure and from the vigorous realism of such phrases as "there make the jar," or "justles with the Almighty." Samuel Willard's sentence, in his *Mercy Magnified* (1684),

There is a great deal goes to the eternal life of a soul, and thou hast none of it; thou wantest the love of God, which is better than life; thou wantest grace which is indeed the inward principle of life in the soul; thou wantest the promise which is the support of the soul here in this life,

hits its mark because of its balance and its flavor of simple speech. Hooker writes of "meditation," in *The Application of Redemption* (1659):

> The second End of Meditation is, *It settles it effectually upon the heart.* It's not the pashing of the water at a sudden push, but the standing and soaking to the root, that loosens the weeds and thorns, that they may be plucked up easily. It's not the laying of Oyl upon the benumned part, but the chafing of it in, that suppleth the Joynts, and easeth the pain. It is so in the soul; Application laies the Oyl of the Word that is searching and savory, Meditation chafeth it in, that it may soften and humble the hard and stony heart: Application is like the Conduit or Channel that brings the stream of the Truth upon the soul; but Meditation stops it as it were, and makes it soak into the heart, that so our corruptions may be plucked up kindly by the Roots.

The pattern is plain; its effect is enhanced because it is clothed with images thoroughly familiar to men and women who weeded gardens and treated one another's ailments.

3

Not only in his prose but in his poetry the Puritan displayed his fundamental literary creed. Early New Englanders wrote a great deal of verse, and in it, as in their prose, they chose the methods which seemed to them best adapted to their audience and most consonant with the Puritan view that all good writing must teach. Of course distrust of sensuous appeals does more injury to poetry than to prose, and the Puritan's verse suffered accordingly. Too often his poems are merely versified prose, expounding a useful lesson. Too often they are flat reiterations of pious truisms, adorned with some of the poetic artifices which the seventeenth century appreciated more than the twentieth. The devices were the more innocent ones sanctioned by the time, the ones least likely to arouse unruly and dangerous emotions; but some of them were intricate and "witty" to a degree uncommon in Puritan prose. The New England colonist gave a little more license to his verse writers than to the preacher or the writer of theological tracts, but he still kept them on a tight rein. The result is that their feeling, however genuine, too often quite fails to reach the readers of their verse.

That they wrote as much verse as they did, however, is sufficient refutation of the old heresy that Puritans were "hostile" to poetry. They were not. They found in it a way of expression necessary to them, but their theories limited their freedom in writing it. Also their utilitarian attitude toward all literature often put verse in the light of a luxury, since there was so much that needed to be said in sober prose. Most of the poetry written in New England before 1760 was never printed; most of it was circulated, if it was circulated at all, in manuscript, or committed to the pages of diaries or volumes of family memorabilia.

There were exceptions, though, and some New England verse found its way into print in the seventeenth and eighteenth centuries. The almanacs, indispensable to colonial farmers and fishermen, gave space to many stanzas, and there were even a few whole volumes of verse. Most famous of these is the "Bay Psalm Book," *The Whole Booke of Psalmes Faithfully Translated into English Metre,* printed in Cambridge, Massachusetts, in 1640, celebrated not for any poetic merit in its clumsy stanzas and tortured lines but because it was the first book issued in the English colonies in North America. Its authors, Richard Mather, John Eliot, and Thomas Welde, all devout and learned ministers and capable craftsmen in prose, knew that they were not writing poetry and said so. They wanted a literal translation of the Psalms which would fit metrically the tunes familiar to Puritan congregations. Accuracy and serviceability for worship were more important than literary excellence. The book was designed to be useful to ministers and their flocks, and was therefore a proper offering to God. If it was rough and graceless in form, it did not matter, since, as its authors wrote, "God's altar needs not our polishings."

Other New England books had more pretensions and more success as poetry. Most famous in its own day was Michael Wigglesworth's *Day of Doom* (1662), a colonial "best-seller." Its jog-trot ballad measure seems to us curiously inappropriate for an account of the Judgment Day, but it has a few flashes of sensitive poetic expression. So have some of Wigglesworth's other poetic efforts. But he was first of all a Puritan divine, and saw his main task as the teaching of sound Christianity. Therefore he chose a meter familiar to his readers, and versified standard Puritan doctrine, hoping that the rhyme and rhythm might make it more gratefully received and more easily remembered than it could be in prose. That he succeeded seems to be proved by the fact that *The Day of Doom* had at least ten editions before 1760.

Anne Bradstreet's verses were never as popular as Wigglesworth's; but they were well enough received to make possible three editions before 1760. The daughter of Thomas Dudley, steward to the Earl of Lincoln and, later, Governor of Massachusetts, she married Simon Bradstreet and came with him to Massachusetts in 1630, when she was seventeen. She had apparently read widely, and although she was a faithful Puritan wife, she could not always accept in entire docility the sterner aspects of the New England variety of

Calvinism. The last stanza of her little poem on the death of a grandchild is revealing:

> By nature Trees do rot when they are grown.
> And Plumbs and Apples throughly ripe do fall,
> And Corn and grass are in their season mown,
> And time brings down what is both strong and tall.
> But plants new set to be eradicate,
> And buds new blown, to have so short a date,
> Is by his hand alone that guides nature and fate.

The simplicity of the diction and the limited but accurate imagery carry a genuine emotional effect until, suddenly, Anne Bradstreet realizes that she is perilously close to writing rebelliously against God's decrees. She pulls herself up in the last line. It falls flat, even metrically, because it is dictated not by real feeling but by deference to orthodox doctrine. In other poems she is content simply to versify learning, sedulously imitating the pious French poet Du Bartas, whose work, in the English translation of Joshua Sylvester, she loved. Many of her pages are dull; many are merely "instructive" verse, using the devices of poetry but rarely rising above the attitudes of prose. But there are also pages in which she wrote simply and well of things close to her heart, and let her emotion, although always decorously expressed, warm her lines. Her *Contemplations,* for example, although overformal by modern standards, is a brave attempt to express poetically some sense of the physical beauty of Massachusetts; her lines in praise of Queen Elizabeth have defiant vigor and wit:

> Now say, have women worth? or have they none?
> Or had they some, but with our Queen is't gone?
> Nay Masculines, you have thus taxt us long,
> But she, though dead, will vindicate our wrong.
> Let such as say our Sex is void of Reason,
> Know tis a Slander now, but once was Treason.

Many a minor English poet of her day, more celebrated than Anne Bradstreet, wrote nothing that is better than her best, even though her best conforms to the Puritan's utilitarian view of art and to his distrust of the frankly sensuous.

A host of other New England colonial poets published only an occasional verse, or are known in print only by lines prefixed to books or collected by Cotton Mather in his *Magnalia*; but many of them left poems in manuscript. Mather says, for example, that the Reverend John Wilson, a pioneer divine in Boston, left at his death enough verse to fill a folio; but a very small book would contain all of it that was put into type for his contemporaries. He was a diligent anagrammatist, addicted to the then admired device of rearranging the letters of a man's name to make a phrase which could be used as the theme for a set of verses. Such contrivances seem to us mere ingenuity, but we should not forget that in Wilson's time anagrams were sometimes thought to have a mystic significance, and that to write verses on themes suggested by them was an intellectually reputable pursuit. Here, as in most Puritan poetry, the modern reader is handicapped by the fact that it is poetry written to meet outmoded standards. The great English poets who were publishing, and were winning applause, while the colonial New Englanders were constructing rhymes in the intervals of arduous lives in a "wilderness," adapted those standards to the uses of great poetry. The New Englander usually followed the convention expertly enough, but rarely made his finished work memorable for anything but competent craftsmanship. He was partially cut off from the tradition of great poetry by his specifically Puritan theories. He was reluctant to stir emotions too deeply, and he disliked the Anglicanism or Catholicism of many of the poets who might have taught him most. He was hampered by the lack of an artistically experienced audience, and he was too often blinded to poetic values by his intense concentration on the idea that the writer's first task was to put useful doctrine into the most immediately intelligible form. This is not to say that the Puritan was emotionally cold or poetically insensitive; there are proofs to the contrary in both Wigglesworth and Bradstreet. Nor is it to say that he could never write memorable lines; there are several in Urian Oakes' *Elegy upon the Death of the Reverend Mr. Thomas Shepard* (1677), and others in the usually awkward rhymes which Edward Johnson sprinkled through his *Wonder-Working Providence.* Any reader with a taste for good technique in expository or didactic verse will be rewarded in the pages of Benjamin Tompson or Richard Steere, who, for all their defects in imagination, were good enough workmen to give pleasure by the neatness with which they satirized New England's foibles or used the devices of Dryden and his school to make useful precepts and sound learning palatable to the colonists.

4

The greatest poet of New England before the nineteenth century was Edward Taylor, a Puritan minister of Westfield, Massachusetts, in the late seventeenth and early eighteenth centuries. His work, and his apparent attitude toward it, illustrate admirably the working of the Puritan theory of poetry, and his successes and failures are useful indices of the general poetic condition of the New England he knew. Very little of his verse was published in his day, but he left enough in manuscript to fill a large volume, with the request that it be not printed. We cannot be sure why this request was made, but Taylor probably knew that his poetry was not quite orthodox, and that it might seem to the more sober of his brethren a reflection upon his godliness or upon his understanding of man's sinful nature. His poetry is, in general, more sensuous, richer in luxurious imagery, and more daringly expressive of an essentially mystic emotion, than that of most Puritans. There are in Taylor decorated altars, jewels, spices, perfumes; there are strong echoes of such poets as John Donne and Richard Crashaw; there are whole poems which play more directly than most Puritans approved on men's love for color, gems, scents, and the delights of the flesh. Of course Taylor's poems were pious in intent; he was passionately devout—but he chose to express his pious devotion in terms which, as he may well have recognized, savored strongly of this world. He seems to have been not only more imaginatively endowed than his contemporaries, but also more defiant than they of the restrictions imposed on poets by the Puritan's fear of the passions of fallen man. For us his poetry gains by this. Where Bradstreet and Wigglesworth give hints of poetic power, Taylor gives proofs; where other Puritan poets rise only to ingenious expression or deft exposition in verse, lighted by very occasional flashes of imaginative insight, Taylor at his best writes poems so vivid in emotional evocation that they attain an artistic immortality quite independent of their doctrine.

Taylor's virtues do not stem merely from his enlargement of the limits of conventional Puritan practice; one source of strength in his work is his skill in using the kind of image most dear to Puritans—the homely image drawn from the simplest daily experience of simple folk. With this goes his adroit use of homespun diction, made more effective often by a contrast between the earthiness of a word (or a figure) and the loftiness of his theme. The soul is a "Bird of Paradise" in a "Wicker Cage," and there it "tweedles" praise to God. God "grinds, and kneads up into this Bread of Life, . . . the Purest Wheate in Heaven, his deare-dear Son." The result is "Heavens Sugar Cake." Man is to be a "Spinning Wheele" for God:

> Thy Holy Worde my Distaff make for mee.
> Make mine Affections thy Swift Flyers neate,
> And make my Soule thy holy Spoole to bee.
> My Conversation make to be thy Reele,
> And reele the yarn thereon Spun of thy Wheele.

The poem goes on to the weaving and dyeing of the cloth, until man is at last "Cloathd in Holy robes for glory."

The image is ingenious in the typical "metaphysical" mode, and is effective by virtue of its realism. No Puritan could have taken exception to it except possibly in so far as its ingenuity might seem to him to smack too much of current Anglican verse, and to be too apt to delight the reader to the point of distracting him from the truth the poem was written to express. But many Puritans might have had doubts about

My Lovely One, I fain would love thee much,
 But all my Love is none at all I see;
Oh! let thy Beauty give a glorious touch
 Upon my Heart, and melt to Love all mee.
 Lord, melt me all up into Love for thee,
 Whose Loveliness excells what love can bee,

or

Shall I not smell thy sweet, oh! Sharons Rose?
 Shall not mine Eye salute thy Beauty? Why?
Shall thy sweet leaves their Beautious sweets upclose?
 As halfe ashamde my sight should on them ly?

Was there not room for fear lest such lines work perilously on the carnal nature of sinful man? There might be offense, too, in

But now my Heart is made thy Censar trim,
 Full of thy golden Altars fire,
 To offer up Sweet Incense in
  Unto thyself intire.

Censers, golden altars, and sweet incense had Biblical precedents, to be sure. But was not this verse too redolent of the ritualism against which the Puritans rebelled? There are other lines of the same sort in Taylor; others, too, in which love fills heaven, love runs over, blood is linked with love. The intensely emotional tone of many of Taylor's poems, and their specifically physical connotations, might well frighten critics who believed the senses could betray the reason, and had no use for the dangerous "enthusiastic" idea that man could ever achieve on earth a rapturous union with God.

Today, fortunately, no such scruples get in the way of our appreciation of Taylor's imaginative power and dramatic skill. His emotions may have been too strong for the tightest bonds of Puritan theory, but he adroitly used some Puritan literary conventions to give contrast and dramatic tension to his work. His constant use of homely and realistic diction and imagery brings ecstatic religious vision and the actualities of earth together in his verses, striking poetic sparks from the contrast. Again and again he makes articulate the drama inherent in man's quest for a beauty which is beyond earth but realizable only in images of earthly delights.

5

Taylor died in 1729. By then New England had changed greatly. The old religious fervor had abated; the concept of a universe centered in God had weakened before that of one centered on man; and more and more colonists, especially in the properous seaboard towns, were interested in trade and in aping the amenities of English society rather than in conquering new lands for Christ. They paid lip service to the old theology, and church membership was still a mark of social respectability; but the zeal for teaching and the fierce concentration on the dilemma of sinful man had lessened, and literature reflected the change. More and more the grace and urbanity of the English periodical essayists came to be admired; the robust vocabulary and rhetoric of the original colonists were toned down to the level of easy fluency; concrete realism often gave way to well turned generalizations couched in abstract terms. In verse Taylor's ardor and his love of dramatic contrast were replaced by smooth couplets and neat stanzas obviously reminiscent of Dryden, Watts, and Pope. Between 1700 and 1760 New England produced plenty of good prose and plenty of graceful verse; but much of it seems tame when compared with earlier work because the feeling behind it was less intense. "Good sense" was in vogue; "reasonableness" and "politeness" were more important than they had been to Puritan preachers and tract writers. Compare almost any line of Taylor, or almost any stanza, however clumsy, of *The Day of Doom* with this bit from a "Poetical Meditation" by Roger Wolcott of Connecticut, published in 1725:

> Vertue still makes the Vertuous to shine,
> Like those that Liv'd in the first week of time.
> Vertue hath force the vile to cleanse again,
> So being like clear shining after Rain.
> A Kind and Constant, Chearful Vertuous Life,
> Becomes each Man, and most Adorns a Wife.

True enough, any Puritan would have agreed; but few earlier Puritans would have put it so blandly, with so little sense of man's helpless vileness before God or of the miracle of God's grace vouchsafed to his elect. The change in attitude—and in style—from the earlier writers, shown in Wolcott and many eighteenth century New Englanders, illustrates some of the ways in which deism, the new rationalism, and changed English literary fashions affected the original Puritan outlook.

There were some literary gains. The newer theory flowered in Benjamin Franklin's best essays, skillfully written by a "sensible" man for "sensible" folk, with their eyes on this world more than on the next, and in the scientific and philosophical works of Jonathan Edwards. The brilliance of the prose in which the Reverend John Wise defended the original New England church polity in *The Churches Quarrel Espoused* (1710) and *Vindication of the Government of New-England Churches* (1717), shows how much he had learned from English stylists of the school of Dryden and Swift.

Furthermore the increasing secularization of society, the relaxing of the old dominant preoccupation with religion, opened the door to pleasant excursions in fields unvisited by the earlier Puritans. Mather Byles, for example, the nephew of Cotton Mather, was a minister, but achieved almost as much fame for his punning as for his preaching. He was also a rhymer, and an admirer of Pope and of the English poets of his day, and dashed off a few verses which his ancestors would have considered too trivial—or too frivolous—for a divine. The early Puritans had humor, of course—to take but two examples, Samuel Sewall in his diary and Nathaniel Ward in his *Cobler,* showed theirs; but usually the seventeenth century colonial preacher would have considered it a waste of paper and ink to display wit (in the modern sense) or humor in published writings. Nor were there, in the early days of Massachusetts, merchants like Joseph Green, ready to entertain themselves and their less pious neighbors with verses on the joys of drinking, or on the death of Mather Byles' cat, or with even more direct ridicule in rhyme of the minister of the Hollis Street Church. New England's notion of the purpose of literature changed fast after 1700. Good writing was seen no longer as simply a way of serving God by communicating divine truth as directly as possible; there was room for work designed merely to entertain. There was also an increasing interest in discussions of purely literary and stylistic matters. John Bulkeley, in 1725, wrote for Wolcott's *Poetical Meditations* a preface which is pious enough but devotes more attention than do most earlier colonial writings to purely literary values. Cotton Mather's famous essay on style, inserted in his *Manuductio ad Ministerium* (1726), a manual for theological students, takes a broader aesthetic view than the preface to the "Bay Psalm Book" or Michael Wigglesworth's unpublished "Prayse of Eloquence."

It is unlikely that more than a few pages of poetry and prose of New England before 1760 will ever achieve popular literary immortality. There are, none the less, memorable passages not only in the chronicles and histories, but in the great mass of sermons, tracts, essays, poems, and pious verse written by the colonists; and there are hundreds of other passages which lack the stamp of greatness but still have interest for, and may give excitement to, the modern reader who can read them with the understanding they deserve. That understanding involves first of all some knowledge of colonial conditions, some realization of the circumstances under which they were written and of the purpose and the audience for which they were designed. It involves, too, an appreciation of the literary conventions which were accepted by our forefathers and, in spite of serious limitations, had value. Order, logic, clarity, are still virtues in writing, even though the devices by which we try to achieve them are unlike the Puritans'. Homely imagery, earthy phrasing, and the use of simple and realistic figures to make abstract ideas or emotions concretely realizable are traits still characteristic of much of the best American writing. Emerson admired "language of nature." He found it in the speech of a "Vermont drover" and said that "in the 17th century, it appeared in every book." For an example he cited Thomas Shepard's "And to put finger in the eye and to renew their repentance, they think this is weakness." Obviously he was thinking of the homeliness so characteristic of Puritan prose; obviously too, much of his own best work shows the same quality. Emerson, and others, found in the Puritan's stylistic theory something adaptable to the needs of the idealist in any age. The early New Englanders' eyes were on God; but they were busy men with a wilderness to subdue and the divine will to carry out on earth.

Jonathan Edwards wrote on science and philosophy more effectively and more attractively, at least for modern readers, than most of his seventeenth century predecessors. Such men were exceptional, but they profited from some of the new methods in English prose popularized in the late seventeenth and early eighteenth centuries—methods by which many other New England writers before 1760 made their work palatable. The Puritans' literary practice grew out of the search for some way to express both the spiritual emotion that controlled them and their vigorous desire to make practical use of it, and to teach others to do so, in daily life. They never succeeded, perhaps, in realizing their aim, either in literature or in life, but only those of us who are too limited in vision to see the gallantry of their quest will refuse them respect for what they did and wrote.

6. JONATHAN EDWARDS

THE East Windsor parsonage where Edwards was born October 5, 1703, was a rambling Connecticut farmhouse which easily accommodated the eleven children of Timothy and Esther (Stoddard) Edwards. In the gently sloping meadow at the rear, by a brook, the youthful Jonathan built the booth where he and his boy companions came to meditate and pray. It was in the immediate neighborhood that he observed the flying, or balloon, spiders in his twelfth or thirteenth year and reported on them in an account celebrated as the earliest natural history essay written on the subject. Timothy encouraged his only son in tasks that required painstaking accuracy, and the boy's imaginative mind responded to the discipline. The son was under the tutorship of a parent better remembered as a teacher than as a preacher, one who was especially successful in preparing students for Harvard and Yale. The power to evoke an "admirably rich and delicate description," as William James characterized *A Treatise Concerning Religious Affections* (1746), was foreshadowed in the youthful considerations of natural phenomena, of insects and rainbows, seen on a Connecticut hillside. Thus endowed, the boy entered Yale College in the autumn of 1716.

The pattern of Edwards' thinking was first displayed in the "Notes on Natural Science" and "The Mind." They were responses to courses in "natural philosophy," or physics, taken in the junior and senior years. This was the time when his conning of the new science, through the pages of Newton and Locke, bewitched him into self-discovery. The quiet young man, whose dependability won him the honor of a college butlership, as supervisor in the dining hall, was already a citizen of the realm of mind. The "Notes" pose the questions: What is reality? What are the metes of human knowledge? Wherein consists true liberty? And, most important of all, is it possible for a man to love anything better than himself?

Here Edwards first attempted to integrate the principles of morals, art, and being. The note on "Excellence" concludes:

Wherefore all Virtue, which is the Excellency of minds, is resolved into *Love to Being*; and nothing is virtuous or beautiful in Spirits, any otherwise than as it is an exercise, or fruit, or manifestation of this love; and nothing is sinful or deformed in Spirits, but as it is the defect of, or contrary to, these.

However technical as doctrine, this early attempt to set down a philosophical ideal on nine sheets of foolscap is the kernel of everything that later took root. It is Edwards' first effort to harmonize emotion and reason, mercy and justice, fate and free will. To read the world in terms of love was Edwards' unique contribution to the philosophic system of Calvin.

All his study of theology, undertaken in the two graduate years after he received his bachelor's degree in 1720, was now absorbed into abstract reflections, as were the scientific speculations. The idealism of "The Mind" and of the better known "Of Being" may or may not be traceable to the English idealist George Berkeley. One thing is sure. The stretch of Edwards' mind is observable from his youth. Rumors of new and exciting speculative theories were in the air: that the world of the senses is a direct expression of divine ideas; that mind and spirit are more important than their manifestation in matter. Such perceptions he had doubtless discussed, for they are convictions toward which he was moving.

The final and certainly determining event in his student years, described so charmingly in the "Personal Narrative" written twenty years after, was his mystical conversion at seventeen: "I often used to sit & view the Moon, for a long time; and so in the Day-time, spent much time in viewing the Clouds & Sky, to behold the sweet Glory of God in these Things: in the mean Time, singing forth, with a low Voice, my Contemplations of the Creator and Redeemer." All that he witnessed as manifestations of the sensible world became shadows of divine truths. The concrete image henceforth was to be the symbolic fact. From now on, nature was an analogy, as it has been felt by mystics from the beginning of time. Among American men of letters in the next century, Bryant came to express it in his own way; and Emerson, most articulately of all.

The apprentice preaching in New York during 1723 at a newly congregated church in William Street lasted but eight months. Edwards' haste to accept an invitation by a group in Bolton, Connecticut, may imply that the world of wharves and brick houses was not congenial to the New England youth now first separated from homestead, woodland, and meadows. The "new Sense of Things" as reflected in the universe round about, which had first possessed him at college, was never to alter.

A pressing community need released him almost immediately from his Bolton commitments. In 1724 his alma mater offered him the senior tutorship at a most stormy moment in the early days of the college, a position which Edwards held for two years, acting virtually as president. Then came the call as colleague pastor to his grandfather's church at Northampton. The aged "Pope" Stoddard, who dictated church polity in a manner no Boston minister dared emulate, would shortly retire. Edwards was settled in February, 1727, and in the same year married Sarah Pierrepont of New Haven, a woman of spirit and great sensitivity. These were the years when the burdens of raising a family and the task of preparing biweekly sermons and writing an occasional book occupied him fully. Indeed, the stately Mr. Edwards, spare of limb, was becoming an author of repute, though his townsmen would recall him walking, lost in thought, across the village common or riding with loose rein through the back pastures, his coat dotted with paper slips, notes set down lest he forget the ideas which absorbed him. It was Sarah Edwards that encouraged this life of plain living and high thinking, and uncomplainingly shared with her husband the heartbreaks of the later Northampton years. She accepted as he did, without self-pity or remorse, the humble missionary station after their transfer to the small Stockbridge Indian outpost in 1751.

2

The root of the Northampton trouble which led to Edwards' dismissal in his forty-seventh year from the most influential Connecticut Valley parish can be traced to the idealism implicit in the youthful notes on "The Mind." Edwards had been embroiled in "issues" from the day he matriculated in Yale College at the age of thirteen. His forthright honesty clearly produced them, and he was now willing to court his dismissal because any earlier doubts were resolved. The good of mankind was inseparable from the manner in which that good must be obtained. The *Farewell Sermon,* preached in July, 1750, spotlights the drama of his life in mid-passage. "You need one," he concludes, remarking of a successor, "that shall stand as a champion in the cause of truth and the power of godliness." And the opinion ruefully evaluates his administrative limits, not his principles.

The willingness of Edwards to accept into church membership only those who professed "renovation of heart," a conviction of spiritual regeneration, seemed intolerable to the majority. The shadow of his grandfather Stoddard, dead these twenty years, was yet upon the community, for Stoddard had taught his congregation to believe that under special circumstances the sacred seal of the Lord's Supper might in itself be a "converting ordinance." That is to say, Edwards was at last convinced that the sacrament was for those only who felt it to be the symbol of a conversion already achieved by the participant. His tragic realization of the place of evil in the scheme of things, his conviction of the irreversible reality of human isolation, were now fully reasoned. The revolution he was effecting in an attempt to abrogate Stoddard's decision, and the issue he joined, were to be made clear in the treatises he would soon write in the frontier settlement at Stockbridge during the remaining eight years of his life. For the moment he seemed an isolated reactionary, lost to the times because he would not compromise with them. Need religion be more than regular church attendance, profession of a reasoned belief in godly living based on good breeding and humanitarian interests in the welfare of one's neighbors? Edwards thought it should be. He was ready to express himself in a series of independent metaphysical speculations which have in fact given permanent direction to spiritual culture in America.

3

Edwards did not codify his analysis until after the apparent failure of his career in 1750. Of the five works which compass his scheme, only *Religious Affections* was written before he left Northampton. The remaining four appeared very late. *A Careful and Strict Enquiry . . . of That Freedom of Will . . .* was issued in 1754; *The Great Christian Doctrine of Original Sin Defended,* in 1758, the year of his death; and the *Two Dissertations* on "The Nature of True Virtue" and "Concerning the End for Which God Created the World"—capstones of his philosophical edifice—were brought out posthumously in 1765. The orthodox theology of Calvinism, on which Edwards had been nurtured in East Windsor and at Yale College, was not a shackle limiting the range of his ingenious faculties. Taking, as he did, all human nature for his province, he absolutely required some frame of reference. Calvinism served him admirably as material for the creation of a new idealism.

In a strict sense Edwards, like Emerson, did not construct a systematic philosophy; but the pattern of his interpretation of man's struggle is laid out in the early "Notes," and the later treatises expound the doctrine. From Locke he took the concepts that knowledge must be supplanted by faith, that man's ideas are derived from sense-impressions, even though he diverged widely from Locke in his exposition of the limits and value of knowledge. To Edwards the process was intuitive: man cannot achieve moral grace by an act of will or reason, but must passively receive it through the senses. From Newton, Edwards learned to observe how immutable natural laws, working harmoniously, reflect the great Geometrician. He began by attacking the problem of man's limitation and failure. His weapon was the language of Calvinistic theology.

Calvinism was never synonymous with Puritanism. Archbishop Whitgift, who crowned James I, was a Calvinist; but not so the men he drove to seek out a new plantation in the Bay Colony. Boston and Salem were not touched by Calvinism, nor the dynasty and followers of the Mathers. Edwards, better than any other spokesman, articulated it as a working philosophy, and this Connecticut Valley phenomenon was carried by his supporters into New Jersey and Virginia. Edwards as the first American Calvinist did not emphasize, like Thomas Shepard, Thomas Hooker, and other leaders among the seventeenth century Puritans, the covenantal relation between God and man, whereby the Sovereign was as fully bound by the contract as the subject. Edwards' Calvinism made the Deity more awesome and arbitrary. It emphasized sin as a property of the species. The "immensity and spirituality of the essence of God," in the words of Calvin, were not to be apprehended by an act of reason or bound by man in too legal a contract.

At great pains Edwards reasserted the reality of evil and the assurance of salvation, not to all, but to the "elect." Those so saved, he emphasized, are the regenerate: men and women infused by some external, supernatural grace which they are powerless to win by inclination alone. The regeneration is passively received by way of a new sense. Men may not be sure of election, but they must never cease yearning, with a heart laid passively open to receive the mystical grace. To see God in a rainbow or a buttercup is a reassurance and a challenge. Both the pantheism and the mysticism of Edwards are harmonized in a Calvinistic dogma.

In common with all Puritans, Edwards made clear distinction between the two activities of God, and set them forth in the "Treatise on Grace," written during the Stockbridge years but not published until 1865. There is first God's "common grace," working through secondary causes, to be seen in his providence—his decreeing will—observable in events; and in his commanding will—the Bible. There is secondly, and most important, his "supernatural grace," his regenerative power, an emanation, a new radiation reaching directly to man, overleaping regular channels. It is the supernatural grace that is peculiar to the elect, for it is an irresistible force depending on no antecedent condition or preparation. It reaches beyond the flawless regularity, the implacable justice of cosmic laws. Such mystic union cannot be rationalized. But this "Divine and Supernatural Light, Immediately Imparted to the Soul by the Spirit of God," as Edwards called it in the title of one of his earliest published sermons in 1734, is coexistent with God's common grace. Without the lesser, the greater cannot work. Since God's decreeing will is clear to all who will read their Bible, the preacher is under obligation to advocate hell-fire and brimstone now and then, in order to remind men forcibly that "conversion" is a matter of immediate urgency. The minatory sermon, though seldom used by Edwards in fact, is especially associated with the Calvinism he expounded, and was a traditional part of the Puritan ideology. Edwards' sermon on the sovereignty of God and depravity of man, *Sinners in the Hands of an Angry God* (1741), has fascinated and horrified succeeding generations of readers as much, apparently, as it did the hearers at Enfield, Connecticut, when it was first delivered; but, removed from its contextual place in the scheme of salvation which Edwards expounded, it tends to misrepresent him as one who despised men when in fact he loved them as fellow beings sometimes forgetful of the warnings of a compassionate Father.

The position of Edwards has thus far been stated in the language peculiar to Puritan theology. When it is reassessed as a living philosophy its idiom is seen to have universal truth. Edwards was Calvinistic especially in that he asserted the persistent reality of sin. Its existence, he felt to be inevitable and inescapable. Created free, with power of choice, man has yet one compulsion laid upon him: that he shall not, as a human creature, overstep the limits which his humanity had fixed. He must not seek to be as a god. The fruit of the tree of knowledge is not his to eat. For Edwards there was a twofold significance to the story of Adam's fall, and in both instances the implication, though tragic, was spiritually invigorating. Act and consequence are inseparable. For Adam's wrong act there must be an appropriate consequence which men call justice. Yet men know that as *human* beings their blindness and ignorance are so necessary that, if justice is to be satisfied, the doctrine of God's absolute sovereignty, with respect to salvation and damnation, can admit of no doubt. "The doctrine has very often appeared exceeding pleasant, bright, and sweet," Edwards remarks in his "Personal Narrative." "Absolute sovereignty is what I love to ascribe to God."

And the second implication is profounder still. Had Adam been allowed to remain forever in Eden where the fruits hung ripe for his picking and no physical problems taxed his ingenuity, what conceivable pleasure could he or his descendants ultimately have found in such virtual condemnation to the life of Lotus-Eaters and Struldbrugs? It is at this point that the concept of Mercy or Redemption is required, for were there no mitigation of justice somewhere, man could have no purpose in living. "Use every man after his desert," said Hamlet testily to Polonius, "and who should 'scape whipping?" No theme more surely postulates the issue of Being. Milton had chosen it for his great epics because he believed it the profoundest subject in the world. And Edwards as a Calvinistic metaphysician expounded the theme with originality. His efforts to uncover the roots of religious experience were greater even than those of William James, since James did not share his conviction that the roots were discoverable. The attempt schematically begins with the "Treatise on Grace," already mentioned, and with the *Freedom of the Will*. It concludes with the essay on God's end in creating the world. The projected *History of the Work of Redemption*, a vast design which was to have epitomized his philosophy by embracing all three worlds, heaven, earth, and hell, was left unfinished.

4

In order to understand *Freedom of the Will,* it is necessary first to know the problem Edwards had to meet. The fact that the treatise is a polemic, directed at certain contemporary "heresies," is today inconsequential except in so far as Edwards hacked at them to provide a clearing on which to establish his city of God. Any child of the eighteenth century knew that the proper study of mankind is man; and Edwards began and ended with man. His probing of the psychology of desire is a courageous facing of the rigors of existence, one that avoids the cosmic optimism of thinking mere flawless regularity is enough. *Freedom of the Will* is an essay on human liberty wherein the will and the emotions are seen to be indistinguishable: "And he that has the Liberty of doing according to his will," Edwards says, "is the Agent or doer who is possessed of the will; and not the will which he is possessed of." Morality, then, is an emotional, impulsive process, not a rational one. Edwards does not deny man's freedom, but states that it is qualified by man's "previous bias and inclination"—by such antecedent complexes as inheritance and childhood conditioning. Here are established both the basis of motivation—that is, self-love—and the limits of achievement. Shades of Mandeville and Hobbes! Had Edwards been their apologist he could hardly have argued their position more cogently. The fact that Edwards had never read Hobbes, though he considered him by way of secondary sources to be a "bad man," gives added force to Edwards' philosophical integrity. "Let [Hobbes'] opinion be what it will, we need not reject all truth which is demonstrated by clear evidence, merely because it was once held by some bad man." The will, then, is passive, the creature is "possessed" by it, and the doctrine of necessity equates with Greek fate. Both transcendentalism and pragmatism have roots in a Puritan past, and this essay with its insistence on passivity is one of them.

To follow the scheme of man's relation to the cosmic plan as it is seen to unfold in Edwards' analysis, one must note that he had established at this point the causal relationship of reason and emotion. A resolution of the struggle between justice and mercy must be attempted, and Edwards faced the issue in the essay on *Original Sin*. Though it was not completed until shortly before his death, it assembled material Edwards had long been pondering: What is the cause of evil? Where are its roots? The logical objection to the position Edwards assumed is that, since God is admittedly the creator of man's moral capacity, any apologist of "original sin" must find God the author of it. Edwards met the argument by contending that sin is original in the sense that it is a "property of the species," that God ordained a system which allows it, that therefore necessarily sin will come to pass. But the sin, Edwards contended, is man's act, not God's; hence the punishment is just. The system which God, the All-Good, ordained, is indeed desirable. Nothing but suffering will answer the Law. The thought is St. Paul's, and is integral with all Christian thinking. If this be tragic, it is the tragedy of an infallible nexus. Let more comfortable men stress the benevolence of Deity, Edwards insisted. Logic and the experience of mankind give no warrant for the assumption. Sin is a universal malady, common to all mankind, one which they must endure from their coming hence until their going thither. It is one illness definitely not contracted from rats, lice, and other vermin. Thus man is unique among creatures. To Edwards the story of the origin of evil, traced to our own hereditary taint, was beautiful as well as disturbing. The fact that it is disturbing should not lead us to deny its truth. Its beauty is manifest by the incentive which man is hereby given to contemplate the mystery of God's inscrutable design. Boldly to avow the reality of sin is to enhance the terror of God's sublimity and compel acknowledgment of humanity's dependence.

The essay does not make easy reading, but the conclusion justifies the labor. "It appears particularly, from what has been said," he remarks in final summary, "that all oneness, by virtue whereof *pollution* and *guilt* from *past* wickedness are derived, depends entirely on a *divine establishment*. . . . And all communications, derivations, or continuation of qualities, properties or relations, natural or moral, from what is *past,* as if the subject were *one,* depends on no other foundation." And here is the second of the elements which gave later transcendentalists a kinship with their inherited past: truth is forever and everywhere one and the same.

A Treatise Concerning Religious Affections has long been widely known as a notable discussion of the psychology of religion. It grew out of Edwards' concern for the problems of human destiny, and constitutes a minute observation of revival meetings when they were recurrent during the 1730's and 1740's. Indeed, his hospitable reception of George Whitefield, the most spectacular exhorter of the century, his endorsement of the many "awakenings," made him suspect among the more urbane ministers of the colony. Though Edwards' support made itinerant evangelism theologically acceptable for the next hundred years, the real importance of *Religious Affections* was not felt until later. Like William James, he was concerned with the psychology of religion in general, and with abnormal psychology in particular; and he analyzed the soul's experience with utmost acumen. The experience is emotional, not rational, Edwards believed; and he traced the steps and gave his witness to the workings of the Holy Spirit, reintroducing emotion as a valid shaper of the good life. He perceived the philosophic meaning which lesser exhorters overlooked: "that the essence of all true religion lies in holy love; and that in this divine affection, and an habitual disposition to it, and that light which is the foundation of it, and those things which are the fruits of it, consists the whole of religion." This was Edwards' pattern for living. What he later systematized in *Freedom of the Will,* he was accounting for in the emotions of men. The union of man and God lay through the mysteries of the heart, and Edwards' bold examination established him as a student of the psychology of mysticism. His care, here as always, is to avoid identifying mere intuition with the voice of God, or fusing God and nature into one substance of the transcendental imagination. The work in this respect is unique and remains an initial force in one cultural tradition, through Emerson to the present.

The Nature of True Virtue (1765), properly a sequel to *Religious Affections,* is something of an achievement, for it is mysticism shaped by dogma. It proceeds by contending that acts receive moral quality from the motives that inspire them. True virtue consists of love to Being in general and thus to God as the sum of being. Since no man, Edwards concludes, can have this love unless he is supernaturally charged by some immediately imparted agency, no man can actively work toward becoming truly virtuous. If such a doctrine seems to imply that man should be glad to be damned for the glory of God, it also presents a surpassing moral ideal. How supreme the love can be! How complete becomes the virtuous man's humility when he is able to love others rather than himself! The virtuous man is motivated by good emotions—good because of their beauty, not because of their usefulness or benefits. In the companion dissertation, *Concerning the End for Which God Created the World,* he pushes the implications to final limits. God created the world as the Supreme Artist or Genius, for the pure joy of creating. "It is certain that what God aimed at in the creation of the world, was the good that would be the consequence of the creation, in the whole continuance of the thing created, . . . aiming at an infinitely perfect union of the creature with himself . . . to satisfy his infinite grace and benevolence." God intended the emanation of his fullness, Edwards here states, since beauty, goodness, and existence are all manifestations of the same Principle. The union is one for man to establish, not by will or action, but through passive receptivity. The essay is written for those who would hear, in Milton's phrase, "the unexpressive nuptiall Song."

Edwards has been analyzing pure goodness in a manner no poet has successfully done. Milton and Goethe both succeeded in portraying evil. Edwards, believing that sin is inherent—that man, to the extent that he partakes of common humanity, is "possessed" as well by good will as by bad—is presenting the conclusion that the good man is the continent of Satan. The convincing symbol of goodness must *contain* evil—experiencing it, transmuting it, dissolving it. How could so magnificent a system, Edwards implies, be postulated without the damnation of sinner and election of saint? He has added to Calvinism the mystical and pantheistic overtones; and thus emerges a symbol of sensuous experience philosophically derived.

Each of Edwards' great treatises was written to answer the arguments of insignificant publicists. The issues concerned him, not the stature of the opponents. The recognition of the dislocation as extended to the social order, the tragic vision, though less central in Edwards' thinking than in that of novelists and poets who re-create human action, is none the less clearly present. "Dear children," he said, addressing the youth of the congregation assembled to hear him preach his Farewell Sermon, "Dear children, I leave you in an evil world, that is full of snares and temptations. God only knows what will become of you." Edwards' treatises are documents to which men may turn for enlightenment on a subject of inescapable concern to man. Most of them were composed in a frontier stockade, in a wilderness village beset by trivial bickerings, by one who, while he set spelling lessons for Indian boys, was giving shape to the American destiny.

As a writer of prose, alike in his sermons and in his treatises, Edwards was sensitive to the requirement of his aim. The dissertations hold to the integrity of the syllogistic method, the sermons avoid flights of oratorical fancy. His ear for prose cadence was developed by conscious attention, and he was expert in writing a "plain" style which, in those moments when he abandoned the syllogism to describe the memory of some boyhood experience, effectively communicates the glow of his own heart.

5

Edwards' call to the presidency of the College of New Jersey followed ten years of great productivity and increased renown. His almost immediate death in 1758 deprived the young institution of a celebrated name. "Edwards of New England," as Boswell refers to him, was better known abroad than at home, where he had never been intimate with the religious spokesmen of his time. Inevitably one contrasts him with Franklin, already something of a power, though by no means yet the world figure he was shortly to become. The two, born in the same decade, in the same province, are recognized counselors of their century. Might Edwards, who never did so, have enjoyed meeting Franklin? Neither of them, one suspects, would have understood the other. Both were speculative, ingenious, and basically concerned for the welfare of mankind. But Franklin, with a patriarchal wisdom never the birthright of Edwards, was the mediator. Taking men and things as he found them, he knew how to mold issues without sacrificing principle. Edwards was an austere logician whose compassion yearned toward mankind rather than toward men. He was a dweller in the Augustinian City of God, where the symbol suggests the meaning, where reason and emotion alike are disciplined by contemplation of the principle itself.

Edwards' mystic doctrines were variously reshaped in the nineteenth century; but the tragic intensity, the dwelling upon the reality of sin, the violent imagery, the concern with symbolism were downright shocking, as Holmes acknowledged, to the men of a later generation. To many, but not to all. One thinks first of Hawthorne who, though a skeptic, transmitted much of the essence of Edwards into fiction. Is there not the elf-child Pearl, humanized only when her mother's sin is expiated? Is there not the recriminatory violence of one Maule, and the minatory apostrophe of lonely Judge Pyncheon? And Hawthorne's friend Melville, darkly brooding of a summer's night in the Stockbridge hills, expressed similar aspects of man's incapacity, failure, and turbulent striving. Emerson dedicated Transcendentalism—which never fought Edwardean Puritanism, but absorbed it—to a new preoccupation with the old symbolism of nature. "We do not determine what we will think. We only open our senses, clear away, as we can, all obstruction from the fact, and suffer the intellect to see." Emerson too was well aware, as he speaks here in his essay on "Intellect" of the will's limitation, of the correspondence of the thing and the word, the object and the spirit. Whitman's bold language shot into fresh tangents, but he wrestled with good and evil, the flesh and the spirit, in poems such as "Chanting the Square Deific." Did the idealism within the pessimism of Henry Adams, intensely cultivating self-analysis, attempting to piece "the singulars" together into rules of art through the symbols of the Virgin and the dynamo, derive more than he would have conceded from a New England inheritance? The voice, through these many American years, is the voice of Hawthorne, and Melville, and Emerson, and Whitman, and Adams. But the hand is the hand of Jonathan Edwards.

7. WRITERS OF THE MIDDLE COLONIES

BETWEEN the Wilderness Zion of the Puritans and the plantation colonies of the South lay the provinces which for want of any common characteristics save their intermediate location have been known as the middle colonies. Yet the fact that these provinces—New York, New Jersey, Pennsylvania, and Delaware—were not dominated like New England by a single theological system or like the southern colonies by a peculiar social system, was itself a most significant common characteristic. By virtue of their linguistic and cultural variety, their relatively democratic social and political institutions, their easy tolerance, and their material prosperity, they were the typically American region.

Few areas of the earth embraced such a conglomerate population. There were Dutch patroons on the Hudson; Anglican, Jewish, Huguenot, and Dutch Calvinist merchants in New York; English Quakers and transplanted New England Puritans on Long Island and in New Jersey; English and Welsh Quaker merchants and farmers in Philadelphia and the surrounding counties; industrious German sectarians farming the fertile hinterland of Philadelphia; hardy Scots-Irish Presbyterians on the frontiers; descendants of Swedish and Finnish traders along Delaware Bay; Negro servants and slaves; Iroquois, Delaware, and Susquehanna Indians. This mixed race, restless and inquiring, was always on the move; by the middle of the eighteenth century it could no longer be contained in the region drained by the Hudson and the Delaware and had begun to spill over into the watershed of the Susquehanna, where it entered the arena of Anglo-French imperial conflict. Here were the people from whom, as Crèvecœur was to write, "that race now called Americans have arisen."

Most of the books produced in the middle colonies were concerned with the topography and history of the inner and the outer worlds; few of them were written with conscious literary intent. In the older towns, however, where economic prosperity had created a stable society, a vital literary culture was coming into being. In spite of a relatively late start among the English colonies, the region advanced rapidly towards cultural maturity, and the quarter-century preceding the Revolution witnessed in New York and Philadelphia a literary flowering which foreshadowed the intellectual leadership to be assumed by those centers in the early years of the Republic.

2

Over the greater part of the middle colonies religious freedom prevailed, resulting in a typically American babel of sects and churches. The most distinctive note was contributed by the Quakers, a religious minority whose ideas, operating as a leaven, have had an influence in American life quite out of proportion to their numbers. It was a note of persistent moral idealism, drawing its strength from a religion of pure inner experience, and manifesting itself practically in the quick response of a sensitive conscience to human suffering.

The central figure in early American Quakerism was William Penn, perhaps the greatest of colonial statesmen, who organized the colonies of New Jersey, Pennsylvania, and Delaware on the basis of religious toleration, political democracy, and pacifism. He was a prolific writer on theological, moral, and political subjects, but his chief claim to attention as a literary figure rests upon his moral and religious aphorisms, of which the most extensive collection is *Some Fruits of Solitude* (1693). A singular compound of devout Quaker and man of the world, Penn distilled into his maxims a morality which was at once intuitively religious and shrewdly utilitarian, prefiguring in its latter aspect some of the sayings of Poor Richard. In *Fruits of a Father's Love* (addressed to his children on the eve of a voyage to Pennsylvania in 1699) he described the Inner Light, the root principle of Quakerism, as

> the Light of Christ in your Consciences, by which . . . you may clearly see if your Deeds, ay and your Words and Thoughts too, are wrought in God or not. . . . And as you come to obey this blessed Light in it's holy Convictions, it will lead you out of the World's dark and degenerate Ways and Works, and bring you unto Christ's Way and Life, and to be of the Number of his true self-denying Followers.

The characteristic literary expression of Quakerism was the journal or spiritual autobiography. There were in the colonies scores of obscure men and women of uncommon spiritual sensitivity who traveled in the ministry as "public Friends," and left these records behind not as monuments to their own spiritual achievements but as guidebooks to others on their inward odysseys. Concerned primarily with inner states rather than outward events, the journals followed a more or less uniform pattern, beginning with a record of divine intimations in childhood, followed by an extreme compunction over youthful frivolities, passing through the spiritual conflicts of adolescence to "convincement" of the truth of Quakerism, and conversion, in which the will was utterly surrendered to the divine leading. As if repeating one another, most of the journalists recorded the same turning-points in later life: entrance upon the vocal ministry, the adoption of "plain dress," the decision to curtail the volume of outward business, and the awakening of the social conscience.

As the structure of the Quaker journals tended towards uniformity, so did the style. Its keynote was an austere simplicity. "Ye that dwell in the Light and walk in the Light," George Fox, founder of the Society of Friends, had urged, "use plainness of speech and plain words." William Penn's advice was to the same purpose: "Affect not Words, but Matter, and chiefly to be pertinent and plain: Truest Eloquence is plainest, and brief Speaking . . . is the best." The emphasis on plainness had been part of the total Quaker revolt against the "world" of the mid-seventeenth century when English literary prose had been loaded with farfetched tropes, inkhorn terms, learned quotations, and other ostentatious rhetorical trappings. In pursuing the ideal of unadorned simplicity, the Quakers were careful to strip their writings of superfluities that served only to please the carnal mind. In their insistence upon plainness of diction, they fell in with, indeed they anticipated, the trend of English and American prose style. Failing to match in syntax the simplicity which they achieved in language, the Quakers retained in their writing an archaic structural element which was to distinguish the plain style of Woolman from that of his contemporary Franklin. Just as the "plain dress" of the eighteenth century Friend was essentially the costume of Charles II with its ornaments removed, so the basic sentence structure of the Quaker journals remained tortuous and intricate in the manner of Browne and Burton, while the diction had all the simplicity and plainness of Swift and Defoe.

The uniformity of the Quaker style blurred but could not wholly erase the individualities of its users. The robust piety of a seagoing Philadelphia Quaker was revealed in the *Journal, or Historical Account, of the Life, Travels, and Christian Experiences, of that Antient, Faithful Servant of Jesus Christ, Thomas Chalkley* (1749); for all its austerity, Chalkley's language retained a salty flavor as he related the nautical and spiritual adventures of a life spent in the triangular trade with the West Indies and England. With the *Journal of the Life, Travels, and Gospel Labours of . . . Daniel Stanton* (1772) the Quaker style showed signs of becoming stereotyped; after repeated usage expressions which had originally been vivid metaphors of spiritual experience—"to dig deep," "to outrun one's Guide," "to keep down to the root"—came to be colorless, drained of imaginative content. In the hands of the saintly John Churchman of Nottingham, Pennsylvania, on the other hand, the Quaker style could be a subtle and sensitive instrument. Thus in his journal (1779) he described the manner in which a religious "concern" to travel "in the love of the Gospel" to Europe had come to him:

> One day walking alone, I felt myself so inwardly weak and feeble, that I stood still, and by the reverence that covered my mind, I knew that the hand of the Lord was on me and his presence round about, the earth was silent and all flesh brought into stillness, and light went forth with brightness, and shone on Great Britain, Ireland, and Holland, and my mind felt the gentle, yet strongly drawing cords of that love which is stronger than death, which made me say, Lord! *go before, and strengthen me, and I will follow whithersoever thou leads.*

The possessor of the sweetest spirit, the tenderest social conscience, and the purest prose style among all the eighteenth century Quakers was John Woolman, the tailor of Mount Holly, New Jersey. He was early convinced, as he wrote in his *Journal* (1774) "that true Religion consisted in an inward life, wherein the Heart doth Love and Reverence God the Creator, and learn to Exercise true Justice and Goodness, not only toward all men, but allso toward the Brute Creatures." Humanitarianism was in the air in the eighteenth century, but the source of Woolman's social concern lay deeper than the transient mood of an age. The poignant consciousness of God's infinite tenderness and love was constantly renewed in him, and these moments of mystical awareness were the wellsprings of his dedicated life, causing him eventually to realize that he was so "mixed in" with the mass of suffering humanity that henceforth he could not consider himself as a distinct and separate being. This realization impelled him, as he traveled to the southward, to labor lovingly with the planters, urging them to renounce slaveholding, which struck his sensitive spirit "as a Dark Gloominess hanging over the Land." It led him to travel unarmed on a visit to hostile Indians on the frontier that he might "feel and understand their life, and the Spirit they live in"; to sympathize with the poor brutalized sailor lads on the Atlantic crossing; and to seek the elimination of the seeds of war from society.

In *Some Considerations on the Keeping of Negroes* (1754, 1762), he spoke out clearly for racial equality, and called attention to the deleterious effects of slavery on the slave owners. His *Plea for the Poor* (published posthumously in 1793) and *Conversations on the True Harmony of Mankind* (first published in 1837) left no doubt that he was equally sensitive to other forms of social injustice, that he was conscious of the rift opening up even in the midst of provincial plenty between the wealthy merchant and the workingman. "To labour for a perfect redemption from this spirit of Oppression," he wrote, "is the Great Business of the whole family of Christ Jesus in this world."

The ideal of perfect simplicity by which his life was guided led him in his writings to strip away every superfluous word and phrase. The man who insisted upon traveling steerage to England because he "observed sundry sorts of carved work and imagery" on the outside of the more comfortable cabin, and "some superfluity of workmanship of several sorts" in the cabin itself, applied the same rigorous standards to his own prose, eliminating from it everything designed merely to please the "creaturely" mind. By banishing non-essential or merely decorative adjectives, adverbs, and modifying phrases, he laid bare the structure of the introspective process. His prose was lacking in warmth and grace and color, but it had a purity which enabled his essential meaning to emerge unclouded, uncolored, undistorted, like something seen at the bottom of a clear spring of water. Thus in spite of his indifference to art, or because of his scorn for the merely ornamental, Woolman created out of the plain style which was his inheritance a medium of expression that was a triumph of functional art. In its crystal purity it was, as William Ellery Channing was to perceive, continuous with the saintly simplicity of his life.

In the realm of purely religious writing the many sects and churches of the middle colonies produced nothing to match the distinctiveness and literary charm of the Quaker journals. But in the field of philosophical speculation, a field which was alien to the Quaker mentality, learned Anglican and Presbyterian divines exhibited notable intellectual acumen and vitality. American philosophy in general has tended to oscillate between the poles of absolute idealism and naïve realism, and it was characteristic of this region of diverse peoples and liberal intellectual climate that it should have fostered, almost simultaneously, both of these diametrically opposed systems—the one originating in Ireland and given currency here by an Anglican clergyman, the other stemming from Scotland and reformulated by a Presbyterian minister.

Samuel Johnson, a Yale graduate who took orders in the Church of England, was at one with the unphilosophical Woolman and with the young Jonathan Edwards when he wrote: "I must account it the greatest perfection and happiness of every intelligent creature to depend on a perpetual intercourse with the Deity for all his happiness and all his hopes." Reacting from the Calvinism of Yale, Johnson moved towards rationalism in religion, composing a "rhapsody" called "Raphael; or, The Genius of English America" in which he pleaded for the use of reason in the pursuit of truth. He drew back as the realization dawned that in the ordered universe of Newton and Locke there was no room for the idea of God as a sustaining presence. At this point the philosophical idealism of Bishop Berkeley came to his rescue, providing a rationale for the sense of the divine presence and a safeguard against skepticism and materialism. Johnson's *Elementa Philosophica* (1752), the first philosophical textbook written and published in America, was dedicated to the Irish bishop, whom he followed closely in insisting that spirit was the only substance, that matter existed only in the mind of the perceiver, and that nature was simply the succession of ideas that God presented to our minds. Johnson's textbook was used at King's College in New York, where he was President, and at the College of Philadelphia, where the Anglican William Smith was Provost.

Idealism enjoyed a brief vogue at the College of New Jersey; but it ended abruptly in 1768 when the Reverend John Witherspoon came from Scotland to be President, bringing with him the Scottish philosophy of common sense. As a theologian Witherspoon occupied a commanding position wherever the influence of Calvinism extended. Quite as much as Johnson he was concerned to vindicate the Christian religion from the corrosive attacks of rationalism and natural science. Dismissing idealism as "a wild and ridiculous attempt to unsettle the principles of common sense," he bluntly maintained that the existence of an object was completely independent of the mind that perceived it. Furthermore, as the external senses assure us infallibly of the existence of the material world, so through the "internal senses" we are made aware of the existence of God and the validity of Christian principles. This naïve realism was the more successful in combating the deists and materialists in that it made use of their own empirical methods. "It is safer," wrote Witherspoon, ". . . to trace facts upwards than to reason downwards." With its empirical methods and its uncritical acceptance of hard facts, the realistic philosophy which Witherspoon introduced into America found a congenial environment. Radiating from Princeton, its influence was to permeate American thought for a hundred years until it came to be regarded as "the American philosophy."

3

Although the broad region occupied by the middle colonies formed the keystone of the colonial arch, it was almost *terra incognita* to English-speaking people until the last third of the seventeenth century. The forested reaches of the Alleghenies and the Ohio River valley hardly entered the consciousness of Englishmen in the colonies or the mother country until the middle of the eighteenth century, when pioneer traders and settlers from the middle colonies came into fateful conflict there with outposts of the French empire. As each of these areas was successively opened for settlement, the colonists rushed into print with accounts of the lay of the land, its flora and fauna, its aboriginal inhabitants, and the momentous affairs being transacted there. These utilitarian reports and chronicles were in the oldest tradition of American literature; but they differed from the exuberant accounts of the Elizabethan sea dogs and traders in that they were informed with something of the scientific spirit that entered British thinking after the middle of the seventeenth century.

The earliest accounts of the region were sober, factual reports, designed to attract settlers but distinguished by accuracy in observation and moderation in language. Thus Daniel Denton in his *Brief Description of New-York* (1670) declared:

> I . . . have writ nothing, but what I have been an eye-witness to all or the greatest part of it: Neither can I safely say, was I willing to exceed, but was rather willing the place it self should exceed my Commendation.

He did not hesitate to compare the New World favorably with the Old, both in economic opportunities and in natural beauties:

> Yea, in *May* you shall see the Woods and Fields so curiously bedecke with Roses, and an innumerable multitude of delightful Flowers, not only pleasing the eye, but smell, that you may behold Nature contending with Art, and striving to equal, if not excel many Gardens in *England.*

William Penn, whose *Letter to the Free Society of Traders* (1683) was the first comprehensive report on Pennsylvania, was a Fellow of the Royal Society, and the scientific temper was apparent no less in his meticulous survey of the natural resources of his colony than in his first-hand observations on the culture of the Lenni-Lenape Indians. Fifteen years later, his account was expanded and brought up to date as *An Historical and Geographical Account . . . Of Pensilvania and of West New-Jersey* by the Welsh Quaker Gabriel Thomas, who added to Penn's sober and temperate language a certain Celtic sparkle and playfulness. With ebullient optimism he enunciated the theme of the promise of American life, setting over against the incredible bounty of nature on the shores of the Delaware a dismal picture of the laboring poor in England "half-starved, visible in their meagre looks, that are continually wandering up and down looking for Employment, without finding any, who here need not lie idle a moment." Only occasionally did Thomas' penchant for hyperbole or his enthusiasm for his new home lead him to transcend the facts, and when he did, it was in a manner that would be regarded in years to come as the typically American vein of humor:

> There are among other various sorts of Frogs [he solemnly reported], the Bull-Frog, which makes a roaring noise, hardly to be distinguished from that well known of the Beast, from whom it takes its Name.

From these early reports and chronicles stemmed two types of writing—

natural history and political history—both dominated by a utilitarian purpose and both characterized by the spirit of careful observation and accurate reporting. These books stood in contrast to much of the contemporary writing in the other provinces in that they were the work not of clergymen, but of lawyers, physicians, teachers, and merchants—men of affairs with a cosmopolitan outlook limited neither by theological dogmatism nor by parochialism and excessive provincial pride. The historians among them wrote from a broad imperial point of view, and the writers on natural history were always conscious of belonging to the international community of scientists. Both groups wrote primarily for a European rather than a colonial audience.

Lieutenant Governor Cadwallader Colden of New York was both historian and scientist. Indeed he was a typical eighteenth century *virtuoso,* equally at home in history, medicine, botany, mathematics, physics, and metaphysics; he was a correspondent of Linnæus and Gronovius in Europe and of the leading members of the Royal Society in England. His *History of the Five Indian Nations* (1727) was drawn largely from Jesuit sources, eked out by his own experiences among the Mohawks. Using these same materials a century later, Francis Parkman was to create a magnificent historical drama. Colden lacked Parkman's historical perspective, his dramatic power, and his architectonic skill in relating incidents to a single overarching theme. His narrative consisted of a succession of apparently unrelated forays, council fires, and peace treaties. The chief distinction of style was contributed by the Indians themselves, whose formal orations, faithfully reproduced, were studded with picturesque and striking metaphors. However inadequate his achievement, there was grandeur in Colden's conception, nor was he unmindful of the momentous lesson implicit in his formless narrative; his avowed purpose was to demonstrate that the Five Nations were of crucial importance to British America as a buffer against the French and a means of holding the West.

"I have sometimes thought," Colden declared, "that the Histories wrote with all the Delicacy of a fine Romance, are like *French* Dishes, more agreeable to the Pallat than the Stomach, and less wholesom than more common and courser Dyet." Thirty years later, William Smith, Jr., an able New York lawyer, found himself in agreement with this dictum, although in politics he was ranged on the opposite side from Colden. Smith's *History of the Province of New-York* (1757), written to dispel British ignorance of colonial affairs, was a full-dress chronicle of New York under British rule, with a prologue on the Dutch period and a comprehensive concluding survey of the trade, religion, and politics of the province at mid-century. The narrative was written for the most part in plain, lawyerlike English, but it was punctuated and enlivened by a series of brilliant set-pieces in the form of mordant sketches of the royal governors. Smith's design, he confessed in his preface, was "rather to inform than please":

> The ensuing Narrative . . . presents us only a regular Thread of simple Facts; and even those unembellished with Reflections, because they themselves suggest the proper Remarks, and most Readers will doubtless be best pleased with their own. . . . no Reins have been given to a wanton Imagination, for the Invention of plausible Tales, supported only by light Probabilities; but choosing rather to be honest and dull, than agreeable and false, the true Import of my Vouchers hath been strictly adhered to and regarded.

Animated thus by a scientific ideal which tempered his partisanship, Smith produced a work second among colonial histories only to Thomas Hutchinson's *History of the Colony of Massachusetts Bay*.

In Pennsylvania, historians were preoccupied with the problem of the Indian on the frontier, and scientific objectivity gave way before the emotions aroused by that ever-present reality. Another William Smith, Provost of the College of Philadelphia, enlisted his literary talents on the side of the aristocratic Proprietors, and launched two vigorous salvos of polemic history against the Quaker-dominated Assembly. In his *Brief State of the Province of Pennsylvania* (1755) and his *Brief View of the Conduct of Pennsylvania* (1756), he taxed the peace-loving Quakers with excessive republicanism and with having appropriated money for hospitals and libraries at a time when the frontiers lay open to Indian incursions. He exploited all the resources of the skilled propagandist, including cold statistics, gruesome atrocity stories, and charges that the Quaker opposition was "a factious Cabal, effectually promoting the French Interest." Charles Thomson, a teacher in the Friends school in Philadelphia, endeavored in his *Inquiry into the Causes of the Alienation of the Delaware and Shawanese Indians* (1759) to vindicate the Quaker policy of seeking the friendship and respect of the Indians. With sober and painstaking scholarship, though not without an obvious bias, he recounted the story of Indian relations in Pennsylvania, a story filled in his telling with fraud and chicanery on the part of the whites and climaxed by the infamous "Walking Purchase" of 1737 by which the Indians had been deprived of a large portion of their patrimony. More than a century of dishonor was to pass before another American, Helen Hunt Jackson, would come forward with an equally strong and well documented plea for justice towards the dispossessed red man.

Lewis Evans, Philadelphia mapmaker, was, like Colden, both historian and scientist, although something of the polemic spirit infected the historical and political portions of his *Geographical, Historical, Political, Philosophical and Mechanical Essays* (1755–1756). These essays, written in the first instance as analyses of his own pioneer map of the middle colonies and the Ohio River valley, contained some of the earliest descriptions of the American landscape west of the Alleghenies. "To look from these Hills into the lower Lands," he wrote as he stood high in the Alleghenies gazing westward, "is but, as it were, into an Ocean of Woods, swell'd and deprest here and there by little Inequalities not to be distinguished, one Part from another, any more than the Waves of the real Ocean." As Evans had hoped, his essays attracted attention in England, where no less a personage than Dr. Samuel Johnson thought them an indication that literature was gaining ground in America. The treatises, Johnson pontificated, were written "with such elegance as the subject admits, tho' not without some mixture of the American dialect, a tract of corruption to which every language widely diffused must always be exposed." No doubt the lexicographer was distressed by Americanisms like *branch, fork, creek,* and *run,* his pedantry thus blinding him to a significant manifestation of the vitality of the English language in America.

Evans' companion on his first reconnaissance of the Appalachian plateau was John Bartram, a tireless collector of botanical specimens from the American forest. Natural history in the eighteenth century was an exciting adventure of identifying and classifying thousands of newly observed forms of life, and a whole continent lay open before the sharp eyes of this simple Philadelphia Quaker turned deist who corresponded with the leading scientists of Europe. The laconic style in which Bartram set down his observations was a product of the Quaker tradition of plain speech reinforced by the spirit of scientific accuracy and objectivity. Traveling through the verdant Susquehanna valley in the summer of 1743, he allowed himself to note only that

> the land hereabouts is middling white oak and huckleberry land. . . . we went up a vale of middling soil, covered with high oak Timber, nearly west to the top of the hill . . . from whence we had a fair prospect of the river Susquehanah.

Even in the midst of the gorgeous exotic scenery of Florida, the taciturn Quaker naturalist, distrustful of emotion, permitted himself only a restrained scientific curiosity. He remarked in a letter to Franklin that his journal contained only his "observations of particular soils, rivers, and natural vegetable productions," adding in a revealing comment, "But there was no artificial curiosities in those provinces as temples, theatres, piramids, palaces, bridges, catacoms, oblisks, pictures." A century hence, more sophisticated writers like Hawthorne and Henry James would be regretting the absence of these "artificial curiosities" from the American scene. And within a few years Bartram's own son was to interpret the American landscape in a manner which required no reference to a remote and storied past to establish its romantic character.

William Bartram, who spent the years between 1773 and 1778 botanizing in the Floridas, Georgia, and the Carolinas, added to his father's scientific curiosity a sensibility to form and color, a rich and varied vocabulary, and a pantheistic philosophy, all of which were to make a strong impression upon the romantic poets of England. His volume of *Travels* (1791), which has attracted attention from literary historians chiefly as a document in the history of romanticism in England, deserves attention on its own merits as an authentic literary masterpiece of early American romanticism.

The younger Bartram was a painter in water colors as well as a poet. He looked upon the strange and beautiful tropical landscape with all the freshness and acuity of vision which had distinguished the earlier observers; but he had the priceless advantage of an artist's eye and a richly varied verbal palette. His style—the most distinctive and accomplished style developed by any writer in the middle colonies—was loose in structure, fluent in movement, heavily ballasted with Latin botanical names, equally apt for detailed delineation and for rapid narrative. Whether he was describing a furious battle of alligators or the flowering shrub which he named the *Franklinia Alatamaha,* a tropical thunderstorm or that "inchanting and amazing chrystal fountain" that was to meander through the wondrous landscape of Coleridge's "Kubla Khan," William Bartram wrote with conscious artistry. The measure of his success can be judged by this description of a fish observed in Georgia:

> It is as large as a man's hand, nearly oval and thin, being compressed on each side; the tail is beautifully formed; the top of the head and back, of an olive green, be-sprinkled with russet specks; the sides of a sea-green, inclining to azure, insensibly blended with the olive above, and beneath lightens to a silvery white, or pearl colour, elegantly powdered with specks of the finest green, russet and gold; the belly is of a bright scarlet red or vermilion, darting up rays or fiery streaks into the pearl on each side; the ultimate angle of the branchiostega extends backwards with a long spatula, ending with a round or oval particoloured spot, representing the eye in the long feathers of a peacock's train, verged round with a thin flame-coloured membrane, and appears like a brilliant ruby fixed on the side of the fish.

Occasionally Bartram lapsed into rhapsodic ejaculations, full of pseudo-classic epithets and periphrases, revealing that, for all his romanticism, he was not wholly emancipated from eighteenth century conventions. His attitude towards the Indian owed something to his Quaker background, but probably more to the current literary stereotype of the noble savage; nevertheless, his observations on the culture of the Creeks, Seminoles, and Cherokees were anthropologically sound. His romantic pantheism, which so attracted Wordsworth, sprang from the union of his ancestral Quakerism, with its ideas of divine immanence, and the scientific deism which he absorbed from his father; he was probably unconscious of the degree to which the two influences merged in such a passage as this: "Let us rely on providence, and by studying and contemplating the works and power of the Creator, learn wisdom and understanding in the economy of nature, and be seriously attentive to the divine monitor within." With William Bartram the middle colony tradition of scientific observation and description reached a culmination. In his *Travels* the raw materials with which his predecessors had been struggling for a century were finally given form by the shaping hand of a scientific observer who was also a sensitive artist.

Not until thirty years had passed did any other American naturalist emerge to carry to greater heights the work of the Bartrams in what was to be a great American tradition of writing about nature. Starting also from Philadelphia, John James Audubon studied and painted the birds of the neighboring areas, extending his journeys eventually from the Alleghenies to the Mississippi and from the Cumberland Gap to the Louisiana bayous. He intended that his *The Birds of America* should include every American bird known to man. The great folio of beautifully colored plates was accompanied by five volumes of text, *Ornithological Biography* (1831–1839), in which species and their habits are set against romantically described landscapes and lively narratives of Audubon's adventures on the frontier. "My work," he said, "shall be not a *beacon* but a *tremendous lighthouse!*" And so it has proved to be. The light from it has thrown into undeserved shadow the pioneering work of his quiet Quaker predecessors, the two Bartrams.

4

Self-conscious literary life in the middle colonies was associated chiefly with the colleges established in the mid-eighteenth century. In two respects educational ideals in the middle colonies differed from those which had led to the founding of the older colonial institutions: education was conceived primarily as training for civic responsibility, and the English language was given a place beside Greek and Latin as a proper subject of college study. Both William Livingston in *The Independent Reflector* (1752–1753) and William Smith in *A General Idea of the College of Mirania* (1753) echoed Archbishop Tillotson's dictum that classical or speculative learning which had no practical usefulness was "but a more specious and ingenious sort of idleness, a more pardonable and creditable kind of ignorance." Regular opportunities for practice in English rhetoric and oratory were provided in disputations and literary exercises held in the college halls. The ideal college graduate in the middle colonies was thus not primarily the polished country gentleman or the learned minister but the useful and responsible citizen, skilled in the elegant and persuasive use of his mother tongue.

William Livingston, a brilliant lawyer and leader of the liberal party in the politics of provincial New York, did much by precept and example to foster this ideal. In 1747 he published a poem entitled *Philosophic Solitude,* a faint echo of *The Choice,* an enormously popular English poem written a half-century earlier by the Reverend John Pomfret. In correct heroic couplets, with a slight Miltonic flavoring, Livingston's poem described the simple felicity of life in a rural retreat, and culminated in a mild paean to a Deity whose existence was inferred, in typical eighteenth century fashion, from the beauty and harmony of the creation. Both the mood and the measure of the poem harked back to Augustan England. It is interesting chiefly for its revelation of the influences which had formed Livingston's mind and tastes. In enumerating the authors whose works he would chose for his library, he named the writers of classical antiquity; the French authors Fénelon and Montesquieu; Milton, Dryden, Pope, and Isaac Watts among the English poets; Raleigh, Swift, and Addison among the prose writers; and Bacon, Boyle, Newton, and Locke, chief architects of the eighteenth century cosmology.

Livingston's strong sense of social responsibility led him to place his literary gifts at the service of the liberal causes to which he was committed. He was the principal author of *The Independent Reflector* (1752–1753) and *The Occasional Reverberator* (1753), two series of periodical essays in the tradition of Trenchard and Gordon's *Independent Whig.* Although he denied any literary purpose ("In subjects meerly literary," he wrote, "I shall rarely indulge myself"), he achieved genuine distinction as a writer of prose. His style was formal and balanced, barbed with satire, full of carefully contrived antitheses and climaxes, rising occasionally to a pitch of stately eloquence. For vigor and trenchancy it was unsurpassed by any other periodical writing of the day either in the colonies or in the mother country.

Livingston left no room for doubt about the cause in which his literary talents were enlisted.

> 'Tis the cause of truth and liberty [he wrote]; what he intends to oppose is superstition, bigotry, priestcraft, tyranny, servitude, public mismanagement, and dishonesty in office. The things he proposes to teach are the nature and excellence of our constitution, the inestimable value of liberty, the disastrous effects of bigotry, the shame and horror of bondage, the importance of religion unpolluted and unadulterate with superstitious additions and inventions of priests.

Himself a Presbyterian and the descendant of Dutch Calvinists, Livingston nevertheless deplored sectarianism, and was suspicious of any interference by the church in secular affairs. In theology he was a liberal, believing religion to be "plain and simple, and to the meanest capacity intelligible." In politics he was a Whig, bent upon vindicating the authority of the provincial Assembly against the encroachments of the royal governors.

When it became known that the proposed college in New York was to be chartered by the Crown as an Anglican institution, Livingston launched a literary campaign to have it incorporated by the Assembly and kept free from denominational control. Returning again and again to the attack in successive numbers of *The Independent Reflector,* he underlined the importance of intellectual freedom, not neglecting the opportunity for animadversions upon Harvard and Yale where the tender minds of the future ruling classes, he maintained, were filled with illiberal Puritan doctrines that were bound to filter down through the whole of society. Behind Livingston's plea for academic and religious liberty one could detect stirrings of a more far-reaching revolt against authority that was to culminate before many years in a revolution.

Livingston's liberalism and literary skill made him something of a hero to the undergraduates at the College of New Jersey who gathered in Nassau Hall every afternoon at five under President Witherspoon's direction to hear orations declaimed by their fellow students. Livingston's essays were frequently used for declamations, and one of the two undergraduate literary societies at the College was named after Livingston's pseudonym, "The American Whig." The leading figures in the American Whig Society were three young men destined soon to take prominent parts in the founding of a national literature. As undergraduates Philip Freneau, Hugh Henry Brackenridge, and James Madison expended their literary energies chiefly in directing coarse and vigorous satires against the rival Cliosophic Society.

For the Commencement of 1771 Brackenridge and Freneau composed a long poem in blank verse called *The Rising Glory of America.* Their imaginations were fired by the same imperial vision which had inspired Colden and Evans. They foresaw new towns springing up along the Ohio, and "nations" on the Mississippi, American poets arising by the Susquehanna, in the Alleghenies and the Tuscarora hills, a new civilization burgeoning on the Appalachians, in the Carolinas,

> and the plains
> Stretch'd out from thence far to the burning Line.

Moved to hyperbole by their regional pride, they celebrated New York as the "daughter of Commerce" hailing from afar

> her num'rous ships of trade
> Like shady forests rising on the waves.

And Philadelphia they hymned as

> mistress of our world,
> The seat of arts, of science, and of fame.

At the College of Philadelphia Provost William Smith held sway as a sort of provincial Great Cham of literature. Like Dr. Samuel Johnson, his English contemporary, he is remembered not so much for his writings as for his personality and his influence on younger writers. The little circle of poets which he gathered around him in the fifties and sixties was the first self-conscious poetic "school" in America, the first group of American writers who regarded poetry not as a handmaid to ethics and religion but as a craft to be practiced for its own sake. The *American Magazine and Monthly Chronicle* (1757–1758), which Provost Smith edited, served as a vehicle for their literary efforts, establishing itself in the brief twelve months of its existence as the most brilliant and original literary periodical in colonial America. The artistic vitality of the group was further manifested by the fact that it included the first American composer of secular music, Francis Hopkinson; the first American dramatist whose work was professionally performed, Thomas Godfrey; and the first American painter to achieve international recognition, Benjamin West.

Even before the founding of its college the Philadelphia region could boast of considerable classical learning. Between 1718 and 1730 David French, Prothonotary of the Court of Newcastle in the "Lower Counties" (Delaware), had rendered into English verse some of the frankly pagan and sensual odes of Anacreon. The Quaker James Logan, who had come to Philadelphia as William Penn's secretary and had remained to become Pennsylvania's most distinguished scholar-statesman, published a translation of the *Moral Distichs* of Dionysius Cato in 1735 and of Cicero's *De Senectute* in 1744. His publisher, Benjamin Franklin, hailed the former as "the first translation of a classic which was both made and printed in the British Colonies," and the latter as "a happy omen that Philadelphia shall become the seat of the American muses." The classics were not neglected at the College of Philadelphia; but by the fifties the tide was beginning to set in another direction.

The college poets of Philadelphia were caught in the same crosscurrents and confusions of taste that affected English verse in this transitional period between the decline of the classical ideal and the emergence of full-blown romanticism. It is instructive to compare them with their English contemporaries, Collins, Gray, and the Warton brothers. There was the same devotion to the Pindaric and Horatian ode-forms and to the youthful poetry of Milton;

the same addiction to the stock epithets and personified abstractions of the Augustans mingled with glimmerings of sentiment that forecast the Romantic mood; the same scholarly urbanity alternating with effusive sensibility. If the poetry of Philadelphia was derivative, so was the best English poetry of the day. Before condemning these provincial poets out of hand for seeking their literary inspiration abroad, one should reflect that they regarded themselves after all as English poets, that they had no indigenous poetic tradition to draw upon, that they lived and wrote in an academic atmosphere, and that, like many later American poets, they felt, or professed to feel, radically out of sympathy with the bustling mercantile society in which their lot was cast. The day of appreciative patrons is past, lamented Nathaniel Evans, young Anglican clergyman,

> And we are in a climate cast
> Where few the muse can relish;
> Where all the doctrine now that's told
> Is that a shining heap of gold
> Alone can man embellish.

The artificialities of the moribund pastoral tradition exercised a singular fascination over the Philadelphia poets. Thomas Godfrey and Francis Hopkinson were at one with Nathaniel Evans in his resolution to naturalize the eclogue in America, to

> wake the rural reed
> And sing of swains, whose snowy lambkins feed
> On SCHUYLKILL's banks with shady walnuts crown'd.

Streams bearing the names of Schuylkill and Delaware appeared in many of their poems, but the landscape through which they flowed was always the conventional bucolic backdrop derived from Theocritus, Virgil, and Pope, further conventionalized by the persistent use of such "poetic" epithets as "spicy vales," "gay, enamell'd groves," "the finny brood," "the feather'd tribe."

No doubt Provost Smith must be held partly responsible for the vein of academic classicism in the poets of his circle, but he also encouraged them in the expression of an inchoate Romanticism. His own principal literary contribution to the *American Magazine* was a series of essays written under the pseudonym (itself a typical pre-Romantic stereotype) of "The Hermit," in which a didactic purpose was invested with an atmosphere of romantic melancholy and awe at the sublimity of nature. In praising the work of his special protégé Thomas Godfrey, the untutored son of a glazier, he employed phrases which betrayed his sympathy with the emerging Romantic conception of poetry. He wrote of the young poet's "poetic warmth," his "elevated and daring genius," and cited Godfrey's own lines as descriptive of his work:

> In beautiful disorder, yet compleat,
> The structure shines irregularly great.

Godfrey's "Night Piece" (1758), written in the stanza of Gray's "Elegy," was redolent of the atmosphere of contemporary "graveyard" poetry; and his *Court of Fancy* (1762) and "The Assembly of Birds" (1765) reflected the current revival of interest in Chaucer. Francis Hopkinson's "Description of a Church" (about 1762) was an American echo of the current English vogue of Gothicism. All three of the major poets of the group shared their generation's adulation of Milton, and paid him the homage of imitation. They were in their happiest vein when they took their inspiration from the Elizabethan and Caroline lyrists. In his lines "To Celia," Thomas Godfrey succeeded in capturing something of the gay *insouciance* of Waller and Herrick:

> When in *Celia's* heav'nly Eye
> Soft inviting Love I spy,
> 'Tho you say 'tis all a cheat,
> I must clasp the dear deceit.
>
> Why should I more knowledge gain,
> When it only gives me pain?
> If deceiv'd I'm still at rest,
> In the sweet Delusion blest.

Both Evans and Godfrey died young, and Provost Smith, suspected of Loyalist sympathies, was under a cloud in the seventies; but Francis Hopkinson was to live on into the first years of the Republic, providing a link between the literary life of the provincial metropolis and that of the political and cultural capital of the new nation. This "pretty, little, curious, ingenious" man, as John Adams described him, was the most versatile of the group: he was a musician and composer, an amateur portraitist, a poet, satirist, and writer of graceful Addisonian essays, as well as a dabbler in science, a lawyer and judge, and a member of the Continental Congress. During the Revolution he exploited the satirical vein first revealed in the pungent humor of his burlesque fragment "Dirtilla" a decade earlier. To the patriot cause he contributed a number of rollicking ballads like "The Battle of the Kegs" (1778) and a series of political allegories in verse and prose of which *A Pretty Story* (1774) and "Date Obolum Belisario" (1778) were the most effective.

Combining in his own person a gift for pure literature and a readiness to devote his talents to the public weal, Hopkinson carried into the literary life of the Republic the ideal which had flourished in the college towns of the middle colonies. In 1787 he celebrated the adoption of the Federal Constitution with a ballad called "The New Roof: A Song for Federal Mechanics," employing an elaborate metaphor which he had used earlier in prose to defend the Constitution against its traducers. In vigorous and homely images he sang:

> Come muster, my lads, your mechanical tools,
> Your saws and your axes, your hammers and rules:
> Bring your mallets and planes, your level and line,
> And plenty of pins of American pine:
> *For our roof we will raise, and our song still shall be,*
> *Our government firm, and our citizens free.*

In 1788 he dedicated to George Washington a volume of songs of which he had composed both words and music. In these stanzas, with their Shakespearean echo and their romantic imagery, the lyric note which had been intermittent with the poets of colonial Philadelphia finally reached clear and sustained expression:

> The traveller benighted and lost,
> O'er the mountains pursues his lone way;
> The stream is all candy'd with frost
> And the icicle hangs on the spray,
> He wanders in hope some kind shelter to find
> "Whilst thro' the sharp hawthorn keen blows the cold wind."
>
> The tempest howls dreary around
> And rends the tall oak in its flight;
> Fast falls the cold snow to the ground
> And dark is the gloom of the night.
> Lone wanders the trav'ler a shelter to find,
> "Whilst thro' the sharp hawthorn still blows the cold wind."
>
> No comfort the wild woods afford,
> No shelter the trav'ler can see—
> Far off are his bed and his board
> And his home where he wishes to be.
> His hearth's cheerful blaze still engages his mind
> "Whilst thro' the sharp hawthorn keen blows the cold wind."

Already the various race which inhabited the middle colonies was revealing through its spokesmen certain traits which were to become constants in the American character. A strain of idealism, of stubborn faith in a higher law and a deeper reality behind appearances was combined paradoxically with a shrewd realism, an insistence upon hard facts and utilitarian values. The literature that came out of the experience of these archetypal Americans, a literature which achieves first rank in the writings of Benjamin Franklin, expressed something of the freedom and newness of the American continent with a freshness of feeling tempered by the objective spirit of scientific inquiry. And around the newborn colleges of the region was springing up a promising literary life that was to reach its flowering in the early days of the young American republic.

8. BENJAMIN FRANKLIN

BENJAMIN FRANKLIN, though he was born in Boston, was little affected by its earlier, sterner traditions. His father was a tradesman who had come from England in 1683, and the son grew up in a generation to which the theocratic concepts of the founders of New England seemed remote if not preposterous. He enjoyed *The Pilgrim's Progress,* particularly because it "mixed narration and dialogue," and he read other books by Bunyan; but the inquiring boy soon tired of his father's "books of dispute about religion" and preferred Plutarch's *Lives* and Xenophon's *Memorabilia.* Neither the polemic habits which Franklin first picked up nor the Socratic method to which he turned during his juvenile disputatious period stayed with him long. Reading the orthodox arguments against the deists when he was fifteen, he was converted to a lifelong deism. Reading the arguments in favor of natural religion at nineteen, he set out to prove that whatever is is right, in a pamphlet called *A Dissertation on Liberty and Necessity, Pleasure and Pain* (1725). As he did not linger with theology, neither did he with metaphysics. He burned all but a few copies of his *Dissertation,* and would not bother to print a short treatise on prayer which he wrote at twenty-four. "The great uncertainty I found in metaphysical reasonings disgusted me, and I quitted that kind of reading and study for others more satisfactory."

Yet here and there in Franklin traces of theology, New England and older, appear. From either or both of two epitaphs printed by Cotton Mather in his *Magnalia* Franklin probably took for his own *Epitaph,* written at twenty-two, his often repeated image which compares the resurrection of a man with a new edition of a book; and he was certainly indebted to Mather's "Essays to Do Good." In Franklin's *Articles of Belief and Acts of Religion,* composed in 1728 for his own spiritual guidance, there is a strain of Puritan self-searching as well as a philosopher's code of morals. In his efforts to attain moral perfection he made laboratory notes on his daily successes and failures in a manner much like that prescribed by Loyola in his *Spiritual Exercises,* which Franklin may not have heard of. In one of his electrical papers, where he speaks of "adoring that wisdom which has made all things by weight and measure," he seems to be quoting from Augustine. Years of experience brought Franklin to the conviction that "God governs in the affairs of men." But the divine government, Franklin held, was a vast order to be studied, not a mystery to be sought in ardor and torment. However intense his youthful perturbations were, he soon mastered them and thereafter lived at reasonable peace in his spacious universe.

2

His life was one of the great lives of all time, and his writings are full of great, if fragmentary, autobiography. It is hard to distinguish between the plans Franklin made and the instincts which impelled him. In his boyhood he wanted to go to sea, disliked his father's trade of tallow chandler, and at twelve was apprenticed to his brother James, a Boston printer. While the younger brother was speedily learning the printer's trade, he was also teaching himself the writer's art. He began with broadside ballads, now lost, on contemporary incidents, then took to prose in painstaking and skillful imitation of Addison's *Spectator*. Franklin was "extremely ambitious" to excel in writing prose, which he afterwards said had been "a principal means of my advancement." His *Dogood* papers, contributed to James Franklin's *New England Courant* in 1722, were Addisonian but also Franklinian, remarkably precocious for an apprentice of sixteen. Before Benjamin Franklin had completed his apprenticeship he had outgrown his status, and he ran away from his brother-master in 1723 to Philadelphia, thereby committing an act which in a tradesman of that age was almost as culpable as desertion in a soldier.

In Philadelphia, and in London in 1724–1726, Franklin worked at his trade as a journeyman. During his voyage home, recorded in a lively *Journal* which is the earliest of his autobiographical writings, he drew up a Plan for his future conduct as if he were making a "regular plan and design" for a poem. He resolved to be frugal, industrious, and strictly truthful, and to speak ill of nobody. That he made such resolutions seems to indicate that he thought he then lacked such qualities, at least in a sufficient degree. His self-discipline had begun. This discipline, and the impassioned inner life of his next few years, did not interfere with Franklin's swift and simple success in business, but did enlarge his mind in preparation for his subsequent career on wider stages. In 1729 he acquired a newspaper, the *Pennsylvania Gazette,* and in 1733 he began to publish an almanac called *Poor Richard* which was soon famous throughout the British colonies. In 1736 he was chosen clerk of the Pennsylvania Assembly, and in 1737 appointed Postmaster of Philadelphia.

One of the least solitary of geniuses, Franklin, while striving to perfect his own character, had been no less busy in his efforts to improve the society in which he lived. The Junto, the club of young tradesmen whom he brought together in 1727, founded in 1731 the subscription library which has survived as the Library Company of Philadelphia; and in 1736 the Union Fire Company, the first in the town. From these Junto beginnings, Franklin and its members and later a widening circle of public-spirited men, particularly after he was elected to the Pennsylvania Assembly in 1751, went on to reform the city watch, encourage the paving and lighting of streets, propose the Academy which was to become the University of Pennsylvania, establish the Pennsylvania Hospital, organize the armed defense of the Quaker province, and generally to develop in Philadelphia the forms of active and enterprising life which made it long the chief city of America.

Philadelphian and Pennsylvanian, Franklin was at the same time American. His *General Magazine, and Historical Chronicle, for All the British Plantations in America* lasted for only six months in 1741; but the American Philosophical Society, which he initiated in 1743 in the hope of uniting American scientists everywhere in a common effort, is still the first of American learned societies as it was the earliest. In 1753 Franklin became the Crown's joint deputy postmaster general for North America. In 1754 his Plan of Union was adopted by the Albany Congress which had been called by the Crown in the desire to see the English colonies united against the French power in Canada. The Plan of Union having been rejected, Franklin had to go back to affairs in Pennsylvania, where he was a leader in the struggle of the people of the province against the British proprietors. That struggle was for Franklin a rehearsal of the part he was afterwards to play in the struggle of the United Colonies against the British Parliament.

In brief intervals snatched from business and politics Franklin incredibly found time to perform the experiments in electricity, mostly in the years 1747–1753, which made his the first great name in that branch of science and produced, in his successive volumes of *Experiments and Observations on Electricity* (1751–1774), the principia of electrostatics. In 1752, apparently in June, he flew his famous electrical kite; in October of that year he announced in *Poor Richard* the invention of the lightning rod. These achievements brought him the official thanks and compliments of Louis XV of France, the Copley gold medal of the Royal Society in London and election to the Society, and honorary degrees from Harvard, Yale, and William and Mary. When, in 1757, Franklin was sent to London to manage the appeal of the Pennsylvania Assembly from the proprietors to the King, he went not only as Pennsylvania's agent but also as, what David Hume called him, America's "first philosopher, and indeed the first great man of letters, for whom we are beholden to her."

For the years down to about 1757 Franklin's *Autobiography* (first published in Paris, 1791) tells the story that is known round the world. But in countless letters and other private and public papers written afterwards it is easy to find as full, if not so formal, a record of his later life. He returned to America for a short stay in 1762–1764, only to go back to England with Pennsylvania's petition to be made a royal, not a proprietary, province. He returned again in 1775–1776, to serve in the Second Continental Congress, and by it to be sent to France as commissioner—and in time minister—from the rebel colonies which had declared themselves the independent United States of America. Everywhere his renown grew, as wizard in science and wit in letters, philosopher and sage, beloved friend to men, women, and children. Yet his method in dealing with affairs remained essentially what it had been in Philadelphia. By deft and tireless persuasion he sought to draw like-minded people together to bring a just political order out of the confusions of prejudice and special interests. The English thought him too American, the Americans thought him too English. As he had risen from local to intercolonial concerns in America, so he rose in England to imperial concerns, and worked year after year for a broader conception of the British Empire. When his vision of that Empire as "the greatest political structure human wisdom ever yet erected" was ruined by the outbreak of hostilities between the parts on the two sides of the Atlantic, he turned himself with all his weight and charm to the business of uniting America and France, not only in resistance to England but also in support of the rights of man in any nation. What he did was of less importance than what he was. When at last, in 1785, he left Europe for America again, he was the most famous private citizen alive. His life had roused the universal curiosity with which his *Autobiography* was greeted the year after his death by contemporary readers, and its record has ever since been cherished in virtually every language that has a printing press. He had written his biography, so far as it went, as well as he had lived his life.

3

Not only his final *Autobiography* but also a large part of his written work had followed the steps of his life, recording it. In his youth, whether as Mrs. Silence Dogood in the *New England Courant,* or as the Busy Body in the *American Weekly Mercury,* or as Richard Saunders in *Poor Richard,* Franklin assumed a fictitious role and wrote in the first person. When in time he put off these disguises and wrote as himself, he continued to write more or less autobiographically, whether in his accounts of his scientific experiments or in his records of his diplomatic activities or in his statement of the various ideas upon which he hit in many fields of speculation. Though he wrote always with care, drafting and revising, he looked upon writing as his means, not as his end. With all his inventive gifts he invented no new forms of writing, but was satisfied with those ready at hand, and with the fresh uses he could put them to.

When late in 1732 Franklin issued his first *Poor Richard,* for the year 1733, he was simply a printer risking his money and labor on an almanac, as many other printers were then doing in America and Europe. His brother James, now removed to Newport, had an almanac called *Poor Robin.* An earlier English almanac, *Appollo Anglicanus,* had been compiled by an actual Richard Saunders. Benjamin Franklin, taking over the name of Richard Saunders for himself as compiler, and adapting the title *Poor Robin* to *Poor Richard,* fell smoothly into step with a familiar tradition. His circumstantial prophecy that a rival almanac-maker, Titan Leeds, would die on the coming October 17, merely imported to Philadelphia the hoax played by Jonathan Swift on John Partridge in London twenty-five years before. *Poor Richard's* forecasts of sunrises and sunsets, high and low tide, lunations and eclipses through the year were mathematical and naturally the same as those in any other almanac. What was new in Franklin's almanac was the humorous character of Poor Richard the philomath, and the range of laconic wisdom tucked in along the margins of the crowded pages.

Poor Richard, in his annual appearances from 1733 to 1758, did not in reality tell much about himself. He lived in the country, made some profit out of his almanac but had to share it with the printer, engaged in altercation with his wife Bridget, and was pestered by people who wanted him to tell their fortunes. Yet the brief strokes with which he was displayed, year after year, were drawn with a skill which could have made Franklin a first-rate novelist if he had cared to write novels. The earliest well-known character of fiction created by an American, Poor Richard, though only an outline, is still as amiably, eccentrically alive as ever.

The marginal Sayings of Poor Richard are some of them in character, more of them not. For they come from Franklin's, not Poor Richard's, reading and reflection during that formative quarter-century. He drew upon such identifiable sources as Rabelais, Bacon, La Rochefoucauld, Dryden, Swift, Pope, Prior, Gay, anthologies of verse, and collections of proverbs. Besides sayings in English, there are also a few in Latin, Spanish, French, German, and Welsh. Now and then Franklin set down one of his own recent moral conclusions, as in 1739: "Sin is not hurtful because it is forbidden, but it is forbidden because it is hurtful. . . . Nor is a duty beneficial because it is commanded, but it is commanded because it is beneficial." La Rochefoucauld's "Cunning and treachery are the offspring of incapacity" became, either directly or through some intermediary version, in 1751 Franklin's "Cunning proceeds from want of capacity." Franklin, returning to the matter in 1754, spoke more definitely in his own idiom: "A cunning man is overmatched by a cunning man and a half." In 1749 he formulated his thoughts about revenge with a neatness found in none of his predecessors: "Doing an injury puts you below your enemy; revenging one makes you but even with him; forgiving it sets you above him." In one of the most characteristic of all his sayings, not yet traced to any earlier source, Franklin in 1752 summed up his principle of tolerance for erring mankind: "The brave and the wise can both pity and excuse when cowards and fools show no mercy."

So many of Franklin's sources remain unidentified that it is impossible to tell with precision how much he only passed on, and how much he added to, the stream of proverbial wisdom which flows down from the past through him into the living human language. But it is easy to see that he bettered most of the sayings which he reworked, thanks to his genius for terse clarity and his delicate ear for cadence. For example, since 1572 a common English-Scottish proverb had been put by several writers into as many forms: "A gloved cat can catch no mice"; "Cuffed cat's no good mouse-hunt"; "A muffled cat was never good mouser." In 1754 Franklin gave it the form which it has since kept: "The cat in gloves catches no mice." The Scottish "Fat housekeepers make lean executors" became in Franklin, in 1733, "A fat kitchen, a lean will." A saying as old as Chaucer or Shakespeare, in one set of words or another, and printed in 1670 as "Three may keep counsel, if two be away," was pointed up by Franklin in 1735 to "Three may keep a secret if two of them are dead." As far back as Plautus it had been said that no guest is welcome longer than three days. Lyly in *Euphues* and Cervantes in *Don Quixote* had compared guests with fish as soon ill-smelling, and Herrick in his *Hesperides*. Franklin may have come upon the saying in John Ray's *English Proverbs* (1670) as "Fresh fish and new come guests, smell by they are three days old"; or in James Kelly's *Scottish Proverbs* (1721) as "Fresh fish and poor friends become soon ill sar'd"—that is, ill savored. In Franklin's handling the proverb settled in 1736 into its vernacular idiom and cadence, "Fish and visitors stink in three days," which sensitive editors print with a politer verb.

If the merely prudential maxims of Poor Richard, which are in fact fewer than the others, are better known than all the rest put together, this is partly an accident of printing. In July, 1757, when Franklin was crossing the Atlantic to London as Pennsylvania's agent, he wrote a preface, longer than usual, for the next year's almanac, which was to be the last edited by him. That preface, known as *The Way to Wealth,* has since then been reprinted more often than anything else by Franklin except his *Autobiography*; while the less specialized sayings have lain unread in the original almanacs or have had to be content with few and limited reprintings. Consequently the prudential part of Poor Richard's counsel has been mistaken for the whole of Franklin's wisdom. But it must be remembered that in *The Way to Wealth* the imaginary speaker, Father Abraham, is an old man at a country auction urging people not to pay more for things than they are worth, and quoting Poor Richard as his authority. Of course he restricts himself to the economical maxims, and has no occasion to quote Poor Richard on all the larger topics with which he had concerned himself. Franklin, for whom frugality was discipline, not nature, had insisted too much on penny-saving and so left behind him a reputation which belies his character and is contradicted by his career.

4

Though Franklin early made up his mind that any writing, in order to be good, ought to be "smooth, clear, and short," and though his own writing from first to last invariably had those merits, he experimented with more different styles than have been commonly noted. They ranged from the sly bawdry of his letter of advice to a young man on marriage (dated June 25, 1745, and called by Franklin *Old Mistresses Apologue*) through the homespun splendor of the opening paragraph of his neglected *Some Account of the Pennsylvania Hospital* (1754) to the elevated and harmonious prose of certain of his later political papers, not to mention the varied tones of sharp wit and easy candor and warm affection in his private correspondence. Slow and hesitant in speech, in English as well as in French, he was at his best only when he could write what he had to say. He is immensely quotable, yet never annoyingly sententious. His years of practice at adapting and perfecting maxims for *Poor Richard* no doubt bred in Franklin the habit of felicity, but it was his felicity, not something borrowed from other writers.

"If you would not be forgotten as soon as you are dead and rotten, either write things worth reading or do things worth the writing," Franklin said in *Poor Richard* for 1738. In his own life he aimed to do both, though his writing, as the pressure of affairs upon him increased, frequently lagged behind his living. By the end of 1741 he had invented the Franklin stove, which he described in his *Account of the New-Invented Pennsylvanian Fire-Places* (1744). This was at once a promotion pamphlet written for a Junto friend to whom Franklin had given the right to manufacture the stoves and also, in effect, the first published contribution to science by a member of the new American Philosophical Society. Franklin, secretary of the Society, found its members less active in general science than he had hoped they would be, and he himself turned aside in 1747 to the special electrical studies which brought him fame. His originality in research was equaled by the force and grace with which he reported his discoveries to the learned world and to general readers alike. It never occurred to them, or to him, that such writings did not belong to literature in the large true sense of that term.

Nor did it occur to Franklin that he was free, however well his electrical studies were under way, to confine himself to them in the midst of the public troubles which beset Pennsylvania and the rest of America. Though he retired from business in 1748, his interests expanded rather than contracted. In August, 1750, he had observed that the pigeons in a dovecot on the wall of his house increased in number as fast as he provided room for them. From this he proceeded to his germinal idea, expounded in *Observations concerning the Increase of Mankind, Peopling of Countries, etc.* (published 1755), that population depends on subsistence and will grow as long as supplies hold up. His idea developed into a confidence that the people of America must before long outnumber the people of the British Isles, and the conviction that the coming change in the balance of population must demand a new organization of the British Empire in respect to its dominions overseas. This confidence and this conviction guided Franklin in all his political and diplomatic efforts down to the American Revolution, and were implicit if not explicit in his Canada pamphlet called *The Interest of Great Britain Considered* (1760), *The Examination of Doctor Benjamin Franklin* (1766) before the House of Commons, *Causes of the American Discontents before 1768* (1768), and many of his more casual pieces. Though he had to suit himself in his particular actions to events as they came, he was remarkably consistent in his major principle.

His fundamental political consistency is sometimes lost sight of in the bewildering, if charming, variety of his scientific, moral, and humorous utterances. He did not cease to seem a wizard and a wit while he became a more and more important politician. In 1769 he brought together a "corrected, methodized, and improved" edition of his *Experiments and Observations on Electricity . . . To which are added, Letters and Papers on Philosophical Subjects*; and in 1773 he aided in the publication in French, at Paris, of a still more extensive collection of the *Œuvres de M. Franklin.* In the scientific papers there were then bound to be many "conjectures and suppositions," as Franklin had earlier insisted. "I own I have too strong a penchant to the building of hypotheses; they indulge my natural indolence." But to his readers it appeared that here was the evidence of a tireless mind inquiring with masterly ease and success into all the mysteries of nature. They could only wonder, since they could not know which of his guesses (in fact the majority of them) would be confirmed by later experiment, and which would turn out to be inadequate or erroneous

While it might seem strange that a politician was also a scientist, it seemed stranger still that he could moreover be so delightful a humorist. Humor, with a satirical intent, was one of Franklin's social and political methods. His specialty was the hoax. As early as 1730, in his fictitious account of *A Witch Trial at Mount Holly,* he ridiculed the witchcraft superstition. In *Exporting of Felons to the Colonies* (1751) he gravely proposed that as a kind of return for the felons the Americans might export rattlesnakes to Britain. In a letter *To the Editor of a Newspaper* (1765) he made fun in London of tall tales about America with his comment on the pursuit of the cod by the whales into American fresh waters: observing, with unquestionable though elusive accuracy, "that the grand leap of the whale in that chase up the Fall of Niagara is esteemed, by all who have seen it, as one of the finest spectacles in nature." In 1773 he parodied the British claim of a right to rule America in *An Edict of the King of Prussia,* wherein Prussia made what Franklin offered as a parallel claim on Britain. In 1782 he printed in Paris his *Supplement to the Boston Independent Chronicle* purporting to prove that the British commanders in America had paid regular bounties to Indians for scalps from American settlers they had killed. Readers fooled at first by such hoaxes might soon see through them, but they would also see these matters in a new perspective, and would remember Franklin's serious meaning as well as his witty expression of it.

The bagatelles with which Franklin amused himself and his circle at Passy, near Paris, while he was Commissioner or Minister to France, were merely a further, lighter application of his hoaxing method. Because Madame Brillon smilingly refused his smiling request that she be more than daughter to him, he wrote, and printed at his little private press, *The Ephemera* (1778), a fantasy on the passage of time and philosophic resignation. When Madame Helvétius declined his proposal of marriage, Franklin in *A Notre Dame d'Auteuil* (1778?) lightheartedly told her how he had slept and gone to the Elysian Fields, where he had found her former husband now married to Franklin's former wife. "Here I am; let us avenge ourselves." If gallantry was expected of a diplomat in France, Franklin could be a master in that pleasant art; just as, if he was expected to be a sage, the Solon of the New World come back to the Old with news of a Golden Age ahead, he could be sage and Solon. These were not disguises he put on, as with Poor Richard, but his own character touched up with deft dramatic art. The years had taught him how to become fully what he was.

The most substantial writings of his later years, outside his *Autobiography,* belong to the literature of diplomacy, in which no other writer has surpassed him. Even his routine dispatches, if any can be called that, were written with a statesman's grasp of the diplomatic situation, a philosopher's insight into the minds and motives of the persons involved, and a wit's happy knack at making everything alive and intelligible. About two of the most interesting chapters in his diplomatic history Franklin was too busy to write much: the passage and repeal of the Stamp Act, and the negotiation of the treaty of alliance with France. But he told as much as it was then possible for any one man to know about three other important chapters, in his *Tract relative to the Affair of Hutchinson's Letters* (1774), *An Account of Negotiations in London for effecting a Reconciliation between Great Britain and the American Colonies* (1775), and *Journal of the Negotiation for Peace with Great Britain* (1782). For the first two of these affairs Franklin remains the chief and almost the sole authority: of all of them he is the classic chronicler in whose pages the bones of those old controversies get up and walk in convincing flesh and blood.

For writing out these chapters at such length Franklin had different specific motives. His narrative of the Hutchinson affair was his vindication of his conduct though it had cost him his Crown office. His story of his negotiations with the British ministry during the winter of 1774–1775, set down on his voyage home while those events were still fresh in his memory, was his testimony that he had done everything he thought possible to avert hostilities. His detailed record of the early peace negotiations in Paris was intended not only for the Continental Congress but also for his fellow commissioners, not one of whom was in Paris when the first moves were being made. But in every case Franklin wrote autobiographically because he had already begun his *Autobiography,* and knew that these recent events must have a place in what was yet to be written.

5

He had begun the *Autobiography,* which Franklin himself never called anything but his Memoirs, at Chilbolton, the house of Bishop Jonathan Shipley near Twyford in Hampshire, in August, 1771. Shipley, pro-American among the British bishops, had a large family which was devoted, young and old, to Franklin whom they regarded as a modern Socrates. They asked him for anecdotes of his childhood, so different from theirs, in far-off Boston. They insisted, at least the older among them, that he owed it to the world to tell the story of his life. Their suggestion seems to have roused a responsive impulse in him, and the unusual expectation of "a week's uninterrupted leisure" furnished him an opportunity. In "the sweet retirement of Twyford, where my only business was a little scribbling in the garden study," as Franklin later put it, he wrote the first part of his *Autobiography* in the thirteen days of his visit, and probably less than that. Since no form of writing was so natural to him as autobiographical letters, and since he had written many of them to his son William, now royal Governor of New Jersey, the father cast his Memoirs in the form of an autobiographical letter to the son. On the first day of writing, it appears, Franklin began with a rush of family anecdotes about his ancestors, his parents, and his early childhood; then, again it appears, he resolved to write "more methodically" and drew up the Outline which thereafter he followed, not too methodically, through all four parts down to the year 1757. The first part is the happiest and sunniest of them, with its carefree recollections of one of the best known of all boyhoods.

After that August, 1771, Franklin for thirteen years found no time, or impulse, to resume his story. On his voyage home in the spring of 1775 he was expected, by his eager friends at Twyford, to do it, but he chose instead to write for his son about the past winter's unsuccessful negotiations. The outbreak of the Revolution interrupted any plans for the Memoirs that Franklin may have had. Not till 1784 did he turn back once more to his youth and go on with the narrative. He had left the manuscript of the first part in America, and could not remember exactly where it broke off. Estranged from his son, who had sided with the British government in the late conflict, Franklin would not now write as to him, and did not feel disposed to give so much space as before to "little family anecdotes of no importance to others." What he wrote in 1784 was "intended for the public" which, through certain of Franklin's close friends and advisers, was demanding that he recount the instructive adventures of his rise to world renown.

Yet even in the congenial air of triumph at Passy, after the peace, Franklin wrote only a short second installment of his Memoirs. Living so richly in the present as he did, he found it difficult to relive the remote past. For that he needed a more pressing personal vanity or literary ambition than he had. His last voyage home to America, in the summer of 1785, he spent on scientific speculations which interested him more than his own history. And at home, where there was no such leisure as he had looked forward to, he put off his Memoirs, in spite of many urgings, till August-October, 1788, when he wrote the third part. He was now too old and infirm to plan, or hope, to do much more. In November, 1789, he sent revised (and somewhat formalized) copies of Parts I–III to friends in France and England, asking their advice whether to publish the work at all. After that he wrote the few pages of the fourth part, probably in the last weeks of his life. The final lines of the manuscript are crooked, as if he were writing in bed.

Because Franklin had delayed so long, his Memoirs met with strange fortunes for so desired and desirable a book. It first appeared in 1791, in an unauthorized and unexplained French version, promptly retranslated into English by some unknown London journalist. That version was often reprinted, even after Franklin's grandson in 1818 printed an authorized version from one of Franklin's revised copies of 1789. Not till 1868 was the original manuscript discovered in France, and the *Autobiography,* including the hitherto omitted fourth part, printed as Franklin had written it.

This bungling introduction of a masterpiece did not too seriously handicap it. The meat of the matter was there in any version, as it was in time to be in any language. This was of course not the earliest of autobiographies. Augustine had told of his struggles between flesh and spirit, Benvenuto Cellini of his fiery life as artist and lover, Rousseau, very recently, of his career among raptures and neuroses. Franklin, telling his straightforward story in a language so transparent that few readers noted his amazing art, seemed to them hardly to be writing a book. This was a life. The book fixed the mode which most realistic autobiographers have since then followed. Franklin is still known to the world at large for his *Autobiography,* which is a fragment, and for *The Way to Wealth*, which is only a selection from his memorable sayings. Probably he will always be best known by these pieces of himself he left behind. Posterity can hardly be trusted to fit the whole of him together in one record if he could never do it. Nor has posterity a good excuse for asking that a man who did so much should have somehow managed to do less in order to write and publish more.

Franklin, summing up his world and at ease in it, left behind him the essence and living image of colonial America in the years when it was realizing its power and achieving its independence. The first to be called the father of his country, he came, after the rise of Washington's fame, to be thought of rather as his country's grandfather. In America, more than elsewhere, he has been popularly remembered for his grandfatherly qualities of prudence, geniality, humor. But the history of his fame has been notably marked by the rediscovery, decade after decade, of his other qualities of originality, audacity, and searching wit. One after another his prophetic forecasts have been justified by events. It increasingly appears that he conformed to the revolutionary spirit in his age, not to its complacency. Revolutionary as well as prophet, he helped shape the future. If he was full of contagious energy in the eighteenth century, so is he in the twentieth. No other early American writer is anything like so well known as he, so often reprinted, or so widely read and enjoyed. A large part of the American character lay in him as in a seed, and it has gradually unfolded by a process not unlike that of his own individual growth. Some great men cast a shadow over posterity. Franklin throws a light, which has affected American life, literature, and science ever since his own day and is still undimmed. He survives as a tremendous national symbol, and yet has never ceased to be a familiar and beloved person.

THE REPUBLIC

---inquiry and imitation

9. REVOLUTION AND REACTION

By 1763 the British colonies on the North American continent had attained a degree of political and economic maturity which ill fitted them for the restraints and prohibitions of British colonial policy. Moreover, the conquest of French Canada by the combined forces of Great Britain and her colonies produced in America an exuberant confidence and expansionism which led Benjamin Franklin to urge the extension of the British Empire—and the liberty for which he believed it stood—around the globe. This lusty sense of power and freedom constantly overset the best-laid schemes of British imperialists who sought, after 1763, to curtail the liberties of Americans with direct taxation by the British Parliament and a stricter enforcement of the Navigation Acts. Balked in their efforts to bend the Empire to their ideals, Americans directed their newfound feeling of unity and strength into the struggle for independence from the mother country.

In order to protect their liberties from the efforts of English administrators to centralize in London power over the Empire, Americans turned—as they had repeatedly done in the past—to Locke, Harrington, and other philosophers of the natural rights school. Their first line of defense against British tyranny was natural law, upon which, they contended, the British constitution itself was based. "Who," asked John Dickinson of Pennsylvania, "are a free people? Not those over whom government is reasonably and equitably exercised but those who live under a government so constitutionally checked and controlled that proper provision is made against its being otherwise exercised." By this philosophy, King and Parliament could not do what God and Nature had clearly forbidden. Above all, they could not impose taxation without representation. God and Nature, to Americans, were Reason; and they sought to apply the cardinal principles of the Enlightenment—the faith in reason and human perfectibility—to the British Empire. Until 1776, far from seeking to destroy the Empire, they strove to ensure its prosperity and perpetuation by bringing it into harmony with the laws of nature. But what the laws of nature were, Englishmen and Americans could not agree: "Were my countrymen now in England dipped once in the River Delaware," remarked an Englishman, "I dare say, that it would make an almost miraculous change in their opinions." Americans stoutly insisted upon the privilege of interpreting natural law—which, Englishmen objected, was to submit the laws of the Empire not to God or Nature, but to a "Jury of Bostonians" with Sam Adams and James Otis as judges.

Because of its universality, natural law became a bond of union among Americans, giving New Englanders and Carolinians alike a common ground upon which to rest their case against British oppression. As a philosophy of the liberty of the individual against the state, natural law was one of the most fruitful sources of democratic ideas. Whether debated by the Rev. John Wise as determining the proper form of government for New England churches, or by Robert Beverley as determining the relationship of the Virginia planters to the mother country, the issue of natural rights *vs.* civil authority was familiar to thinking Americans at least a century before the Revolutionary War.

When applied to the problems of empire, Americans' interpretation of natural law led to decentralization and the exaltation of local liberties. Fearful of the authority of the government at Westminster, they glorified their provincial assemblies into local parliaments, bound to the mother country only through a common king. In the opinion of Englishmen, these ideas pointed not so much to liberty as to provincialism and isolationism—in short, to the break-up of the Empire. When compromise failed, Americans declared their independence—and in so doing inherited the problem which the English government had been unable to solve: how local liberty in the Empire could be reconciled with the existence of central government.

2

Conflicting ideologies gave rise to a war of words which raged for ten years before Americans and Englishmen resorted to blows to settle their differences. During the decade before Lexington, the colonists sought to persuade the British government by means of arguments, reinforced by nonimportation agreements directed against British merchandise, to respect their rights. Literature became a weapon in the struggle for liberty: the art of whipping up public opinion by propaganda became the chief study of many American writers. As the conflict grew more embittered, less attention was paid to the niceties of the constitutional argument as developed by James Otis and John Dickinson: British atrocities, the wickedness of the ministry of Lord North, and the depravity of the English people increasingly became the subject matter of American pamphleteers and newspaper writers. This literary outpouring materially helped to prepare public opinion for the

Declaration of Independence and to sustain American morale during the days that tried men's souls. Edmund Burke said that Americans sniffed tyranny in every tainted breeze: it would be more exact to say that they read about it in their newspapers.

As long as the revolutionary movement remained an effort to win for Americans the rights and privileges of Englishmen within the Empire, the colonists were united and "Toryism" was relatively unimportant; but when the goal of independence and Republicanism was held up to Americans early in 1776 by Thomas Paine, it became apparent that the revolution was to be a civil war in which Americans fought Americans. A large number of colonists—perhaps one-third of the population—continued loyal to Great Britain, not merely out of love for King and Parliament and veneration for the mother country, but because they feared that a democratic upheaval would be the first result of American independence. The Declaration of Independence gave these conservatives no comfort. In pronouncing that "all men are created equal," Jefferson seemed to have opened the floodgates of revolution at home; it was now certain that the patriot leaders intended not only to sever the connection with Great Britain but to usher in a new order based upon the principle that government was created for the welfare of the common man.

Not all conservatives took the hard and thorny road that led to Toryism and exile; many threw in their lot with the patriots and, in consequence, the revolutionary party itself became a battleground between radicals and conservatives. Conflict centered on the questions of who should rule at home and how democratic the United States was to be. Some patriots resisted all reform and strove to confine the revolutionary movement within the narrow channel of resistance to Great Britain; others wished utterly to sweep away the old aristocratic order and to turn the country over to the new men—chiefly from the small-farmer class—who boldly promulgated the right of the majority to rule. But neither radicals nor conservatives won a clear-cut triumph: it was rather the moderate reformers who carried the day. Over the protests of the embattled reactionaries, the state churches were disestablished and the principle of religious freedom avowed; primogeniture and entail were swept away; slavery was abolished, usually by gradual means, in the Northern states; and the preambles of the new state constitutions proclaimed that the people were the source of all political power. Yet in most of the states "the people"—in the sense of those qualified to vote and to hold office—remained essentially the same; and the West was denied its fair share of representation lest it should seize control of the state governments from the conservative East.

These reforms were the most important achievements of the Enlightenment in the United States during the revolutionary period. The eighteenth century was the era of enlightened despots: for a brief span in European history, philosophers were kings. It was a period when ideas, long germinating in the minds of philosophers, began to bear fruit in the form of humanitarianism. Thus the United States was conceived in an age of reform—but it was reform from above, the work of paternalistic and arbitrary rulers. The American patriots of the revolutionary generation proved that republicans were not less enlightened than despots and that the people themselves could do, and do better, what kings and philosophers sought to do for them.

The changes introduced by the Revolution did not destroy aristocracy in the United States. In abolishing primogeniture and entail, Jefferson believed that he was striking a blow at the roots of aristocracy; but he soon found that he had merely lopped off one of its limbs. Privilege had yielded only a few of its outer defenses to the democrats: its citadel remained unshaken. Moreover, the Revolution spawned its own aristocracy: the *nouveaux riches* created by privateering, profiteering, and speculation, having already moved into the houses of the departed Tories, quickly adopted their manners and ideas. These beneficiaries of the Revolution became the backbone of the Federalist party and the most redoubtable enemies of the "principles of 1776."

Perhaps the greatest service rendered by the Revolution to the cause of democracy in the United States was throwing open the West to settlement. Quite rightly, many British statesmen had foreseen that, once Americans were permitted to stream unimpeded across the Alleghenies, the cause of authoritarian government would be gravely weakened. But the westward advance was too powerful to be long held in check by any governmental fiat: the Federalists sought to oppose the growth of the West and, like the British government before them, went down to defeat. The party of Jefferson, on the other hand, allied itself with the West and thereby with the future of American democracy.

If the American Revolution seemed to many democrats an "unfinished" revolution, it likewise fell short of the expectations of those who wished to establish a powerful national government. During the darkest hours of the Revolutionary War, these patriots had been sustained by the hope that the United States would emerge from the struggle a strong and united nation. But under the Articles of Confederation, the republic was weak, disunited, and seemingly drifting into anarchy. To alarmed nationalists, the United States seemed a certain victim of hostile European states; yet the mass of Americans remained unconscious of their danger, unheedful of warnings that weakness was an invitation to attack.

Instead, the American people, spurred on by a postwar depression, attempted to apply the ideals for which they had fought to conditions at home. They demanded laws for the benefit of debtors, fair representation for the West, office holding open to all, manhood suffrage, and curbs upon the power of wealth—in short, Jacksonian Democracy fifty years before Jackson became President. The small farmers gained control of many state governments and proceeded to enact legislation in their own interest; and where the conservative, privileged class refused to yield, as in Massachusetts, the people rose in armed rebellion.

These events produced a sharp reaction in favor of strong government. The people, who in 1776 had been hailed as the source of wisdom and virtue, now began to be regarded as a "great beast" which must be kept securely under leash. To reconcile order with liberty and to create a strong central government capable of resisting foreign foes and American populists alike, plans for "a more perfect union" were drawn up at the Constitutional Convention held in Philadelphia in 1787. Here was contained the answer of American statesmen to the problem that had wrecked the British Empire: how local liberty could exist alongside strong central government. It was also the answer of Americans to the age-old problem of whether man lives for the state or the state is his servant, created for his benefit. Despite the strong feeling against popular "licentiousness," the framers of the Constitution made clear that Americans were not to be mere creatures of the state but citizens endowed with inalienable rights beyond the reach of government.

3

If a nation had been created by the American Revolution and the Federal Constitution, the question remained: What kind of nation was it to be? Was the United States to become an industrialized country of cities, with an aristocracy of wealth looking to the federal government for bounties and protection, or was it to be a country of small farmers, led by an aristocracy of talents, and with the fostering of individual liberty the paramount concern of the states? Herein lies the crux of the struggle between Jefferson and Hamilton, between Republicans and Federalists—the struggle that was to preoccupy the American mind until, merging with the slavery question, it produced the elements of civil war.

The contest between Jefferson and Hamilton, involving as it did the future of American civilization, was intensified by the outbreak of the French Revolution. In the United States, discontented democrats hailed the work of French revolutionaries and began to clamor for a second American revolution, to be based upon the principles of "Liberty, Equality, and Fraternity" and directed against the home-grown brand of aristocracy and privilege. Conservatives rallied to the defense of the established order, resolved to resist any change whatever lest it prove the opening wedge for revolution.

In this struggle, Thomas Paine's *The Rights of Man* became the Bible of the radicals while conservatives found an arsenal of arguments in the counterrevolutionary writings of John Adams and Alexander Hamilton. The New England clergy—the "black regiment" of war days that had given its congregations rebellion and theology in approximately equal measure—now fulminated against the infidelity and license of the French Revolution, picturing the horrors that awaited Americans if they followed in the footsteps of the French. "Shall our Sons become the disciples of Voltaire and the dragoons of Marat," exclaimed the Reverend Timothy Dwight of Connecticut, "or our daughters the concubines of the Illuminati?" But American democrats staunchly upheld the cause of revolution both at home and in France: in their eyes, opposition to the French Revolution was "a war of Kings and Nobles against the equal Rights of Men" and the Federalists were reactionaries who sought to deny the American people the freedom that was their birthright.

4

It is significant that even before the Constitution had been adopted, an ardently nationalistic school of American writers had appeared: the so-called Hartford Wits. The idea that the United States was to be the new Athens of the arts and sciences had been frequently expressed during the Revolution: as long as they remained British colonists, it was said, Americans had reflected all the prejudices and insularity of Britons, but now, as free men, they stood prepared to embrace the world, drawing inspiration from all cultures and all men. In the eyes of some patriots the separation had come just in time: another generation of British rule, said an American, and the colonists would have "learned to eat and drink, and swear and quarrel like Englishmen." Happily, their eyes had been opened in time and they could now perceive that France, for example, was "the most enlightened nation in the world" and its people the most civilized and polite. France had polished and refined Europe: the next step was for this gifted nation to remove the last vestiges of colonialism from the United States. To Thomas Paine, the alliance of the United States with France was like a breath of fresh air stirring among the dead leaves of provincial America, promising a golden age of American literature. "We see with other eyes," Paine exclaimed; "we hear with other ears; and think with other thoughts than those we formerly used. . . . Every corner of the mind is swept of its cobwebs, poison and dust, and made fit for the reception of generous happiness."

In this frame of mind, Americans rushed into print to proclaim their declaration of intellectual independence, grimly determined to stand and die in the literary trenches rather than submit to any return to colonial bondage in things of the spirit. Inevitably, they were led to use American scenes and materials—and thus helped prepare the way for the American Renaissance of the nineteenth century. If America had not come of age in literature—and the work of these early writers is the best evidence that it had not—at least the first stirrings of a vigorous and promising adolescence were evident.

Yet polemics continued to engross the American mind: Philip Freneau, the most promising poet of his generation, spoke as Jefferson's champion against Hamilton and devoted to politics talents that belonged to literature. Party warfare tended to make the American a "newspaper reading animal," to borrow the phrase of an English traveler, and to make American writers propagandists and pamphleteers. Seemingly a grave disservice was thereby done to the cause of literature; but, by developing a great mass of readers, the newspapers made possible a wide and expanding market for books.

By 1820, the triumph of democratic ideals and the ending of the menace of foreign intervention enabled Americans to turn their attention to the business of settling and developing the continent. The purely polemical phase of American literature was passing, and writers could give literary expression to something more enduring than the political passions of the day. America, it began to be recognized, in its size, color, and diversity furnished the man of letters with a wealth of material for his pen. No longer wholly concerned with hewing out a livelihood from a forest wilderness, and now imbued with a desire to exploit the literary resources of their country, Americans were prepared for the long awaited, and long delayed, American Renaissance.

10. THE MAKING OF THE MAN OF LETTERS

Education was the first need, and the colonial schools and colleges had made a good start toward providing it. The early colleges survived the era of revolution and maintained well into the following century their modified classical curricula, their small and socially selected student bodies, and their emphasis on preparation for the law, the ministry, and public life. To the eight colonial colleges were soon added Virginia and many others. The church drew fewer of their graduates, and the law and politics more. Gradually there was less temptation to send likely youth to Oxford or Cambridge, London or Edinburgh, for the fundamentals that make a gentleman.

On the other hand, the habit of going abroad for advanced study in medicine, the fine arts, science, and still to a large extent the law became even more firmly established in the first half-century of independence, and, particularly in science, continued to our own day. The American-born president of the British Royal Academy, Benjamin West, spread his giant historical canvases on the walls of Windsor Castle and Greenwich Hospital, and trained almost all our early painters in his London studio, at least until one of them, Charles Willson Peale, broke the tradition and helped to found in 1805 the Pennsylvania Academy of the Fine Arts. Similarly our early physicians went as a matter of routine to Edinburgh and London for their training until they in turn could establish medical schools at home. And the study of language and literature took George Ticknor, Longfellow, and many another young professor to England and Germany during the years that followed. The former colonists were typically adolescent in their attitude toward their parent cultures. They cultivated the strut of independence in voice and manner while sedulously learning from and aping their elders.

On other levels of education, this attitude brought good results. The rampant nationalism of the lexicographer Noah Webster and the geographer Jedidiah Morse did much to popularize a more genuine and less traditional system of elementary and secondary schooling, combating the limitations of the colonial grammar schools, dame schools, and private tutors of the socially privileged. The district and "charity" schools which, after the Revolution, provided the democratic foundations for our modern system of public instruction, were slow of development. Although Massachusetts had had a public-school law since 1647, most of the state constitutions made no such provisions, and even the federal constitution was silent on the subject. During the eighteenth century, the training of youth was still a responsibility of the home.

Into this situation, Webster in 1783 injected his "blue backed speller," a challenge to traditionalism and complacency. On the principle that learning must be close to experience, it proclaimed an American language and set out, by properly training the youth, to make this country "as independent in *literature* as she is in *politics*—as famous for *arts* as for *arms*." The campaign was carried forward by his own reader, grammar, and dictionary, by Morse's *The American Geography,* "calculated early to impress the minds of American youth with the idea of the superior importance of their own country," and by Jefferson's proposal of 1817 for a comprehensive plan of mass education, starting with county schools and culminating in a university in which should be taught "all the useful sciences in their highest degree."

It was a century or longer before natural democratic man took his place in the councils of the colleges. In spite of the liberal and rational views of such planners as Franklin, Jefferson, and even the American Samuel Johnson, first president of King's College (Columbia), the classical and theological ideals of the colonial period, born of sedulous loyalty to the tradition of Oxford and Cambridge, persisted through early national days. Our first literary men had a colonial training and a colonial heritage. They were the select few, presumably masters of Latin, Greek, logic, rhetoric, theology, mathematics, and perhaps science in its early form of natural philosophy. In college, "that temple of dullness, that roost of owls," as Joseph Dennie described it, discipline was strict and learning carefully divorced from life. Occasionally the more spirited students were rusticated for misbehavior as was Dennie, or dismissed outright, as was James Fenimore Cooper when, it is reported, he opened the door of a friend's room by a miniature blast of gunpowder tucked into the keyhole.

Other and better outlets for youthful spirits were the literary and debating societies, such as the Linonia and Brothers societies at Yale, the American Whig Society in which Freneau and Brackenridge were active at Princeton, and the Philomathean and Zelosophic societies at Pennsylvania. These groups were usually paired, and their rivalries provided the focus of undergraduate life. They supplemented the classroom by promoting debate on current topics in politics and literature, sometimes so successfully that the resulting pranks and brawls led to petty bloodshed. But, most significant for our purposes, their surviving libraries show a preponderance of the currently imported and popular books, which must have compensated for the narrowly academic collections built up by the administrations. It was out of them rather than the formal classroom that the modern American college grew, and it was in their meetings that the combative and creative interests of our later political and literary leaders were formed and nurtured.

2

Once out of college, the American youth found even less stimulus to a purely literary life. If he had learned to read, analyze, and declaim in the classroom, he had also learned in his societies to debate current issues and to enjoy current English and American books. His mind might be stored with Latin and Greek, theology, logic, rhetoric, and mathematics, but his veins secretly pulsed with the gentle rhythms of Addisonian prose or the emphatic couplets of Pope while his ears rang with the phrases of Patrick Henry and Samuel Adams. It was all very confusing and thwarting if one wished to write, as college graduates do. The simplest answer to the problem was to read for the law, and then to enter the political or business world, saving literature for the idle moment and watering it down to belles-lettres. There were so many immediate issues to be settled; there was so much work of the pioneering world to be done!

For one thing, there were no publishers in the modern sense, and few printers would take a chance on a book by an American when English authors could be pirated at will. Franklin had republished *Pamela* in 1744, and the example had been followed with no qualms by later printers. These printers, of whom there was a steadily increasing number in all the coastal cities, were primarily equipped to issue broadsides, currency, pamphlets, newspapers, and occasionally a magazine. Until about 1825, American authors published their own books, taking all or the greater part of the financial risks. Most of our printers had learned from the example of Hugh Gaine, of wartime notoriety, to change their opinions with the weather and to seek out such business as the market afforded. Our first publishers in anything like the modern sense—Isaiah Thomas and Mathew Carey, who had ambitions and ethics of their own and the initiative to implement them—were exceptions. Yet even these two were primarily printers, only incidentally publishers.

The reading public, which grew rapidly during this period, was also in part responsible for hampering the immediate encouragement of native work because the prestige of English authors more than satisfied the increasing demand for popular forms of literature. Colonial libraries had been composed of the works in the classics, history, philosophy, and theology which their owners had learned to value in college; and the stock-holding subscribers to the libraries of pre-Revolutionary days like the Philadelphia Library Company, the New York Society Library, and other athenaeums and library societies from Providence to Charleston, merely extended the pattern to New Orleans (1805) and to Boston (1807). Even though these societies bought generously from the lists of native printers, their subscribers demanded even more urgently the London imprint and the standard or popular work.

The craze for novel reading which hit the British public toward the close of the eighteenth century, and the subsequent popularity of the Romantic poets and the familiar essayists of the early nineteenth, soon found reflection in this country. American presses were reprinting English novels in quantity before 1790, and long listings of "new books (mostly travel and fiction) by the ship Electra from London," sales of private libraries, and offerings of "books, fancy articles, &c. for Christmas" were occupying almost as much space in the newspapers as were announcements of importations of gloves, cotton goods, wine, tea, salt, and soap. Cooper could not hope to find a publisher who would pay him adequately for his first success, *The Spy,* in 1821; but when it appeared, in December of that year, there were four booksellers in New York City alone ready to advertise that they had it for sale.

The novelist Charles Brockden Brown was the first American, and the only one before Cooper and Irving, to attempt the literary profession by reliance on the book market alone; and he failed. He experimented with a bookseller as well as with local printers as publishers for his American Gothic tales. The list of fiction in the circulating library of one William Caritat (1804) supplies the causes of Brown's failure with both, and the reason why he, like so many of his fellows, turned from writing to magazine editing for subsistence. Caritat, a fashionable bookseller, in that year had some two thousand French and English novels on his shelves, reprinted in this country or directly imported. A study of this list reveals why Brown was hopeful of the popular moral tale of horror as a medium for his literary ambitions; but it also explains why his inspiration dried up so suddenly in the face of foreign competition.

3

Our printers were quicker than our authors to learn how to profit by the unequal situation. By the time *Waverley* appeared in 1814, the war was on, and Scott became its principal victim. John Miller, a hack publisher of London, acted as agent for his most successful American counterpart, Mathew

Carey in Philadelphia. It was his task to see that the sheets, or even the proofs if he could get them, of any potential British success were in Carey's hands by fast packet (about thirty days) almost before the bound volumes had appeared in the London bookshops and well before any of them could be imported. Carey paid Miller, not the British author or publisher, for this service. "We have rec'd *Quentin Durward* most handsomely," he writes Miller on June 17, 1823, "and have the same completely in our own hands this time." He had won the race if he could be first to get sufficient copies to the local booksellers and into the van of the picturesque Parson Weems, peddling his wares through the countryside and fiddling his way to the hearts of his customers.

When the sheets of a new book were received, they were at once divided among three or four typesetters who worked night and day in shifts and sometimes produced a reprint in twenty-four hours. Even one or two days' priority assured financial success. It is perhaps significant that when this traffic was at its height, about 1815, popular books of American authorship were virtually nonexistent. The first group of writers had given up the struggle and were depending on a precarious magazine market to issue the literary by-products of their more substantial pursuits, while the second had not yet overcome the increasing obstacles to success. It is also significant that almost all the prominent early American printers of books—the Wileys, Appleton, the Harper brothers, and the Careys, as well as other and lesser men—were violently opposed to any form of international copyright.

The problem remained unsolved until about 1825, when Irving and Cooper discovered the cause of the difficulty. They were the first to realize that Noah Webster's patriotic zeal had overreached itself, for the Copyright Act of 1790 allowed protection only to American authors, whereas in England protection could be claimed under common law or gentlemen's agreement on the basis of prior issue and regardless of the author's nationality. For an entire literary generation this legal difference had remained unnoticed and merciless pirating gone unchecked on both sides of the water. Both British and American authors suffered; but British prestige made the lot of the American hopeless. "What publisher," wrote Cooper to Carey, "will pay a native writer for ideas that he may import for nothing?"

Great as this temporary sacrifice of native talent may have been, perhaps it was a necessary preparation for the writers who were still to come. However unethical the copyright situation, it built up and educated a reading public in a great European literary tradition, and it taught American writers that they could not compete with that tradition by imitation alone. The full force of this education would not be felt for another generation, when the spirit rather than the mere forms of older cultures had been absorbed and the values rather than the bare facts of the American experience had begun to be understood by native writers.

4

If the book market was, in this transition period, practically nonexistent for the American author, the outlets for his work provided by the magazines and the theater were little better. The four principal post-Revolutionary magazines of the eighteenth century—the *Columbian,* Carey's *American Museum,* the *Massachusetts Magazine,* and the *New-York Magazine*—all were addicted to the scissors and the paste-pot, although they occasionally published original essays, poems, and tales with scrupulous anonymity. Dennie's *Port Folio* occupied the central place among American literary magazines during the first quarter of the nineteenth century and achieved the longest run of any such journal up to that time. It offered safe harbor to John Quincy Adams and Richard Rush when their impulses turned from diplomacy to poetry and essay, and to men like Charles Brockden Brown and Dennie himself, for whom writing was an end in itself. The ambitious "Knickerbocker" authors, Irving, Paulding, and their friends, long before the *Sketch Book* days, relied on the newspaper and the pamphlet rather than on the book or the magazine for their Addisonian *Salmagundi* essays, as did Dickinson and Paine for their political tracts during the Revolution and Halleck and Drake for their verse satires, *The Croaker Papers,* in 1819. Yet even the scant market provided by the magazines and newspapers, by an ironic paradox, may have had some bearing on the cultivation of the tract, the essay, the short story, and the lyric poem by American authors at a time when novels were obviously the choice of their readers.

The theater too afforded little encouragement to native talent. Probably there was no time during colonial days when some form of play-acting had not been practiced, however primitively or secretively. The problem of what to do about it was among the first of the agenda of our forefathers. As early as 1610 it had seemed wise to Virginian authorities to forbid the immigration of actors from England because of the evils associated with them. In 1665 three young men of Virginia were charged with "acting a play of ye Bare and ye Cubb." New England's hostility toward the drama has been proverbial, yet in 1712 Samuel Sewall was disturbed by "a Rumor, as if some design'd to have a Play acted in the Council Chamber, next Monday." In Charleston, South Carolina, the "Court room" was used for theatrical performances (in 1735) long before a regular theater was established. In the meantime New York had probably had its first taste of professional acting about 1700 when Richard Hunter apparently was granted a license to present plays. By 1732 there was some sort of "play house" in New York. Strolling players turned up from time to time in many of the major towns and cities of the Atlantic seaboard: Boston, New York, Philadelphia, Annapolis, Williamsburg, Charleston. Sometimes a nucleus of professional actors (generally British) worked in conjunction with local amateurs. In the absence of adequate theaters, performances took place in coffeehouses, stores, or barns. Occasionally, to avoid arousing the ire of municipal authorities, a flimsy, impermanent structure was devised or adapted on the outskirts of a town.

The more consecutive history of the American theater begins about the middle of the eighteenth century. In 1749 a "Company of Comedians" presented the tragedy of *Cato* in Philadelphia. New York was accorded its first notable Shakespearean performance on March 5th of the next year when, with the permission of his Excellency the Governor of the Province, the "Comedians" presented *Richard III*—"Wrote originally by *Shakspere,* and alter'd by Colly Cibber, Esq." Another notable "first" was the presentation of *The Merchant of Venice* at Williamsburg, Virginia, on September 15, 1752, by the "American Company." This occasion was the more historic because it marked the first American production and performance of the Hallam family, among them Lewis Hallam the younger, who was to dominate "the stage of the New World" for "nearly a quarter of a century." It was this initial performance of which John Esten Cooke wrote a glamorous (and not entirely accurate) account in his *Virginia Comedians* (1854). From about this time on, the record indicates a rapid expansion of the theatrical activities, professional, amateur, and "unofficial." When authorities frowned, plays were sometimes advertised as "readings" or "lectures." Private performances, which were hard to censor or suppress, whetted the appetite of play lovers. Students at some of the colleges began to put on performances despite administrative disapproval. In a moment of irritation one former tutor of Yale College complained to the president (in 1777) that students had "left the more solid parts of learn^g & run into Plays & dramatic Exhibitions chiefly of the comic kind & turn'd College . . . into Drury Lane."

The professional theater slowly acquired confidence and prestige. The establishment of more or less permanent buildings was a material gain. The first of these, the Southwark Theater on South Street, Philadelphia, was built in 1766. A brick-and-wood structure painted "a glaring red," it lasted fifty-five years as a theater before becoming (what the opponents of playgoing did not fail to mark) a distillery. The John Street Theater (opened in 1767) in New York was of the same general type as the Southwark. In Annapolis a theater was built in 1771; and Charleston's "elegant" new theater, larger than either the Southwark or the John Street Theater, was opened on December 22, 1773.

With the erection of substantial buildings, the play business became more and more institutionalized. A common practice was to have performances on

Mondays, Wednesdays, and Fridays, with the bill changed for each night. Performances generally began at six or seven o'clock, and the standard bill included a regular play and an "afterpiece," which might be a farce or ballet or a comic opera. The "society" which attended was of course mixed, but it was by no means riffraff. In the South, ladies of the better families were often seen at public amusements, as Josiah Quincy of Boston noted to his astonishment when visiting Charleston in 1773. The frequency and virulence of tirades against the theater everywhere lessened in proportion to the increasing social distinction of its patrons. When General Washington himself attended dramatic performances—as, the records indicate, he did on scores of occasions—who should presume to say that the theater was an altogether degrading and iniquitous place? Alert managers learned to advertise the fact that he would be present, sometimes with a party including brilliantly appareled ladies. Surely on occasions such as these the theater had "arrived." But the best that can be said of it in this period is that it was not a bad imitation of the British. Where Byron and Keats failed, American poets can hardly be blamed for inadequacy. It produced a successful actor in John Howard Payne, whose fame rests equally on his playing of Young Norval in Home's *Douglas* and on the perennial "Home, Sweet Home" from his own *Clari*; but it failed to make a playwright out of himself or his friend Washington Irving, however hard they tried.

5

For self-protection as well as for sociability, these writers gathered together in mutual encouragement societies. The most famous of such groups was the "Hartford Wits," originally composed of four men of varying political views—Joel Barlow, John Trumbull, Lemuel Hopkins, and David Humphreys—but later to include Timothy Dwight, Elihu Hubbard Smith, and many others who shared with them either an enthusiastic patriotism, a religious conservatism, or a love of rhyming couplets. When Dr. Smith moved to New York City in 1793, he became the center of the Friendly Club, a group composed of William Dunlap, Charles Brockden Brown, Dr. Mitchell, and Noah Webster. The fellowship which gathered about Dennie's *Port Folio* in Philadelphia, known as the Tuesday Club, and Peter Irving's Knickerbocker group on the *Morning Chronicle* of New York, were not dining and writing clubs in as strict a sense; but they performed similar functions, as did the later Bread and Cheese Club which forgathered with Fenimore Cooper in the "Den" back of Charles Wiley's bookshop in the City Hotel, and which survives as the Century Association in its dignified home off modern Fifth Avenue.

Under such circumstances, the false literary dawn of the nineties and the

"dark ages" which followed seem to lend themselves to ready explanation. Not only was the creative genius of our best minds channeled into politics and practical affairs, not only were we intellectually dependent on England long after we obtained political independence, but we had as yet inadequate means for producing a literature of our own. The struggles of Poe, Cooper, Irving, Halleck, and Bryant did not meet with even modest success until well after 1825; the first half-century of our national life was spent mainly in preparing for the writers and readers to come.

11. THE WAR OF THE PAMPHLETS

EVEN though excellence in the deliberately "literary" forms of literature had to wait more settled times, the Revolutionary era was ideally suited to the pamphlet. The writer of 1776 might have said of his book, as George Gascoigne said in 1576 introducing Humphrey Gilbert's *New Passage to Cataia:* "It is but a Pamphlet & no large discourse, & therefore the more to be borne withall: since the faults (if any be) shalbe the fewer, because the volume is not great."

The first three hundred years of American history coincided with the age of the pamphlet. In these centuries, pamphleteering became a distinct profession with its own techniques and forms, the pamphlet the dominant vehicle of propaganda and debate. Promotion of colonies in the sixteenth century and the rise of contending religious sects, political revolutions in the seventeenth century, the issues of imperial organization and national wars in the eighteenth century, finally the American and French revolutions at the end of the pamphlet era, were episodes perfectly suited to brief, controversial, and popular treatment.

The literary controversies of the American Revolution were conducted in little books—books inexpensive to print (though well printed), cheap to buy, easy to read, and, more significant, easy to write. About nine thousand books, newspapers, and broadsides were emitted by some two hundred American presses between 1763 and 1783; of these, perhaps two thousand were pamphlets on the political issues of the day. This is the corpus of literature of the American Revolution—a couple of thousand little books with their pretentious and formidable titles, intended for instant circulation, designed to change men's minds, addressed to urgent problems, sometimes touching the universal issues that confront men everywhere, any time, in civil society.

In a literature of such fugitive productions and such voluminous mass, individual dimensions were likely to be slight. The man and his book had to be considered in relation to a host of men and their books which, taken together, expressed the thoughts and feelings of two million Americans embroiled in a common experience of appalling magnitude. The pamphlet, even a great one like Dickinson's *Farmer's Letters* or Paine's *Common Sense,* never stood alone. It took its place in the stream of action and the stream of thought. Nor did its influence end with its publication. Often an essay would have prepublication readings, as did Otis' *Rights of the British Colonies* before the Massachusetts Assembly, and Governor Stephen Hopkins' treatise on the origin and nature of law before the legislature of Rhode Island. Sometimes, too, it would have public readings after publication, around a drumhead in a militia camp or in meetings of the Sons of Liberty. Some loyalist tracts received public burnings after being heard. Frequently, a little book had appeared first in a newspaper, or was reprinted in news columns afterward. Moreover, it was the nature of the pamphlet to evoke other pamphlets—rejoinders, refutations, responses of all kinds. Samuel Seabury's five "Westchester Farmer" tracts explain and are explained by the prodigious rejoinders of young Alexander Hamilton. One little book did not make a literary figure, nor a political leader. Only when a man had written several pamphlets, and developed in them a reasoned, coherent program of thought and action, did he rise to personal eminence as a writer among writers.

Some men did just that. A few pamphleteers—Otis, Dickinson, Paine, Franklin, Jefferson, Hamilton, Seabury, Galloway—wrote so effectively and so often that for them the little book became a literary career. Each had something more than ordinary to say; each, through special insights or unusual learning, saw in discrete instances of political conflict the permeating principles of universal application that enabled Americans to feel their cause akin to the historical purpose and destiny of man.

The pamphleteers of the Revolution received their training in local political struggles in each colony before 1765. There were American political pamphleteers before there was any unifying American point of view. The Parson's Cause in Virginia had produced the early tracts of Patrick Henry; Daniel Dulany argued a taxation question in Maryland; the prolonged attempt to overthrow the Penn family's proprietorship in Pennsylvania occasioned pamphlets from the famous Franklin and from men like Joseph Galloway and John Dickinson who were not yet so famous; in Boston James Otis, Josiah Quincy, and a brace of Adamses became the leaders of a radical faction in Massachusetts politics. All these writers developed in their partisan little books the contentious tone familiar to America from the religious polemics of the Great Awakening; but the orientation of their thinking before 1765 was narrowly provincial. A sense of purpose common to all America was lacking. After 1765, however, provincial issues were swallowed up in imperial polemics. When the British government embarked on its program of reforming the Empire, American writers rose from local squabbles to general political principles. The Stamp Act and the laws of Parliament which followed not only forced the several colonies into a kind of union; they also obliged the American pamphleteers to rise above their local orientation and become philosophers. The philosophy of the pamphleteers gradually won Americans from fundamentalist attitudes of colonial political thinking to secular attitudes of revolution.

2

The literary career of James Otis comprehended the early stages of the movement (1761–1769). Massachusetts-born and Harvard-trained, Otis in 1761 was a successful lawyer in his middle thirties. His sister, Mercy Otis Warren, was a playwright, poet, and historian, whose *History of the Rise, Progress, and Termination of the American Revolution* (1805) was to stimulate the patriotism of a generation. Otis had published a textbook in Latin prosody and composed another in Greek, but his tastes were not really academic. He was by nature partisan and worldly. An eloquent courtroom speech against the new parliamentary measures made him the chief spokesman of the local radicals, and as leader of this faction he wrote the five pamphlets on which his great reputation rests. They were controversial and intemperate works, reckless and sometimes coarse, but they stated tersely and vividly (if not always logically) an American constitutional theory. The first tract, *A Vindication of the Conduct of the House of Representatives of the Province of Massachusetts Bay* (1762), written in angry tone on a trivial issue of local politics, developed the principle of representative taxation as a basic requirement of constitutionally limited government. The second, *The Rights of the British Colonies Asserted and Proved* (1764), marked Otis' transition from local to imperial issues. Written "amid the continual solicitations of a crowd of clients," after "one single Act of Parliament has set people a-thinking, in six months, more than they had done in their whole lives before," this pamphlet was a testament of fundamental political faith. Supreme power, Otis asserted, was *"originally* and *ultimately* in the people." The people delegated power to whom they pleased, but only as one man gives another a possession to hold in trust for him. Thus government was a fiduciary trust. "The *end* of government being the *good* of mankind, points out its great duties: It is above all things to provide for the security, the quiet, and happy enjoyment of life, liberty and property." The tract, conservative in spirit, was designed to justify opposition to Parliament. Otis hoped to persuade Americans "to behave like men, and use the proper legal measures to obtain redress." The next year, in an acidulous pamphlet, *Considerations on Behalf of the Colonists* (1765), he retorted to the English writer Soame Jenyns, stressing the dependence of the colonies on Britain but warning:

"Revolutions have been. They may be again." In later pamphlets the violence of his writing increased, at times approaching "a mere shriek," and the contours of his thinking failed to alter with changing issues. After 1769 he was silent, living in a disordered half-world until he was struck down by a bolt of lightning in 1783. But his work had really reached fruition, for in his virile tracts he had exhibited the literary technique of resistance, and had given, in Moses Coit Tyler's words, "a conservative and law-respecting race, a conservative and lawful pretext for resisting law, and for revolutionizing the government."

A large amount of James Otis' fame is due to the repeated encomiums heaped upon him by John Adams, from whom we have the only contemporary description of Otis' Writs of Assistance speech. Although Adams continued to praise the older man as long as he lived, he produced himself four essays on the Stamp Act more profound than anything Otis was capable of, treating the new measures as episodes in the ageless struggle in western civilization between corporate authority and individual rights. These essays, originally published in newspapers, were issued in pamphlet form as *A Dissertation on the Canon and Feudal Law* (1768)—the first of a long series of distinguished works by Adams which are more properly considered as philosophical literature than as political pamphlets. To Adams also is due much of the reputation of the Rev. Jonathan Mayhew, whom he termed a "transcendent genius." Author of a dozen significant published sermons and tracts, Mayhew represented the spirit of the Enlightenment in New England dissent, and epitomized the combination of religious leadership with political emancipation. Just before his death at the age of forty-six he published *The Snare Broken* (1766), a sermon on the repeal of the Stamp Act in which he justified civil disobedience even to the point of rebellion. The "great and primary law of nature" was self-preservation, he averred, and the measure of political action (as of spiritual truth) was now as always private rather than public judgment.

A bewildering number of little books by a host of young men had appeared before the Stamp Act controversy was over. One, by an older hand, appealed to readers in all provinces. Daniel Dulany, eminent Maryland statesman whose gracious personality and immense learning had placed him, in the Chesapeake colonies, at the very summit of the newest American profession, the bar, wrote a brilliant, persuasive tract against the power of Parliament to legislate for the colonies, *Considerations on the Propriety of imposing Taxes in the British Colonies* (1765), which went through many editions and endured as a strong influence in American constitutional thinking. "No taxation without representation" had been a slogan to Otis; to Dulany it became the foundation principle of free government.

3

The Stamp Act also marked the beginning of John Dickinson's leadership as a writer of the little book. Dickinson was thirty-three years old in 1765, a product, like Dulany and so many other leaders of the middle colonies, of the wealthy farm-proprietor group of the Chesapeake Bay region. He had prepared for three years at the Middle Temple, and had built a conspicuously prosperous business as lawyer, merchant, and landowner. Studious, frail, modest, diffident, he lived elegantly in the most polished Philadelphia society; he wrote with good humor and poised assurance. "The cause of *liberty* is a cause of too much dignity to be sullied by turbulence and tumult," he observed. "Those who engage in it should breathe a sedate yet fervent spirit, animating them to actions of prudence, justice, modesty, bravery, humanity and magnanimity." Dickinson's literary career extended over forty years and ranged over many subjects. The basic principles of his philosophy were broad enough and his mind was fluid enough to adapt to the successive crises of revolution, constitution, nationalism, and democracy. Dickinson stood between extremes. He was moderate in all things. He presented the picture of the thoughtful legislator, the adroit political manipulator, the able administrator, moving slowly but firmly toward well defined goals. His extensive learning, his ever keen sense of political conflict, his winning style as a writer, his analytical ability, and his impelling moral convictions gave his books immediate popularity and imposing stature. Tyler has called the appearance of the *Farmer's Letters* "the most brilliant event in the literary history of the Revolution."

The early pamphlets of Dickinson on Pennsylvania politics—he wrote eight in five months—not only reveal his mastery of this technique of propaganda, but also reveal how ephemeral the tract on transitory issues could be. When he turned to the greater questions of colony and empire he explored permanent values of freedom and order. His powerful state papers and pamphlets on the Stamp Act made his voice the most effective of the resistance movement, since he wrote for a broader audience than Otis had reached. Dickinson described all the various classes of colonial society and their relations with one another, analyzing the economic situation of each class, and the meaning of freedom for each. He warned that while the colonists were instinctively loyal, oppression would undermine that loyalty: "we never can be made an independent people, except it be by *Great-Britain* herself," he declared, "and the only way for her to do it, is to make us frugal, ingenious, united, and discontented."

When the Townshend Acts were passed, Dickinson wrote his *Letters from a Farmer in Pennsylvania* (1767–1768), which were published in all but four of the twenty-five American newspapers, and in eight book editions; Richard Henry Lee edited them in Williamsburg, Otis in Boston; in England Franklin wrote a preface for the first of two editions; in France also two editions were published, translated and edited by a noted liberal. Dickinson made a triumphal tour of England, was awarded an honorary degree by Princeton, was toasted in John Wilkes' prison lodgings in London; he was to be known for the rest of his life as "the Pennsylvania Farmer." He formulated the American interpretation of the British constitution in terms of the principles of liberty.

> For WHO ARE FREE PEOPLE? [he asked]. Not *those,* over whom government is reasonably and equitably exercised, but *those* who live under a government so *constitutionally checked* and *controuled,* that proper provision is made against its being otherwise exercised.

He developed a theory of imperial federation in which colonies and empire were perfectly balanced. In such an empire, Americans could "support the character of *freemen* without losing that of *faithful subjects.*"

From 1774 to 1776 Dickinson led the moderate party in the Continental Congress; and he wrote many of the state papers of that body. As chief executive of two states, Delaware and Pennsylvania (1781–1785), he wrote proclamations and messages on the nature of political power, on the suppression of vice and immorality, on social inequality, and on free governments as the expression of the American spirit. He participated in the Constitutional Convention, wrote the *Letters of Fabius* (1788) urging ratification, and in 1797, when American politics turned upon the axis of the French Revolutionary Wars, produced his most reflective and most eloquent pamphlet, another series of *Letters of Fabius* (1797), in which he recommended the French cause, enjoining his countrymen:

> Let us assert and maintain *our true character—sincerity* of thought, and *rectitude* of action; and convince the world, that *no man,* or *body of men,* whatever advantages may for a while be taken of our *unsuspecting confidence,* shall ever be able to draw this nation out of the direct road of an honest, candid, and generous conduct.

The length of Dickinson's career, and the distinction of his writing, made him one of the most constructive and successful pamphleteers of his generation—among them all, one of the surest of his ground. In a "chaos of politics and morals, in which strength and weakness, safety and ruin, virtue and iniquity, strangely met together, and wrought in wild conjunction," he strove for order and principle, for intellectual integrity. "I am acting a very small and a very short part in the drama of human affairs," he told his critics. "I shall little trouble myself how your applause or your censures are bestowed."

4

The year 1774 was the watershed of Revolutionary literature. The meeting of the First Congress gave continental expression to all the various bodies of opinion. Production of pamphlets increased, and the state papers of the Congress, instead of emphasizing the areas of agreement among the American writers, polarized the elements of disagreement. Three parties appeared: moderates like Dickinson, loyal extremists of the right, and the independence party of the left. The loyalists were among the ablest literary figures. They had a worthy cause, and they were as American in their orientation as the moderates and independents, expressing—only with different emphasis—the same intellectual and emotional currents that moved in the revolutionists. There was a loyalist philosophy, akin to the fundamentalist conservative philosophy of all social crises. Jonathan Boucher, Virginia clergyman, developed in bold sermons the theme of a natural aristocracy and a divinely ordained government. Robert Proud, pedantic Latinist and schoolmaster, argued in almost medieval spirit that men were born to obey. But not all Toryism was backward-looking. By more realistic men a positive reform program was developed, which can be seen in such spirited essays as *A Friendly Address to all Reasonable Americans* (1774) by President Myles Cooper of King's College, and the five great "Westchester Farmer" pamphlets (1774–1775) of Samuel Seabury. Most original of the loyalist writers was Joseph Galloway of Pennsylvania, whose plan for union between Britain and the colonies was first presented to the Continental Congress where it was rejected, then published in various pamphlets, and after Galloway's migration to England developed through three more stages, the last appearing as late as 1788. Galloway's productivity included more than a score of the little books. His nobly conceived plan of a federal empire was one of the significant intellectual achievements of the American mind of this period.

Meanwhile, after 1774, the extremists on the left steadily gained adherents, and with the beginning of hostilities in April, 1775, independence tracts secured an ever widening audience. The war itself was the cradle of a more exuberant literature, in which the poetic careers of Philip Freneau, Francis Hopkinson, and John Trumbull were nurtured. These satirists as well as radical leaders like John and Samuel Adams continually urged independence; but at the end of 1775 America was still paralyzed by indecision. Then in January, 1776, a new little book appeared in Philadelphia, by a writer theretofore unknown, who with this work began to assume international significance as a pamphleteer of revolutions. The pamphlet was *Common Sense,* its author the one-time English artisan, Thomas Paine.

Paine belonged to no country, his doctrines to no age. Of all the writers of the American Revolution, he was the least American in background, in spirit, and in purpose. He had not participated in the fifteen years of constitutional debate that had qualified the colonial mind for contention and produced such achievements as Galloway's simple federalism and Dickinson's complex matrix of constitutional limitations, for throughout these years he had been still in England. His cause was not America; it was revolution. He differed in every essential respect from the major writers who had preceded him: his learning was slight, his personal standing inconsequential, his ability in systematic philosophy or organized presentation of argument almost nonexistent. Still, having missed the previous debates with their constitutional metaphysics, he was uninhibited by them. He felt, he sensed, he reacted. He did not complicate his emotional processes with intellectual refinements. He was the exotic radical, the revolutionary prototype. He wrote with urgency, excitement, and bold simplicity; he furnished straightforward, uncomplicated guidance for artisans, mechanics, and farmers. He carried the new philosophy to the masses of the American people, and turned the resistance movement into revolt.

Once a corset maker of Thetford in Norfolk, later a sailor, then a careless exciseman, later still a teacher, successively a tobacconist, a grocer, and once more a crown servant, Paine had lived a singularly disorganized and unfulfilled life before he came to America in 1774 at the age of thirty-seven. Possessed of a lively intellectual curiosity but lacking the capacity for sustained application, he had learned a little about a great many subjects. He became an editor in Philadelphia just as the cumulative force of the resistance movement was supplied with a national focus, the Congress, and in Pennsylvania was entering a proletarian phase. He responded both to the aspirations of the lower classes and to the humanitarian zeal of such enlightened men of position as Benjamin Franklin and Dr. Benjamin Rush, who were his patrons. His newspaper articles on abolition, women's rights, dueling, titles, and the freedom of British India constituted a significantly different preparation for writing revolutionary tracts from that furnished by local political contention and legal study to Henry, Otis, Dickinson, Dulany, and Galloway. The battle of Lexington awakened Paine to the magnitude of the Revolution in a way that constitutional arguments and congressional papers had not. Deciding that, "in a country where all men were once adventurers," his recent arrival did not preclude his uttering opinions, he set out to win America's thoughts from dependence to independence. He concluded that the issue had passed beyond the subtleties of constitutional law, had indeed become a matter to be solved "by man's instincts for truth, decency, and fairness"—that is (Dr. Rush suggested the title), by *Common Sense.*

The impact of the pamphlet was amazing. In a few months more than a hundred thousand copies were published in America and four European editions appeared. The total number eventually circulated was not much less than half a million. Every contemporary felt its effect. Washington found it "working a powerful change in the minds of many men." A South Carolinian declared it had made independents of a majority of Americans. Seldom if ever had a book enjoyed such an immediate popularity. Paine rejected all political theorizing over sovereignty and federalism; he scoffed at loyalty to George III. Instead, he presented the doctrine of separation as inevitable: a continent could not remain subject to an island. "The period of debate is closed," he wrote. "Arms, as the last resource, must decide the contest." In violent language he attacked "the royal brute of Britain" and ridiculed the institution of the crown. "Of more worth is one honest man to society, and in the sight of God, than all the crowned ruffians that ever lived." He painted the picture of three million Americans "running to their seacoast every time a ship arrives from London, to know what portion of liberty they should enjoy," and he contended that the colonies had reached a maturity that made their state of pupilage both farcical and dangerous. Finally, he challenged America to build a freer state than existed anywhere in the world:

> O ye that love Mankind! . . . Every spot in the old world is overrun with oppression. Freedom hath been hunted round the globe. Asia and Africa have long expelled her. Europe regards her like a stranger; and England hath given her warning to depart. O! receive the fugitive; and prepare in time an asylum for mankind.

Paine was, like Jefferson and Rousseau, a master rhetorician. In this lay the strength of his appeal. His arguments were crudely simple, his presentation of issues blandly elementary. The canons of good taste scarcely applied to his works; he was not above referring to the stricken George III as "His Madjesty," and he approached the subtleties of politics with blundering passion. But his very simplicity and the heat of his febrile writing brought him the attention of masses of readers whom the careful, reasoned arguments of others had not touched. "The world is my country; to do good my religion," he exclaimed, and in the confident way of inspired agitators he proselyted for his faith.

That faith contained two stable and enduring elements: a belief in the ability of natural reason to govern, and a conviction that all men everywhere were united in the fellowship of freedom. Neither idea was original, nor had Paine as profound an appreciation of their meaning as had certain of his greater contemporaries. But he proved better able than anyone else to translate them into the vernacular of the common man, and his books were then and have ever since been range-lights of liberalism.

Common Sense made Paine the spokesman of the independence party. *The American Crisis* (sixteen papers he contributed at irregular intervals to the *Pennsylvania Journal* during the next seven years) made him the journalist of the Revolution itself. The first *Crisis* opened with the famous words that became a battle-cry:

> These are the times that try men's souls. The summer soldier and the sunshine patriot will, in this crisis, shrink from the service of their country; but he that stands it *now,* deserves the love and thanks of man and woman. Tyranny, like hell, is not easily conquered; yet we have this consolation with us, that the harder the conflict, the more glorious the triumph.

He attacked the complacency of those who wished for peace in their day, if it meant war for their children's generation; and he praised the sturdy resolution of the patriots who had endured the defeats of the first year of campaigning.

> I love the man that can smile in trouble, that can gather strength from distress and grow brave by reflection. It is the business of little minds to shrink; but he whose heart is firm, and whose conscience approves his conduct, will pursue his principles unto death.

Later numbers dealt with the threatening issues of the war years: financial chaos, loyalist opposition, military conspiracy, national union, a just peace, and adequate government. Busy with minor offices and with many essays besides the *Crisis,* Paine became enmeshed in the details of political life. His essential philosophy remained, but he did not again achieve the originality, the vitality, the unifying definition of the American overcause that had in *Common Sense* helped to make "thirteen clocks strike together."

But there was no confusion in his philosophy of freedom. "My own line of reasoning is to myself as straight and clear as a ray of light," he wrote; and as he watched the slow and painful victory of the American people he developed the concept of revolution as the emancipation not of Americans alone but of common men everywhere from the worship of their antique idols in their antique symbolism. Revolutionism became Paine's basic faith. It had little application in American politics after the peace, even less after the reforms in government of 1787–1789. In this country, the Revolution was over. In Europe it was just beginning, and Paine, who went abroad in 1787, was its self-appointed evangel. Like Archimedes, he felt that, "had we a place to stand upon, we might raise the world." The French Revolution gave him his platform. Ineffectual in his efforts of personal leadership, he gave all his intense convictions and restless energies to his writings. *The Rights of Man* became a textbook for world revolution, and has remained the democrat's breviary of two continents. *The Age of Reason,* confronting the connection between political and theological doctrine—always present but never before so explicit in his thought—stated the case of deism crudely but so overtly that Paine incurred the enmity of hosts of the common people who had once been his admirers and followers. *Agrarian Justice* was an examination of the problem of poverty. Could civilized man, who begat poverty, eliminate it by social action? To answer this question in the affirmative, Paine proposed a system of state taxes and pensions. He had moved from the democracy of the seventies to the nationalism of the nineties.

The French Revolution ended, as the American had; France entered a constructive, aggressive phase, to which Paine had little to contribute. He returned to a strange America in 1802, spent a few pitiful years, poor, ill, and outcast; he died in 1809. Thriving on social turmoil, he languished in times of peace; apt to stir emotions, he affronted sober judgment; yet he had wrought marvelously in the processes that undermined the ancient pieties of men; he had crystallized the conviction that reason, rather than accepted authority or revelation, is the surest guide in politics, religion, and morality; and he had added to the vocabulary of politics stirring phrases of courage, determination, and faith that have not lost their magic in the passing years. If doubt still lingers as to which nation should take Paine unto itself, there is at least no doubt that, in giving memorable expression to American life at its most decisive moment, he made his place in the formative literature of the new republic.

5

There was only one Otis, one Dickinson, one Galloway, one Paine; yet the age of the little books produced many other notable literary careers. There was, for example, gentle Anthony Benezet, whose humanitarian ministry of good works included five sensible tracts on abolitionism, the slave trade, temperance, Quaker doctrine, and the treatment of the Indians. There was the vain, half-educated mountaineer, Ethan Allen, who wrote pamphlets on the Vermont controversy, an account of his captivity during the war, and shared in a barbarous presentation of deism, *Reason the Only Oracle of Man* (1784). Most copies of this tract were accidentally destroyed by fire and some were burnt on purpose; but enough remained to cause a brief uproar among orthodox clerics, and it has unaccountably received serious attention by historians since. There was Benjamin Rush, scientist, philosopher, reformer, statesman, and educator, whose great works on chemistry, diseases, medicine, and madness do not entirely eclipse the scores of essays and tracts he wrote on social and political questions. And there were many more. But for several years after the peace (1783) fewer pamphlets emerged from the run of little books to achieve either literary distinction or a wide audience. Controversy scarcely abated, but the issues of controversy were not so often the great universal issues of political experience. Religious contention, social reform, currency problems, and economic ills were the subjects of the little books, while larger books were appealing to the dominant moods. War-nurtured nationalism was gratified by the publication of military journals and patriotic histories of the Revolution. These were noncontroversial works that were not part of the literature of propaganda and debate.

The proposal of the new Constitution in 1787, however, was the occasion for another spate of pamphlets, in volume second only to that the independence controversy had caused. The debate on ratification extended over twenty months, and produced examinations of first principles of political organization as searching and as significant as any of the revolutionary pamphlets of the previous decade. Historical traditions have conferred such an accolade upon *The Federalist* that other tracts of literary merit, particularly those opposing the Constitution, have been all but forgotten. Yet writers of ability, reputation, and learning, in little books simpler and more popular than the great classic of Madison, Hamilton, and Jay (which was "not well calculated for the common people"), laid the cases for and against the Constitution at the bar of public opinion. Elbridge Gerry's *Observations . . . By A Columbian Patriot* (1788), criticized the new plan as a scheme "of military combinations, and politicians of yesterday." In New York the partisan leader George Clinton attacked the proposed frame as tyranny and corruption, in *Letters of Cato* (1787–1788), to which Alexander Hamilton, as *Caesar,* replied. Albert Gallatin, Luther Martin, James Monroe, Patrick Henry, George Mason, and Samuel Chase were among the pamphleteers who wrote little books and newspaper essays against the Constitution; but the most effective antifederalist tract, and one of the most persuasive pamphlets of the whole period, was Richard Henry Lee's *Letters of the Federal Farmer* (1787–1788), which went through four editions in as many states in three months, and became a handbook of the opposition to the new frame of government. It evoked vigorous rejoinders, among them an elaborate refutation by Timothy Pickering. Lee's writing was spare and firm. He preserved a calm dignity. His arguments were careful and thorough. He was neither narrow nor contentious in spirit, but earnest and constructive. "We are making a constitution, it is to be hoped, for ages and millions yet unborn," he wrote, and warned that the defects in the proposed instrument would doom it to failure. Lee spoke for what he termed "the honest and substantial part of the community," as Henry and Gallatin spoke for the lower income groups. His *Letters* were a powerful influence in bringing about the first ten amendments (the Bill of Rights) which as Senator from Virginia he helped put through Congress in the following year (1789). The pamphlet also deserves notice as the principal literary achievement of this sturdy, quiet, somewhat austere character who had been throughout a long public life above the reproach either of interest or of enthusiasm. Ever since his bold oration against slavery in the House of Burgesses in 1759, Lee had been in the forefront of the resistance movement. His stately petitions and official papers had been on a plane with Dickinson's. He it was who had written and introduced the resolution of independence in 1776; he had shared in composing the North-West Ordinance, had served long in Congress as member and for a while as president. Above all the Virginia statesmen, Lee represented what the classically trained revolutionary generation meant when it spoke of Roman virtues.

On the other side of the ratification question were writers equally distinguished and apparently even more effective. Dickinson's *Letters of Fabius,* published in a Wilmington newspaper, helped to make Delaware the first state to ratify. Noah Webster, John Jay, Edmund Randolph, Alexander Hamilton, James Iredell, Hugh Henry Brackenridge, Hugh Williamson, and Tench Coxe joined the lists of the Constitution's champions, under a bewildering array of pseudonyms. James Wilson, ineradicably Scotch, inordinately learned, incurably romantic, had led the Convention through its most tortuous philosophical difficulties. To the ratification polemic he contributed a precise explanation of the principles he had concocted, *Address to a Meeting of the Citizens* (1787), pronouncing the Constitution "the best form of government which has ever been offered to the world." Trained in law by John Dickinson, associated with him in opposition to the Stamp Act and later regulations, author of the *Considerations on the Nature and Extent of the Legislative Authority of the British Parliament* (1774) and other pamphlets, Wilson had always represented the opinions of the Philadelphia mercantile and professional classes. His style was sober and heavy, his arguments sometimes turgid, but he had attained a very extensive influence. His lectures on law at the University of Pennsylvania mark the beginning of the public study of jurisprudence in America. His brilliance as a thinker and writer and his effectiveness as a statesman were alike marred by his immoderate speculations in land companies. Perhaps because his life closed amid sordid scenes, his substantial contributions to American literature and statecraft have been insufficiently valued.

6

Of all the little books of 1787–1788, none has a stronger claim upon the student of literature than *The Federalist,* written by Madison, Hamilton, and Jay. These papers formed the best exposition of the principles of the new government, and after its adoption gained the authority almost of constitutional law. They appeared first in New York newspapers, and were issued in two volumes in March–May, 1788; republished in many American cities and in two French editions during the nineties; praised by German reviewers; and reprinted on the occasion of South American and Central European revolutions in the nineteenth century. *The Federalist* occupies a unique place in American journalism, for it summarizes the most original contributions the revolutionary generation of pamphleteers made to the discussion of government. As Paine's *Common Sense* marked the height of revolutionary radicalism, so *The Federalist* signalized the success of the conservative, constructive, consolidating processes which shaped the new nation in postrevolutionary molds. The ideas of distributive powers, checked by correlative limitations upon power, the colonists had found in their political texts: Montesquieu, Harington, Sidney, and Locke. They had given their own expression to these ideas in their first pamphlets on imperial organization in the Stamp Act year. Dulany, Wilson, Dickinson, and especially Galloway had proposed a federal scheme for the empire, and Galloway had developed his proposals into a well articulated structure of administrative and legislative units. The members of the Constitutional Convention, though young men, had in one sense been truly as Gerry had charged "politicians of yesterday," for they were directed by the writings and experience of the previous two decades. *The Federalist* papers, written by a strangely assorted trio—a conservative New York lawyer, a convinced monarchist and nationalist, a pedantic constitutional theorist—were the result not so much of the discussions behind the closed doors of Independence Hall during that hot summer of 1787, as of all the American experiments, literary and actual, with federal forms since the dimly remembered days of the Confederation of New England. This book was a sort of codification of American conservative thought. It signalized as much the end of an era as the beginning of a nation.

The ratification controversy was the last great American chapter in the age of the pamphlet. The form itself did not disappear; every national election and every national issue for many years was to see a flood of the little books. But American writers were already by 1790 presenting larger and longer works to an expanding reading audience. The pamphlet, a ready instrument in conflict, was being relegated to a minor place in the currents of reconstruction and nation building. The literary career of Tench Coxe, our first original economic thinker on a national scale, bridged the two eras. Most of his score of works (1787–1820) were pamphlets, varying from thirty-eight to one hundred thirty-five pages in length; but his *View of the United States* (1795) ran to more than four hundred pages, and was popular enough to appear in three editions in one year. Coxe and his contemporaries had to be more than pamphleteers, because the processes of thought and opinion set in motion by the pamphlet literature of the Revolution had been completed. The techniques of communicating major ideas in simple words had been refined to a point where the philosopher, the political leader, the reformer had an almost instantaneous hearing in the public forum. The newspaper and the magazine at one level, the printed book at the other, took the place of the pamphlet. The age of the little book, like the American Revolution itself, had come to an end.

12. PHILOSOPHER–STATESMEN OF THE REPUBLIC

No less contemporaneous in its inspiration than the writing of the pamphleteers, but far more substantial and enduring, was the writing in all forms of those philosopher-statesmen who did most by thought and action to bring the First Republic into being.

The founding fathers were men of remarkably broad interests with an uncanny aptitude for political analysis and for the adaptation of theories to practice. There are some who describe this phenomenon as no more than the heritage of humanism which the American enlightenment merely reembodied. Certainly the statesmen who shaped the Republic in its first form were confronting essentially the same issues as those formulated by the Renaissance humanists: the attempt to reconcile speculative thinking on the nature of man with the immediate task of creating a new political and social order. But these modern humanists differed from More and Erasmus in being under more pressure to apply their theories to the urgent task at hand. Yet there is something breath-taking about the reembodiment of broad humanist principles in a struggling and relatively unsophisticated people, beset on every side by the problems of living. The "fathers" therefore deserve either spontaneous admiration or informed respect, whether we study their ideas and actions as we find them, or trace their intellectual heritage to another age.

Of the first statesmen of the Republic, four—Jefferson, Madison, John Adams, and Hamilton—trained their sights higher than any of the others. Addressing themselves to more than practical considerations, they seemed to be genuinely inspired by the historical uniqueness of the experience open to them, to launch a new civilization on a large scale. In final outcome, they proved equal to the challenge of planning republican government, and they could only have become so because they tried to understand not only the buried sources of power, but the moral objectives of good government. In a sense they were, as Hamilton once contemptuously declared, "speculative" thinkers and "empirics." Even Hamilton belonged to the company he criticized, for he, with the others, assessed what he already found in existence as social habit and political tradition; he built upon that which was already "given," and recommended, according to his lights, the best direction of change.

Jefferson, the greatest of them all, was conspicuously devoted to the theory and practice of good government. Further, he was actively critical of his own methods of establishing political judgments, and he was intellectually prepared to examine the logical, philosophical, scientific, or sentimental elements in his views of society. He learned to style himself an "ideologist," identifying himself with his friends the French philosophers, who had founded a school of thought known as "Ideology" in the Napoleonic period. Hamilton, Madison, and Adams as well as Jefferson contributed characteristic ways of thought, individual tempers of belief which were to be important not only in the era of the Republic but for America thenceforth. The principles of the four philosopher-statesmen taken together almost define the range of our national ideology—our objectives, our character as a people, our economic and social patterns, our "Americanism."

The challenge of creating a new form of government gave rise to an atmosphere of intellectual adventure, in which the Platonic vision of the philosopher-king could for one brief period take on American reality. "Until philosophers take to government, or those who now govern become philosophers," Plato had boldly written, "so that government and philosophy unite, there will be no end to the miseries of states." In the timeless analogy of the cave in the *Republic,* the philosophers who struggle to free themselves from the chains of ignorance and superstition make their way to the light outside. They see the truth. Loving its clarity, they would bask in its light. But the thought of the chained multitude below gives them no rest, and they understand, as Platonic seekers of truth must, that they cannot fail to carry glimmerings of light to the poorer minds who inhabit the cave.

The four great philosopher-statesmen of the American "Enlightenment" conform admirably to the Platonic pattern. They grope in authentic Platonic fashion for the true principles of social order, accepting the responsibility of administering the affairs of their less farsighted fellow men; yet they reject the Platonic ideal as an explicit inspiration. They are willing to exemplify it if they must; but justify it, direct from its ancient source, never. Plato, even for Jefferson who had the most developed philosophic predilections of the group, was too full of metaphysical flights and trances to prove sympathetic to the common-sense orientation of the new nation. Yet the double drive of philosophy and leadership, thought and action, vision and its fortifying concrete detail is heeded by Jefferson, Madison, Adams, and even Hamilton. From the time of Franklin to the present this double drive, common to all humanity but intensified by life in a new continent, has dictated a double destiny for the American nation and a dualistic orientation for its literature. In the great period of American political literature, both forces were present without fatal conflict, and lend a peculiar divided charm and predictive importance to this body of writing.

2

In its literary guise, the issue faced by the philosopher-statesmen was the reconciliation of potent ideas with traditions of style formalized by eighteenth century English writers and imitated by our early writers of fiction, essay, and poetry. The methods of belles-lettres were inadequate to the urgent demand for clear and effective expression. These public-minded men wrote their state papers, their reports, their tracts, and their letters with some care for the form as well as the content, but they subordinated the formal demands of art to the immediate need for communication. John Adams, who was himself a tyro in the "literary" essay, had made it all too plain: "substance" was to take precedence over "elegance." He had written: "The simplest style, the most mathematical precision of words and ideas, is best adapted to discover truth and to convey it to others, in reasoning on this subject [politics]." That Adams himself, who once boasted that he had never had "time" to compress his written pieces nor to prune them of repetitions, did not always live up to the severe criteria of clarity and communicability he invoked, in no way affects the importance of the ideal. Amusingly enough, some of Adams' most notorious departures from this standard produced his best prose, the nervous and animated passages so eloquent with his erratic brilliance. Jefferson and Madison never quite forsook the rounded and urbane prose line which by now seems characteristic of the Virginia political dynasty with the notable exception of George Washington, who strove, not always successfully, to restrict himself to a "plain stile." Yet even the Virginians never hesitated to put communication and content above consideration of style or form. Madison, ever judicious and temperate, best conformed to the utilitarian ideal. In criticizing a political pamphlet, he commented that it would have been "much improved by softer words and harder arguments," and he found the style attractive in that it had "the artless neatness always pleasing to the purest tastes." Hamilton, in the calculated fixity of his desire to convince, to silence the opposition by a brilliant show of fire before an enemy gun could shoot, did not hesitate to employ rhetorical ornament and insistent, obvious rhythm. Although he too agreed that "our communications should be calm, reasoning, serious, showing steady resolution more than feeling, having force in the idea rather than in the expression," he often lapsed into purple passages whose melodramatic tones are as trying as they are insincere.

Throughout, the unorthodoxy of this political literature is a consequence of the fact that these statesmen were primarily devoted to the issues and principles growing out of a serious national undertaking. The motivation of interest seems to have been so compelling that communications tended to become direct colloquial exchanges, discussions of ideas, selfless presentation of the "argument" without stopping for artifice or formal discipline. For this reason it is a great pity that the most often quoted of their political "classics" have tended to come from the public documents and official papers of the nation's archives, rather than from the enormous correspondence which more truly characterizes this age of statesmen. This correspondence, in fact, should be the mainstay of our knowledge of the political thought and of the social continuum of the early Republic. In a sense, its excellence may be regarded as the nation's unearned reward for having once lived in an age with inadequate media of communication. It is hardly an exaggeration to say that there is no Jefferson, no Adams, and no Madison without the body of letters they left. To understand Hamilton and Madison, notes for their speeches in the Constitutional Convention and elsewhere must be added to the justly famous papers they separately contributed to *The Federalist* (1787–1788).

All the statesmen had been trained in Congress or had read deeply in the law. None in the country knew better than they the amount of power that could be borrowed from the logical ordering of material, the legal-rhetorical habit of defining terms. A truly impressive endurance also marks the longer writings of Jefferson and his colleagues, as they patiently investigate detailed charges and sternly cleave to the political issues under discussion. Their writing is suffused with a kind of lofty passion born of the consciousness of the cosmic importance of the "infant nation" with which they identified themselves so intimately. What a terrible disaster it would be, they seem to say, if the "ark, bearing as we have flattered ourselves the happiness of our country & the hope of the world" (Madison's phrase), should be shipwrecked! It is not surprising that an earnestness of moral tone is the keynote of this literature which in general is neither original in metaphor nor polished in style.

On occasions, the utilitarian limitations upon expression are conceived of as a moral question, intimately related to the simple and severe needs of republican society. Jefferson, gentle lover of the fine arts, was keenly aware that America differed from Europe in being not yet ready for the highest and most cultivated art-forms. His journals of travel through Italy and France conscientiously record technical improvements in agriculture and contain long passages on how to make wines and cheese. This attitude is at war, all through Jefferson's varied European sojourn, with such projects as the adaptation of Palladio's Villa Rotunda to his plan for the second Monticello and his general enthusiasm for the ancients in literary form and moral leadership, and to the highest expression of what was then "modern" music, painting, "beauty" in general. John Adams, prone to state reasons for his actions, epitomized the stage of American literary and artistic needs by declaring:

It is not indeed the fine arts which our country requires; the useful, the mechanic arts are those which we have occasion for in a young country as yet simple and not far advanced in luxury, although perhaps much too far for her age and character. . . . The science of government is my duty to study, more than all other sciences. . . . I must study politics and war, that my sons may have liberty to study mathematics and philosophy, geography, natural history and naval architecture, navigation, commerce, and agriculture, in order to give their children a right to study painting, poetry, music, architecture, statuary, tapestry, and porcelain.

Jefferson had clearly announced that in "a republic nation, whose citizens are to be led by reason and persuasion, and not by force, the art of reasoning becomes of first importance," and had recommended the speeches of Livy, Sallust, and Tacitus as "pre-eminent specimens of logic, taste and that sententious brevity which, using not a word to spare, leaves not a moment for inattention to the hearer." Amplification, he thought, was the "vice of modern oratory," and he avoided speech-making when he could. But it was Jefferson who developed that flowing and "felicitous" line for which John Adams, the Continental Congresses, and all America since came to know him—the rhythmic yet thoughtful line that moves unchecked in our most famous public *Declaration,* in our early official papers and documents, and in that remarkable corpus of Jefferson letters with which no subsequent political correspondence can compete.

Madison we have noted as the advocate of the tightened composition of logical demonstration. He felt that the "only effectual precaution against fruitless and endless discussion" was the definition of our political terms. Hamilton nursed a notorious and constitutional fear that republican government would not weather the storm; but in his *Federalist* essays, when he was promoting the cause of the new constitution, he shared the general excitement over political innovation.

The people of this country, by their conduct and example [he wrote], will decide the important question, whether societies of men are really capable or not of establishing good government from reflection and choice, or whether they are forever destined to depend for their political constitutions on accident and force.

Adams, paternal watchdog of his beloved New England, had further called attention to the specific virtues found in the self-government local to his region. These virtues he kept in mind from his early directives on government in his influential letters, "Thoughts on Government" (1776), to his last review of the revised constitution of Massachusetts, half a century later. Madison added to his theoretical contribution a practical demonstration of superior journalism in the unique service he performed by reporting the Constitutional Convention. Demonstrating selfless honesty, patience, and comprehension, he early set a high standard for American political reporting. Thus, in different ways, the statesmen of the American Republic demonstrated their sense of a supreme political mission, and it was this dominant aim of constructing a government compatible with freedom which gave unity to their writing—not in the sense of formal arrangement or style, but in the homogeneous conviction which flowed from their dedication to political ends.

The very issue of English versus American idiom adds the final touch to the thesis that there was a separate quality in American political writing as early as the formative years of the new Republic. The British critics who mocked American writing for forsaking "purity" of standard English form and style were met with singular equanimity. Jefferson, for example, whose use of the word "belittle" in *Notes on Virginia* (1784) had been the occasion for reproof by the *Edinburgh Review,* was unperturbed. Languages, he explained, had always grown by innovation. They fattened on flexible adaptation and change. Who would expect a vast new American nation, with its very different regions, to bind itself in an iron cask of ready-made English speech and prose? No, "neology" must clearly replace purism, since the price of purism was stagnation.

> Had the preposterous idea of fixing the language been adopted by our Saxon ancestors, of Peirce Plowman, of Chaucer, of Spenser, the progress of ideas must have stopped with that of the language . . . what do we not owe to Shakespeare for the enrichment of the language, by his free and magical creation of words? [To be sure] uncouth words will sometimes be offered; but the public will judge them, and receive or reject, as sense or sound shall suggest.

No matter how often the debates in Congress, or the individual statesmen in writing, might call upon the eloquent models of antiquity; no matter how much the balanced sentence of the English essayists, Addison and Steele, or the English political theorists of the seventeenth and eighteenth centuries might be copied—a sense of the American scene in all its heady potentialities was so strong in the minds of these architects of the Republic that they could scarcely avoid giving direct expression to nascent American culture. In the authentic idiom of American thought and speech the statesmen of the greatest experimental democracy in history put pen to paper.

3

The ideology of American democracy began its career with a set of political principles termed "Republican." Although John Adams was quick to warn of the shifting meanings of "Republic," the term became a fixed pole of reference in American political theory, directly contraposing that other pole, Monarchy, against which the Revolution had been waged. Adams himself believed in republican doctrine and, like the other political leaders of his day, made standard references to the ancient republics as the historical alternative to monarchy and to feudal hierarchic society. Almost everyone in early America agreed on the minimal connotation of the term, either explicitly or by implication. Like late eighteenth century philosophers elsewhere, they understood that a republic was a government which derived its power from the people "originally," referred back to the people for an ultimate court of appeal in "crucial" questions transcending the ordinary affairs of legislation, and exercised its granted powers through representatives chosen by a majority of the voting citizens. In theory, at least, these voting citizens were further supposed to represent the "will of the people"; and, while they confided specific powers to their representatives, it was understood that a republic was essentially a government of laws rather than of men.

Were one to try to locate the maximum adherence to this republican ideal, one could project an imaginary political line with the left terminal point designating "maximum faith" and the right terminal point "minimum faith." We should then have to place Jefferson at the left and Hamilton at the right. John Adams accordingly must occupy the middle ground, to the left of Hamilton and the right of Jefferson; but he is also to the right of Madison, who is closer to Jefferson on most fundamental political matters—although it is important to note that Madison is sometimes closer than either Adams or Jefferson to Hamilton in economic questions.

Had Jefferson written no more than the initial draft of the *Declaration of Independence* he would probably have earned his place on the radical left of our American political line. The achievement of the *Declaration,* if it proves nothing else, certainly establishes its author's title to the greatest pen in the patriotic cause. Certain contemporaries, either through faulty judgment or through jealousy of his ability to fashion a line of fundamental national policy that could sing itself into the country's ears, challenged the author on the score of "originality." Madison was incensed, for he knew that it was absurd to cavil thus.

> The object [he protested] was to assert not to discover truths, and to make them the basis of the Revolutionary Act. The merit of the Draught could only

consist in a lucid communication of human Rights, a condensed enumeration of the reasons for such an exercise of them, and in a style and tone appropriate to the great occasion, and to the spirit of the American people.

But if the content of the *Declaration* alone is not enough, Jefferson is established in his preeminence on the left by his *Notes on the State of Virginia* (1784), the first American book to become an accidental "expatriate," published in England and France in pirated versions before it reached print in the country of its origin. This series of informal essays ranges far and wide over disputed questions in philosophy, science, politics, and morals, and is the natural discourse of a born humanistic rationalist. Proud of his friend's prowess as a thinker, Madison once observed that Jefferson was "greatly eminent for the comprehensiveness and fertility of his genius, for the vast extent and rich variety of his acquirements; and particularly distinguished by the philosophic impress left on every subject which he touched." And then, as if the *Notes* had come to mind, Madison hastened to add: "Nor was he less distinguished from an early and uniform devotion to the cause of liberty, and systematic preference of a form of Government squared in the strictest degree to the equal rights of man."

Although Madison had been a friend, follower, and co-worker of Jefferson's for many years when he wrote this tribute, it is notable that in all the advancing and receding waves of historical interpretation the residual significance of Jefferson's contribution to the American tradition has grown rather than diminished. Of American Presidents, this statesman of the "Enlightenment" most closely approximates the Platonic philosopher-king. No other incumbent of the Presidency, and no other of the liberal philosophic spirits of his age—many-sided men like Franklin, Benjamin Rush, and Thomas Cooper—could match Jefferson's happy union of learning, independence, and competent judgment in diverse fields such as social morality, government, education, natural science, agriculture, and the arts. What Washington began to do for the American personality by example and by the sheer weight of personal decency and leadership, Jefferson molded into an intellectualized ideal of social order. The entire development of American affairs, as the definition of our national ideology, is consequently more indebted to Jefferson than it is to any other single man.

This is not to say that Jefferson was an illustration of that cliché, the crusader of eighteenth century enlightenment who preached the gross "goodness" of man and the inevitable rational progress of society. Jefferson, who never wearied of reading history—he knew excellently the classical and the best of modern historians—had come to recognize the hazards of evil in human as in social affairs. He had so acute an awareness of the consequences of entrenching evil men in public positions that he concluded no society would be safe without an informed, alert citizenry participating actively in government. Devoted to human possibilities of growth, he outdistanced the faith of the other philosopher-statesmen—although Madison and Adams both had their areas of hope and solid, if less generous, funds of good will. Another way of viewing the difference between Jefferson and all others is to recognize his philosophy of education for what it was—a conscious "ideological" program to create right-thinking, tolerant citizens whose management of local affairs would be but a neighborly orientation for their wise judgment and activity in the affairs of the Union. It was a program fitted to practical needs and political responsibilities, and yet attuned to the highest cultivation of the arts, the sciences, and belles-lettres.

If it was Jefferson who recommended the fullest participation in political control, just as he sustained the greatest confidence in the educability of the American people, it was Hamilton who had most concern for government as a force, who saw little to worry about in its suppressive intrusions upon local or personal rights. It must be understood that the whole of the political line ranging from Jefferson to Madison to Adams and to Hamilton operated within realistic limits. Each statesman feared different contingencies, each phrased his hopes in typical or unique terms, each seized upon symbols of approbation or aversion sympathetic to his own personality and to the range of his ideational life. One might almost conclude: therefore, the republic was made possible—through the very variety and divergence of the founders' visions, ideas, and wishes.

Hamilton, for instance, saw very clearly the vast economic potentialities of America if the government would ally itself with the possessors of large fortunes and legislate in the direction of the expansion of financial and commercial activities. In the "people" Hamilton held virtually no stock. He thought they might listen to a debate and repeat with fair accuracy another man's line of argument, but were by and large susceptible to the flatteries and the manipulations of natural politicians. When left to his own selfish and irrational devices, the "great beast" might actually retard the productive energy of the nation, rather than build it up.

It was some time after Hamilton's memorable project of the *Federalist* (1787–1788)—that lucid exposition of constitutional republican government, not always consistent in its internal logic, but always impressive in its powerful defense of the need for national unity—that he began to voice his gloomiest thoughts about the survival of the republican experiment in self-government. "It is yet to be determined by experience whether it be consistent with that stability and order in government which are essential to public strength and private security and happiness," he wrote in 1792, having already tasted the strength of Jefferson's principled opposition. He seemed eager to give voice to his fear that republicanism might not "justify itself by its fruits." His progress Tory-wise, away from what he had called "the fair fabric of republicanism . . . modelled and decorated by the hand of federalism," was complete. In this shortsightedness Hamilton showed himself less of a philosopher and less of a statesman than one would desire. Were it not for the towering importance of certain of his administrative and governmental principles, his temperament and the transparency of his self-interest would hardly qualify him as a philosopher-statesman. But there is great penetration in his theory that the extension of national prerogative is indispensable for achieving internal uniformity and efficiency in a genuinely "central" government. And there is undeniable truth in his perception that this is the first essential of defense against foreign powers. Another realistic principle of capitalist development appreciated by Hamilton early in the nation's life was that it was a direct obligation of the government to foster the development of the productive resources and activities of the nation—by whatever combination of interests might prove effective. The first of these principles figures in Hamilton's masterful *First Report on the Public Credit* (1790), when he unhesitatingly decides, "If the voice of humanity pleads more loudly in favor of some [classes of creditors] than of others, the voice of policy, no less than of justice, pleads in favor of all." The second principle is the key argument of his classical treatise on protectionism, the *Report on Manufactures* (1791).

By a peculiar concentration of interest, Hamilton attained a definiteness in the body of his belief which sounds surprisingly modern in tone. Read today, his justification of strong, efficient government comes close to a native American defense of totalitarian political management. But, clever though his analysis was, it did not succeed in reconciling the two inseparable demands of prospering republicanism: national power, exercised to the full by an unimpeded, energetic central administration, and mature responsibility vested in the people of a free society.

The conservatism and legalism of John Adams and Madison explain almost as much about the success of the American Republic as they do about the absence of their names from most of the emotional appraisals of the early American tradition. Adams was a testy man, given to incalculable fits of temper that could shake his soul and harden his behavior to the utmost expression of stubbornness. Madison was naturally prudent, neither commanding in person nor captivating in his imaginative vistas. He did not permit himself the occasional exaggerations of the genius which he himself detected in Jefferson, while Adams, unlike Hamilton, kept steadily in view his high duty to guard the national interest and subordinate his own political welfare to the paramount needs of the American Republic. Adams was therefore saved from the extravagances of Hamiltonian ambition. Since the "mean," in politics, is not golden—not, at any rate, in the "memory of the race"—both Adams, the unorthodox Federalist, and Madison, the conservative Republican, paid the political price of hewing to the Aristotelian middle. Without Adams, the preservation of the dignified ideal of lawful, responsible government and a great example of Bolingbroke's ideal "Patriot King" who comes to guard like an "angel" the destiny and the long-range interests of his country might not have been realized. Without Madison, the amelioration of factional (including "class") strife would not so early have been made a governmental objective; nor would the allocation of sovereign power in the federal and in state contexts have found so subtle an expositor.

The surety of republican foundations, one might say, depended upon the Jeffersonian "left," with its key insights that the preservation of individual freedom and the moral development of cooperative society were the ultimate objectives of free society. It depended upon the Hamiltonian "right" with its knowledge that governments need effective organization and the power which comes from having the substantial productive and financial forces in the nation solidly united behind the administration. The stability of the Republic and its true course depended much upon the labors of Madison, with his realistic conviction that the main purpose of a government is the protection of the many and diverse economic interests into which every country is divided—and with his belief that this protection can be accomplished through a limited, federal republic capable of preventing the monopolistic dictation of one faction or combine over the people of the nation. The experienced conclusion of the elder Adams, that republicanism would not dispel the disparities of wealth and station and their attendant aristocracies, was a grave note of warning. When Adams added that the chief function of wise governors would be to protect the separate but "balanced" powers delegated to them, by compact with the people, and thus prevent tyranny, chaos, or the anarchy of the impassioned mob, he further safeguarded the Republic from what the ancients had been pleased to characterize as the "inevitable" degeneration of the good society.

The main task of republican government, in the long view of John Adams, appeared to be the prevention of excessive power in the hands of any one group. Believing that "vice and folly are so interwoven in all human affairs that they could not, possibly, be wholly separated from them without tearing and rending the whole system of human nature and state," Adams had to put his trust in the rare statesmanlike leaders who would possess wisdom to formulate just laws, and discipline to abide by them. Adams thought the network of checks and balances would defeat the ambitious and power-hungry few who might design to capture government for their private ends, and would insure fair representation of the interests of every region in the nation, thereby allowing the propertied and "responsible" citizens who were the mainstay of each region a voice in governmental affairs. By these devices, he thought he could make the most of fallible human nature. A republic, devoted to the interests of the people and operating through their own representatives, should be the outcome of these precautionary mechanisms. Adams accordingly thought his own republicanism as firm as that of anyone, including the leader of the Republican party, his good friend and occasional enemy, Thomas Jefferson, who, in Adams' opinion, differed from himself only in that he was for "liberty and straight hair. I thought curled hair was as republican as straight."

Madison's starting point was less psychological and more sociological. It began with the observed differences in group interests, differences which he took to calling "factions." Factions for Madison were special-interest groups arising out of the fundamental conflict present in every society between those who are rich and maintain their riches, and those who are poor and struggle to relieve their condition.

> All civilized societies are divided into different interests and factions [he wrote in the crucial year 1787], as they happen to be creditors or debtors—rich or poor—husbandmen, merchants or manufacturers—members of different religious sects—followers of different political leaders—inhabitants of different districts—owners of different kinds of property, etc.

The advantage of modern republicanism over other governments Madison expected to find in its ability to impede the full force of factional combinations, preventing them from controlling the state, and from usurping the rights of one or more minorities. Madison as a Virginian feared the added danger that the majority (the North) might suppress the rights of the minority (the South), and contended in a letter to Jefferson:

> Where the real power in a government lies, there is the danger of oppression. In our Governments the real power lies in the majority of the Community, and the invasion of private rights is chiefly to be apprehended, not from acts of Government contrary to the sense of its constituents, but from acts in which the Government is the mere instrument of the major number of the constituents.

Madison thus called to the attention of all men the inflexible requirement that democracies protect the civil rights of minorities from the real or reported "will" of the majority.

Madison and Adams made more of property rights than Jefferson did, but neither of them deserted the democratic theories of natural rights, popular sovereignty, limited government, antimonarchism, and antiaristocracy. Nor did the two conservatives ever approach Hamilton's justification of plutocracy. Both Adams and Madison inclined to the ideal of a republic which was economically agrarian at base, but supplemented by mercantile and manufacturing interests. Madison perhaps a little more than Adams realized the vital role of credit and of government-financed expansion of the country's natural resources and communications—the role which John Adams' son, John Quincy Adams, was to develop fully in his program of "Internal Improvement." Theoretically, therefore, it was Hamilton, of doubtful birth, who thought most exclusively of the moneyed interests of the country, partly because he saw in them the source of national strength, while Jefferson, graceful and learned "landed squire," cared most deeply about the widespread independent well-being of the "people," farmers and laborers included. Adams and Madison, aristocratic in taste in the typical styles of Massachusetts and Virginia, but far from dazzling in the family fortunes to which they were born, were actively promoting a scheme of society favorable to widespread middle-class prosperity and power.

4

The ethical theories of these men had pronounced influence upon the political and economic views they maintained. As character is the inner side of habit in the individual, so in society its outward crystallized structure is government. Save for these four philosopher-statesmen of the Republic, the American character might never have been given more than haphazard or perfunctory significance. Jefferson, Madison, and John Adams all understood the importance of character for those who would be leaders in a republic, and Hamilton sometimes did but sometimes paid only lip service to the ideal. Jefferson and Madison and Adams advocated that "the purest and noblest characters" (Madison's phrase) should serve as the people's representatives, since they alone would do so from the "proper motives." Because these men dedicated themselves to the cause of their country before they consulted their immediate personal needs, the inceptive principles of the American republic betoken seekers of truth and wisdom, and good citizens in the Roman sense, rather than mere men of office.

Jefferson, perceiving that government was necessary for the release of man's fullest potentialities, liked to speak of it as of secondary or instrumental value—a habit which was later perversely construed to mean that government was evil. The range of realistic political choice for Jefferson lay entirely between repressive government and republicanism, and he identified the essence of republicanism as "action by the citizens in person in affairs within their reach and competence, and in all others by representatives, chosen immediately, and removable by themselves." For this reason, a republic was the "only form of government that is not eternally at open or secret war with the rights of mankind." To achieve republican freedom, citizens must pay a price, the wakefulness of "eternal vigilance," and therefore a citizenry trained in the principles of government, an educated citizenry, is the indispensable support of freedom.

Thus, subtly and indirectly, a moral climate had been postulated for the America in which republicanism was to be tried. Benevolence and moral sense, self-created will rather than coercive force, are the dynamic daily agents in free society as well as the purely theoretical factors of its ethics. "Natural" moralism is opposed to the reputed "natural" rule of force, which Jefferson saw as the breeder of authoritarian society, whether of "kings, hereditary nobles, and priests" or, in the language of a later day, of leaders, demagogues, and commissars. Jefferson's agrarianism, so often made the catchword for his variety of democracy, is in reality a by-product of an almost sentimental preference for the simplicity of classical republicanism joined to the supposed purity of "primitive" Christianity. Yet when Jefferson realized that the evolution of his nation demanded the self-sufficiency and expansion of her manufacture and trade—when he perceived that free society would be jeopardized if it were unable to defend itself on the high seas—he protested that "he . . . who is now against domestic manufacture, must be for reducing us either to dependence . . . or to be clothed in skins, and to live like wild beasts in dens and caverns. I am not one of these; experience has taught me that manufactures are now as necessary to our independence as to our comfort." Despite this, Jefferson's instinctive trust reposed in the fair and free interchange of nation with nation, as in citizen with citizen—which is to say that he was a man of peace, conceiving productive society basically as a peaceful society, an earnest judgment in which he was fully joined by James Madison.

Economically and politically, to Hamilton's expert eye, the softer fringe of social morality was not a subject for enthusiasm nor even for belief. "The seeds of war are sown thickly in the human breast," Hamilton had written, and the rivalry that precipitated wars, in his view, stemmed partly from "the temper of societies," and partly from the human disposition to "prefer partial to general interest." Coming to terms with self-interested reality was accordingly Hamilton's basic preoccupation, whether that "reality" meant strong armies and navies for defense against foreign powers, or a strong system of national credit. His ultimate separation of himself from his idealistic associates, whom he termed "political empirics," finds expression in an important unfinished paper called "Defence of the Funding System" (about 1795), where he identifies the "true" politician as one who "takes human nature (and human society its aggregate) as he finds it, a compound of good and ill qualities, of good and ill tendencies, endued with powers and actuated by passions and propensities which blend enjoyment with suffering and make the causes of welfare the causes of misfortune." Afraid to warp this fundamental human complex by urging a happiness not suited to it, the true politician supposedly aims at the social measures designed to "make men happy according to their natural bent, which multiply the sources of individual enjoyment and increase national resources and strength." The great objective of the statesman should thus be to find the cement for compounding diverse elements of a state into a "rock" of national strength.

Governments would not need to be afraid to take power, Hamilton believed, could they strip themselves of false attitudes of modesty. In the logic of economic stability and national expansion, of credit and appropriations and "sound policy" versus the misguided pleadings of "common humanity," Hamilton saw an unanswerable imperative: to wit, that the "sacred" right of property must be defended by the laws and by the constitutions of the land, and that even the non-propertied groups in the community should protect property rights lest the "general principles of public order" be subverted.

John Adams, the self-styled "John Yankee" who could not bear to kowtow to "John Bull"—nor for that matter to any foreign power—seems more at home in Jefferson's and Madison's company than he is with Hamilton, the "boss" of his own party. Without Adams, the democratic precedent of the New England meeting hall, the training green, and the system of self-support for local schools, churches, and cultural institutions might have spoken only with muffled voice in the American tradition. The political "virtues" of Massachusetts even Jefferson commended, pointing to that state as the best exponent of the theme that knowledge is power. In Adams' championship of New England there is a nucleus of national pride useful and perhaps necessary to a rising nation. To this Adams personally added the dignified appeal that, however much republican government consisted of equal laws justly administered, it further required consistent benevolence and encouragement for the arts and sciences. Almost a humanist but never quite freed of a Puritan sense of guilt and sin, Adams privately reveled in the classics just as Jefferson did. The late correspondence which flourished between the two aged statesmen as they enacted the roles of sages in retirement, with great éclat, is a phenomenon of tireless learning and peppery jest, joined in a correspondence the like of which is not known in the annals of American statesmen.

5

Such were the philosopher-kings of the American Enlightenment. However often they may have erred—in description, in prognosis, in emphasis, and sometimes in behavior as statesmen—they seem to have possessed that rare wisdom about human and political affairs which never quite exhausts its power to suggest. On occasion, it restores its own original vitality and suffices to sanction an important change in national or international policy. We know that in the curious reversals of history, the truths of an age are likely to suffer sea change. As Lincoln pointed out, the maxim "All men are created equal," once thought a self-evident truth, is termed a "self-evident lie" once we have "grown fat, and lost all dread of being slaves ourselves." So it may be with the far-ranging insights and veridical principles of the philosopher-statesmen of the Republic. Since the advent of the Jacksonian age—a "calamitous" Presidency in Madison's prediction—the objectives of tempered democracy have been often ignored or ingeniously misinterpreted. As the letters and state papers of the Republican era again come under review, it is apparent that democratic ideology can still benefit by its own very articulate original. The foundation of our national literature is present here, in the practical literature of ideas, as well as in the imitative experiments of the deliberately "literary" work of the day.

13. POETS AND ESSAYISTS

THE writing of the pamphleteers and of the philosopher-statesmen thus frequently rose to the level of literature, but it did not satisfy the demand for a national expression in that first of the arts. Independence to be complete, declared the poet-politician Freneau and many another young man, must produce for America its own Miltons and Addisons and Swifts, its Popes and Goldsmiths and Wordsworths. The times that tried men's souls demanded iron purpose, tempered to the single task of creating the framework of a strong republic; but the coming of peace brought the need and the desire for fuller expression of the national "genius."

Here was a paradox: On the one hand, patriotism demanded a national literature; on the other, the urgency of events made its creation seem an idle and unworthy occupation. The difficulty, of course, lay in the sophistication of art developed by the English neo-classical writers and as yet unsuccessfully challenged by the romantics. The standards and forms for the epic, the pastoral, the novel, the essay, the comedy, the tragedy, which had evolved in the self-conscious literary atmosphere of eighteenth century London, could not easily be bent and stretched to contain the ideas and the experiences of the young republic; yet bent and stretched they must be if that republic were to have a literature of its own. Imitation of established or current literary modes contended therefore with the unruly spirit of nationalism during the first half-century of independence in an effort to create overnight an American literary tradition.

Young men all over the new nation fumbled for words to explain themselves and the busy tumult about them. None were more active than the group in Connecticut, known as the "Hartford Wits." But practical considerations often sprawled into the path of literature. John Trumbull would have liked nothing better than to be allowed to become a man of letters, an "American Swift," the sting of whose satire reminded contemporaries of their comic inadequacies. Couplets came easily to him. He liked the tone of Prior and Churchill, the quick cantankerousness of Pope. Such satirical pose allowed him to correct without seeming pontifical, to flick incisive little wounds into complacency and pretense:

Were there no fools beneath the skies,
What were the trick of being wise?

He could do this kind of thing rather better than he could write seriously in the mood of Milton or Gray, though the notebooks in which he experimented privately indicate that he did not easily convince himself of his own limitations. It was gratifying to be admired, as he was admired, to be compared publicly with Pope, applauded as equal to Samuel Butler and Jonathan Swift. But the young man was also a Trumbull, with reputation to maintain and his way to make in the world. Satire, even when good-naturedly modulated, hurt people, and people who were hurt turned in anger. Their humorless opposition made difficult, perhaps impossible, the road to judgeship and political renown which a sensible young man should follow.

The lesson was learned early, when Trumbull's sprightly, but corrective essays, first called "The Medler" (1769–1770) and then, less truculently, "The Correspondent" (1770–1773), led him into controversy. It was learned most pertinently when *The Progress of Dulness* (1773) landed him in the midst of distressingly public quarrels. Today the poem seems innocently amusing, well worth an evening's reading. There is good humor behind Trumbull's probings into the aspirations and hapless adventures of the dullard ministerial student Tom Brainless, of the fop Dick Hairbrain, and of the modish young belle Harriet Simper. Idiosyncrasies of manners, dress, and education, religious bigotries and reading habits are dissected with such impish skill that we chuckle as we remember similar small absurdities among our own neighbors. We recognize Tom, Dick, and Harriet as ancient literary types, long familiar in England, but livened by Trumbull's deft wit into characters whose foibles seem distinctively American. The author's contemporaries read more knowingly into the poem to discover local men or favorite local institutions impiously ridiculed, and they struck back at him viciously in print and with ominous threats of violence. He replied manfully, denying what he could of personal intention, but affirming the satirist's traditional responsibility to expose incompetence and dishonesty wherever he found them.

Such undignified public wrangling certainly could not be permitted to continue. Little was accomplished, except that a young man's career was jeopardized. Thus Trumbull learned to soften his stroke: his next, and most popular, satire, the Revolutionary *M'Fingal* (1776), was so cautious in ridicule both of Tory and of Patriot that it could be reprinted in London without apparently causing a ripple of comment. Perhaps Honorius, who ranted pompously at the town meeting with which the poem opens, was intended to represent John Adams, with whom at the time Trumbull was studying law; certainly no such satirical intention could be openly expressed. *M'Fingal* is effective burlesque of the bombastic oratory of the early Revolution; it is ironical in analysis of Tory argument, but is not pitched in a key calculated to incite vacillating men to action. Even in 1782 when Trumbull lengthened the poem, he reached his now more strongly patriotic climax only with the tar-and-feathering of Tory M'Fingal and the ignominious hoisting of his ally, the constable, to the "sublimest top" of a liberty pole. The verse is competent, objectively humorous, sometimes quotable:

> No man e'er felt the halter draw,
> With good opinion of the law.

Such moderation helps explain the enormous post-Revolutionary popularity of *M'Fingal,* which went through some thirty editions and was frequently quoted in political campaigns and school readers during the next half-century. Avoiding extremes, it became a well of good-tempered ridicule into which later countrymen of whatever political persuasion could dip for aptly phrased commentary on affairs of their own times. John Trumbull seems to have been little moved by the American Revolution: he viewed it dispassionately, not quite as a disinterested spectator, but as one who allowed himself neither shrill cries of triumph at patriot successes nor thunderous encouragement when victory seemed remote. *M'Fingal* is the least topical of Revolutionary satires, and the best worth reading. We may overlook its literary debts to Swift and Butler, accept its impertinent burlesque of Virgil and Milton, forget even the minor position to which it must be assigned in the history of the English mock-epic, and still enjoy what it has to say of our ancestors and, obliquely, of us.

Though by 1782 Trumbull had virtually abandoned literature for a more respectable career as a jurist, his influence remained pervasive among contemporaries in New England. As tutor at Yale until 1773, he had led friends and students to an examination and imitation of modern English authors—to Addison, Pope, and Milton. "I have learned more about English style from Jack Trumbull," said one of his students, "than from any other man." David Humphreys probably expressed the opinion of many of his Yale friends when he playfully blamed the "ill company" which he kept with Trumbull for having induced him to "turn scribbler." Trumbull's was a witty and intellectual leadership which appealed to young men. When he looked forward to the literary future of America in his *Essay on the Uses and Advantages of the Fine Arts* (1770), he struck a spark which glowed to fine imitative fire among his younger friends:

> This land her Steele and Addison shall view,
> The former glories equall'd by the new;
> Some future Shakespeare charm the rising age,
> And hold in magic charm the listening stage.

It was not for lack of trying that Trumbull's protégés failed. Literature to them was the hallmark of superiority, a method of instruction whereby men who knew the way pointed it clearly to their less fortunate fellows. Such a guide was David Humphreys, whose armload of solid volumes taught industry and patriotism and humble recognition of the wisdom of one's betters. Such, too, was Timothy Dwight, who grew to be one of America's giants, created in the image of his own honest ambition. One of Yale's great presidents, a teacher whose solidly authenticated theological doctrines spread through all the expanding young country from the close-written notebooks of his students, he became an oracle whose voice inspired no one so greatly as himself. People like his brother-in-law, William Dunlap of New York, who read William Godwin and wrote plays, found him narrow and censorious. They called him the "Protestant Pope of New England," but they squirmed under the confident vigor of his disapproval.

At nineteen Dwight conceived a poem, an epic of high moral purpose which would combine the sublimity of Milton and Fénelon with more modern notions of what a great poem should be. Its rhyme would be the heroic couplet of Pope's Homer. Its theme would be Biblical—Joshua's hard-won entry to the promised land. When fourteen years later *The Conquest of Canaan* (1785) appeared, readers had little trouble convincing themselves that patriotic analogy was intended, that Joshua was Washington, and that other American heroes strode thinly disguised through its eleven tedious books. "He who would learn," suggested William Cowper in England, "by what steps the Israelites possessed the promised land, must still seek his inspiration in the Bible." Another Englishman, Thomas Day, whose *Sandford and Merton* was a best seller on both sides of the Atlantic, defied "the most resolute reader to wade through" Dwight's poem "without yawning an hundred times." The elements so storm in sympathetic energy with the martial strivings of its heroes that Trumbull suggested it be provided with lightning rods. In it also, says the best and most sympathetic of Dwight's critics, stalwart eighteenth century Americans with Hebrew names talk like Milton's angels and fight like prehistoric Greeks.

After 1785 Timothy Dwight left literature almost as completely as did John Trumbull. His single subsequent trial at belles-lettres was a charming bucolic and didactic poem called *Greenfield Hill* (1794), which represents the landscape and the people of a small Connecticut village. The scene is perhaps less familiar to one who knows New England than to one with some acquaintance among the poets of England. Lines are so admittedly imitative of Beattie, Dyer, Gray, Goldsmith, Thomson, and Pope that any reader, if he pause at all over the poem, may simply hold in one hand a copy of, say, *The Deserted Village* and, with *Greenfield Hill* in the other, completely deflate Dwight as a creative artist. He was not essentially a creative artist:

he was a moralist, a powerful and successful teacher, a righter of great wrongs. With a practical job to do, he did it effectively by taking what he could where he could find it. Yet the America of his day, with his concurrence, accepted him as one of her principal men of letters. The fault was as much with America as with Dr. Dwight.

As a moralist, Dwight was most persuasive in his sermons, where he could undisguisedly correct to his own pattern. He is strongest in protest, as in *The Triumph of Infidelity* (1788) which attacks what Dwight interpreted as the influence of Voltaire in America. It is a bitter and a coarse poem, published anonymously and never, even in the face of public accusation, acknowledged by Dwight. As a clergyman, he was fond of talking of the "Duty of Americans," "The Genuineness and Authenticity of the New Testament," and "The Nature and Danger of Infidel Philosophy," and he simplified, explained, and defended his theology in a series of sermons delivered to many college generations at Yale. Outsiders found him an autocrat who talked so much they could get no word in themselves. He puttered every day in his garden for his health's sake, and he spent the long college holidays exploring byways of northeastern America. His wanderings are recorded—where he had been, what he had seen, what needed correction—in a journal which, published as *Travels in New-England and New-York* (1821–1822), preserves not only delightful pictures of countryside and people but also a candidly revealing self-portrait of its author.

Other men from Yale turned in other directions. Younger than Trumbull and Dwight, Joel Barlow grew in New England under the influence of both until search for livelihood took him to Europe. There, always impressionable, he found in new masters exciting new sources of enthusiasm. He was to move familiarly among the liberal political circles of Horne Tooke, William Godwin, and Joseph Priestley, to absorb the intoxicating doctrines which promised rights to all men. He would advise with Lafayette on the future of France, with William Hayley on the future of poetry, or with Mary Wollstonecraft on the future of women. Futures fascinated him, and he overflowed with optimistic good talk. His friends remembered him as "so far gone in Poetry, that there is no hope of reclaiming . . . him."

As one of the international gadflies attracted by the bright promise of the French Revolution, Barlow joined in the attack on Edmund Burke, until that stout-hearted statesman brushed him off contemptuously as "Joel the Prophet." His *The Conspiracy of Kings* (1792) unleashed a young man's best store of conventionally rhymed invective against the designs of scheming and undemocratic men. Less heatedly, his *Advice to the Privileged Orders* (1792) defended in prose the superior claim of human rights over property rights and sounded the revolutionary's traditional warning that a better day must dawn. Fox applauded the pamphlet in Commons, but the Pitt ministry ordered it burned and the author arrested. Thereafter, like his friend Paine, Barlow became a marked man, for people were attracted by his simple logic and paused to think—nothing seemed more dangerous. The French Assembly voted him an honorary Citizen of the Republic. But friends in New England were shocked: they wished there were some way to "relieve him of his enchanted castles"; Barlow's brains, they thought, needed settling. Sober Noah Webster could not understand what maggot gnawed at his old schoolmate. John Adams considered even Tom Paine "not a more worthless fellow."

Before this, as a young man at Yale, Barlow had also conceived an epic. He hurried it to completion as *The Vision of Columbus* (1787), in nine rhapsodic books which told of the past, but particularly of the future of the brave, new American world. A young man's poem, and choked with little of the pedantry of Dwight's epic, it nevertheless breaks down in spite of—or perhaps because of—its breathless verve and easy patriotism. Barlow had dashed off page after page at single sittings, and neither his imagination nor his control of verse was equal to the strain. Yet failure in poetical technique and confusion of thought never quite dull the *Vision's* assertive enthusiasm. Foreshadowings of Barlow's later and less restricted notions of human freedom are there, sufficiently submerged beneath conventionalities to allow his conservative friends to greet the poem with hosannas of loud praise. That more precise critics in England found it pretentious, as they found Dwight's epic pretentious, was unimportant; that critics in England noticed it at all was a sign of success.

Within a year after publication of the *Vision,* Barlow had left New England to become the apostate whose change of political coloration increasingly distressed old friends. He poured out his heart in long letters to his young wife, as he was to do every time they were separated during the next thirty years—in letters which Ruth Barlow faithfully preserved and which re-create today an idyl of married love which is, quite inadvertently, among the finest monuments of her husband's career. There is humor and playfulness in Joel Barlow, sincerity, and a great fund of often completely impractical idealism. Homesick for New England and corn-meal mush (though he detested the word), he composed the mock-epic *The Hasty Pudding* (1796), a completely American adaptation of an ancient gastro-literary theme, and a poem so admired by anthologists that it sometimes promises to be all that remains of Joel Barlow.

Barlow developed into one of the most cosmopolitan and useful Americans of his generation, Minister Resident to Algiers, Ambassador to France, adviser and confidential friend to Jefferson and Madison. He worked with

Fulton on the steamboat; thrilled to the promise of the age of canals. As he grew older his enthusiasms were more controlled, but he never lost them. Nor did he ever forget the epic which had not been exactly right as he first presented it. When he had mulled over it for twenty years, it was ready again, rewritten and expanded for second publication as *The Columbiad* (1807), and heralded by public fanfare such as no American book had received before. It was a beautiful volume, a credit to American printers and bookbinders, a collector's item enhanced by engravings from his friend Robert Fulton. It is better articulated than the *Vision,* more mature and more correct in versification; but *The Columbiad* is best known today as one of America's great failures, the book nobody reads, the tin-plated epic.

The tragedy of Joel Barlow is not that he is not remembered, but that he is remembered for the wrong thing. Every textbook pauses for a paragraph to review the epic failure of *The Vision of Columbus* and *The Columbiad.* Few remind us of the armor of bright prose with which this early American Lochinvar girded himself as he crusaded for doctrines which never quite spread from the new Western world. Like Timothy Dwight, Barlow was a greater man than his writings ever reveal him. Like too many others of his time he still awaits the biographer who will detail his sincere and wholehearted small contribution to the articulation of democratic thought.

These three—Trumbull, Dwight, and Barlow—are traditionally listed as outstanding among the larger group, variously called the Hartford Wits, the Yale Poets, or the Connecticut choir. There were others: Humphreys for the bulk of his earnestly patriotic verse is sometimes admitted as a fourth; Richard Alsop, Noah Webster, Lemuel Hopkins, Mason Cogswell, and Theodore Dwight, to list them in an arbitrary, rough order of excellence, were the principal remaining members—not to forget the younger Elihu Hubbard Smith, never completely of their company, who extracted from them generously when he edited our first all-American anthology in 1793. The aim of the Wits was chiefly political and remedial: in one combination or another they produced *The Anarchiad* (1786–1787), *The Echo* (1791–1805), *The Political Greenhouse* (1799), and other serviceable satires directed against the absurdity of anyone disagreeing with solid, New England views. Such barbs more often than not found tender marks and called for retaliation, until the acrimonious exchange produced some of the most readable, if not the most refined verse of those times. It was a rough-and-tumble battle of poets with shirt sleeves rolled, the effects of which lasted long enough for Fenimore Cooper half a century later to throw his weight in satire against the New Englanders, not realizing perhaps that another man of letters from the Middle States, Philip Freneau, had already done the job very well indeed.

2

"The writings of an aristocratic, speculating faction at Hartford, in favor of monarchy and titular distinctions," wrote Freneau, "are sufficient to convince any candid person that the old *insular* enemy to independence and prosperity in America has her hired emissaries at work in that part of the union." The Wits, he continued, openly profess the same principles as the "old, defunct Tories of 1775." His statement, of course, was not quite true, but the men of Connecticut had found in this hard-bitten veteran an opponent who could stand to them blow for blow. Freneau represented, as did the apostate Joel Barlow, the democratic principles of Jefferson, even of Thomas Paine. Therefore he was an enemy, subject to attack as a party tool and, in contrast to the epic poets of New England, a "mere writer for newspapers": by others far less original than he, he was ridiculed as an imitator, a plagiarist. Literature had so become the handmaiden of politics that, "amidst the mutual clamours of contending parties, not one reader in a thousand cares three cents about the literary honour of his country."

It was not, as James Madison said more pointedly, the time for poetry. Nor perhaps could it be expected to be. Men in leather aprons rose early to insure expansion of American commerce; hands toughened at the plow were raised in committee room or assembly; come-uppers were coming up, and there was no time for dallying. Literature was for ladies, for clergymen with leisure, or for young men who had not yet found more proper and productive work. But America had then among her young men one poet whose talent, caged within the utilitarian necessities of his times, was allowed frequently to beat itself to doggerel. Might-have-beens have no place in literary history, but the early promise of Philip Freneau, displayed in the Keatsian insight of "The Power of Fancy" (written in 1770) and the philosophic searching of "The House of Night" (written possibly in 1775), foretold achievement which could have placed him among our greater poets. Even thwarted, he developed the most original, though not consistently original, poetic voice of his generation. He sang of American men and American achievements, of his fine hope for America, and of the bitterness of his disappointment that she seemed so often to fail. He had none of the mellow inclusiveness of Walt Whitman, and he wrote more often in anger than in understanding, but not before Whitman was his country to produce a poet more completely or more devotedly her own.

As a young man at Princeton Freneau had also written prophetically of the future of his fair Western world. With his classmate Hugh Brackenridge he composed *A Poem on the Rising Glory of America* (1772) as a commencement piece which, like Trumbull's, looked forward to more than a march of material progress.

> I see a Homer and a Milton rise
> In all the pomp and majesty of song, . . .
> A second Pope, like that Arabian bird
> Of which no age can boast but one, may yet
> Awake the muse by Schuylkill's silent stream, . . .
> And Susquehanna's rocky stream unsung, . . .
> Shall yet remurmur to the magic sound
> Of song heroic.

This was not only a schoolboy's poem of optimistic augury. It was the personal dedication of a young poet, steeped in the lore of his calling. Freneau would be a poet, and he would sing a clear new song. Where are the glories of yesteryear? he asks in "The Pyramids of Egypt."

> —all, all are gone,
> And like the phantom snows of a May morning
> Left not a vestige to discover them!

Vast and unexplored, filled with promise such as the modern world had never known, America would be his theme, she and the opportunities she offered for fulfillment of the ideals of which great poets had always sung. An apprentice to the art of these, his masters, Freneau soon developed his own elastic lyric idiom which, avoiding much of the stereotyped pattern of his contemporaries, contained echoes of young Milton and promise of young Keats. Thus at eighteeen he invoked his muse in "The Power of Fancy":

> Wakeful, vagrant, restless things,
> Ever wandering on the wing,
> Who thy wondrous source can find,
> Fancy, regent of the mind; . . .
> Come, O come—perceiv'd by none,
> You and I will walk alone.

This was the kind of poetry for which busy America could make no room, and it was what Freneau most wanted to write. Nevertheless, when revolution broke over America, he dutifully put poetry behind him, though not without hesitation and false starts, to enlist his talent for rhyming in the shrill war of words which played accompaniment to military and political maneuverings. Mercurial, sensitive, quick to speak in anger, Freneau in his satire showed neither the moderation of John Trumbull nor the infectious good humor of Francis Hopkinson. He spat derisively at every enemy, whether among the faint-hearted in America or among the false-hearted abroad. He wrote jubilant songs on patriot victories, spurred laggard spirits when defeat seemed most certain, and denounced the "gorged monsters," "infernal miscreants," "foes to the rights of freedom and of man" who "spare no age, no sex from lust and murder." He became the authentic "Poet of the American Revolution," who wrote of what he had known at first hand as a militiaman, of what he had suffered in his poet's pride as a prisoner of war. With the memory of his experience hot within him, he wrote *The British Prison-Ship* (1781), as intensely bitter a poem as America has ever produced. He called on his countrymen to "glut revenge on this detested foe" which pants "to stain the world with gore." Banish them forever. "Defeat, destroy and sweep them from the land." Then only might America be free for, among other things, the kind of poetry which Freneau wanted most to write.

This hatred for England, bred of his war years, colored the rest of Freneau's life and his literary production. What had been America's crime, except that she had raised her arm to stay an assassin's knife? Pride, greed, lust, avarice, each cruelty which kept mankind in chains was exhibited by that same land from whose poets he had drawn his early poetic vision. As the Revolution dragged through its last weary phases, Freneau, now editor of the *Freeman's Journal* in Philadelphia, found it necessary to combat not only the foreign tyrant but new tyrannies of compromise with and imitation of England which appeared within his own country. Drawn ever deeper into petty quarrelings, he became increasingly disillusioned. How many fine sentiments were on people's lips, how few in their hearts! With what faint courage men of letters in America faced their future! He ridiculed David Humphreys who seemed sycophant in seeking literary honors, just as he later ridiculed Washington Irving for seeking reputation abroad. Would America ever be truly independent of England?

> Can we ever be thought to have learning or grace,
> Unless it be sent from that damnable place?

One of Freneau's unique characteristics was complete sincerity in meaning exactly what he said. His were no catchwords designed to rouse the rabble to defense of special privilege. He had learned to speak plainly, in simple idiom, of simple things which common men understand, about things like liberty and the right of every man to happiness. When, after ten years of patriotic satire, he retired from controversy in 1785 to become a sea captain plying between New York and Charleston, he avoided the grandiose schemes, the epic attempts which had attracted him as a collegian. He turned to simpler subjects, less traditionally poetic—to rugged, unpretentious themes like "The Virtue of Tobacco," "The Drunken Soldier," "The Pilot of Hatteras," "The Roguish Shoemaker," and, best loved of all, "The Jug of Rum." He wrote of "the red-nosed boy who deals out gin," "the quack that heals your negro's bruise," the ranting evangelist, native Americans all, "who did as they pleased and who spoke as they thought." No poem was very long, none very serious, and all were greatly popular among men who read their newspapers quickly.

Here was what America seemed to want, simple songs of American things, in stout American idiom, brightened with humor which recognizes even its own shortcomings. No moth-wing aspiration here for the sentimentalist, no learned claptrap for the intellectual. These were clearly stamped as of domestic origin, songs of and for the people. The pity is that the more finely wrought poems that Freneau produced during these busy years were unrecognized and virtually unread. In England Sir Walter Scott purloined a line from the elegiac stanzas "To the Memory of the Brave Americans" who fell at Eutaw Springs; Thomas Campbell took another from the contemplative "The Indian Burying Ground." But "The Wild Honey Suckle" (1786), which surpassed them all, was seldom reprinted during the poet's lifetime. The tone of muted wonder and the fresh clarity of diction which here consider the "frail duration" of beauty amid American swamplands place Freneau chronologically at the head of America's poets. Burnsian it is, and written in the year which greeted the Kilmarnock edition of the Scotch poet; Wordsworthian, too, and twelve years before *Lyrical Ballads*. America cannot afford to forget "The Wild Honey Suckle," for here at last were fused the two elements of native scene and native expression, and here, too, was poetry.

Moods productive of poetry were seldom allowed to Freneau again. When principles for which the American Revolution had been fought seemed threatened and democracy held in contempt among his countrymen, he emerged once more as a partisan propagandist who lashed out courageously, even boisterously, to defend rights of the common man, the poor soldier fleeced of his earnings, or the farmer crowded to poverty by greed of industrialists. Hard-headed and sharp-tongued, he became the first powerfully effective crusading newspaperman in America, and lost, as editor of the *National Gazette* (1791–1793), much of his reputation as a popular poet. Plain people still understood him as he reduced national issues to their own plain language, but men in power struck back with blows that left permanent marks. Alexander Hamilton wrote him down publicly as a liar. Washington damned him as a rascal. The Wits of New England, when they could not withstand the logic of his argument, attacked him as a poet. But he saved our Constitution, said Jefferson, when it was "galloping fast into monarchy." Few men have done more, and with less reward. When defeat of John Adams in 1800 made the place of the common man seem at length secure, Freneau retired again, to the sea, finally to a "few sandy acres" of homestead in New Jersey, to rephrase, more quietly now, his tenacious convictions. He continued to publish volumes which sold poorly, or unnoticed verses in obscure periodicals, even after he was seventy; but America passed him by. Bryant remembered him only as "a writer of inferior verse . . . distinguished by a coarse strength of sarcasm."

Freneau's coarse strength can be better understood and better treasured today. His stubborn refusal to compromise seems even admirable, as he extended it to include "such rhyming dealers in romance" as Joel Barlow, who failed to forge their songs to the simple, democratic temper of America. As editor of the *Time-Piece, and Literary Companion* (1797–1798), Freneau had offered its columns for the display of poetical wares from his countrymen. And what had he received? Echoes of English verse, sentimental and saccharine, as beaux and bluestockings parried traditional compliments, prettily phrased and insipid. Where was American virility, the solid, self-assertive strong phrases in which a new country should sing herself to the world? Nothing was more popular than the limpid lines with which young Joseph Brown Ladd, as "Aroeut," addressed his fair "Amanda," or which Robert Treat Paine as "Menander" exchanged in Boston with the "American Sappho," Sarah Wentworth Morton, known to each reader of sensibility as "Philenia," the "warbling eloquence" of whose harp stirred such polite, such sad and sweet response. The air was filled with melancholy strains inspired by Goethe's *The Sorrows of Young Werther,* with liquid rhapsodies distilled from Ossian, with inconsequential nonsense hung—so spoke one critic—with "garrish ornament and tinsel decoration, which are necessary to satisfy expectation." Against this background, Freneau's unpretentious work stands out, homespun among faded satins, durable, woven of native fiber to a pattern adapted to native requirements.

Like his verse, Freneau's prose became progressively more indigenous. During the Revolution he had been satisfied with that stock figure of the eighteenth century periodical essayist, the learned hermit who surveys the world from a quiet, woodland retreat. The voice with which "The Pilgrim" (1781–1782) pleaded for simplicity or railed against bestial servilities of Englishmen was a deep-throated expression of Freneau's new-found national creed, but the words were old, and the mood and the setting. "Tomo-Cheeki, the Creek Indian in Philadelphia" (1795–1797), an unidealized American aborigine who found strange foibles among his white neighbors, represented an advance, but along trails already clearly marked by Goldsmith and Montesquieu; "Hezekiah Salem" (1797), the defrocked Yankee deacon who spoke variously and sometimes amusingly in ridicule of domestic eccentricities, was more genuinely a home-grown product; but most American of all was "Robert Slender." As first presented in 1788, he was a stocking weaver who liked to record sly observations on such things as young men in love, the frustration of garret-pent poets, or the peculiarities of American businessmen; but he grew as Freneau grew until, when resurrected in 1800 to comment on the upheavals which brought Jefferson to power, he had become a native type whose literary and political descendants have been numerous among us. He was the simple country boy, who knew nothing of affairs except what he read in the newspapers. His rustic interpolations and naïve misgivings, his optimistic assurance that everything must come out right are in the best tradition of American political burlesque.

Freneau's failure is most simply explained by his headstrong refusal to compromise his conception of a literature divorced completely from "that damnable place" which had threatened American liberties. He had few followers, no imitators, for he was not quite respectable. He was a radical who, even when right, went too far. He addressed the wrong people, and proper people scorned him. His strictures on the writings of contemporaries went unnoticed or were explained as grumblings of a disappointed man who prostituted his own talents to politics. His nativism thus became an undercurrent which was seldom to emerge during the next fifty years, and never in the pristine and unworkable state in which he conceived it. In person he was known as an opinionated gaffer, eccentric in insisting on smallclothes and cocked hat long after they were out of fashion. So also in poetry he refused the easy sentimentality which became popular in America. His stark and didactic idiom, founded on rational principles of human justice, seemed old-fashioned and harsh in the 1820's beside the smooth, more modern phrases of Fitz-Greene Halleck and Rodman Drake. His prose, for all its sturdy independence, was seasoned so strongly with reference to local events that it repelled all but the most expertly trained palates. Forgotten in his own time, too seldom remembered in ours, he left as his testimony:

> To write was my sad destiny,
> The worst of trades, we all agree.

This worst of trades attracted few experienced workmen. Almost everything presented as literature was apprentice work by young men who later in self-protection turned to other things. We read copybooks in which students painstakingly traced moods and themes in which other men had succeeded. Scott, Byron, Moore, even Gray and the older poets were eagerly read in America: in what better manner might young men write if they too wished to be read? "Piddling poetasters," their practical countrymen called them, and this they were, swaying sensitively, as young poets must, to every breath of influence. They sang of solitude, of broken harps, and of genius—how they liked the word!—allowed to wither unrecognized. Theirs were juvenilia beside which Freneau's simplest "newspaper verse" seems extraordinarily mature.

3

Americans were proud of their newspapers. What other country on the face of the globe could boast a larger proportion of readers? This was America's literature—she had no time for more. Almost every newspaper or short-lived magazine had its poets' corner, and had also its essayists dressed in motley patched with shreds of Addison, Swift, Goldsmith, or Johnson. Noah Webster's homely "The Prompter" (1790) was popular and inspirational. Brockden Brown's "The Man at Home" (1798) contained the first draft of scene and incident later to find place in his novels. William Wirt's "Letters of the British Spy" (1803) was panoramic in literary learning. Each was corrective, some were pointedly satirical. Thomas Greene Fessenden was "Christopher Caustic"; New York had its "Tobey Tickler," Boston its "Tim Touchstone," and Philadelphia its "Tobey Scratch-'em," all lampooning with the conventionalized audacity of their English betters. Following them came the Irvings and James Kirke Paulding who in *Salmagundi* (1807–1808) simply did so much better what had often been done before.

Satire was condoned as a useful occupation, but polite literature was something quite different. William Wirt inquired of St. George Tucker whether being known as an author would harm his legal reputation and seemed not at all surprised at the older writer's answer that it very well might. At best, what sensible men liked to call "scribbling" was what they also liked to dismiss as "an avocation of idle hours," something almost surreptitious, certainly anonymous, for one dared not acknowledge many hours idle. Only a few hardy souls attempted literature as a livelihood; and they failed, like Freneau, and like Brockden Brown who capped his brilliant brief successes as a novelist with hack work little above that of an almanac maker.

Fresh from brilliant journalistic triumphs in New England, Joseph Dennie was also resolved to make writing a profession. He was equally resolved to create a standard for native literature in no degree inferior to that demanded in England. In fact, to this young Harvard man the standards were the same. His own prose rang so true that Timothy Dwight could claim him as the "Addison of the United States, the father of American belles lettres." Hawthorne recalled him as "once esteemed the finest writer in America," and Irving began his career in the contagion of Dennie's influence. It was as "Oliver Oldschool," a precise and opinionated champion of tradition, that he first edited the *Port Folio* (1801–1808) in Philadelphia, just as it was as

"The Lay Preacher" who restrained American folly that he had made his earlier reputation. Like Freneau, he was contemptuous of the sentimental and the extravagant: "a childish taste prevails and childish effusions are the vogue." Unlike Freneau, he refused even by implication to accept inferior products just because they were linsey-woolsey from homemade looms.

A critic rather than a creator, Dennie himself produced little that recommends him to our day. His essays seem prim, crotchety, sometimes sophomoric. His humor is condescending. His occasional easy familiarity is that of a well informed superior who stoops self-righteously to instruct. Above all else, however, he did love literature and had a sound, sure taste when his prejudices allowed him to exercise it. He printed long extracts from his favorite English authors. He solicited original verses from Thomas Campbell. He recognized and helped promote the early promise of Leigh Hunt. He was the first American critic to notice Wordsworth. He spent charming hours with Thomas Moore, who contributed to the *Port Folio* and remembered his visits with Dennie as among the "few agreeable moments" of his American tour. He gathered young men about him, and many a fine, literary talk they had together. "Mr. Dennie," said Moore, "has succeeded in diffusing through his cultivated little circle that love of good literature and sound politics which is so rarely characteristic of his countrymen."

Someone like Dennie was necessary to America—after him came the *North American Review* (1815) and the flowering of literary New England. He helped draw together, bind up, and package for many generations a conception of literary purpose irrevocably tied in with politics and respectability: authoritative sanction was given for lifting the literary embargo against England; standards were reimported and the level of excellence set high. He supplied an atmosphere in which Irving could grow to favor and Cooper to favor and disfavor, in which Freneau could be disregarded and Bryant hailed as a fresh, clear American voice; which made it possible for Longfellow to flourish, and necessary for Emerson to sweep aside the debris of tradition in clearing a path for Whitman.

Not everyone was convinced: "Dependence is a state of degradation, fraught with disgrace; and to be dependent on a foreign mind, for what we can ourselves produce, is to add to the crime of indolence, the weakness of stupidity." But, for all the protest of Freneau or anyone else, literary independence was as unrealized by 1820 as when Trumbull had called for it half a century before. After Campbell published *Gertrude of Wyoming* in England, Rodman Drake rephrased in the twenties the old complaint:

> No native bard the patriot harp hath ta'en,
> But left to minstrel of a foreign strand
> To sing the beauteous scenes of nature's lovliest land.

14. THE BEGINNINGS OF FICTION AND DRAMA

The history of fiction and of the drama during this period runs parallel to that of poetry and the essay. Here too the impulse to produce an independent, indigenous literature vied with the natural tendency to carry on a distinguished European tradition.

The vogue of the novel, so pronounced in England during the latter half of the eighteenth century, was reflected in America by imported reading until about 1790. Then native authors began suddenly to write stories of their own in the three current British fashions: the sentimental (or domestic), the satirical, and the Gothic. The first to succeed was the sentimental. Its usual theme, seduction, not only permitted the discreet exploitation of thrills but lent itself to those moral lessons which made fiction acceptable. Thus William Hill Brown's *The Power of Sympathy* (1789), usually reckoned the first indubitably American novel, was designed "to represent the specious causes, and to expose the fatal consequences, of seduction . . . and to promote the economy of human life." This formal reassurance prefaces a story compounded of seduction, narrowly averted incest, abduction, rape, and suicide. The main plot tells of a young man who, upon learning that his sweetheart is really his half-sister (by a liaison), shoots himself—a copy of Goethe's *The Sorrows of Young Werther* lying on the table beside him. The secondary plot tells of an unprincipled Lothario who triumphs over the virtue of his wife's sister. The victim dies by taking poison. The diction employed by Brown is decorous to the point of obscurity, and the episodes are only obliquely described; but between the lines lie the very elements against which moralists were inveighing as likely to inflame the passions if not corrupt the heart. Still, the story was, as the title page made clear, "founded in truth." The secondary plot was so patently based on an actual case in contemporary Boston that Brown was prevailed upon to suppress his book.

Connecticut and New York soon received similar lessons—and thrills. Susanna Rowson's *Charlotte Temple* (London, 1791), one of the most popular novels ever written, relates the tragic experiences of a young English girl lured to New York on the promise of marriage, only to be abandoned there by her lover and to die in childbirth. Old-fashioned in its rhetoric, the story is nevertheless told with a sincerity and power that can be felt even today; and indeed the novel still sells. Like *The Power of Sympathy,* this narrative is based upon an actual history, that of Charlotte Stanley whose mortal remains (according to legend) lie in Trinity Churchyard under a tombstone now inscribed "Charlotte Temple." Whether as love story or as a moral emblem, *Charlotte Temple* has attracted millions of readers; it went through some 160 editions (many of them incredibly garbled) before 1860.

The Connecticut Valley also had its lurid fictional warning when Hannah Foster published *The Coquette* (1797). The novel closely followed the case of Elizabeth Whitman, daughter of a trustee of Yale College, who put her confidence unwisely in a "gentleman" speculatively identified by some as Aaron Burr and by others as Pierrepont Edwards, son of Jonathan Edwards. Her death in childbirth occurred at a tavern in Danvers, Massachusetts. In the novel the heroine (Eliza Wharton) is the victim partly of her own vanity and partly of the unscrupulousness of a glamorous military man. The narrative is quietly unfolded by means of letters, but the moral is inescapable, and Eliza's tragic end added to the mounting calendar of advice to young women.

All three of these novels are in the general stream of Richardsonian fiction in that they picture females in distress. Two of the three are told in letter form with a great deal of analysis of the "heart." All are at times heavily didactic in tone, but since the same lessons could have been conveyed by straight prose, it must be inferred that the authors preferred to be novelists rather than moralists. The quality of fiction they represent is not high. Settings are almost negligible, and dialogue sparse and generally inept. *Charlotte Temple* is the most touching as a story; *The Coquette* is the most finished as a novel; *The Power of Sympathy* is the most uncompromising as a tract.

2

The satirical novel was not so prolific as the sentimental, for its irony was disturbing to the Calvinistic mind, and its humor, often arising from sordid picaresque episodes, was objectionable. Yet the use of satire is one of the first signs of intellectual maturity, of the writer's consciousness of his art. Hugh Henry Brackenridge's *Modern Chivalry* may therefore be listed as among our more important achievements in the last decade of the eighteenth century. This massive work—as long as four or five average-length novels—was published in installments between 1792 and 1815. In outward form it is a picaresque or "rogue" novel; its intellectual core consists of a satire on bad government.

As a picaresque story *Modern Chivalry* contains many of the stock elements and devices of eighteenth century British fiction. Chief of these is the framework of roadside adventures experienced by a master and his servant—a parody, in effect, of Don Quixote and Sancho Panza. In *Modern Chivalry* the protagonist is a fifty-year-old Squire, Captain Farrago, who is described as a "peripatetic philosopher" engaged in a trip through Pennsylvania. His servant is the Irishman, Teague O'Regan, a blundering, conscienceless, irrepressible oaf who passes ingloriously from one ludicrous scrape to another, to be rescued and lectured (vainly) by his master on each occasion. Some of these scrapes are of a low order; on one occasion Teague tumbles into bed with a chambermaid, who resists his advances. When she screams for help, Teague manages, with what the author ironically calls presence of mind, to cast suspicion on a Presbyterian preacher. Urged to confess so that an innocent man should not suffer, Teague at first refuses; and he finally consents to do so only if the minister pays him "smart money": it "is a thankless thing to do these things free, you know."

But *Modern Chivalry* is no mere sequence of rogue incidents related for amusement. Teague is a walking embodiment of some of the ills of a raw republic, and his crude actions stimulate Captain Farrago's (i.e., Brackenridge's) analysis of governmental abuses. The author's basic intention was serious: he proposed to examine the state of American "democracy" as he had seen it in operation. For years a judge in Pennsylvania, he knew at first hand the rough politics of democracy; yet his point of view in *Modern Chivalry* is generally that of an objective observer.

Modern Chivalry has often been called a satire on democracy; but Brackenridge was not opposed to democratic government. Indeed he explains that to him it is "beyond all question the freest." His target in *Modern Chivalry* is not democracy itself but rather its incompetence and corruption. Teague is the fulcrum on which his satire turns. Crude and illiterate as he is, Teague is everywhere invited to assume positions for which he is totally unqualified except by a certain good-natured acquiescence. Had it not been for the interference of Captain Farrago, he would have become a preacher, a member of the Philosophical Society, and an Indian treaty maker. When on one occasion he disappears, the Captain not unnaturally fears that he will find him speaking in the Congress or lecturing at a university; but this time Teague is employed as an actor, a post for which he is as little fitted as any. Before he has finished, Brackenridge has touched satirically upon legislation, the practice of law, the ministry, higher education, the press, dueling, scientific research, political chicanery, and Jeffersonion economy. His general method is to show Teague in an incongruous situation from which he is somehow extricated by the Captain, and then to pass on to appropriate philosophical reflections regarding government and society.

But incompetence is only one of the threats to democracy; the other is corruption in high places. The untutored and arrogant masses are themselves vulnerable to exploitation from above:

> The demagogue is the first great destroyer of the constitution by deceiving the people. . . . He is an aristocrat; and seeks after more power than is just. He will never rest short of despotic rule.

Thus Brackenridge thrusts at Hamiltonian politics and at the excessive power of the courts. The "rage of mere democracy" and the aristocratic urge toward domination are the Scylla and the Charybdis between which a democracy must sail. "The great moral of this book," he concludes, "is the evil of men seeking office for which they are not qualified." It was this lesson—urged when the air was full of theories of the natural rights of man—which Brackenridge tried to teach his countrymen. To him liberty is neither an abstraction nor an inalienable right; it is something sought and worked for intelligently. Because he loved democracy, he became one of its sternest critics.

Brackenridge was a deliberate craftsman with a definite theory of writing and a calculating eye on his public. He set a high value upon clarity, and he quoted with approval Swift's injunction concerning style—proper words in proper places. Embellishment for its own sake he frowned upon, and he believed that the proof of good writing is "that when you read the composition, you think of nothing but the sense." Yet he enriched his own page with many an allusion to the Greek and Roman classics, which more than any modern models (excepting *Don Quixote*) influenced his writing.

At the same time he thought of himself as an American writer. Occasionally oppressed by his lonely existence in a western wilderness, he "sighed for the garrets of London," but he was in general reconciled to his environment, and he never became (like his contemporary Joseph Dennie) an outright Anglophile. Although he seldom referred specifically to American writers, he once asserted that English is better written in America than in England, and his own prose could stand comparison with most of the best that eighteenth century England produced. He said that he intended *Modern Chivalry* for "Tom, Dick and Harry in the woods"; but its quality was such as to appeal primarily to the intelligentsia. His was one of the ripest minds of the era. While the lady novelists were dispensing simple, serious lessons in morality for young folk, Brackenridge was teaching his fellow men how to be good citizens. His was the harder task. To it he brought not only the wisdom of observation but also his wide reading from Plato to Swift.

3

Charles Brockden Brown, exemplar of the American "Gothic," was the first of our writers to make a profession of literature and the first to approach the stature of a major novelist; few have failed of "greatness" by so narrow a margin. Powers, Brown indubitably possessed; his failure lay in his inability to focus and sustain them. His work drew praise from a wide diversity of other writers as well as from critics domestic and foreign. Shelley was fascinated by him; in the opinion of one of his biographers, "nothing so blended itself with the structure of his interior mind as the creations of Brown." Keats found *Wieland* "a very powerful book." Applause came from many other foreign writers, including Thomas Hood, Godwin, and Hazlitt. In America his gifts were recognized by Poe, Cooper, Neal, Dana, Hawthorne, and others. The scene depicting the maniacal frenzy of Wieland deeply impressed Whittier, who wrote: "In the entire range of English literature there is no more thrilling passage. . . . The masters of the old Greek tragedy have scarcely exceeded the sublime horror of this scene from the American novelist."

The common factor in most of the tributes to Brown is their recognition of his originality: there was no writer quite like him even among the contemporary pre-Romantics to whom he was in some ways akin. The nature of Brown's power eludes exact definition, but its property is to compel the reader's attention irresistibly not only to the exciting narrative but also to the gravity of whatever philosophical or moral problem is implicit in it—whether it be religious obsession (as in *Wieland*), criminology (as in *Edgar Huntly*), philosophic anarchism (as in *Ormond*), humanitarian reform (as in *Arthur Mervyn*), or marriage (as in *Clara Howard* and *Jane Talbot*). His fiction was outwardly sensational, yet no device for heightening the reader's interest in tense action—and Brown commanded Gothic devices—completely effaces the reader's awareness of his high seriousness as a student of mankind.

Brown took himself seriously too. He was a writer of great ambition—perhaps too much so for the good of his health. During his bookish boyhood and effervescent youth he conceived (partly under the stimulus of Elihu H. Smith and William Dunlap) the most grandiose schemes. He would write a trilogy of epics. He would analyze the basic causes of man's misery and propose remedies. He would serve the cause of perfectibility. He would classify all knowledge. He would found important magazines—on a scale suggested by the prospectus of one of them: "to extract the quintessence of European wisdom; to review and estimate the labours of all writers, domestic and foreign." He was in fact attracted by so many ideas that his work suffered from the dispersion of his energies. The air was full of liberal theories which he brought to his desk for eager observation. He was excited by ideas which he could not finally or fully endorse, yet he acquired the reputation of a radical, for in his fiction he discussed the most "advanced" theories: freer divorce laws, political rights for women, deistic religion, a more humane treatment of criminals, amelioration of the lot of the peasant class. Many of these ideas he probably first encountered in Godwin's *Political Justice* (1793), but even less than Godwin could he implement radical thought. He was less interested in machinery than in motives. He never devised a coherent program of reform because he lacked the final qualification of the true crusader, a dynamic urge to act. He remained a liberal Utopian dreamer, resting his hopes for mankind somewhat vaguely in the rule of reason, the rejection of the incubus of Calvinism, and an appeal to benevolence in the human spirit.

In *Wieland* (1798), his best novel, Brown seems to have used for his plot an actual case of murder committed under the influence of hallucination in Tomhannock some years before; but the tone, coloring, and motivation are his own. The action is laid in the environs of Philadelphia, where Theodore Wieland has lived in pastoral tranquillity with his wife and sister until events begin to play havoc with his delicately poised mental health. He becomes the victim of a religious melancholia and hears a mysterious "voice." Actually this voice is at first the voice of a wandering, experimental ventriloquist, Carwin, who uses his special powers some eight times altogether in situations ranging from the trivial to the tragic. Finally Wieland, far gone in a religious psychosis (for which Carwin's experiments are only partially responsible), hears a heavenly "voice" (not Carwin's this time) which commands him to slay his wife and children. This he does. He is prevented from extending his dubious benevolence to his sister Clara only by the intervention of Carwin, who calls upon him to "hold!" This command brings him back to reality; but his realization of his deed converts him into a "monument of woe," to be delivered from ineffable remorse only by death.

The story, despite serious structural defects, is intrinsically as well as historically important. On the derivative level, it is obviously Richardsonian in its presentation of a persecuted heroine (Clara) carrying on in the face of incredible difficulties. Gothic terrors beset her, for she lives in seclusion in a house architecturally ideal for nocturnal terrors. Yet these horrors take on a degree of reality because of the seriousness with which Brown treated—apparently for the first time in American fiction—a case of dementia. In addition there is a Faustian motif: the ventriloquist's chief trait is his appetite for knowledge, and he pleads that his "only crime" is "curiosity." His dismay in contemplating the tragedy that he in part induced may have given Mary

Shelley the idea for her Frankenstein. Says Carwin: "Had I not rashly set in motion a machine, over whose progress I had no controul, and which experience had shewn me was infinite in power?" *Wieland* derives its strength not merely from the exploitation of sensation, but from the blending of the Gothic method with philosophical, psychological, and moral implications to create a powerful, even if unbalanced, book.

Like his own Carwin, Brown had a vast curiosity. In *Ormond* (1799), as chaotic a book as he ever wrote, he presented a glamorous, superman-like villain with a high intelligence and a low opinion of bourgeois conceptions of good and evil. His principles he has absorbed in part through contact with the secret society of the Illuminati on the Continent. He scoffs at the conventions of marriage, religion, and private property. His conduct is commensurably extravagant and violent. Yet opposite this almost caricatured villain Brown placed Constantia Dudley, who seemed to Shelley "a perfect combination of the purely ideal and possibly real." In *Arthur Mervyn* (1799–1800) there is a serious study (with emphasis on civic responsibility) of the problem of yellow fever, which Brown had observed in epidemic proportions in Philadelphia. In *Edgar Huntly* (1799) he provided his country with its first detective novel. The story has thrilling moments, but its action is finally bungled. At the same time it reflects Brown's interest in the Godwinian theme of morbid curiosity and its relationship to crime. Its "cave scene" may have inspired Edgar Poe as a source for "The Pit and the Pendulum," and Cooper, who at first scoffed at *Edgar Huntly,* later imitated its author.

Clara Howard (1801), Brown's next novel, is relatively free from the violence of the preceding stories, being mainly a love story told with emphasis upon an ethical dilemma. *Jane Talbot* (1801) treats of the problem of a sensitive young lady who makes a loveless marriage although she has met her real affinity before the wedding. The problem is handled with a finesse that surprisingly adumbrates certain stories of Henry James. The relative quietness of these last two novels reflects Brown's awareness of the relationship between a writer and his public. He was a conscious craftsman. His first three novels had made him a reputation, but they had not sold well. In April, 1800, he wrote, "Book-making . . . is the dullest of all trades." When his brother suggested that perhaps the public would find more interest in novels less devoted to "the prodigious or the singular," he gloomily agreed, and he promised less extravagance and more emphasis on "daily incidents" of the sort that the public presumably cared for. Yet he never succeeded in becoming a popular writer, and indeed produced no novels after 1804.

A late eighteenth century novelist, Brown was inevitably influenced by foreign models, for American models were almost nonexistent. Yet he was keenly aware of his position as an American writer. Even as the author of Gothic fiction, he bravely attempted to use native materials. He prided himself on the fact that in *Edgar Huntly* he had opened new sluices of power:

> Puerile superstition and exploded manners, Gothic castles and chimeras, are the materials usually employed for this end. The incidents of Indian hostility, and the perils of the Western wilderness, are far more suitable; and for a native of America to overlook these would admit of no apology. These, therefore, are, in part, the ingredients of this tale, and these he has been ambitious of depicting in vivid and faithful colours.

Europe's example was to him by no means an unmixed blessing, for, he said in *Clara Howard,* "Our books are almost wholly the productions of Europe, and the prejudices which infect us are derived chiefly from this source." A substratum of American democratic thinking underlay his romantic theorizing and his moral speculation.

Without being overtly doctrinaire, Brown was unquestionably a moralist in his fiction: idea and scene coalesced to form art. His most sensational narrative episodes were the artistic counterparts of his philosophic probings into the causes of man's unrest. Even those of his characters who (like the protagonist in *Ormond*) were antisocial in act and creed revealed the basic problems of humanity. Final remedies Brown did not in most cases propose: he was not a "didactic" writer. He merely described the human tragedy with a skill great enough to enable him to produce many memorable scenes of high seriousness and compelling interest. Constantly interrupted by illness and the exigencies of business, he wrote rapidly during the time available to him, and he revised little. He rose brilliantly to heights of eloquence and as suddenly bogged down in bombast, bathos, or incoherence. Had he been able to sustain his flights, he might have been a great tragic novelist.

4

In this period the novel could experiment, with relatively few restrictions, but the drama suffered under enough handicaps and discouragements to founder any ordinary enterprise. Legal statute, clerical frowns, the exigencies of war, yellow fever, the copyright bogy—these and other factors operated to prevent the conception and hinder the growth of the American theater.

Moralists might indict the theater as the "House of the Devill," and lawmakers might legislate against it as contrary to the public good; but no amount of opposition could effectively stamp out a form of entertainment based on the virtually instinctive will to "make-believe." Not that the opposition ever capitulated completely or permanently—it was renewed, for example, during the Revolutionary War—but its severity was relaxed from time to time. At the end of the eighteenth century the American theater was pretty well established, but original American drama was far from arrival. Repertories were mainly foreign; it would have been folly to expect a native drama to compete with royalty-free plays such as *Richard III* or Dryden's *Amphitryon* or Farquhar's *Beaux' Stratagem.*

In the beginning, however, there was no thought of an American drama. To be sure, many Americans experimented with the dramatic form; but they had little hope of seeing their plays professionally produced. Out of some forty plays written prior to 1787 fewer than a half-dozen were even intended for production on the regular stage, although many of them were presented by amateurs. The first complete and unquestionably American play to be performed publicly and professionally was presented in 1767. Gradually more American writers entered the field, and between 1790 and 1820 the variety and vigor of native production was so great that our failure to bring forth a single great dramatist or a single great play is the more remarkable.

The first American play of record acted on the American stage was Thomas Godfrey's *The Prince of Parthia,* written before 1763, published in 1765, and produced at the "New Theater," Philadelphia, April 24, 1767. That the play was a tragedy was perhaps consonant with the prevailing sobriety of our national thinking at the time. That it was Elizabethan in pattern and Oriental in subject matter is not to be wondered at. The population of this country at the time was in effect that of Englishmen transplanted, but scarcely rooted, in a new land. Given the circumstances, it was natural for a playwright to utilize the tested and the universal rather than the new and the local. *The Prince of Parthia* is a reasonably good play. It tells of dark passions and violent action in the ancient and remote kingdom of Parthia. Epic enterprise and fierce personal tensions combine in melodrama sincerely conceived. Brother fights brother; father and son compete for the favors of the same woman; wife instigates the murder of husband—these are some of its bloody data. At the end the heroine, falsely told that her lover is dead, takes poison; it remains for the hero to dispatch himself on his sword. Plot elements and language from Shakespeare, and Beaumont and Fletcher, obviously inspired but did not completely dominate Godfrey's work. In *The Prince of Parthia,* tradition was put to good use by the first native American dramatist.

There was a good deal of interest in the drama during the Revolutionary War. The British, who were active in promoting it, converted Faneuil Hall for a time into a theater. Some plays were written, and a few of them remain as interesting mixtures of colonial art and politics. Tory views were sometimes dramatized, as in the anonymous farce *The Battle of Brooklyn* (1776 *)

* Except as noted, dates of plays are those of first production.

which lampoons General Washington and his officers. Notable among patriotic plays were Mrs. Mercy Warren's *The Adulateur* (published 1773), a satire on Governor Thomas Hutchinson, and *The Group* (about 1773), which bitterly satirized those persons who acquiesced in the abrogation of the Massachusetts charter. It is possible that Mrs. Warren also wrote *The Blockheads,* a coarse satirical answer to Burgoyne's satirical farce, *The Blockade,* which had been played in Boston in 1776–1777. These plays by Mrs. Warren and others are not of sufficiently high quality to command enduring interest, but they are reminders of the fact that the Revolutionary War was one of the factors responsible for the awakening of interest in the drama.

5

By the time Royall Tyler wrote *The Contrast,* the nation had emerged as an independent political unit; but its social pattern was still equivocal. *The Contrast,* the first American comedy to be presented in America, was performed at the John Street Theater in New York on April 16, 1787. It was and is an excellent acting-play. Its universally interesting theme of urban sophistication vs. rural naïveté had a peculiarly appropriate application in post-Revolutionary America, when the British, having lost political control, were still able to patronize us culturally.

The central situation in *The Contrast* shows an English cad maneuvering for the hand of a pure American girl while at the same time he is making dishonorable overtures to another intended as a "companion" to his wife. Of course he loses out ignominiously. The characterization of the "fashionable" elements in the dramatis personae is done with the authentic tone of a writer who knew his Sheridan—for *The Contrast* has much in common with *The School for Scandal*—but the prologue sounded a national note that was well sustained:

> Why should our thoughts to distant countries roam
> When each refinement may be found at home?

Patriotism was further emphasized when "Yankee Doodle" was sung during the performance. Beyond this, the action was made interesting to Americans by local references and the celebration of the American character. Colonel Manly's success in breaking up a sinister stratagem (and in his suit of the young lady he has saved from a Chesterfieldian fop) constitutes an endorsement of the American way of life in 1787. Our own social institutions must set the standards of individual behavior.

The success of *The Contrast* on the stage was probably due also to the adroitness with which Tyler manages his dialogue and to the introduction, for the first time on the American stage, of a fine example of Yankee rustic, Jonathan, whose combination of sturdy, though not inflexible, New England morality and childlike innocence makes for rollicking comedy, especially in the scene in which he unwittingly attends a theater and tries to carry out the foreign servant's instructions as to how to succeed in an amour. The play scene is almost worthy of Fielding, whose Partridge is a literary cousin of Jonathan. Jonathan's attempted amour ends in a rebuff which helps to clarify his thinking: "If this is the way with your city ladies, give me the twenty acres of rock, the Bible, the cow, and Tabitha, and a little peaceable bundling."

The Contrast was a lusty embodiment of American ideals in a play which, without pointedly ignoring English tradition, made its own way. Subscribers to its publication included, among other eminent people, George Washington and General Humphreys. Tyler also wrote other dramatic pieces, including a musical farce (a popular type at the time), but his fame as a dramatist remains vested in *The Contrast.*

The mixture of opportunity and handicap that confronted early American dramatists is further illustrated by the production of James Nelson Barker, who experimented with masque, domestic comedy, topical (political) drama, romantic comedy, and historical play. His *Tears and Smiles* (acted 1807), a sentimental comedy, reopens a vein which Tyler had mined profitably in *The Contrast,* with the foreign menace to our native institutions—this time French instead of British. Barker had "never even seen a Yankee," but at the request of the actor Jefferson he supplied Nathan Yank. The play was a moderate success. His next play, *The Embargo* (acted 1808), illustrates a current trend toward realistic political discussion. Its text has been lost, but when it was produced at "Old Drury" (the Chestnut Street Theater) in Philadelphia, a riot was instigated by those of the merchant class who objected to Barker's pro-administration bias. The drama was evidently becoming a social force to be reckoned with.

Barker's *The Indian Princess* (1808), the first "Indian play" written by an American and produced on the stage, told of the adventures of John Smith and Pocahontas, with perhaps less emphasis upon the dangers threatening Smith than upon the romantic love between Rolfe and the Princess, as well as among the lesser personnel. Realism was here no major aim of Barker. The outcome of events is happy: a conspiracy to kill the white men is quashed, and there comes (as Lord Delawar puts it) a "pairing time among the turtles." John Smith survives to envisage a time when "arts, and industry and elegance shall reign" in "this fine portion of the globe." Called a "melodrame" (a sign of increasing French influence on our theaters), *The Indian*

Princess is a light, actable play, with music and a masque added in deference to popular taste.

Superstition (acted 1824), Barker's most ambitious work, is a carefully wrought drama based on an aspect of the Regicide Judges' story, a very creditable early treatment of a theme later used by Cooper, Hawthorne, Paulding, Longfellow, and others. It is a sober and serious study of a solemn chapter in American history. If it fails to be really memorable, the reason is that Barker's derivative language was not quite equal to sustaining the mood in which the play was pitched.

Barker led an extremely active public life, and his plays form only one expression of his constant concern for the public good. He was no blind believer in an untutored democracy. He realized, as his use of the witchcraft theme in *Superstition* showed, the havoc that might be wrought by an "unthinking crowd." Yet he was basically American and republican. He was furthermore a proponent of an American theater even though he seems to have connived at manager William Wood's ruse of passing off one of his plays (*Marmion,* acted 1812) as by a British dramatist. Without being fanatically nationalistic, he staunchly did his part in building a native tradition in the drama. Compared with Tyler, he seems more earnest but less of an artist. Compared with Dunlap, he seems less significant by reason of the latter's more voluminous production and more intense devotion to the cause of the drama.

6

One of the most influential names in the earlier cultural history of America is that of William Dunlap. He fell short of genius in any single category, but he achieved distinction in several. Playwright, theatrical manager, painter, historian of the drama and of the arts of design, novelist, biographer, diarist, periodical writer, entrepreneur, he escaped the obscure fate of many men who have exhibited so much versatility. Called the Vasari of America for his services to painting, he might also be called the father of the American drama and theater. His devoted service to the drama was motivated by his conviction, "The rise, progress, and cultivation of the drama mark the progress of refinement and the state of manners at any given time and in any country." All the arts were having their troubles in America at the time of Dunlap's ascendancy, roughly from 1790 to 1820. When a man like John Adams could say, "I would not give sixpence for a picture of Raphael or a statue of Phidias," there was obviously much missionary work to be done. Dunlap objected to the practice of singling out the drama for attack. He believed that "the fine arts [are] all connected, and must stand or fall together . . . if the drama is injurious to a state, so are literature and the arts." As manager, designer, producer, and writer of plays, he exerted an influence which helped to elevate and stabilize the theater in a chaotic period. If as a writer he lacked imaginative powers of the first order, he was extremely useful to the young nation at a time when it greatly needed standards of taste and technique.

The plays Dunlap presented were both a reflection and a cause of conditions in the theater. As producer he responded to public demand; if he frequently presented Shakespeare, he also presented many of the mediocre plays of Kotzebue, that darling of the Continent as well as of the American theater about 1800–1805. But even in his partial concessions to public demand, he knew good taste and good technique even though he did not always exercise them. He himself wrote and adapted some sixty plays. If one failed to succeed, he could be ready with a new one in ten days to two weeks. He had the advantage of his own versatility; he could keep control of most of the production factors himself. First and last he experimented with many varieties of drama: comedy, farce, melodrama, tragedy, heroic plays, romantic drama, opera, domestic drama, and patriotic "spectacles" lying between drama and pageant. The scenes of his plays include America, England, Germany, France, Russia, Italy, and South America.

His first play, *The Father, or American Shandyism* (acted 1789), was a creditable but not really distinguished work written under the influence of *The Contrast.* Dunlap himself thought that the best of his plays was *The Italian Father* (acted 1799), for which he used as a model Dekker's *The Honest Whore.* Considered critical opinion now points to *André* (1798) as probably his best. It is a tragedy based on the last days of the British officer. Dramatic tension is established by a young American's attempt to save André out of gratitude for the latter's generous behavior to him. But General Washington, to whom young Bland applies, denies the appeal on the ground of patriotism. Complications arise when the British threaten to execute Bland's father (their prisoner) if André is hanged. Since the outcome of the action was known to the audience in advance, the success of the play depended on the power of Dunlap (and the actors) to invest the drama with high seriousness of mood and resourcefulness in episode. High seriousness the play does attain, but the action tends to crumble away into a diversity of separate scenes which, despite unity of time, fail to cohere. The blank verse in which the play is written is mobile and not without apt echoes of Elizabethan dramatists. The public did not greatly favor the play in its original form; but Dunlap thriftily revamped it and presented it as a patriotic spectacle with music. In this form, known as *The Glory of Columbia,* it was a commercial success. But as a dramatist Dunlap exhibited more craftsmanship than high art. To him the text, in any case, was only one of the elements upon which the prosperity of the theater depended.

All the factors of production and management interested Dunlap. He frequently inveighed against the star system, for he sensed the danger that playwrights would be guided by the whims of the star instead of the principles of sound, balanced drama. He studied the physical conditions of the theater as well as the use of appropriate sets and properties. He observed that an overlarge theater could affect a play adversely, for besides making it impossible for actors' facial expressions to be seen, it "requires an exertion of the actor's voice which destroys its melody, and renders variety of intonation impossible." He was extremely meticulous in working out details of staging, especially for Shakespeare. He once searched "several books" in order to find out what were the right banners to use for "the Britons under Cymbeline." His intelligent interest in the merging of the theater arts was exemplified when during a production of *Hamlet* he painted an interpretation of the play scene. Harassed by practical production problems and beset by the temptation to pander to the masses, Dunlap never really relinquished his high ideals.

As a producer-playwright Dunlap was not unduly concerned to stress American themes. Indeed he even queried "how far we ought to wish for a national drama, distinct from that of our English forefathers." He thought that the process of Americanization should be gradual rather than hasty and arbitrary, but in one sense he did wish the drama to be "national": he believed that most of the ills of the theater—which he attributed to the "necessities and cupidity of managers"—could be removed by a system of government patronage, citing in support of his view the experiences of Germany and France. Time and again in his *History of the American Theatre,* he reverts to this possibility of saving the drama. Perhaps such a system would have made his own career more tolerable, for he was in constant difficulties and went into bankruptcy at one time.

In his later years Dunlap had very little active connection with the theater, returning to painting and to miscellaneous writing for his somewhat precarious livelihood. In 1832 he produced his *History of the American Theatre,* a work which, despite evidences of hasty composition, remains a monument to a man who did more than any other one person in his time to promote the welfare of the American theater and drama.

7

During this period the novel fared better than the drama: Brackenridge's *Modern Chivalry* and Brown's *Wieland* probably reached a higher level of achievement than any of the plays that appeared. Yet for a long period the harvest is singularly meager in both forms. The familiar explanations of this condition are the lack of affinity between Puritanism and art, and the overinfluence of Europe. Probably the latter factor was the more deleterious. Puritanism was a direct deterrent, but it waned to a point at which it should have ceased to hamper a real artist. The influence of Europe, particularly England, was more subtle and pervasive, taking various forms. England provided us with a language and a tradition. With a ready-made literature at hand, was it not natural for us to defer our efforts? Long after we had won our political independence we remained, as Barker said, "mental colonists." A kind of provincial snobbery prevented many Americans from seeing such merit as there was in national productions. Certain critics, as he noted in the preface to his *Tears and Smiles,* had coined the opprobrious term "Columbianism" to apply to "every delineation of . . . American manners, customs, opinion, characters, or scenery. . . . They can never pardon the endeavor to depict our national peculiarities, and yet they will listen with avidity to Yorkshire rusticity, or Newmarket slang." Such an attitude was fostered by the British who, having lost the war, continued to belittle our cultural progress.

There were notable exceptions: John Howard Payne, for example, had a considerable success as an actor at Drury Lane, and his tragedy *Brutus* ran fifty nights in one season. Yet he was later to be the victim of "much prejudice" and "persecution" because of his American principles. During the first two decades of the nineteenth century an inglorious literary warfare was carried on between England and America. It was Irving's purpose in "English Writers on America" to allay this ill-feeling. He reminded England that it was beneath her dignity to attack us; and he bade Americans think indulgently of England as a "perpetual volume of reference." Yet perhaps it was unwise to seek to end this literary war by appeasing both sides. Perhaps it was necessary that we should fight for our literary independence too.

15. THE AMERICAN DREAM

WHILE the citizens of the United States were thus struggling to create a literature fitting to the assumed grandeur of the national destiny, the idea of America was becoming itself a part of the cultural tradition of Europe. As a state of mind and a dream, America had existed long before its discovery. Ever since the early days of Western civilization, peoples had dreamed of a lost Paradise, of a Golden Age characterized by abundance, absence of war, and absence of toil. With the first accounts of the New World, it was felt that these dreams and yearnings had become a fact, a geographical reality fraught with unlimited possibilities. The first navigators had landed, not on the rocky coast of the northern part of America, but in islands swept by balmy breezes, inhabited by natives of peaceful dispositions, living without toil or industry on the natural productions of a generous soil. Their nakedness, their disconcerting absence of shame, their simplicity seemed to indicate that in some incomprehensible way they had not been as much tainted by original sin as had the peoples of Europe.

From the very beginning travelers' relations provided an inexhaustible store of material and arguments in the great debate, opened since the early days of the Renaissance, between the enemies and the defenders of the European form of life. Critics of a society which was becoming every day more closely knit, more sophisticated and artificial, never tired of comparing the simple, virtuous, and "natural" life of the Indians with the complicated, restless, and greedy existence of civilized men. Undoubtedly Shakespeare had these people in mind, when he made the honest old Counsellor Gonzalo, in *The Tempest,* draw a picture of the ideal commonwealth he would establish in an island if he were "king on't":

> All things in common nature should produce
> Without sweat or endeavour: treason, felony,
> Sword, pike, knife, gun, or need of any engine,
> Would I not have; but nature should bring forth,
> Of its own kind, all foison, all abundance,
> To feed my innocent people.

This is the "soft primitivism" also found in the French poet Ronsard or in the story of *El Villano del Danubio* retold by the sixteenth century Spanish writer Antonio de Guevara or even later in Cervantes' description of the Island of Barataria under the rule of good Sancho. To a philosopher like Locke it offered a true image of a condition which had existed before personal property and compacts had laid the foundation of human society such as we know it, for then "all the world was America." But though neither Locke, nor Vico, nor Montesquieu intended to use their praise of the savages as an argument destructive of our form of society, such was clearly the purpose of the Frenchman Lahontan, in his *Dialogues between an American savage and the author* (1703), and to a lesser extent of Jean-Jacques Rousseau. Whether they intended it or not, these advocates of a more or less complete return to nature were the forerunners of some of our modern anarchists and communistic utopians.

Admirers of a harder form of primitivism also found abundant material in the travelers in the northern parts of America, particularly in the Jesuits' relations. The good Fathers were steeped in the classical tradition, and they were delighted to find in the Indians replicas of Greek and Roman exemplars of stoic and republican virtues. On the other hand, it is no less certain that Hobbes derived from travelers' accounts his unsympathetic reconstruction of the natural state of mankind. But such pessimistic views were exceptional; what prevailed was the picture of a boundless and generous land, preserved from the evils of our modern society, and it is significant that Thomas More in 1516 set a precedent followed by countless imitators in locating his ideal state of Utopia in the newly discovered world.

This dream of an Earthly Paradise was, of course, a mirage—but it was more; it was a revolutionary force, let loose in the Western world, because it proved that the whole of mankind had not been irremediably condemned by some inherent vice to toil, suffering, oppression, war, famine, and misery. Man's faulty organization of society and not man's nature was responsible for his unhappiness. America as an idea was already at work pointing the way in the never-ending and hitherto chimerical quest of happiness.

If it had not been confusedly felt that the New World held out a hope to the whole of mankind, the indignation against the atrocities committed by its European conquerors might have been less vehement. The first eloquent outburst of indignation came from a Spanish missionary, the famous Las Casas, as early as 1552. His *Brief Relation* was translated into English in 1556 and into French in 1579, and in the Latin original was circulated throughout Europe. It marked the beginning of a long protestation in the name of humanity against the use of unjustified violence and the enslavement of innocent peoples. It was the proclamation of the rights of the so-called inferior peoples, echoed again and again during the eighteenth century. From the very excesses of the conquerors rose a new conception of the right of conquest and the right of colonization.

2

The implication was clear: what our civilization had failed to accomplish would perhaps find its fulfillment in the newly discovered lands. This "infant world, still quite naked and at the breast" suddenly presented to a senescent world another chance, perhaps the last one, to build anew the city of man.

By the middle of the eighteenth century, despite the vogue of the primitivistic dream in literature, this view had become singularly definite. The American Indians occupied a larger place than ever on the stage, in poetry, and in works of fiction, and more than ever their simple and natural virtues were opposed to the corruption of civilized men. It was only too plain that any reform in Europe would entail an enormous effort, and that new structures could not be erected without destroying the buildings still sheltering a discontented society; but in America persecuted peoples could find not only a refuge but an opportunity to lay the foundations of a better society. This dream was not limited to the British colonies, for the French had attempted in Brazil and in Florida about the middle of the sixteenth century to establish such settlements. Whether the Jesuits had succeeded or not in doing it in Paraguay was a moot question among the philosophers. At any rate, it was known that the French Huguenots, after the Revocation of the Edict of Nantes, had found a refuge in New England, on the banks of the Hudson where the Palatines had joined them, in Pennsylvania, and in the Carolinas. New England as well as Virginia had been the subject of a considerable body of "promotion literature," intended to counteract the recital of the trials and sufferings of the first colonists.

Among the British colonies, Pennsylvania occupied a privileged rank. Even the wildest dreamers among the philosophers never entertained seriously any scheme which would bring man back to a stark state of nature. The real problem was to find a form of society which would enable man to preserve his native qualities while enjoying all the benefits resulting from his association with his fellow beings; and such was the formula proposed at the end of the century by Godwin in his famous *Enquiry concerning Political Justice*. But long before Godwin the French *philosophes* thought they had discovered such an ideal commonwealth in the "republic" of Pennsylvania. To a large extent, the propaganda carried on in Europe by William Penn, in order to attract desirable immigrants, was responsible for that impression.

Pamphlets and leaflets containing enthusiastic descriptions of the advantages offered to the colonists were printed in English, Dutch, German, and French and distributed among the would-be immigrants. The Quakers, themselves a persecuted people, had substituted purchase from the Indians for conquest by force; they were true republicans using the equalitarian "thee" and recognizing no man as their master; they were philosophers who had abolished all the artificial trappings of religion, and who worshiped God in their hearts. The noble Quakers inherited all the virtues of the noble Indians, and Voltaire could declare, in his *Lettres anglaises* (1734), that Penn had brought to this earth the Golden Age, hitherto believed an invention of poets but now existing in Pennsylvania. Thus was developed through the eighteenth century a semiphilosophical and semisentimental body of literature dealing with the good Quakers and culminating in the *Histoire philosophique des deux Indes* of Abbé Raynal, in which the author contrasted the humane and philosophical development of the republic of Pennsylvania with the atrocities committed by the Spanish, the Portuguese, and all the European nations in the course of their colonial conquests.

Even admitting that the British colonists had not succeeded in establishing everywhere the city of the philosophers, the fact remained that liberty in America was much more the result of conditions inherent to the soil than the product of reasoned efforts. Such was the conclusion reached in 1774 by the editor of the *Gazette de France,* the official journal of the Court:

> Those of our navigators who have studied this half of the Northern American Continent, maintain that an inborn love of liberty inherent to the soil, the sky, forests, and lakes prevents this still young country from resembling the other parts of the Universe. They are convinced that any European transported under this climate will be affected by this particular condition.

Whether through some providential design or, as Montesquieu and his disciples would have said, because of the "nature of things," the stage was already set for an unprecedented political experiment. During the earlier part of the eighteenth century, Voltaire and Montesquieu had represented England as the classic land of liberty. But Montesquieu himself had admitted that he had described not England as he had seen it, but England as it might be if the principles of the British constitution were integrally applied. American liberty, however, did not rest upon ancestral institutions and traditions; it was a new revelation, and as such it was described by Thomas Pownall, a former colonial governor and a friend of Benjamin Franklin, in his *Memorial addressed to the Sovereigns of America* (1783). It was a

New System of Things and Men, which treats all as they actually are, esteeming nothing the true End and perfect Good of Policy, but that Effect which produces, as equality of Rights, so equal Liberty, universal Peace, and unobstructed intercommunication of happiness in Human Society. . . . This is a Principle in act and deed, and not a mere speculative theorem.

This was the burden also of Crèvecœur's *Letters of an American Farmer* (first printed in English, then in French, and broadly circulated between 1780 and 1790), and of Thomas Paine, who came to Philadelphia to tell its citizens in January, 1776, that theirs was much more than a quarrel with the King of England:

The cause of America is, in a great measure, the cause of all mankind. Many circumstances have and will arise which are not local but universal, and through which the principles of all lovers of mankind are affected, and in the event of which their affections are interested.

To the enemies as well as to the friends of the Anglo-Americans, it appeared from the very beginning that from the Revolution would come answers to the problems affecting the future development of Western civilization. It was generally conceded by clear-sighted observers, even in England, that the revolt could not be crushed once for all by force. Sooner or later, the colonists would win their independence. Furthermore it would be utterly impossible to limit the conflagration, which would spread from the British colonies to the other colonies of the new world and to all European colonies, all over the globe. This meant the disappearance, or a deep transformation, of economic factors on which rested the economic structure of Europe. It meant the end of monopolies, of exploitation of colonies for the sole benefit of the metropolis; it meant also that the trade of all nations might enter hitherto restricted areas. It meant eventually the freedom of the seas and consequently the complete reorganization of international life.

This was clearly perceived in England and explains the exclamation of Horace Walpole upon hearing the "black news" of Saratoga: "Nothing will be left of England but the vestige of her grandeur." In France it was hardly less keenly felt by Turgot, Vergennes, and even such a liberal as Abbé Raynal, who dreaded the consequences which would follow the collapse of the colonial system.

Even more important and fundamental was the answer given to the social and political problem which had become acute during the eighteenth century and was simply the problem of government. Very different were the forms of government adopted by the former colonies; but all rested on the doctrine of popular sovereignty proclaimed in the Declaration of Independence and developed in the declarations prefixed to most of the state constitutions. The theory was not new, but the undertaking was unprecedented. It was an attempt to form a society in which essential natural rights would be preserved, and government from above be reduced to a minimum. Such a form of government was not to be granted by sage legislators more or less divinely inspired or by an impersonal state substituted for the monarch; it was to be determined by the decisions of the citizens, whose collective body constituted "the people." It cannot be said that all the implications of the initial expression of the Constitution, "We the people," were at first fully understood even by the philosophers. The Italian-born citizen of Virginia, Mazzei, had to explain to the French in 1788 that "the people" was not the rabble, but was constituted of all the inhabitants of the land. Mirabeau fought in vain to make the deputies in the National Assembly meet and proclaim the Declaration of the Rights of Man in the name of "the people." The old prejudices prevailed in 1789: the Deputies preferred "Nation" to "People" and the "French people" was recognized only in the preamble to the Constitution of 1793. Joel Barlow, friend and disciple of Jefferson, had to remind the French in particular and the Europeans in general in his *Vision of Columbus,* published in Paris in 1793, that the people was this

> fraternal family divine
> Whom mutual wants and mutual aids combine.

Condorcet himself, who, because of his efforts in favor of the rebels, had been made a "citizen of New Haven" with several members of the philosophical group gathering around Madame d'Houdetot, was puzzled to know how the will of the people could be ascertained and wrote to his colleagues of the American Philosophical Society of Philadelphia to inquire what mathematical computations would enable the Americans to have a true representation of the people. Despite these reservations, the magic words uttered in Philadelphia echoed, to quote Condorcet again, "from the Guadalquivir to the banks of the Neva." Enthusiasts like Lafayette hailed the beginning of "the American era," and Dr. Richard Price, Benjamin Franklin's old friend, could declare in 1785:

> Perhaps I do not go too far, when I say that, next to the introduction of Christianity among mankind, the American Revolution may prove the most important step in the progressive course of human improvement.

Even before the final success of the Revolution, its first repercussions were felt in Europe. Nowhere were they more direct and more instantaneous than in Ireland, where ever since 1763 the progress of independence had been anxiously followed. "Look to America," cried Grattan two months after Yorktown, and already, on June 14, 1782, Henry Flood had proclaimed in the Irish House of Commons:

A voice from America shouted to Liberty, the echo of it caught your people as it passed along the Atlantic, and they renewed the voice till it reverberated here.

This fervor reached its maximum in France. It has often and justly been pointed out that the French Revolution was in fact the daughter of the American Revolution. The French Declaration of the Rights of Man follows very closely the Virginia "Bill of Rights" of 1776. The American precedent was quoted in the National Assembly and in the different assemblies which vainly tried to establish a permanent regime during the ensuing years. If later Fench historians have attempted to trace the main principles of the Declaration of Independence to Montesquieu and Rousseau, it does not seem that such indebtedness ever occurred to the French contemporaries of Jefferson. Yet, as Chamfort, the French moralist, pointed out, Louis XVI had acknowledged the legitimacy of popular government and signed his abdication when, in February, 1778, he signed a treaty of alliance with the young United States. Almost a hundred years later, Lamartine, at the end of his career, was no less justified in declaring with poetical emphasis:

One would need the discernment of God himself to distinguish America from France after their respective causes had been fused together during and after the American Revolutionary war.

3

The fight for independence had been won and a stable government established through the countless efforts of obscure American citizens, but popular imagination is fond of heroes who seem to embody all the characteristics of a people and an epoch. From the Revolution emerged two towering figures, living symbols of the country they had created: George Washington and Benjamin Franklin.

The Virginia gentleman called by Byron, after the first abdication of Napoleon,

> the first—the last—the best—
> The Cincinnatus of the West,

enjoyed from the early days of the American Revolution an extraordinary popularity. He was celebrated in epic poems; he appeared as the main character in patriotic dramas; no novel dealing with the Revolution was complete without some episode in which he appeared as a stern, sad, reserved, dignified figure, a great man without personal ambition, entirely devoted to his country, at all times conscious of the tremendous responsibility he was bearing on his mighty shoulders.

To him young Alfieri, in Italy, dedicated one of his odes on America in December, 1781, and seven years later he repeated his tribute "Al chiarissimo e libero uomo il Generale Washington," in the dedication of his tragedy *Brutus*. In a gesture of defiance to the Tories, young Coleridge drank Washington's health in a public inn in 1792. The French volunteers who joined the Americans unanimously acknowledged in him a military genius of the first order. Frederick II was anxious to obtain information on his tactics. Berthier, who later was to become Napoleon's chief of staff, made it a point to visit all the places where the American general had fought, and drew elaborate maps of his battles. In him they saw an organizer who had revolutionized modern warfare by leading to victory against professional soldiers an army of volunteers without any military training, poorly armed, without uniforms, "without shoes and without bread." His fame grew immensely in later years when the French, during their Revolution, had to resort to the levy in mass in order to defend their frontiers, and when Kosciuszko who had served under him attempted to repeat the tactics of his old chief during the insurrection of Poland. When the news of Washington's death reached France, young Bonaparte, then First Consul and still a republican hero, ordered a week of mourning for all the French Army and had his eulogy delivered in the "Temple of Mars" before the veterans of the campaigns of Italy and Egypt.

The foreign officers who served under Washington, the foreign visitors who saw him at Mount Vernon, when under his vine and fig tree he was living as a private citizen, readily acknowledged in him a sterling character, an impressive dignity, and a sort of melancholy most striking in a man who had had such a glorious career and had lived to enjoy the completion of his task. The only discordant notes to be heard in this unanimous praise are found in the correspondence of some French and British ministers during the troubled years between 1793 and 1797.

Of his achievements as a statesman, of the part he played in the making of the Constitution, little was known and little was said. Outside America, the names of his victories were soon forgotten, with the exception of Yorktown. His military glory was eclipsed by the fact that, once the victory was won, he had disbanded his army and resigned his commission to the hands of Congress. As the years passed, the comparison with Napoleon became unavoidable and almost obsessing, and Washington stood more and more as the prototype of the republican hero.

For obvious reasons, the tributes paid to Washington were more frequent and more persistent in France than in any other country; but they were not limited to France. The Italian Carlo Botta, writing in 1809 a *History of the War of Independence of the United States of America,* concluded his account with Washington's resignation as commander-in-chief, a significant and bold allusion to the very different course followed by Bonaparte. According to his memorialist, Napoleon himself sighed at St. Helena, "They wanted me to be another Washington" and attempted to explain that conditions in Europe did not permit him to keep his republican faith. In his "Ode to Napoleon Bonaparte" as well as in the "Age of Bronze," Byron gave Washington as a "watchword" to would-be dictators. Traveling in South America in 1817, H. M. Brackenridge found everywhere translations of Washington's Farewell Address, and at the same time the political magazine published by Chateaubriand deplored that everywhere on the Boulevard were seen portraits of Washington and Bolívar as a sort of tacit protest against the Bourbon restoration. No more eloquent tribute has ever been paid to the republican leader than the pages in which the author of *Atala,* recalling the short visit he had paid to the President of the United States in 1792, contrasted Washington and Napoleon, the man who had built a country and the conqueror who had left only ruins behind him.

The Washington hero-myth persisted throughout the nineteenth century and into the twentieth. Less eloquent than the praise of Chateaubriand, but no less striking, is the chapter at the close of *The Virginians* (1857–1859), in which Thackeray pictures Washington taking leave of his army at Whitehall Ferry, on the Hudson. More qualified and typical of many English appreciations was the estimate of Matthew Arnold, who spoke of Washington as if he had been an Englishman accidentally living in America, and maintained that Americans should think of him as a good model of the English country squire. In France admiration for Washington remained throughout the century a form of opposition to dictatorship and arbitrary power, as may be seen in the lectures delivered at the Collège de France during the Second Empire by Edouard de Laboulaye. Washington appeared again to proclaim "Liberty to the World" in *Le Nouveau Monde,* a play written by Villiers de l'Isle-Adam to commemorate the centennial of the Declaration of Independence. Again, in 1882, when France was obsessed by the fear of a dictator, Joseph Fabre in his book *Washington, libérateur de l'Amérique,* hailed the soldier-citizen. More recently, when many French liberals were seriously alarmed at the progress of totalitarian ideology and the growing popularity of Mussolini and Hitler, Louis Ferrier produced a play on Washington, to revive the old patriotic faith and, in the name of the great American, to preach the republican gospel.

Of an entirely different order has been the fame of Benjamin Franklin in Europe. His mission to France (1776–1784) marked the apogee of his European popularity, but he would not have taken Paris by storm if his reputation had not already been firmly established. His experiments in electricity were known in England through his friend Collinson as early as 1749; the French physicist Dalibard made them available to the French in 1752; and translations into German and Italian soon followed. European scientists saw in him a skillful observer and experimenter, but popular imagination magnified the American "doctor" into a modern Prometheus, a man able to control and play with a force of nature which had filled with awe countless generations.

During his lifetime, Franklin's fame extended throughout Europe even to Austria, the Scandinavian countries, and Russia. He corresponded with the most famous philosophers and scientists of his age, received from them and from monarchs the most flattering messages. He felt as much at home in Paris, although his knowledge of French was far from perfect, as in Philadelphia. After the partial publication of his *Autobiography,* printed in French and in Paris during the Revolution, he appeared as the most striking illustration of the unlimited possibilities residing in the "people," a living demonstration of the fact that in a republican society, where class distinctions do not prevent recognition of talent and genius, a poor boy may seize opportunities and rise to positions reserved to privileged classes in the Old World. No wonder the German historian Georg Forster in his *Reise um die Welt* (1784) saw in Franklin a prophet chosen to inaugurate the Golden Age of humanity, and Chamfort in his *Tableaux de la Révolution Française* (1793) hailed him as the herald of the new era of the common man. Thirty years later, the "child of poverty" who was to become a great South American leader, Domingo Faustino Sarmiento, treasured equally the only two books he had in his possession, the Bible and Franklin's *Autobiography.* As late as 1845, the French historian Mignet included a life of Franklin in a collection issued under the auspices of the *Académie des Sciences Morales et Politiques.* It was reprinted again in 1865 under the same auspices

> as a biography which makes live again a good man, a master of wisdom adapted to every age, every condition, every society, and one of the founders of that American liberty which is not the privilege of a race, or of a given form of government, but pure and simple Liberty.

Franklin had not kept to himself the secret of his extraordinary success in life. Eighteenth century philosophers had vainly attempted to establish a practical code of morality which would not rest on a religious foundation and would be acceptable and accessible to the common man. In Franklin they found no metaphysical speculations, but sound and homely precepts of conduct. "The Science of Good Man Richard," the title generally given to the translations of *The Way to Wealth,* provided a sort of civic catechism soon incorporated in elementary textbooks and still to be found in fragmentary form in many of the readers used by children in the public schools of France and Italy. There is no young European who in his school days has not become familiar with the story of the whistle and anecdotes from the *Autobiography.*

Franklin also contributed another important element to the composite picture of America as it appears to European eyes. He stood, even more than Fulton, as the embodiment of the spirit, bold in its aims and yet practical, which characterizes American science; and the great English physicist Humphry Davy praised his work as justifying not only pure scientific research, but the application of science to the service of man. Franklin was the first to give the impression that through science America could achieve the impossible. Thus was established a popular tradition which was reinforced through the pseudoscientific tales of Poe and carried out in the novels of Jules Verne, in which Americans conquer the interstellar spaces and travel to the moon. Later the tradition, already well established, received a new confirmation in the inventions of Edison, "the wizard of Menlo Park," celebrated by Villiers de l'Isle-Adam, in his *L'Ève Future* (1886) not only as the man who had invented the phonograph but as a sorcerer who through mechanical devices had succeeded in creating an automaton endowed with all the manifestations of a living organism, including feeling and thought.

4

General as this admiration for America was in the days of the Revolution and later, it was accompanied in many quarters by reservations and misgivings. By comparison with the discoverers whose imaginations were haunted by visions of a recovered Earthly Paradise, many eighteenth and early nineteenth century travelers seem particularly unimaginative and "unromantic." To them, as well as to most of the settlers, nature was essentially an obstacle to colonization: it had to be tamed and subdued in order to make room for civilization and provide a living to man. As late as 1770, Oliver Goldsmith in his *Deserted Village* represented Georgia as a "dreary scene":

> Those matted woods, where birds forget to sing,
> But silent bats in drowsy clusters cling; . . .
> Where crouching tigers wait their hapless prey,
> And savage men more murderous still than they.

Occasionally happier notes occur in the accounts of foreign travelers who were sincerely interested in nature, and particularly in botany, like the Swede Peter Kalm, or in glowing descriptions of the Ohio published in Paris shortly before the Revolution and intended to attract French immigrants; but with the exception of Chastellux, who was a philosopher and a poet, the officers who accompanied Rochambeau failed to be impressed by the American scene, and Lafayette was completely blind to the beauties of nature.

British travelers generally deplored a country defaced by unsightly settlements and by forest fires leaving behind them bleached skeletons of trees and horrible stumps. They compared the scarred spaces surrounding the farms, the dreary and unhealthy swamps, and the eroded hills, with the well kept and humanized European countryside. Very few of them showed any real appreciation of American scenery; Isaac Weld was one of the first foreigners to perceive the beauty of autumn foliage, of the majestic landscape of the Hudson between New York and Albany, and of Niagara Falls. Here and there scattered notations could be collected. John Davis, in his *Travels in the United States* (1803), was probably the first European to celebrate the mockingbird. A disciple of Rousseau, he should take first rank among the romantic observers of America.

Frequent as the unfavorable comments of disgruntled travelers may have been, their effects were largely canceled by the works of two writers, the American botanist William Bartram and the French prose-poet Chateaubriand. Bartram's *Travels* was widely reprinted in Europe and was used as a source by Coleridge in "Kubla Khan" and "The Ancient Mariner," by Wordsworth in "Ruth," by Southey in "Madoc," by Thomas Campbell in "Gertrude of Wyoming" (County in Pennsylvania), by Mrs. Hemans, by Shelley, and even by Tennyson in *In Memoriam*.

Bartram's influence was multiplied in a measure difficult to ascertain because he was the chief source of the descriptions inserted by Chateaubriand in *Atala* and *Les Natchez* (1802 and 1826). In many respects, the famous prose-poem of Chateaubriand may be considered not as a revelation of an unknown world, but as a final and perfect expression of the various sorts of exoticism which had flourished during the previous three centuries. Atala and her simple lover are no longer children of nature; they are torn between the traditions, customs, and prejudices of their tribe and a new and higher code of ethics. Unable to solve the conflict, they can only suffer and die; Chateaubriand's poem sounds the funeral dirge of a disappearing race.

A generation later, the novels of Fenimore Cooper were to revive European interest in the Indians and to start a very different tradition. Whatever may have been the intentions of the author of the Leatherstocking tales, the

French public saw in them primarily exciting adventures, with Indians lurking behind the trees, tracking their enemies with uncanny skill, scalping and slaying the white settlers. Balzac, who was a fervent admirer of Cooper, drew abundantly from him to portray not only the half-savage peasants ambushing the Republican soldiers in *Les Chouans,* but also both the criminals and the detectives constantly at war in the jungle of the Paris underworld. Thus gradually through a long series of popular novels and particularly through the many stories of Gustave Aimard, the noble savages of the early discoverers and philosophers underwent a curious evolution to become finally the *apaches,* or gangsters, of the French capital.

At the beginning of the nineteenth century, the success of Chateaubriand's *Atala* could be attributed to the magnificent descriptions of the "scènes de la nature": the Falls of Niagara, the Mississippi, the virgin forest, and the tropical swamps which serve as a frame for the melancholy love story of Chactas and the half-breed Atala. Whether or not his descriptions were embellished and magnified by his poetical imagination matters little here. They were accepted as authentic, for the author had dreamed of the American solitude, he had heard the voice of the desert, he had seen or imagined, with the assistance of Bartram, the swarming life of the swamps, the majestic cedars and the towering magnolias (*grandiflora*). He had done what many of his less gifted successors had confessed themselves unable to do, from Thomas Moore who was content to observe that the sight of the Niagara was "sad as well as elevating," to Frances Wright, who admitted that the Falls "acknowledge at once their power and immensity, and your own insignificance and imbecility." Neither the much more precise descriptions of Volney, in his *Tableau du Climat et du Sol des Etats-Unis* (1803) nor the scientific and minute accuracy of the great British geologist Charles Lyell could modify the deep and lasting impression made by Chateaubriand's little book, translated at once into all the languages of Europe and accepted as a model of description even by several South American writers. This extraordinary popularity was strengthened by Longfellow's *Evangeline* which helped further to arouse, in European travelers, exaggerated anticipations followed by an almost general disappointment when they were confronted by the actual countryside of the Eastern United States.

More serious than this concern for the contemplation of nature was the effort of European observers to find out whether natural conditions in the United States would permit and favor the development of a great civilization. During the last half of the eighteenth century, the French naturalist Buffon and the Berlin academician Cornelius de Pauw answered negatively. Judging from the accounts of travelers, they found the climate enervating, and nature itself so weak that the natives were unable to do any sustained work. Only unfavorable natural conditions could explain the fact that the New World, despite its reported fertility, had never developed a population comparable in density to the populations of Europe or Asia. The creoles (whites born in the colonies), as well as the domestic animals they had brought with them, showed signs of physical degeneration, and the wild species were decidedly smaller than the corresponding animals in the Old World. This was more than an academic question, and its political implications grew apparent as the British colonies progressed towards independence and finally formed a new nation. What faith and what hopes could be placed in the mission assigned by European liberals to the United States if this "young" people was condemned by the laws of nature ever to remain small and comparatively weak? Many of the French officers who had suffered from the extreme cold of a Rhode Island winter before being exposed to the semitropical temperature of the Virginia seashore had come to the conclusion that America was unfit for human beings. La Rochefoucauld-Liancourt and Volney, who spent several summers in Philadelphia, between 1794 and 1799, could but agree with them and insist upon the unhealthy features of the climate and the frequent epidemics.

These were some of the notions that Franklin and later Jefferson attempted to refute; but they did not succeed in convincing their opponents. The controversy found a last echo in Schopenhauer. Facts, however, spoke louder than theories: it was soon discovered that, despite certain unfavorable circumstances which could not be denied, the population of the United States increased at a regular rate independently of immigration, thus justifying the optimistic calculations of Franklin. Malthus provided an explanation: in the rapid development of the new nation he saw a confirmation of his theory that population invariably increases with the increase in the means of subsistence. The native population had remained practically stationary because of the Indians' lack of industry. It had increased as new territories were opened to cultivation and, because new land was practically limitless, it would continue to grow with the progress of agriculture.

Doubts nevertheless persisted concerning the quality of the civilization which the Anglo-Americans, as they were still called, would succeed in establishing. The first reports were far from favorable. French refugees remembering the exquisite life of the Old Regime, supercilious Britishers still considering America as a wayward child, criticized sharply or with indulgent scorn the uncouth manners of the people. In New York, Philadelphia, and Boston they missed the literary and artistic coteries, the salons, the concerts, the frivolous and yet intense intellectual life of the great capitals. Some, like the poet Thomas Moore, were so deeply disappointed as to doubt the soundness of the liberal creed in which they had placed their hope. Even the best intentioned among them fell into the common mistake of judging American society by European standards, and were disillusioned by this unexpected contact with a harsh reality. Once again was confirmed the curious separation between America as a geographical, political, and social entity, and America as a state of mind. Never perhaps had it been more strikingly expressed than in the words of Goethe in *Wilhelm Meister,* when one of the characters declares after a disappointing experience in America:

> I shall return, and in my house, on my land among my home people, I shall repeat: Here and nowhere else is America. *Hier oder nirgends ist Amerika.*

But as Europe grew constantly weaker, torn by continuous wars and domestic strife, while the strength of the United States increased rapidly, the optimistic predictions concerning the future development of the United States made on the eve of the French Revolution seemed amply justified. Already in 1795, during the third year of the French Republic, Pictet of Geneva, summing up the observations of European travelers and the data found in Jedidiah Morse's geography, thought he was justified in examining "the causes of the greatness of America." His was not a great book; but it contained a summation of all the material available at the time, and his conclusion contrasted the country whose inhabitants had been wise enough "to submit themselves to a strong government in order to preserve their liberty," with a Europe apparently doomed "to oscillate between the cheerless tranquillity of despotism and the stormy fury of anarchy." At the same time (1793–1799), impelled by the same considerations, Christoph Daniel Ebeling published in Hamburg an enormous compilation on the United States which was to serve as the main source-book of information for several generations of German scholars.

Even more emphatic were the views presented by the Reverend John Bristed after the fall of Napoleon, the Peace of Ghent, and the reorganization of Europe. In the world of 1818, this British clergyman who had spent many years in America could see only two countries susceptible of growth: the giant Russia and the giant United States. He was too much attached to the European tradition to admire without restrictions the American ways of life; but he had to admit that the sun of Europe was setting, that none of the old nations could compete with a country capable of supporting ultimately a population of five hundred millions through its agriculture, commerce, industry, steam navigation, and mechanical inventions. It was not that the soil was extraordinarily fertile—America was "neither the Garden of Eden, nor the Valley of Tophet"—but a practically unlimited extent of territory which could be reclaimed through the tremendous energy and industry of the inhabitants offered possibilities undreamed of by the crowded populations of Europe.

Very similar was the conclusion reluctantly reached by Abbé de Pradt, the former chaplain of Napoleon, in his study *Des Colonies et de la Révolution actuelle de l'Amérique* (Paris, 1817). The contagion predicted by Jefferson and dreaded by Turgot and Vergennes had reached South America. The Spanish and Portuguese colonies, following the example of the United States, were shaking off the yoke of Europe. Thirty years after the conclusion of the Treaty of Versailles, the revolutionary influence of the United States extended over the whole New World. Considering "What is the future of the United States?" De Pradt answered that according to Franklin's calculations, which so far had proved to be correct, the United States would support 138,400,000 inhabitants by 1919. Nothing comparable had ever happened in ancient or modern times. The American flag was already everywhere, and everywhere the very existence of the United States placed monarchies in jeopardy. Going even further than Bristed, De Pradt concluded:

> No human power can now stop the march of a nation destined to exert its influence all over the world and perhaps to dominate it.

In fact, it was not an influence, it was an "invasion."

Less emphatically, but no less positively, ten years later, Barbé-Marbois reiterated the warning. In the eyes of the old diplomat who had served Louis XVI and known Washington; who, acting for the First Consul, had "sold" Louisiana to the United States and remained in the diplomatic service under Louis XVIII,

> the United States, even without participating actively in the affairs of Europe, will exert through their example, an influence to be reckoned with by the imperial and royal cabinets of Europe. The Prince, whether he be called a king, magistrate, or people will no longer be able to rule without paying due regard to the political liberties of the citizens.

This extraordinary prediction was intended as a lesson to the future ruler of France, since it was dedicated by the old Royalist to the heir apparent of the French throne, "Monseigneur le Dauphin."

Once again Europe was discovering America. All the predictions and misgivings of Montesquieu and his disciples had proved to be false. It was no longer possible to maintain that a republican system of government was inherently weak and that it could survive only in a small territory. Not only was America a powerful country which had recently repelled aggression, but it was the only country that had been able to establish "a stable government, standing without props, while most governments in Europe maintained a precarious existence through measures of expediency."

5

Far more extensive and pervasive than the influence exerted in Europe by the American Revolution proper, and consequently not so easily traced, was a new force, symbolized in the magic word "America" and felt throughout the Old and the New World. This new force was Democracy. All the subterranean activities which neither Napoleon nor the Holy Alliance had been able to suppress completely had slowly prepared the violent explosion which shook all the nations of Europe in 1830. To determine the part played by the American example in the elaboration of the ideas and the fostering of the movements which came to fruition at that time, would require detailed studies which are not yet available. It would be particularly desirable to ascertain the influence of Jefferson, exerted directly and personally through his extraordinarily large correspondence with the lovers of liberty in Europe.

The author of the Declaration of Independence never enjoyed during his stay in Europe the extraordinary popularity carefully exploited by Franklin in the interest of his country. The *Notes on the State of Virginia* (1784), printed in Paris and in London, were not widely circulated, and Jefferson's other writings very seldom appeared in the public papers. But to the *philosophes* he was known as the man who had drafted the "Bill for establishing Religious Freedom," who had proposed a comprehensive plan of public education. By the members of the Committee on the Constitution of the National Assembly he was eagerly sought as a wise counselor. By the Physiocrats he was highly esteemed as a practical philosopher and farmer, interested in developing the agricultural resources of his country. He became later the man who had befriended Volney, Priestley, Thomas Cooper, and Thomas Paine, and was represented as the champion of the oppressed and the protector of political refugees fleeing their country to escape prison, persecution, or worse. As long as he stayed in office he was compelled to observe great prudence in the communications he addressed to his European friends. After his retirement he spoke more openly. He did not conceal the fact that he hated Bonaparte, the man whose ambition had changed Europe into a charnel house. He applauded the first efforts of the South Americans to achieve their liberty and the attempt of the Cortes to establish a more liberal regime in Spain. He advised the Greek Coray, the Portuguese Correa, the Pole Kosciusko, the Spaniard De Onis, and encouraged even more strongly his French friends, Lafayette, Du Pont de Nemours, and Destutt de

Tracy. He corresponded with British liberals like Major Cartwright, and with philosophers like Dugald Stewart, and political and human geographers like Alexander and Wilhelm von Humboldt. He was fully aware that his letters circulated secretly among his friends, but he showed a genuine iritation when his confidence was betrayed and they were printed, on several occasions, in the public papers. He was in fact, and perhaps unknowingly, the leader of a secret resistance movement in Europe during the Empire and the Bourbon Restoration.

The few and still superficial investigations of Jefferson's influence hitherto undertaken are singularly revealing. It seems that at the origin of the Italian *Risorgimento* is to be found a combination of eighteenth century philosophy and French revolutionary theories, with Jeffersonian Americanism acting as a sort of catalytic agent. It may be shown that under the combined influence of Jefferson's theories of government and Destutt de Tracy's *Commentary and Review of Montesquieu's Spirit of Laws,* the Russian "Decembrist" Pestel wrote his book on *Russian Justice* (1825), which led to the promulgation of the first Rumanian code of laws, worked out in collaboration with the representatives of the Rumanian people in 1832. In France again, Auguste Comte acknowledged his debt to the man who had attempted to found the science and practice of government irrespective of theological and metaphysical assumptions. A selection of Jefferson's letters and speeches published in Paris in 1832 led to a long discussion of his political philosophy in Armand Carrel's *National.* The great French critic Sainte-Beuve advised the young French generation to take as a leader and master the man who had proved that one of the first functions of government was to respect the rights of the "individual." No less emphatic and enthusiastic was the *Edinburgh Review,* in October, 1837, proclaiming Jefferson "the recognized leader of the party which had effected the first, possibly the most remarkable of those revolutions, and the one that has had the greatest influence upon the fortunes of mankind." Two years earlier, Richard Cobden had already declared that the time had come to draw lessons from the American example, in words calling for a complete reorganization of the social structure:

> We fervently believe that our only chance of national prosperity lies in the timely remodelling of our system so as to put it as nearly as possible upon an equality with the improved management of the Americans.

Shortly before the Revolution of 1830, the French "doctrinaire," Royer Collard, had declared, "La démocratie coule à pleins bords," and indeed Democracy seemed to be on the point of overflowing its banks and of sweeping through Europe like an irresistible flood. But "Democracy" was now a battle cry rather than a definite program, as "Liberty" had been some fifty years earlier. Even its most enthusiastic apostles had no experience with the working of a democratic system of government. At a time when a complete transformation of the European system was impending, the Americans were the only people who had somehow managed to control and to direct through well laid-out channels this apparently unmanageable force. The United States stood no longer as engaged in an unprecedented and venturesome experiment: the experiment had been conducted in a gigantic laboratory, and it was an undeniable success.

6

Such were some of the thoughts which filled and haunted the mind of the young French magistrate who, in the spring of 1831, crossed the ocean with the official mission of studying the penal system of the United States. Born of a noble family, Alexis de Tocqueville was the grandson on his mother's side of M. de Malesherbes, the fearless lawyer who had presented the defense of Louis XVI before the Convention. Recently appointed to a modest position in the judiciary, he seemed little prepared by his education and family tradition to become, if not an apostle, at least a theorist and an exponent of democracy. He did not venture on his expedition without misgivings and hesitations. He was, as he has told us himself, "under the impression of an almost religious awe" caused by the sight of that irresistible revolution, marching for so many centuries through countless obstacles and now advancing in the midst of the ruins it had accumulated. To determine whether this "phenomenon almost fatal or providential" could in some degree be limited; to discover through what means democracy could be dedicated to the great task of enabling people to govern themselves; to find out some of the reasons which had made it possible for America to avoid the pitfalls into which the French people had fallen—these were the momentous problems that this young man, twenty-seven years of age, had undertaken to solve.

This utilitarian preoccupation, this eagerness to serve his country and the cause of civilization, have secured for Tocqueville a unique place among the critics and historians of America. He had no desire to prove or disprove any theory or system. He had no preconceived idea or prejudice, but as a judge he had been trained to look for the evidence and the facts of a case. His training largely accounts for both the judicial quality and the shortcomings of *Democracy in America* (1835).

That he was an alert and keen observer, susceptible of spontaneous reactions, is amply proved by his recently published journals. He traveled extensively in the United States, interviewed many statesmen and scholars, slept in the huts of the pioneers, and even visited some Indian tribes. But he strove to rise above contingencies; he looked for what is permanent and durable under the changing surface of changing phenomena. To use again Montesquieu's phrase, he was more interested in the "nature of things" than in things themselves. He used observation to establish principles from which, through an extensive deductive process, he could derive logical consequences and ultimately lessons in the art of self-government for the use of his fellow countrymen.

The consequence and perhaps the weakness of this method is that *Democracy in America* does not present a vivid and complete picture of American life, but rather a sort of diagram of what American life might become if the principles which directed its development continued to apply. A not inconsiderable number of Tocqueville's predictions have proved to be false, but for three-quarters of a century his book was accepted as fundamental and authoritative in America as well as abroad, and even today it can be read and studied with profit.

Tocqueville concluded that the pillars on which the structure of American civilization rested were separation of church and state, and an almost excessive decentralization. Obviously, in emphasizing these features of American life, the author had always present in his mind reverse conditions and tendencies in his own country. His conclusion was that the American experiment could not be repeated in Europe, and least of all in France, without a deep moral transformation. His picture of American democracy was presented as an object lesson and not as a pattern to be exactly reproduced.

Two problems, however, were common to Europe and America. The first was how to preserve the liberty of the individual against all tyranny, whether it be the tyranny of the state or the tyranny of the majority. The second problem, no less pressing, was raised by the irresistible leveling and lowering tendencies of modern peoples. As the old aristocracies were doomed and had amply demonstrated their political incapacities, as an aristocracy of riches would entail no lesser evils than those of the old system, as on the other hand, the common people were incapable of solving directly the problems of modern life, the main question was

> for the partisans of democracy to find means of getting the people to choose the men capable of governing and to give them in addition enough power to direct the latter in matters as a whole, but not in the details of their work nor the means of execution.

And in discussing, in a letter to John Stuart Mill, the first part of his work, Tocqueville concluded: "That is the problem. I am fully convinced that upon its solution depends the fate of the modern nations."

Europe and those of the young nations of Eastern Europe and Asia, would meet on the American continent not in a death struggle, but "to join hands and mix together, and this will be the greatest fact in the history of mankind."

His contemporary, Guillaume Tell Poussin, whose ambition was to write "a complement to Tocqueville's great book," emphasized, even more than Chevalier had done, the extraordinary development of applied science in America. In the railroads and steam navigation he foresaw the end of economic isolationism and a sort of industrial democratization of the world originating in the United States. In a book significantly entitled *De la Puissance Américaine* (1845), he foretold the triumph of world democracy, following great struggles in which America would be called upon to participate. Her strength and power, which could no longer be questioned, were consequently a matter of international importance. Nor was this view limited to the French. In the Introduction to his *Philosophy of History,* Hegel, some twenty years earlier, had admitted that

> America is therefore the land of the future, where, in the ages that lie before us, the burden of the old world's history shall reveal itself . . . perhaps in a contest between North and South America. It is the land of desire for all those who are weary of the historical lumber-room of Europe. Napoleon is reported to have said: "Cette vieille Europe m'ennuie." It is for America to abandon the ground on which hitherto the History of the World has unfolded itself.

It remained for a disciple of German thought, Edgar Quinet, in an article published in 1831 in the *Revue des Deux Mondes,* to trace the decay and death of the religions of the Old World accompanying the decline of Old-World civilizations and to predict:

> A new idea of God will surge from the lakes of Florida and the peaks of the Andes: in America will begin a new religious era and will be born a new idea of God.

To a certain extent, but with an interesting modification, this was also the view expressed by the Prussian historian Friedrich von Raumer, in 1845 *(America and the American People)*. In the prodigious growth of the United States he saw an almost divinely inspired achievement of "the Germanic stock marching irresistibly forward." Having little faith in the future development of Asia and Africa, unable to distinguish any indication of a rejuvenation of a sickly Europe, he concluded:

> If we were forced to despair of the future progress of the Germanic race in America, whither could we turn our eyes for deliverance, except to a new and direct creation from the hand of the Almighty.

7

Such were some of the dreams to which America was giving rise. As much as during the eighteenth century, it was, in the early years of the nineteenth, still a Utopian land, or rather a land where Utopias became realities. It was the land where Lezay-Marnesia had hoped to establish a refuge for the French aristocrats and where a few years later Coleridge had planned to establish his Pantisocracy. It was the land where Robert Owen after his unsuccessful experiment in England came to build his New Harmony and where the German Rapp established his communistic village of Economy, sixteen miles from Pittsburgh. The Napoleonic exiles, after Waterloo, had come as "soldier farmers" with General Bertrand to plant "the vine and the olive" in the wilds of Texas and Alabama. It was known that, while the theories of Fourier could not be put to the test of experience in Europe, a group of New England writers managed to conduct a famous if inconclusive experiment at Brook Farm. America was the only country on earth where the French socialist Cabet could attempt to organize colonies of Icarians, because nowhere else could small groups, advocates of a new order, establish and govern themselves locally and practically without any interference from a central government. It was the land where Priestley and Thomas Cooper from England, Comte de Noailles, Talleyrand, and Volney in the troubled last decade of the eighteenth century, General Bertrand, Jérome Bonaparte, and Achille Murat after the fall of Napoleon, had found an asylum. It was the land where the Germans, the Irish, and the French after 1848 were again to come as refugees to seek a liberty which they despaired of establishing in their own countries. It was also a land of hope in another respect. It was an irrefutable demonstration that the representatives from all the nations of the world, thinkers, reformers, and generous poets who had been called to attend an International Peace Conference under the presidency of Victor Hugo, in 1848, were not wild dreamers. The United States of America was a "commonwealth of nations." It had proved the truth of one of Hegel's chief axioms, that Unity dominates the diversity of elements. As long as the United States stood, there was hope that ultimately the peoples of the Old World could be redeemed from themselves. The American dream had become part of the cultural tradition of Europe.

THE DEMOCRACY

. . . the meaning of independence

16. THE GREAT EXPERIMENT

During the years from the nonpartisan reelection of James Monroe in 1820 to the Compromise of 1850, the United States lived very much to itself. Contacts with Europe were slighter than at any time before or since. Transportation by steamship was initiated in the thirties, but it was irregular and unreliable. Communication by cable had not yet been attempted. Consular and diplomatic exchanges were few. As compared with the rate of increase from births, the increase in population from immigration reached the lowest point since 1607. For three decades, Washington and New York and even Boston moved westward across the globe—farther from Europe, nearer the Rocky Mountains.

In the period of the Revolution, American liberals had put into execution European ideas; during the early years of the Republic, conservatives had been equally willing to accept foreign thought. Now, in partial isolation, a new generation adjusted Old World concepts to their own activities and began to create indigenous symbols to represent their own experiences. Out of this ferment there emerged a way of life dominated by the two forces of self-trust and expansion. Each advanced the other, yet at the same time each contravened the other: the thrust of expansion drove individuals and the states farther apart while the pull of self-trust held them together in one nation. More often expressed in action than in words, this diversity within unity found fragmentary utterance in the speeches of Clay, Webster, and Calhoun, and in the social criticism of Bryant of the New York *Evening Post* and of Cooper. In these crosscurrents of opinion, the generation of Lincoln and Emerson came to maturity.

Self-trust, when exercised by a people, is nationalism—in this instance, the brash yet healthy assurance of a youthful country secure in its achievements and its potentialities. Born in the political and philosophical debates of eighteenth century Europe, the doctrine had first taken on a negative form in America, that of hostility to England. Later it had become a self-conscious demand for native arts, native customs, and even a native language—to be created *de novo*. Now, as the frontier moved toward the Pacific, geography gave nationalism a new context. Not only was the United States the first nation founded on the novel principle that the boundaries of a nationality should coincide with those of a sovereign state, but it was also the earliest example of a nationality taking root in the rich soil of an unexploited continent. It is true that the enthusiasm of Americans for national symbols and holidays, for native scenery and customs, and for their own past often paralleled similar enthusiasms in Europe. But the impact of a new world, with its tremendous resources and its ever-present frontier, gave to nationalism in the United States a fresh and gusty incisiveness which sometimes angered and always amazed foreign observers.

This nationalism of the thirties and forties was often provincial, and it was often noisy—never in American history were patriots more vocal. It was at the same time realistic. Statesmen in Washington, as they watched the continental European powers withdraw from the Americas, discovered that the United States could rely on the Atlantic Ocean and on the self-interest of Britain as guarantors of American independence. In 1823 President Monroe was shrewdly capitalizing on the geographical self-sufficiency of the United States and on the foreign policy of Britain when he announced that the young republic had become the protector of a hemisphere: "The American continents . . . are henceforth not to be considered as subjects for future colonization by any European powers," and any attempt of a foreign power to control any independent state in the American hemisphere will be viewed as "the manifestation of an unfriendly disposition toward the United States." It should be remembered that the President and his advisers, Jefferson, Madison, and J. Q. Adams, did not commit the United States to this bold policy until they were assured of the support of Britain. Self-confidence for Americans in that day was confidence not only in themselves but in the only foreign power which maintained a navy capable of striking across the Atlantic.

Meanwhile the American people were congratulating themselves on the success of their experiment in republicanism. The division of opinion in the later eighteenth century between monarchists and republicans now disappeared, and monarchy became a symbol of all that Americans hated. Their republic, on the other hand, was neither the mirage nor the chaos that European reactionaries had anticipated; it was a practical, going concern. Out of the older concepts of natural law and natural rights, American liberals developed the new doctrine of popular sovereignty. Then they defended the republic as the only form of government consistent with that doctrine. (Popular sovereignty was not at that time generally associated with "democracy" because the latter term was not yet in general use.) Americans, as might be expected, were confirmed in their faith by the emergence of each of the French republics, by the founding of the South American republics, by the turmoil in Europe in 1830–1831, and particularly by the revolutions of 1848–1849. Whenever a foreign political experiment collapsed, Americans congratulated themselves again on the happy state of their own nation.

A steadily increasing respect for and reliance on the idea of the Union, one and indivisible, further strengthened egocentric Americanism. Jackson made his position dramatically clear at the Jefferson Day dinner of 1830, when he repudiated a series of toasts from the nullifiers by proposing: "Our federal Union: it must and shall be preserved." Likewise unequivocal was his reaction when in 1832 South Carolina declared that the federal tariff was null and void, and that the state would leave the Union if it were coerced. Jackson issued a proclamation in which he denied that the Union is a league of independent states and insisted that it is sovereign and perpetual. He let it be known also that he would use troops to enforce national laws. Respect for the Federal Constitution continued to grow until that instrument and the doctrine of the Union became, in the minds of nationalists, the two great bulwarks of the Republic.

A people as successful as the Americans considered themselves to be, and as religious as a majority of them were, inevitably credited their triumphs to God as well as to themselves. Reinterpreted in terms of the nineteenth century, the Puritan thesis that God's hand had been evident in every incident in the colonization of New England became the cult of manifest destiny. The United States had been set apart by divine Providence or by fate as the scene of a great, and perhaps a final, experiment in free government. The success of this experiment now made it evident that Americans were indeed a chosen nation. As such, they were destined to bring self-determination and republicanism to Texas, to California, and perhaps even to Canada and Cuba. They were chosen, likewise, to exemplify the ideal state for the imitation of rebels against monarchy in Europe. The honest concern of the American people for the welfare of all mankind gave a certain dignity to this theory of manifest destiny and a comfortable feeling of self-righteousness to its exponents.

The pervasive self-trust of these decades was announced, both by single citizens and by the nation, in a variety of terms. On the frontier, Davy Crockett shouted: "I kin lick my weight in wildcats!" In the White House, the President announced the nation's coming of age in state papers. In office and countinghouse, men said: Much as we owe to Europe, that continent is merely the exhausted past from which our fathers escaped; we find it expedient and profitable to be Americans. Among the older men of letters, Irving and Cooper groped for security, now abroad and now at home; but the young men put their trust in themselves and their new world. Emerson, speaking in 1837 for his egocentric contemporaries both in the United States and in Europe, declared: "If the single man will plant himself indomitably on

17. ART IN THE MARKET PLACE

THE era for the making of the new literature had arrived by 1820, but no one knew the rules or had the blueprints. The air was alive with energy and experiment. Writers were relying more upon journalism and the lecture and less upon the law, politics, and the church for their support. At the same time, American culture began to develop stronger regional characteristics and to strengthen such cultural centers as New Orleans, Charleston, Richmond, Baltimore, Cincinnati, Louisville, Philadelphia, Albany, New York, Concord, and Boston. But as the business of publishing and distributing books and magazines became better organized, these widespread centers looked more and more to New York for the stimulus of literary association and for the market place of literary wares.

The spirit of self-trust and expansion in this period found one form of expression in a zeal over all of America for the country to distinguish itself in the arts, to compel the critics as well as the common readers of England to think highly of the American book. That zeal was doubly felt in the South which, after about 1830, was concerned to justify itself sectionally against the North as well as nationally against Europe. The West as it expanded felt the same double defense to be necessary. Nationalism and sectionalism can hardly be distinguished; both stimulated the demand for "mental independence," both deferred to the critics of the older cultural center. The result was a ferment of literary activity.

2

New theories of education based on the concept of the natural man had already begun to develop a new generation of readers. The textbook reforms of Noah Webster and Jedidiah Morse were carried forward by the matter-of-fact "Peter Parley" (Samuel G. Goodrich) who insisted that cows give milk as well as jump over the moon, and that the first ideas of children "are simple and single, and formed images of things palatable to the senses." Starting with pictures and common experience, he took his imaginary charges over the globe, at the same time covertly attempting "to spiritualize the mind, and lift it above sensible ideas." He wrote or edited in the next twenty years 170 volumes and sold seven million copies. Emerson's philosopher-friend Bronson Alcott followed the same route from sense to spirit for the thirty children in his "Temple School" in Boston a few years later, although his climb from the sensory experience to the "spiritual" was aided by a schoolroom with "paintings, busts, books and not inelegant furniture," which provided "a prop round which tendrils may fasten"; while the Thoreau brothers accepted the conditioning provided by nature for their Academy and took their charges for long walks in the woods and fields of placid Concord.

The theories of Pestalozzi and of Jefferson, thus curiously mixed with sentimental idealism, were to require another century before John Dewey could urge their acceptance in a purer form, but meanwhile primary education developed rapidly. In 1827, when Peter Parley began to write, there were two "infant schools" and fifty-six primary departments in New York City, while a Massachusetts law in the same year required a high school in every town of five hundred families or more. But progress was slow, especially in the South, and it was not until 1850 that a campaign of propaganda and legislative reform, led by Horace Mann, succeeded in establishing, in principle at least, in every Northern state the provision of a common-school education for all children at public expense. "I have faith," wrote Mann, "in the improvability of the race—in their accelerating improvability."

This faith in improvability led to the founding of some five hundred universities and colleges before the close of the century. There were two theories of state direction of higher education: that of New York which followed the French plan of administrative centralization of control over a distributed group of institutions, and the German plan of gathering the various schools of learning into one place and establishing a sprawling mammoth. The latter prevailed in most instances, and the states of the West and South almost without exception created universities within a few years of their admission to the Union. Even cities like Charleston and Louisville had by 1837 set up universities or colleges of their own on this pattern. At the same time, the various religious sects followed the advancing waves of migration and established small denominational colleges by twos and threes in each new state. The pattern of higher education for affairs as well as for ideas, which had been laid by Jefferson in the early years of national life, guided this entire period of expansion and became set as the distinctive form of organization for democratic institutions. Its chief characteristics were elasticity and a blind faith in "Veritas" and "Lux."

The colonial colleges adopted this pattern by a slow breakdown of the fessor Edward Tyrrel Channing, who in his many years of teaching read and castigated the "themes" of Emerson, Holmes, Lowell, Dana, Motley, Thoreau, Sumner, Parkman, and Edward Everett Hale. Compulsory chapel exercises were held twice a day.

The college was not remarkably stimulating to lads of fine intelligence, and the ordinary undergraduate probably gained less information there than is commonly acquired in a good high school of the twentieth century. On the other hand there was at Harvard a serious concern for things of the mind to which even a dullard could scarcely fail to respond. In a time and place almost exclusively concerned with crude "practical facts" it managed to inculcate an interest in abstract ideas and in knowledge for its own sake. It had a character, an idiosyncrasy of its own, which it stamped upon all its sons indelibly. There was a hint of ancient Rome and Athens in this Harvard character, and through the barnlike classrooms and dormitories there blew as it were the bracing air of Plutarch's "Parallel Lives." Most of all to its credit, the place was hospitable to odd and unclassified individuals who did their own thinking and boldly spoke it out. In training most of the New England clergy Harvard had done her share, producing a conventional and conservative culture; but now she was slowly making ready for a different kind of leadership.

4

The pulpit and the lyceum did not supersede other and more traditional agencies for the making of the literary man. The increase in population, the spread of literacy, the improvement in means of communication, the growing sophistication of both urban and rural society, and the technical advances in printing and book production conspired to build up a substantial reading public. George P. Putnam of New York, the first of the great publishers in the modern sense, estimated that in 1845 the combined college libraries in the country contained 600,000 volumes and public collections almost 900,000. "Besides these," he added, "there is scarcely a town of any importance in the Union, but has some sort of a public library, reading-room, lyceum, or athenaeum."

The effects of inventions on the spreading of the printed word soon became apparent. The old methods of hand-set type, handmade paper, and the screw-pressure press had already been superseded by the principles of levers and cylinders when in 1825 the Napier steam-driven press made its appearance. The production of 2,000 copies an hour of the New York *Daily Advertiser* seemed a miracle until in 1847 the Hoe rotary press stepped production up to 20,000. Type casting and hand setting continued, however, for editions of most books, which in 1832 averaged 1,000 copies. Stereotyping of plates was known in this country as early as 1813, but was applied mainly to Bibles and textbooks until about 1830 when the Harpers adopted it as a regular practice for their "omnibus editions" of English reprints and Carey began to use it for Cooper's novels. Paper- and ink-making processes, machine type casting, and new methods of binding and embossing kept pace with these other improvements, and the process of steel engraving in the forties started F. O. C. Darley and others on careers of book illustration which would have been altogether impractical with the less durable wood block, the copper plate, and the lithograph.

Important by-products of these improvements were the appearance of the annual or gift book and of the giant anthology or cyclopedia of literature, scenery, or other matter suitable to fine printing, binding, and illustration. Goodrich attributed the sudden vogue of such annuals as *The Token, Friendship's Offering,* and *The Atlantic Souvenir* to the invention of steel engraving. "Under such seductive titles," he wrote, "they became the messenger of love, tokens of friendship, signs and symbols of affection, and luxury and refinement; and thus they stole alike into the palace and the cottage, the library, the parlor, and the boudoir." Similarly, R. W. Griswold raised the literary anthology to new levels of luxury if not of discrimination with *The Poets and Poetry of America* (1842) and his subsequent collections of prose and of the work of "female poets." And the Duyckincks produced their ten-pound, two-volume *Cyclopaedia of American Literature* in 1855.

Mechanical improvements in book making led in two quite contrary directions. They made it possible to produce far more elaborate books at no increase in cost, to illustrate them more copiously, and to bind them more sumptuously; but competition was so acute that mechanical improvements could not be generally applied until the middle of the century, when the Townsend *Cooper* and the Putnam *Irving* appeared, dignified gentlemanly rows of stocky volumes, with clear type on heavy paper, steel-engraved illustrations, and embossed ornaments on substantial cloth covers. Such books could look down on the humble, paper-bound parts of the 1819–1820 *Sketch Book* as a well disciplined, modern regiment might view ragged mountain guerrillas.

On the other hand, competition called for a continuously increasing quantity of production and lowering of costs. This tendency reached its climax in the late thirties and the forties, when Cooper's novels began appearing in paper wrappers at twenty-five cents instead of a dollar a volume; when mammoth newspapers, four feet long and eleven columns wide, began to print the complete novels of Dickens, G. P. R. James, or Lytton in "extras" of some seventy closely printed pages at ten cents a copy; and when the

two of whi
published th
from 1840 tc
in 1857. *Go*
with its col
continued i
Willis' *New*
and for man
Graham'.
entered into
tributions. I
was content
in a financia
S. Osgood $
same time P
sional poem
for you at $
there is no
attitude was
annual earni
contracted tc
page. "My te
cash on deli
could write
cannot live l
Writing
passage of th
the sole righ
perform, or
play out of
Wallack som
the return ir
as most actin
repertories c
and the tend
specific theat
turns. Forres
much to dig
as it meant th
da Rimini is
century, it w

editions of the poetry of Scott, Milton, Praed, Béranger, Bryant, Hemans, Campbell, and others, made him a sort of court of appeal in matters of taste; but he abused the authority this gave him in his treatment of Poe's life and reputation, and otherwise exercised it with breadth rather than discrimination.

Duyckinck was a man of sounder scholarship, finer taste, and broader human sympathies. Unlike his rival, who fought with Poe, he encouraged Melville when the author of *Typee* was beginning his career and most needed the kind of aid that an editor could give. A graduate of Columbia College in 1835, Duyckinck spent more than a year (1838–1839) in Europe in the expectation of a professorship of literature; when the appointment failed to materialize, he became a sort of *ex officio* professor to countless literary men, many of whom gathered weekly for far-ranging conversations over Roman punch and cigars in the basement of his New York residence. Bryant, Irving, Lowell, Simms, Taylor, and Hawthorne were his close friends. They and many others borrowed books from his well chosen library of some eighteen thousand volumes. As editor, after 1845, of Wiley & Putnam's Library of Choice Reading and Library of American Books, he was a major influence in introducing European classics to American readers and in helping American authors to find an audience. Hawthorne advised him to publish Emerson's poems because he thought Emerson's reputation still "provincial, and almost local, partly owing to the New England system of publication." Simms sought him out on a visit to the North and became one of the distinguished group of contributors to the *Literary World*—as brilliant a literary journal, under Duyckinck's editorship, as this country has known.

The *Cyclopaedia of American Literature* (1855) immediately became and still is a standard reference work. Written and edited with the aid of his brother George, it reflects his comprehensive reading, his widespread acquaintance with living authors, his extensive research in both books and manuscripts, and his indefatigable correspondence in search of facts, as well as his taste and his critical judgment. Here and in his critical articles he declared the superficiality of the popular N. P. Willis and of much of the poetry of even Longfellow and Lowell. Although out of sympathy with the principles of transcendentalism, he never doubted Emerson's greatness and was disappointed in not obtaining some of his work for New York publication; and he unqualifiedly proclaimed Hawthorne and Melville the literary titans of his day. Like most New Yorkers, Duyckinck felt ill at ease in Boston; but his friends included writers from all sections, and his home—like his native city—was a national meeting ground.

Thus mercantile giants like John Jacob Astor and Stephen Girard were not alone in learning before the middle of the century the art of focusing the diverse material of a democratic laissez-faire economy upon their own fame and profit. James Gordon Bennett, Horace Greeley, and William Cullen Bryant became powerful as editors by so marshaling these forces; George Palmer Putnam, E. A. Duyckinck, and James T. Fields did the same for book making; Willis, Graham, and Lewis Gaylord Clark, for the magazine; Edwin Forrest and William Niblo, for the theater; and finally Cooper, Irving, Emerson, Kennedy and many lesser men, for literature. Cooper, Irving, and Willis, by playing their cards with cunning and care, made possible the career of the professional man of letters in America; Emerson did the same for the popular lecturer, as Edward Everett stamped out the pattern for the occasional orator by making of his art a career. By mid-century the American literary man had come into his own.

The increasing millions of new readers created by education and migration could thus be supplied with literary fare only because there was corresponding progress in importing, producing, and circulating the printed word. At first glance one wonders, not why there was suddenly a new generation of native authors, but why this group was relatively small and why it struggled with financial obstacles almost as great as those of an earlier day. The answer to these questions is clear. In a competitive mercantile economy, the writer is in the position of the farmer, a producer of raw materials without protective tariff. Power and profit pass him by unless he too can find ways to play the game. "Democratic literature," wrote De Tocqueville in 1835, "is always infested with a tribe of writers who look upon letters as a mere trade"; Dickens spoke of the "present abject [moral] state" of the American newspaper press; and the elder Longfellow wrote sorrowfully to his son in college, "There is not wealth and munificence enough in this country to afford sufficient encouragement and patronage to merely literary men." Wealth was growing, but for many years it was to be widely distributed and was to fall for the most part into the hands of the literary manufacturer and middleman rather than into those of the author.

18. WASHINGTON IRVING

THUS America was ready for a man of letters: the lights were on; the audience assembled. The mediums for the new culture were exciting. In all those interests of man which we call cultural there was a stir, the unmistakable promise of a future. A few of our writers, a Hawthorne or an Emily Dickinson, were to live "beyond time," that is, not without aloofness to the dust and heat of their own eras. This man of letters, however, for whom the theater, the magazine, the novel, the more civilized society, and the new nationalism called so imperiously, was not to be, like Edwards or Emerson, timeless, but temporal, an inevitable creation and adroit user of those cultural mechanisms and moods; it could not, in this adolescence of our intellectual life, be otherwise. Without a skillful manipulation of these instruments of culture, success in writing was impossible; and without measurable public renown of some kind, any author might hope in vain for readers.

Naturally some of our first men of letters were men of affairs who discovered in themselves surprising talents with the pen. Before he published *The Sketch Book*, at the age of thirty-six, Washington Irving had been a lawyer, a businessman, and a soldier; in his contemporaries' eyes the crown of his career was not this famous volume, but his appointment as minister to Spain. Although at heart a dreamer and a deliberate artist, he was fascinated by these new playthings of culture, and became an urbane participant in the clubs, coteries, and literary and theatrical circles which formed a graceful backdrop to his own preeminence. In spite of his long residence abroad, his links with the "Knickerbocker Group" were real. No writer gauged better than he the demands of contemporary readers, at home and abroad; his essay of manners was not unaware of that of Joseph Dennie in Philadelphia, of Miss Mitford in England, and of Fernán Caballero in Spain. His creative life prospered not in the study, but in the drawing room, the theater, or John Murray's publishing house.

Washington Irving was our first classic. Even in his own time his sketches found their way into the schools and into the libraries beside the English masters; and he early demonstrated his mastery of the form and temper of the nineteenth century essay. Byron, Coleridge, and Scott were among his admirers; he stands on the shelves with Addison, Goldsmith, and Lamb. Yet, contrary to the myth, he never imitated these essayists, nor even Scott; his own style is authentic, born of a temperament, taste, and subtlety of mind which were peculiarly his own. Hawthorne, who worshiped him, and whose writing resembled his in its singular unity of tone, felt, as did all his peers (save the bristling Cooper), the union in him of a sensitive personality and the power to express this completely. His good sense and amiability undoubtedly enhanced his prestige, as Cooper's truculence diminished his; if Irving is now unread, this may be partly the reason. Yet his place, apart from his literary pioneering and his personal charm, is secure.

For Irving is classic not only as a stylist but as a poetic interpreter of legend—local, European, and universal. The monument at the entrance of "Sunnyside" commemorates his triple achievement, in the three figures of Diedrich Knickerbocker, King Boabdil of Granada, and Rip Van Winkle. If we dismiss the romantic story of his life, that of the son of middle-class Scottish parents rising to eminence as a famous American, or if we set aside his brilliant workmanship in prose, there still remains his extraordinary intuition concerning America's heritage of world legend, his fulfillment of his early determination to enrich his country with the "colour of romance and tradition." The tendrils of Irving's finest stories lie deep in human memories and feeling. Rip Van Winkle's return is a symbol of his concept of mutation, an all-pervasive theme in his writings:

> With what singular unanimity [says Thoreau] the furthest sundered nations and generations consent to give completeness and roundness to an ancient fable.

2

In retrospect, Washington Irving's golden career as a man of letters seems the result of a happy convergence of circumstances: the rapidly growing social and literary life of Manhattan; European fashions of writing; his own alert, plastic mind. Spanning the period between the Revolution and the Civil War (1783–1859), he read successively, as they came from the press, the writings of Burns, Campbell, Byron, Scott, and later, with some misgivings, those strange new books of Emerson, Poe, and Hawthorne! The early nineteenth century romantics, particularly Scott, oriented his taste, as the clubs, periodicals, and theaters of the gay, civilized little city directed his talents toward satire, the essay, the drama, and the short story.

Indulged by parents and innumerable friends as the youngest and most gifted child of a large family, he let himself drift in the pleasant currents of parties, gossip, and tea-table authorship. By his twenty-sixth year he had already composed light verse; a life of Thomas Campbell; essays and biographies for the *Analectic Magazine,* of which he was for a brief period the editor; a dim little volume of dramatic criticism (*The Letters of Jonathan Oldstyle, Gent.,* 1802); a symposium of satiric pieces, in collaboration with his brother William Irving and James K. Paulding (*Salmagundi,* 1807); and that energetic burlesque, *Diedrich Knickerbocker's A History of New York* (1809). This was our first remarkable piece of comic literature. Old New York shook with a roar of laughter.

In these years Irving knew the blessing of a light heart which defied his strain of latent melancholy. Of medium height, with chestnut hair, blue eyes, and a peculiarly pleasant, husky voice, he was friendliness itself; never as a person does he seem more winning than in these casual years when he squired the damsels of New York and Philadelphia, journeyed on a holiday trip to the Canadian frontier, played with the study of law in Judge Hoffman's office, or frolicked with *Salmagundi.* He "makes his travels go far," said his friend Henry Brevoort, alluding to a two years' grand tour of Europe bestowed upon Irving in 1804 by his fond brothers. He had returned still less in love with the family hardware business or with the bar; instead he was enamored of his little vellum notebooks, reminiscent of his wandering and germinal of many a later essay and story. Thus he had become almost the habitual dilettante when in 1809 the remarkable satire by "Diedrich Knickerbocker" (one of Irving's many *noms de plume*) revealed to discerning eyes, among them Scott's, his exceptional powers as a satirist. Yet in this very year occurred the great sorrow of his life, the tragic death of his fiancée, Matilda Hoffman; a period of doubt and uneasiness ensued, accentuated by the uncertainties of his future. During the War of 1812 he served as a staff colonel, and in 1815 he again sailed for Europe: he did not know that he was to remain abroad for seventeen years, or that he would return as "Geoffrey Crayon," the famous author of *The Sketch Book* (1819–1820).

After *Bracebridge Hall* (1822) and *Tales of a Traveller* (1824), and a winter in Dresden, he collaborated unsuccessfully in play writing in Paris with John Howard Payne. In 1826 he was on his way to Madrid to translate, at the request of A. H. Everett, Navarrete's history of Columbus. The following three years, mellowing his natural vein of romance, saw him a scholar in the ancient libraries of Madrid (where Longfellow called on him), a dweller with Andalusian peasants in the courts of the Alhambra, and a friend of the German antiquarian Böhl von Faber, and of his daughter Fernán Caballero, the Spanish novelist of manners. Such a life, seminomadic, was entirely congenial. Nevertheless, in 1829, bowing to his brothers' wishes, he accepted the post of Secretary of the American Legation in London. Three years later he returned to his own commonplace country, but not before he had published or prepared for the press four works memorializing his experience in the Spain of a century ago (*The Life and Voyages of Columbus,* 1828; *The Conquest of Granada,* 1829; *The Companions of Columbus,* 1831; *The Alhambra,* 1832).

For Irving this break with European life and thought was momentous. Though only fifty and at the height of his powers, he returned to an America appreciative of his fame but suspicious of his extended exile abroad and of his truancy to European themes. He now permitted a belated Americanization of all his interests. After a pilgrimage to the wild Southwest, he celebrated the wonders of the Osage frontier and other Western explorations in three elegant volumes for the parlor tables of his countrymen (*A Tour on the Prairies,* 1835; *Astoria,* 1836; *The Adventures of Captain Bonneville,* 1837). He was now the friend of Astor and, some said, his factotum; he dabbled in the stock market; and he was discussed for political posts. Most dismaying, he ceased, so far as we can tell, to read or to write for his craft, and on one occasion he admitted to John Pendleton Kennedy that, like most of his contemporaries, he regarded the creation of literature as merely a gentleman's avocation.

Living on at "Sunnyside," except during the years when he was the popular Minister at the court of Isabella II (1842–1846), he became an arbiter of our letters, a benevolent despot of our writers, a symbol of our thin literary culture. Uncomprehending, he beheld the rise of the great New Englanders and uttered pontifical platitudes on Poe's tales and *The Scarlet Letter.* He himself could only rifle again his old notebooks to produce biographies of Goldsmith, Mahomet, and Washington. His work was long since done; the age in which men read eagerly of the romantic wanderer in Europe already belonged to the past. Yet in the pathos of his decline we must not forget the adoration of Poe and Hawthorne; through Washington Irving, writing as an art had been born in America.

3

On all the historic events occurring within his long life of more than three-quarters of a century Irving sets down in letter or essay shrewd comment; but in his pages we look in vain for sustained wisdom concerning the movements of thought behind such events, for penetration of the intellectual life of his epoch. He wrote graphically of many famous episodes, of Waterloo or of the War with Mexico; but of Anglo-French relations or of American imperialism he has nothing to say worth hearing. He lived in England during the ferment culminating in the Reform Bill; but he merely laments the passing of the stagecoach and the yule-log Christmas. From the unrest in England and the democratic upsurge in America he acquired only a sentimental Toryism. On the meaning of democracy, of sectionalism, of the frontier he offers only pretty paragraphs communicating his personal distaste. He was simply a lover of old ways, of the romantic past.

Likewise, on more spiritual problems Irving was properly silent. His personal religious history includes his childhood with Deacon Irving, a Scotch Covenanter, his rapid progress toward skepticism and indifference, and finally, in the later years at Tarrytown, his identification with the Episcopal Church; the story reflects his natural remoteness from religious introspection. On the turmoil of Unitarianism, transcendentalism, evangelicalism, he let fall no word; he merely found New Englanders uncongenial, and popular religions vulgar. His notions on current trends of thoughts had their origin not in an analytical mind such as Melville's, nor even in a passionate partisanship such as Cooper's, but in an indolent temperament and an incurably conservative taste.

Irving's first books, *The Letters of Jonathan Oldstyle, Gent.* and *Salmagundi,* are distinguished by little save high spirits. Yet the other "youthful folly," as Irving ruefully called it, *A History of New York,* is still breathing. Prolix, repetitious, and, in consequence, mercilessly revised by Irving for later editions, it boils over with his boisterous ridicule of Swedes and Yankees, Dutch ponderosities, the pedantry of histories, and Jeffersonian democracy. It is written with gusto, on one occasion breaking into blank verse, and with such an avalanche of satiric allusion, from Cervantes and Rabelais to Walter Scott, that the latter's sides ached, so he wrote Irving, from laughing at its fantasy. In particular, the Dutch personalities of Wouter Van Twiller, William Kieft (a cartoon of Jefferson), and Peter Stuyvesant have crept into tradition, painting, and into the imaginations of subsequent generations of readers. The tough old mock epic may live; it proclaimed not only the breadth of Irving's self-cultivation, but also the vigor of mind that underlay his apparent languor.

Even as Irving corrected the proof sheets of his comic history, lovely Matilda Hoffman lay dying. The decade beginning with the publication of Diedrich Knickerbocker's learned indiscretion and ending with the appearance of *The Sketch Book* changed Irving from a callow youngster to a man; he was still amiable, still shrewd, but he was now meditative, a participant in human suffering. "I know," he wrote, "what it is to be sick and lonely in a strange land." As a refuge he turned again to writing. From boyhood he had faithfully kept journals and notebooks, and now, after his arrival in Europe in 1815, he continued to set down the titles of books, quotations, anecdotes, travel incidents, and his moods of depression; in the blurred pencil lines we may read of his unhappiness in the Liverpool office, of his study of German, of his ecstatic hours with Walter Scott: "Ah," he exclaims, "I knew happiness then!" On March 3, 1819, he forwarded to New York the first number of *The Sketch Book.*

"Crayon is very good," remarked Byron. Some even believed that he was Walter Scott. To us halfway through the twentieth century, all the virtues of *The Sketch Book* seem pallid; we can endure but not applaud the unevenness of the thirty-two pieces, the sickly pathos of such an essay as "The Pride of the Village," the naïve records of Irving's travel in England, the appropriation of the familiar legends. This last weakness in particular has attained an unpleasant emphasis in the scholars' discovery that even "Rip Van Winkle" is dependent on a literal translation from a tale in Otmar's *Volkssagen,* and that "The Legend of Sleepy Hollow" has origins in Bürger's *Der wilde Jäger* and one of the Rübezahl tales. Superficially at least, *The Sketch Book* appears to be dated, embalmed beyond all hope of a resurrection.

Yet beneath Irving's insipidities burned one strong response to life, his sadness or romantic melancholy in the presence of the law of change. The underlying idea in all Irving's best essays is that of flux. The old, forgotten books in "The Mutability of Literature"; the silence of the Boar's Head Tavern, once alive with the mirth of Falstaff; the tombs of Queen Elizabeth and Queen Mary; the grave of Shakespeare; the aged Rip Van Winkle—all declare the terrible brevity of life, the transiency of Man. Wistfully, recalling the tragic alterations in his own life, Irving dwells repeatedly in his public and private writing on "the dilapidations of time":

> How [he lamented in a notebook] the truth presses home upon us as we advance in life that everything around us is transient and uncertain. . . . We feel it withering at our hearts . . . in the funeral of our friends and written on the wrecks of our hopes & affections—when I look back for a few short years, what changes of all kind have taken place, what wrecks of time and fortune are strewn around me.

Perhaps the gossamer loveliness of these sketches suffers under precise interpretations. Their symbolism is probably unconscious, involuntary; the essays' indefinitiveness of emotion may be felt as we read, but not explained. In "Rip Van Winkle" this connotative meaning is the secret of its hold upon our imaginations; in it are all the implications of the grim but romantic theme of *tempus edax rerum.* In retrospect or in prospect, Rip's free youth, prolonged sleep, fanciful dreams, and disillusioning return are all ours. The fragile piece deserves study for its debt to German literature, to American legend, to Thomas the Rhymer, to Walter Scott, and to Irving's own boyhood; for its arresting adaptation in the theater, in song, or in Spanish or

Russian translation, for its revelation of a great stylist. But its soul lies in the symbolic distillation of a universal mood. All of Irving's literary manipulation of his reading, his wandering life, and his melancholy were concentrated in a passion which made him compose the tale during a single night, pouring into it all that he had ever felt concerning man's ceaseless enemy, "time": the German romance of Otmar, stories heard from the lips of Dutch friends, memories of the shadowy Catskills and of the blue Hudson. However outworn, by familiarity, jest, and parody, "Rip Van Winkle" still belongs to the indestructible literature of all peoples.

The depths of Irving's melancholy were not meant for repetition. As the climax of ten years of uncertainty and bereavement, his sadness had nearly spent itself in "Westminster Abbey" and "Rip Van Winkle." In a sense he had spoken; never again was he to recapture the spiritual tension of these essays, even in the moonlight scenes in "St. Mark's Eve," in *Bracebridge Hall,* or in the reveries of *The Alhambra.* A professional writer, bent on consolidating his reputation, he was now destined to do *The Sketch Book* over and over again, for the most part on its lower levels. After a season as "the most fashionable fellow in London," with Gifford, Rogers, Moore, and Scott as his friends and Byron and Coleridge as his admirers, he became the author of the fifty-one miscellaneous tales and sketches known as *Bracebridge Hall* (1822). "The fault of [this] book," said Maria Edgeworth justly, "is that the workmanship surpasses the work. There is too much care and cost bestowed on petty objects."

4

Meanwhile Irving was exploring the vein which was to link his books with the more macabre studies by Poe and Hawthorne. Long before 1817, when he sat in Scott's library and watched the novelist take down from his shelves his copies of Fouqué, Grimm, Bürger, Tieck, and Hoffman, he had shared the popular passion for what Scott called "the supernatural in fictitious composition." His approach to the tale of horror, despite his laborious study of the German masters, was characteristically light; he was fond of pointing his eerie stories with a question or a whimsical smile. Was the specter bridegroom an actual being? Was not the rumble of the Catskill bowlers a thunderstorm? After all, the head on Brom Bones' saddle was a pumpkin! He understood the practical value of success in this lucrative field, but his interest in the supernatural had causes deeper than those of expediency. Late in life he declared that the essential stuff of his life had been reverie. Dreams he could express in his versions of German romantic tales; these stories of the supernatural fed his restless, playful imagination, and in addition, as in "The Spectre Bridegroom," offered provocative problems for his craftsmanship. It is not surprising to hear of him during the winter following *Bracebridge Hall* writing, so rumor had it, a "German novel."

If so, this novel was never finished, and only one of the four sections of *Tales of a Traveller* (1824) showed directly the harvest of Irving's prolonged curiosity concerning the supernatural, from his youthful days in New York through this unlucky winter in Dresden. Beginning in an intensive study of German language and folklore, this had been expended in Saxon balls, skating parties, boar hunts, and an unhappy love affair with the English girl, Emily Foster. Tenacity of purpose was not the dominant trait in Irving's nature. So the ghost stories and the robber tales, at best marionettes, were supplemented with three other sections, one on Italy (rehabilitated from the notebooks of 1805), "Buckthorne," a shallow, semiautobiographical novelette under the influence of Goethe's *Wilhelm Meister,* and flaccid tales of cabbage-growing Dutchmen and of Captain Kidd. Gothic novelists, German romancers, Italian robber stories, legends of old New York—*Tales of a Traveller* is an empty cave of echoes.

The ensuing Spanish episode was to be far more felicitous than the German. In the Madrid libraries and in the matchless collection of the bibliographer, Obadiah Rich, he lingered long, indulging his love of old books and manuscripts. His original plan of translating Navarrete's history proved difficult; finally he abandoned the translation in favor of his own free dream of the great navigator. *The Life and Voyages of Christopher Columbus* (1828), in its eighteen books and one hundred and twenty-three chapters, is a strange compilation of theatrical personages (Columbus is a "man of sensibility"), pageantry, Gothic thunderstorms, treacherous Spaniards, noble savages, mermaids, seas of milk, and careful documentation. Its tantalizing hesitation between history and romance evidently created in Irving—a natural *colorista* in his treatment of Spanish material—an indecisiveness which reached a culmination in the next year in *The Conquest of Granada,* a book which no critic has ever been able to classify. It translates the chronicles but poetizes episode and character. Professedly the work of an old monk Fray Antonio Agapida, it craved respect as history. Yet the two long volumes are really romances, beautiful in their tone and even in their monotonous, flowing style. That such things never happened, we may be sure. Yet few admirers of Irving would cancel, as part of his total achievement, the lofty, melancholy personages of Columbus and the fair-haired "El Chico," Boabdil, the last Moorish king of Granada.

In *The Alhambra,* Irving's "Spanish Sketch Book" as Prescott christened it, the frail Boabdil reappears, the legendary king living happily in the palace or pausing sadly at *El Suspiro del Moro* for his final glance backward at his "city of delights," *bellissima Granada.* In its pages Irving was more at ease; he was not a scholar nor even a historian, despite his myriad footnotes; he was an antiquarian romantic. Released from a pattern of writing which had never won his complete devotion, he was again the easy student of folk-lore, through the black-letter books he had studied for his histories, through his friendship with Fernán Caballero, and through his intimacy with Andalusian peasants in the palace, Dolores and Mateo Ximénez. So he described in the leisurely fashion of *The Sketch Book* the Court of the Lions and the gallery of Lindaraxa; so he revived the ancient myths of mysterious caverns, buried gold, clashing scimitars, and phantom Moors. History, legend, and the ways of Granada blend in a reverie like those inspired by the dim, blue Catskills. Instead of homespun Dutchmen, paynim cavaliers; instead of the pumpkin, the pomegranate. In the book is the gorgeous tapestry of the Moorish past; such stories as "The Legend of the Arabian Astrologer" in Irving's most civilized manner perpetuate the enduring fascination of opulent, barbaric Spain.

If Irving was, as Robert Southey declared, no man to write of the wars of Granada, it is equally true that his books on the Western frontier, which after his return to America in 1832 he published as a capitulation to popular demand, show the same incapacity to set down facts unadorned by sentiment. H. L. Ellsworth's literal record of adventures in the Oklahoma country, on this same journey, reveals by contrast Irving's prettifying of buffalo, wild horses, and the customs of the Osage Indians. *A Tour on the Prairie* (1835) is a drawing-room version of, to do Irving justice, a rough experience, in which he forded streams on horseback and dined uncomplainingly on skunk. Yet in the waving trees of the forest he saw the Gothic arches of the Europe for which he was still homesick; and as he rode with Ellsworth through the blackjack, he reminisced on his creation of *The Sketch Book*. The glimmering lights of the campers, the picturesque dress of the ranger, the bee hunt, the hostile Indians, the undulating reaches of prairie and forest, he refined into a Europeanized idealization of the wilderness.

Sensing the gentle wave of excitement roused by *A Tour on the Prairie* in readers who had never seen a bison or an Indian, he sat in John Jacob Astor's library, and from the diaries of trappers, authentic writing of the frontier, he spun out in *Astoria* an agreeable epic of the overland journey to the Pacific outpost and the voyage around the Horn of the *Tonquin*. In both *Astoria* and the *Adventures of Captain Bonneville, U.S.A.,* also under the patronage of Astor, he relied upon just the right composite of general reading and citation from original sources, upon velvety narrative, upon that "singular sweetness of composition" which had captivated even the hard-bitten Francis Jeffrey. These frontier narratives were not really history, though scholars quoted from them; nor were they humbug, for compared with the actual events they depicted no dream world; they merely reflected the born romancer exploiting materials which belonged to the historian.

However popular, the Western narratives proclaimed one fact: the famous Washington Irving had written himself out. Surrendering in 1839 to Prescott the great theme of the Spanish conquest of Mexico, he attempted little more until, in 1848, he revised his collected works. He now, as he said, read little, and during the four years in Spain as Minister he did not even keep a notebook. He still loved everything Spanish, even the odor of the kitchens, but his beautiful letters to his nieces concerning the court of Isabella II and Espartero remain the sole record in these years of a talent that had gone to seed. Instead of legend, his thoughts were of politics, gossip, and his return to dear Sunnyside and his nieces. Reestablished there, in the last decade of his life, he wearily replundered the old notebooks until Longfellow, who owed so much to the inspiration of *The Sketch Book,* protested at this deterioration. These articles for the *Knickerbocker,* the miscellanies, such as *Wolfert's Roost,* or the third-rate biographies of Goldsmith and of Mahomet hardly bear analysis; little remained but the worn-out themes and the perfunctory grace of the master's style. Of his decline he was conscious, and just before his death he spurred himself to one last effort; but the five huge volumes of his *Life of Washington* mirror in his tired prose merely a stolid marble bust of the founder of the Republic.

5

More and more in retrospect, Irving emerges as both the beneficiary and the victim of the adolescent American culture of the first three decades of the nineteenth century. In this period he formed standards of literary taste from which, for good and ill, he never afterward deviated. To the pre-Victorian drama (he boasted he had seen every actor of his time), to the periodicals, to contemporary idols (not Addison and Steele, but Byron, Moore, Campbell, and Scott), to literary clubs, to growing libraries and still unexhausted private collections of manuscripts, and to lax copyright laws he was heavily in debt. Although he was occasionally capable, as in the libraries of Spain, of almost monastic devotion to learning, yet constructive thought, such as that of the Concord group, was alien to him. His satire, his short stories, his personal essays, were the easy products of his travel, his life in society, his endless casual jottings in his notebooks. Tirelessly he collected these literary *morceaux;* skillfully he amplified them into story or essay; and tactfully he introduced them into the most apropriate cultural medium—the periodical, the annual, or the timely book. He was a superlative literary adventurer.

This is the first, most obvious Irving, the caterer to public taste, hardly more than the hack writer hand in glove with such eminent publishers or editors as John Murray or Lewis Gaylord Clark; this is the Irving cannily alert to fluctuations in literary fashions and sales. Yet from such habits of mind, evident to readers of his self-revealing correspondence with Murray concerning the *Columbus,* developed a second Irving, the man of affairs, the successful American, the substantial citizen of New York (mentioned as candidate for the mayoralty), the grandee of Sunnyside, the Minister to Spain. From the days of Aaron Burr, Irving had hated the sweaty nightcaps of the mob; his Tory soul shrank before Jacksonian democracy. Yet if not openly on the political stage he remained in the wings of this theater. The same disarming tact, the same shrewdness, the same comprehension of public opinion so influential in his literary career, did not harm him in this related role of the observer of American life. These two careers were intimately joined. The America of the forties loved to canonize its literary men, such as a Bryant or an Irving—and so destroy them as poets or essayists. Literary fame might mean public eminence and, turn about, public distinction might enhance literary reputation.

Yet still another Irving—there were really three—commanded the homage of younger American writers who resisted more effectually than he the corrupting influences in our callow culture. If Hawthorne and Poe beheld in their inspirer a journeyman or political meddler, they never said so; in Irving's *Sketch Book* and even in his trifles they perceived the penetrating observer, and his aspirations and his craftsmanship as an artist. This Irving they revered. This Irving wrote tolerable verse and sketched so well that for days in Rome Washington Allston pleaded with him to turn painter. This Irving's notebooks blossomed with delicate sketches; his writing was deeply in debt to this related art; the pictorial quality of his prose is evident both in its metaphors of the brush and in its transference into the drawings of Leslie, Darley, and others, and into the weird beauty of John Quidor's paintings, from "Rip Van Winkle" to "Wolfert's Roost." For this nobler Irving, no self-imposed discipline for the sake of the image or sentence was, as the notebooks prove, too arduous. Ceaselessly he rewrote; indefatigably he revised; his was, in his best moments, the happy, blessed labor of the true artist.

19. JAMES FENIMORE COOPER

Meanwhile, James Fenimore Cooper, a tyro in the more subtle aims of the novel, assumed in the history of our literature an almost giant stature. More casual than Irving toward literary craftsmanship, he triumphed by his interpretation of romantic and realistic life on the frontiers of the forest and the sea, of the development of democracy, and of the meaning of America. A man of action whose career as a novelist was superficially an accident, in him genius was "mainly an affair of energy." In preface, pamphlet, history, and novel he poured out his convictions concerning his era, employing to the full, like Irving, all (except the theater) of the new instruments of culture. Cooper's was not properly a "literary" spirit; he was Agamemnon at a desk (and in the fray, too). Yet his genius left some thirty novels, several volumes of enduring social criticism, and two or three immortal characters. The resiliency of his masculine mind defied in his time devastating attacks from his critics; and his vitality is still contagious. As we read, we breathe the air of ocean and primeval lake; we hear the crack of Leatherstocking's rifle. Not only is Cooper an indispensable critic of growing, bumbling democracy, but a golden story-teller, the creator of our own Arabian Nights of the frontier.

Born in Burlington, New Jersey, on September 15, 1789, of English, Swedish, and Quaker antecedents, he enjoyed a vigorous youth in his father's village, Cooperstown, New York, not far from the edge of the eighteenth century frontier. Here he learned, from the example of Judge Cooper, to restore the traditional right of property to the Revolutionary prerogatives: life, liberty, and the pursuit of happiness. After two years at Yale College, from which he was dismissed for some obscure disciplinary reason, after serving as a midshipman in the United States Navy, after his marriage in 1811 into the family of the aristocratic Westchester De Lanceys, he began, virtually on a wager, his career of the man of action turned fiction writer. His rise to fame seems incredible. Within four years he had written four novels that placed his name second in popularity at home and abroad to that of the author of *Waverley*.

After these preliminaries, after his first fame in literary New York, after the incomparable *Last of the Mohicans,* we may follow him for seven years through England, France, Switzerland, and Italy. His was now a triple role: the cultivated American, with his family, in quest of the traditional experiences of European life; the distinguished author consorting in London and Paris with other notables; and the aroused critic of political and social institutions abroad and, indirectly, at home. Hazlitt saw him "strutting" down the streets of Paris; he was, in contrast to Irving whom he already despised, an unabashed observer in this older civilization.

Before Cooper returned to America in 1833, he had found time, besides aiding Lafayette in the French budget controversy and composing his invaluable commentaries on Europe and a defense of America against the attacks of foreign critics, to publish seven novels, of which three concerned the past of Europe, two the life of the sea, and two that of the frontier. Human energy could hardly do more. When Cooper, refusing an invitation to a dinner of welcome by his countrymen, set foot again on American soil, he was alive with a critical spirit which was to mold his career in America until his death in 1851. His was to be a boundless and often misdirected fervor. For eighteen years he instructed his unwilling countrymen through preface, novel, and libel suit; he lived his full life as country squire and critic of democracy; and he gave to the world his flow of novels. At virtually the height of his powers he died, his personal unpopularity obscuring his brilliance as a romancer of wilderness and sea.

2

An orderly and chronological or a sharp and topical classification of Cooper's writings is almost impossible. He had begun, after his unsuccessful novel *Precaution* (1820), modeled upon Jane Austen or Mrs. Opie, with three types of American subject (the Revolution, the frontier, and the sea); these themes he was to discuss throughout his life. Almost simultaneously he had begun in *Notions of the Americans* (1828) that downright defense of American life which was to animate *A Letter to His Countrymen* (1834) and his many prefaces and articles. In particular, his first frontier novel, *The Pioneers* (1823), explored the subject in which his genius was to find its noblest expression; it began the Leatherstocking series. The five novels in this series were composed over a period of eighteen years, and their chronology, in reference to the prolonged life story of Leatherstocking, is at variance with the order of composition and publication. At the same time the Revolution, the frontier, and the sea crossed and recrossed one another in these and other tales; and through them all crackled the fire of Cooper's criticism of America.

One fact is clear, a by-product of the truism that Cooper's writings are a paradise for the intellectual historian: he cared little for literature as literature. For him, writing was primarily an implement for his convictions about America. Some of his ideas, such as those concerning the Navy or the antirent laws, are as obsolete as those in Melville's *White Jacket or Mardi*; but others anticipate the persistent problems of democracy which now meet our troubled eyes in the newspapers. We should be aware of those which recur: his belief in the moral quality of liberty; his nationalism; his conviction that an aristocracy of worth was not inconsistent with the democratic ideal; his notion that native human character received its most valid self-expression in America; and his concept of the relation of all these ideas to the natural world of forest and sea. With infinite variation in detail these great themes reappear in all his books.

Thus in Cooper's writings we may see America in the early stages of introspection and self-evaluation, America trying to explain its origins and growth and to prefigure its far-off future, and America struggling for a commensurate cultural independence. In his novels and tracts may be found the optimism and fatalism of the frontier, the growth of class-consciousness, the beginnings of imperialism, the stubborn resistance of property-ownership, and a hundred other battles of a century ago. The desire to record these drove Cooper to his pen instead of to the forum; through writing he hoped to resolve these elements into some kind of unity. Having become an author, he was subject to literary influences, but his fundamental conception of writing is suggested in his statement in 1837:

> It is high time not only for the respectability but for the safety of the American people, that they should promulgate a set of principles that are more in harmony with their facts.

Nevertheless he can never be dismissed as a social novelist. Despite his "literary offences," as Mark Twain called them, he stands with Dumas and Scott as one of the great romancers of all time. Thackeray, for example, paid tribute to his heroes:

> Leatherstocking, Uncas, Hardheart, Tom Coffin, are quite the equals of Scott's men; perhaps Leatherstocking is better than anyone in "Scott's lot." *La Longue Carabine* is one of the great prizemen of fiction. He ranks with our Uncle Toby, Sir Roger de Coverley, Falstaff—heroic figures, all—American or British, and the artist has deserved well of his country who devised them.

Here is a puzzle: the contrast between these "great prizemen" and Cooper's own disregard of his famous novels, at which he was accustomed to laugh as "light literature." His attitude toward such fiction was, of course, typical of an era which considered writing a medium for saying what had to be said; even Irving came to believe that he must not take belles-lettres too seriously. Most of our early nineteenth century men of letters disdained, at least outwardly, the aims of the "artist."

Yet Thackeray uses this very word, and not too hastily or too flexibly. If we turn to Cooper's letters or his prefaces we shall find only simple literary principles, such as a story-teller's right to take a poetical view of his subject, or the novelist's definitions of types. Such do not seem, in the deepest sense, to be the reflections of an artist. Yet their simplicity is misleading. The fact is that Cooper cherished unconsciously an allegiance to the traditions of English fiction, precisely as he felt a deep but unanalytical devotion, especially in later life, to one of the traditional churches. We should reconsider his associations with writing not immediately concerned with "American opinions" or "American things."

Such a reexamination discovers in his reading the positive, somewhat naïve tastes which adorned his living. Certain economists and geologists he studied meticulously; he did first-hand historical research for both his fiction and his nonfiction; and he was steeped in Shakespeare. Yet deep literary intimacy, comparable to Hawthorne's understanding of Milton, is absent. His critical opinions were violent, impressionistic; throughout his letters we encounter few penetrative judgments on books, and though there is real dependence on the substance of literature, extremely few allusions occur, except for the poetic captions of his chapters. In his youth he read the lucid poetry of the eighteenth century (Pope, Gray, and Thomson); and he afterward shifted to such popular narrators in verse as Byron, Scott, and Longfellow. We do not need his sarcasms to learn what he thought of the more introspective nineteenth century poets. Shakespeare he held dear, but the writing of other Elizabethans had for him little meaning. Verse of intellectual weight bored him; he was fond of saying that Shakespeare should have written *Paradise Lost*!

Whenever the broader philosophic thought of Shakespeare or Scott touched his own simple code of living, he approved; but he was evidently less moved by such wisdom than by the power of the well told story. Here was a gift which, though he never says so precisely, must have stirred him deeply, like the bold art of historical or biographical narration. Such vital creation was worth a man's attention. Let us not be deceived by the petulance uttered not long before he composed *Precaution:* "much as I dislike writing in general." In the prefaces he sets down theories on the technique of narration. In such matters he was interested.

Thus by reading and by temperament Cooper acquired a devotion to a leading art form of the nineteenth century; namely, narrative. No definition of his work is just without recognition of this interest, however incomplete he was in the exposition of his theories. Perhaps this representation of action was an escape; certainly his study of it as an art form was amateurish; but his intuitional grasp of its methods was impressive. His love of books centered in the depiction of moving events and large natural emotion. His writing, says his daughter Susan,

> was simply the outpouring of his own nature, the expression of his own inmost train of thought, the current of real feeling in his own breast.

Had not his early experiments in verse revealed his incapacity for rhyme, he might well have attempted narratives like Byron's, for poetic feeling, as Balzac pointed out, was a strong element in his mental constitution. Since he loved narrative, he drew his literary life from the English novel. He swallowed it whole, with all its vices, devoting himself to its main purposes of eventful record and broad characterization.

For like reasons he admired the basic characteristics of the English novel form: realistic action, unrefined psychology or character, luxurious description, comfortable denouements, and the use of all these elements for the communication of social ideas. This last function of the English novel, which enjoyed such vogue in the first decades of the century, he emphasized, often to the detriment of his literary reputation. His great original contribution was the theme of the frontier, but this he adapted to the standard concepts of the novel form, concerning which he harbored no misgivings. Rebellion and criticism he reserved for the affairs of his country. In the movements which prophesied the break-up of the novel form or in those which strove for an American literary independence he showed no interest whatever:

> It is quite obvious [he remarked] that, so far as tastes and forms alone are concerned, the literature of England and that of America must be fashioned after the same models. . . . The only peculiarity that can, or ought to be expected in their [the Americans'] literature is that which is connected with the promulgation of their distinctive political opinions.

Accepting, with a surprising docility, a form later used by Hawthorne and Melville, Cooper made the most of its time-honored conventions. With a heavy, humorless style, often drawn into a terrible prolixity, he repeated in novel after novel all the threadbare formulas. He exploited heroic action in battle or single combat; he described secret escape and breathless pursuit; he played with disguises and rejoiced in true love rewarded. So objective was he, so fixed in purpose, so lacking in self-criticism, that he never foresaw how absurd his subservience might appear to later writers, so ridiculous, indeed, that he became a target for satire not to the intellectuals of New England but to other frontier writers such as Mark Twain and Bret Harte. He romanticized famous personages such as Washington or John Paul Jones, and for characters he often created bright-uniformed officers and high-bred maidens, strange blends of musical comedy and convent. In contrast to the natural conversation of his best characters, he frequently penned a dialogue so artificial that we read it with suppressed laughter; such diction represents not life but only the false taste of the novel readers of his generation. Everything suggests his obtuseness to what was happening in the craftsmanship of the novel.

3

Cooper's literary career, beginning with *Precaution* in 1820 and ending in 1850 with *The Ways of the Hour,* covers a period of thirty years during which he issued more than fifty books and pamphlets, exclusive of his articles and communications in periodicals. The main line of his development is difficult to trace; and in it Cooper himself had no interest. He obeyed merely his changing impulses to write on European subjects, on the bad manners of the Americans, on the United States Navy, or on frontier themes to which, had he been more sensitive to the true meaning of his genius, he would perhaps have wholly consecrated his unique powers. For convenience we may let chronology furnish us with an artificial division into three periods. The first includes Cooper's venture into fiction in his thirty-first year, his sudden triumph in his historical novel of the Revolution. *The Spy,* his comparative failure with a similar subject in *Lionel Lincoln,* and his success in special historical material of two distinct kinds—the sea and the frontier.

The second period, which includes the journey to Europe (1826–1833), beginning with *The Prairie* in 1827 and ending, according to our arbitrary division, with *The Deerslayer* (1841), consummates the novelist's richest, most varied performance. From his thirty-fourth to his fiftieth year he bestowed upon his puzzled countrymen his travel sketches, his social criticism, his satirical and allegorical novels, his romances of Europe, additional sea tales, and the three supplementary volumes of the Leatherstocking series. In the third period, which equates the last decade of his life, he played, with strength but with less inspiration, on the now familiar themes. Surveyed in this broad fashion, the three periods tell a fascinating story of his alternate blindness and vision in the creation of fiction.

Cooper's uncritical dependence upon the traditions of the English novel is evident not merely in his first novel, *Precaution* (1820), but in his second, *The Spy* (1821), in which the conventional patterns of mysterious disguise, the near-supernatural, sensibility, realistic comedy, and the mercurial rise and fall of human fortunes in chase or battle create all the surface faults and virtues of this version of a Revolutionary legend. The differences between *The Spy* and its feeble predecessor are real enough, but less so than some critics lacking the courage to finish *Precaution* have admitted. In both novels is the same Cooper, trying an increasingly deft hand at the tricks of story-telling. What delight must have filled his energetic mind as he found in the tale of "neutral ground" opportunities to use the devices culled from his wholesome but unprofessional habits of reading! Halfway through the composition of *The Spy* he must have known himself for a master of his new trade; likewise he must have realized that he had stumbled on themes suited to his unique powers.

One of these themes, invisible in *Precaution,* we may call, for want of a better name, patriotism. Often clumsily handled in *The Spy,* as in his anxious justice to the loyalists as opposed to the predatory skinners, or in his too composed, too benevolent "Mr. Harper"—George Washington transformed into a kind of fairy-godmother—this is basically a profound, almost religious emotion concerning the destiny of America. This feeling he was to express in many different ways, from the petulance of *Home as Found* to the sublimity of certain scenes in *The Prairie*. The feeling seems at best a tenuous, inconclusive weapon for a novelist, but it served Cooper well; indeed, it sheds today a glory on his writings. His meaning is inadequately conveyed in the starched words of Washington, as, at the end of *The Spy,* this Olympian figure attempts vainly to reward Harvey Birch for his unrecognized loyalty:

> That Providence destines this country to some great and glorious fate I must believe, while I witness the patriotism that pervades the bosoms of her lowest citizens.

We smile and rephrase the sentiment for ourselves; yet there remains the sincerity of Cooper's emotion. Consistently throughout his life it led him to expound and defend a Platonic theory of democratic society which, he felt, Europe needed and America did not appreciate.

Less nebulous, but equally suggestive of directions in Cooper's development, is his mastery in *The Spy* of native background; his powers of observation were remarkable. Intimate friends stressed this gift, now suddenly so apparent in these splendid scenes of the river country in autumn. Whenever Cooper's eyes fell on forest or stream he saw much; such details of nature he recombined endlessly for the settings of his novels. Thus the picturesque haunts of Harvey Birch on hillside or in mountain cavern are almost as fascinating as the spy himself.

In this portrait of the peddler-patriot we apprehend another talent of Cooper's, dim in *Precaution* and, like his intuitional sense of America, only intermittently revealed in, for example, Magua, Chingachgook, Leatherstocking—or now, in Harvey Birch. This talent is his capacity for creating truly original and *natural* character. So beset is Harvey by lay figures, such as the bewildered Mr. Wharton or the "lovely maniac" Sarah, that we are likely to lose sight of the unique qualities in the spy himself. This special insight of Cooper's is evident in Harvey, rather than in the tedious Smollettesque echo Dr. Sitgreaves, or even in the robust Betty Flannagan, who excited the admiration of Maria Edgeworth. In fact, Harvey Birch is not imitative at all, except in his incidental resemblance to the Yankee peddler type. Daringly conceived, inviting the contempt of his readers by his avarice, timidity, and meanness, he wins them in the end by the selflessness with which he faces his leader and his God. On this legend of the mysterious patriot who served Washington directly as a spy Cooper first employed that understanding which found fulfillment later in another conception, that of Leatherstocking. Thus he early revealed his comprehension of such natural men; Harvey Birch transcends the conventional formulas which control the hundreds of manikins in his novels.

It is characteristic of Cooper's experimental temper in this early period and also of his restless energy that, instead of following this successful historical novel of the Revolution with others like it, he essays in *The Pioneers* (1823) a fresh approach to American subjects. Conscious perhaps of his newly discovered skill in narrative, he now tells a negligent tale of Oliver Edwards and Elizabeth Temple, and of their union after the heroine is rescued from a forest fire by her lover who is finally revealed as the grandson of old Major Effingham. Jejune devices reappear, but Cooper's interest now centers on a reproduction of the frontier settlement in Otsego County, so dear to him in his youth. In an illuminating preface, written seventeen years after the first publication of *The Pioneers,* he reveals a conflict in his mind, still unresolved prior to the Leatherstocking tales. On the one hand, he is attracted by the imaginative creation of character, as in a Harvey Birch, and, on the other, by a literal accuracy tempting him in this novel to set down a true record of the life and environment of Judge Marmaduke Temple:

> This rigid adherence to truth [he admits], an indispensable requisite in history and travels, destroys the charm of fiction; for all that it is necessary to be conveyed to the mind by the latter had better be done by the delineation of principles, and of characters in their classes, than by a too fastidious attention to originals.

Such in 1823 was Cooper's uncertainty; from it resulted a compromise between a dependable record of his own father's life-history on the New York frontier, and a romance destined to be third in fictional chronology in the series of five great novels dedicated to the life of the forest. Yet he had hit it at last. He had implemented his patriotism, his descriptive power, and his exploration of human character (apart from his innumerable conventional figures); he had begun his long task of memorializing the American frontier experience. Dreamlike indeed, even with their basis of fact, were the clearings of the Otsego settlement, and heroic was the gaunt, angular Leatherstocking in his middle age. Yet these were living places and persons; at least their prototypes had lived in the past. Cooper hoped, as he said later, to show them without "too fastidious attention to originals" and "by the delineation of principles," that is, by the full sweep of his imagination. If he could do this, he would re-create one of the poetic yet essentially true experiences of developing America. He was adjusting his realism and romance in the treatment of native themes. He now trod the actual frontier and there brought to life one authentic inhabitant, a human being susceptible of continuous growth in his imaginative re-creation of the wilderness.

During this same year he had written and published *The Pilot,* a further capitalization of his own experiences. It is easy to attribute the novels of this period to minor incidents: *Precaution* to his annoyance at a weak English novel; *The Spy* to a tale told him by the brother of Mr. Jay; or *The Pilot* to a dinner party at which was discussed the nautical inadequacy of Scott's *The Pirate*. The causes lay deeper. His first novel of the sea was a consequence of his intense interest in the two frontiers; the sea and the wilderness, the water and the forest, were always intimately associated in his mind—witness, in particular, the aqueous quality of *The Pathfinder*.

In *The Pilot* (1823) we may disregard the complicated plot: the love affairs of the lieutenants Barnstable and Griffith with Cecilia Howard and Katherine Plowden, the nieces of the loyalist Colonel Howard; the schemes and ghastly death of the villainous Christopher Dillon; the usual soufflé of escapes, rescues, and pursuits. With variations, such are always staples in Cooper's novels. Beneath the veneer rests the solid oak of *The Pilot*: the passage of the straits by the schooner in the storm; the battle between the frigate and the British man-of-war; and the accurate transcripts of life on the ocean during the Revolution. Cooper's novels of the sea have more authenticity than those of the frontier; he never knew well an Indian warrior. His two years in the Navy, apart from his reading in the sea tales of Smollett and Marryat, enabled him to write with precision of sheet, jib, and compass. The sailors' dread of the land, their love of the open water, their management of schooner and frigate make *The Pilot* an event in the history of the novel of the sea.

Cooper's growth toward the mastery of his "art" is evident not only in this wider frontier of the Atlantic, but in two characters. The pilot himself, a favorite of our school days, is the second in Cooper's gallery of fictionized historic figures. This misty representation of John Paul Jones reminds us of the earlier portrait of George Washington; Cooper never learned that dimness of outline and an aura of mystery did not in themselves create a heroic character. In this man without a country he attempts a tragic hero; instead he achieves a Byronic ghost, a man with secret sorrows, darkened brow, mysterious devotions, and almost comic mannerisms. From our first sight of him in his "calmness bordering on the supernatural" until he waves adieu wearing "a smile of bitter resignation" he is as vague as his platitudes on liberty, of which Cooper evidently hoped to persuade us he was the ardent defender.

Long Tom Coffin is otherwise. He is as real as the *Ariel* itself, whose first timbers he saw laid and whose death he shared. Tom's every salty word, every vigorous action with cannon or harpoon, every simple feeling, reveal these perceptions demonstrated by his creator in Harvey Birch and Leatherstocking; himself a sailor and a man, Cooper could delineate a man of the sea. We welcome Long Tom's entrances as we dread uneasily those of the Gothic pilot, and his death (surely a mistake if we consider the possibilities for him in later sea novels of Cooper's) is closer to our human sympathies than that of Captain Ahab, in Melville's greater novel. Brief as is Long Tom's literary life, he ranks with Leatherstocking.

Presumably we must attribute the unevenness of Cooper's novels to the sluggishness of his self-critical faculty. Such disparities are almost ludicrous in the last two novels published before his journey abroad, that is, the final two in the first period of his writing and the fifth and sixth in his swiftly moving career as a novelist. Few if any novels in his later work, and relatively few from the pens of other writers, have equaled in pompous dullness *Lionel Lincoln* (1824–1825), a well informed but preposterous melodrama told against an oddly contrasting background of Boston on the eve of the Revolution. No character in the novel makes common sense—neither the priggish hero, nor the mysterious father, nor "Ralph," nor the hideous, unconvincing Mrs. Lechmere. *Lionel Lincoln* is a harlequinade of absurd scenes unredeemed save by the two or three battle pieces. Momentarily Cooper throws over us his old spell as the embattled farmers drive the redcoats down the Lexington road or as they release their sheet of fire from the crest of Bunker Hill. Yet such flickers of life are hardly to be mentioned except as hints of the unfaltering genius of the sixth volume, the second in order of publication of the Leatherstocking series, *The Last of the Mohicans* (1826). Here at last was mastery; more profound studies of his great frontiersmen were to come, but never was Cooper, now thirty-five years old, to attain such unerring control over the only technique of art which really interested him; never was he to tell another story with more triumphant suspense.

For many—and this represents one real level in the book—*The Last of the Mohicans* is a breathless, unrelenting chase, unbroken save when Alice and Cora are captured by Magua, and Leatherstocking, Uncas, and Duncan Hayward, thus far the pursued, become the pursuers. Who does not, like Mark Twain, discern extravagances in the plot? Yet the pauses between the climactic rifle shots of "La Longue Carabine" are so brief; the moments of security, so insecure; the very rustle of the leaves in the red man's forest, so ominous that the reader has no peace—nor desires it. This acceleration of event is a convincing indication of the novelist's development: gone is the jerky Cooper, backing and filling between tense incident and dreary moralizing. In this novel too there is time for frontier wisdom, but from the bitter struggle of Hayward and the Indian on the rock until the deaths of Uncas and Magua, action is all!

To this unflagging suspense *The Last of the Mohicans* probably owes its universal fame and its innumerable translations into foreign languages. The student of Cooper will also observe his skill in showing the civilization of the white man through the eyes of the Indians and through the mind of the partly Indianized Leatherstocking. In *The Pioneers* we have glimpses of the wilderness; in *The Last of the Mohicans* we live there. In this novel Cooper is less interested in the trapper than in the Indian, and the latter he counterpoises not so much against his enemies, the whites, as against other types of his own race. The noble young brave Uncas, his father, the honorable chieftain Chingachgook, the treacherous Magua, the venerable patriarch Tamenund—all such commemorate Cooper's first sustained exploration of the Indian's soul. In no other of his novels do we live so intimately with the folk ways of the red man and appreciate so sharply the inevitable conflict of those ways with encroaching civilization.

Aside from their value as studies of the Indian character, in whose depiction Cooper has been so maligned and eulogized, Uncas and Magua epitomize fairly the virtues and vices which Cooper thought worthy of portrayal in human nature: in the former, loyalty, unselfish love, and kindness; in the latter, treachery, hatred, and cruelty; in both, bravery, endurance, and intelligence. Cooper had never seen such Indians, but he had known, with modifications, such men. Intensifying and magnifying these human traits, he placed them in their frontier setting; authentic, Uncas and Magua retain permanent places in the history of fiction. As for Leatherstocking, he has grown younger since his somewhat grumpy role in *The Pioneers*. Wise counselor of the forest, chivalrous protector of women, ruthless enemy, provocative if by no means succinct philosopher, he has now reached full stature, although he is to be younger and more adventurous fifteen years later in *The Deerslayer*.

4

The appearance in the next two years in our second period of two strongly contrasted novels of respectively the sea and the prairie (on which Cooper never laid eyes) is an illustration of the vigor of his imagination. The *Red Rover* (1828) offers a magnificent drama of sailing ships in combat on the vast ocean; *The Prairie* (1827), though not deficient in incident, breathes upon us the peace of Nature and of Leatherstocking's old age and death. The story of the seaman in the Royal Navy who killed an officer and became the notorious pirate, but who loved America, flags and ends in the usual revelations of mistaken identities; the antics of Fid and Scipio Africanus cannot excuse its conventional episodes. Only the storm—perhaps the most titanic in all Cooper's writings—survives, the storm in which the *Royal Caroline* is beaten to a naked hulk.

More slow-moving than *The Last of the Mohicans, The Prairie* tells an adventurous tale in which a kidnaping, a buffalo stampede, and a prairie fire cannot divert our interest from Cooper's powerful conception of the immigrant family of Ishmael and Esther Bush and their sons. These squatters, the villainous Sioux, Mahtoree, or the benevolent Pawnee, Hard-Heart, are subordinate to the noble delineation of Leatherstocking, which, Cooper honestly believed, was to be the last glimpse of his frontier hero. This book, he wrote—not divining the future—

> closes the career of Leatherstocking. Pressed upon by time, he has ceased to be the hunter and the warrior, and has become a trapper of the great West. The sound of the axe has driven him from his beloved forests to seek a refuge . . . on the denuded plains that stretch to the Rocky Mountains.

Enfeebled in arm but not in mind, Natty is still the "philosopher of the wilderness"; he dies as he has lived, serenely, calling out to his Maker, "Here."

Although in this period Cooper published ten more novels, all save the two which recalled Natty from his grave on the prairie (*The Pathfinder,* 1840; *The Deerslayer,* 1841) were marred by that pedestrianism which was so characteristic of him when absorbed by some general aspect of tradition or afflicted by his heavy enthusiasm for reforming his countrymen. Thus *The Wept of Wish-ton-Wish* (1829), clumsily aiming to "perpetuate the recollection of some of the practices and events peculiar to the early days of our history," is a melodrama of King Philip's War enacted against a superficial background of Puritan Connecticut; Cooper alluded to these New Englanders' "very quaint and peculiar dogmas." He was more at home but not more convincing in *The Water-Witch* (1830), set in New York in the same century; instead of the assault on the blockhouse of the previous novel, he offered the pursuit of the pirate, "The Skimmer of the Seas." This book he wrote in Italy, while, with his fatal fertility, he was already at work on a series of three novels with European themes. This trilogy *(The Bravo, The Heidenmauer, The Headsman)* attempted to meet Scott on his own ground, by portraying European society as it would appear to an enlightened American, liberalized by his intimacy with democracy.

Some savage attacks from American newspapers on *The Bravo* crystallized his latent intention: in 1834, he published his vituperative *A Letter to His Countrymen,* in which he assailed these criticisms and prematurely announced his retirement as a novelist. He now embarked upon that fierce warfare of preface, satire, and libel suit which makes the reappearance of Leatherstocking nearly a miracle. His anger found expression in an experiment in allegory, *The Monikins* (1835), and in two complementary novels *Homeward Bound* and *Home as Found* (1838). These latter are ambitious efforts to portray contemporary American manners; the first, spiced with the usual chase and battles, shows a group of cultivated Americans returning to their country in company with less estimable members of society; the second examines American social life in town and country. Cooper's success is debatable; the elegant Effingham brothers, who represent his conceptions of the American gentleman, are as unnatural as his caricatures of our clodhoppers, Mr. Steadfast Dodge and Aristabulus Bragg. Through such charcoal sketches Cooper solidified the growing enmity of his countrymen, earned the nickname of Effingham, became involved in the famous "Effingham" libel suits, and seemed to justify his irritable decision (to which he did not adhere) that he would write no more fiction. Yet in *Homeward Bound* and *Home as Found* he bequeathed to historians sovereign documents of the social issues of the day.

About the year 1840 he had reached the peak of his activity, not only in his quarrels with his countrymen, but in his power over the written word. Since his return to America he had published, besides the works already described, four volumes on his life in Europe, his political primer for his countrymen *The American Democrat* (1838), various reviews, the pioneer history of the American Navy (1839), a masterpiece of tediousness *(Mercedes of Castile)* in the form of a novel on Columbus; and in a demonstration of the fertility of his genius, he completed the Leatherstocking series with *The Pathfinder* (1840) and *The Deerslayer* (1841). These two novels were the immortal answer, had his angry contemporaries only realized it, to all denunciations of Cooper as a man and writer. Once again he moved freely amid forest and lake; forgotten were the self-conscious allusions to his own experiences (as in *Home as Found*), and even the moralizing, which he could never entirely abandon, took on dignity from Leatherstocking's life in the wilderness. Again, all is action; and once more we share his beautiful insight into simple, strong characters, so amazing after the grotesque portraits of the Effinghams.

The Pathfinder is absorbing for its union of the two themes most natural to Cooper in fiction—adventure in the forest and adventure on the water; and in this novel the water is an inland lake, enriching the beautiful panorama of the Ontario frontier. Moreover, he obtains a secondary contrast in Cap, the salt-water sailor, watching with reluctant admiration the exploits of young Jasper Western, the fresh-water pilot of the *Scud*. No other frontier novel of Cooper's attains the variety of episode of *The Pathfinder*; even the standard blockhouse scene is pleasantly off-pattern through the character of the Indian woman, Dew-of-June; and there are no mistaken identities! Only the suspicion concerning Jasper, with his final vindication, reminds us of Cooper's stock artifices. The great central character of the series is in his prime now, like his creator; and the woods are his sanctuary as well as his battleground. Cooper wishes us to feel the deepening influence of the frontier upon this natural man, this true democrat living simply with other men. Possibly some of Cooper's own Quaker heritage enters into the scout's relations with God and Man. Leatherstocking is capable of grief in the loss of Mabel Dunham. Yet Cooper's blessing lies on the idyllic happiness of Mabel and Jasper; united at last, the lovers bid the scout farewell:

> A tread whose vigour no sorrow could enfeeble soon bore him out of view, and he was lost in the depths of the forest.

Thus at this apex of Cooper's intellectual and emotional powers, sustained in *The Deerslayer,* we may observe not only his control over his material—stock characters are few in this final novel of the series—but also his deeper intuitions concerning the moral nature of the scout. In renouncing Mabel Dunham (in *The Pathfinder*), he dedicates his life to the meditative moods of the forest, and because of his conviction, already latent in *The Deerslayer,* the love of Judith Hutter finds him unresponsive. Younger now, if we follow the chronology of Leatherstocking's spiritual development, the affair prepares us for his unwillingness to wed Mabel. In his increasing imaginative grasp on the character, Cooper emphasizes Deerslayer's essential loneliness and his kinship with the forces of nature. Thus he now depicts him in its early years, the brother-in-arms of Chingachgook, taking human life for the first time and acting with youthful energy and intensity. We thrill at the fight for Tom Hutter's "castle" or mourn for the death of Hetty or shudder as Deerslayer awaits the torture; but in this culminating novel we perceive, in particular, Cooper's preoccupation with the spiritual meanings of his immortal character.

5

In *The Deerslayer* Cooper had, unaware of the precise nature of his posthumous fame, made his ultimate bid for immortality through enduring works of fiction. Nevertheless, in the dozen or so novels which were to follow, in our third period, from *The Two Admirals,* in April, 1842, until *The Ways of the Hour,* published in 1850, a year before his death, he retained his zest for narrative. Moreover, in the trilogy of antirent novels, the Littlepage Manuscripts, he reached the zenith of another talent; he became the acute social observer. Thus there occurred no real decline of his innate force as a writer, but only, according to the laws of advancing years, a hardening of prejudices, a narrowing of opinions, and insulation from the new generation in the America he loved so dearly. It is pointless to enumerate the topics which clogged more and more his narratives and aroused his didacticism as his social vision was dissipated into concern for particular and sometimes petty causes: revelation and reason in *Wing and Wing*; Dutch and English land grants in *Wyandotté, Afloat and Ashore,* and *Miles Wallingford*; Christian conversion in *The Oak Openings*; or trinitarianism, against the odd Arctic backgrounds in *The Sea Lions.* Religion, as he himself drew more closely to its supports, and social injustice, as he realized its persistence, were now perpetually the subjects of his lectures to his readers, but his other obsessions were infinite: the Yankees, English pronunciation, or the Bay of Naples. Yet if to these crotchets we oppose a patience unknown to their possessor we may, in such a novel of adventure as *Jack Tier* (1848), learn much concerning Cooper's mind. In *The Two Admirals* (1842) the maneuverings, not this time of single ships, as in *The Pilot* and *The Rover,* but of fleets, make engaging episodes; and, despite the theology and the ever present villainous Yankee Ithuel Bolt, Cooper's complacence about *Wing and Wing,* which appeared only a few months later, is pardonable. Against a blue and gold Mediterranean background, this tale of a privateer and an English frigate is enthralling—more so, indeed, than the standard blockhouse siege in *Wyandotté.* In contrast to Hawthorne, who distilled his study of Puritanism into delicately balanced interrogations, Cooper's exposition of the ideology he detested is opinionated and superficial, though hardly more so than his favorable delineation, in the same novel, of Anglicanism.

It is on his mature mastery of an impartial approach to social history in the guise of fiction that the distinction of his next two novels rests. Published within a year, told in the first person as the recollections of their hero, and relating a continuous story, *Afloat and Ashore* and *Miles Wallingford* are really one novel. The first part is in Cooper's best narrative manner, the action on the sea equaling in suspense that of *The Pilot* or *The Red Rover,* and throughout both parts we take pleasure in Cooper's own autobiography (for the lovely Lucy is assuredly Susan De Lancey, and Miles is Fenimore Cooper). Yet apart from an undeniable subacidity of manner, the two novels are remarkable for their temperate portrayal of eighteenth century life in orchards, meadows, fields, river valleys, and substantial buildings of such American farms as Clawbonny. Here is a serene picture of this solid, almost idyllic America then hardly known at all to European critics of our civilization. Here, as in *Satanstoe* and *The Chainbearer,* is the novel of manners, the fictional re-creation of the best in American society, which Cooper had always hoped to accomplish, blended imperfectly with the romance of action which he did with such natural ease.

This panorama of American life is integrated with the succeeding trilogy, *Satanstoe* (1845), *The Chainbearer* (1845), and *The Redskins* (1846). In the antirentism controversy, now a forgotten issue, Cooper saw the crisis of American idealism, and characteristically aligned himself on the side of the landlords and the rights of property. His now nostalgic patriotism had finally turned him against the equalitarian society of Andrew Jackson's America. Again, in the first of the three novels, and to a lesser degree in the second, he tells a good story, though this virtue is stifled in the preachy *Redskins.* In any case the sequential elements of the three books, as he says in a Preface, depend upon his study of "principles." The romance of Cornelius Littlepage and Anneke Mordaunt, with the usual reticulations of plot and with a black-hearted pedagogue from Danbury, Connecticut, ranks high among Cooper's plots. At the same time the social novelist diverts us from the action to the scenes themselves, to the patroons and the English in the eighteenth century, or to colonial New York, with its "Pinkster" or Dutch Festival. Such interests dominate the trilogy, even in the symbolic character of Thousandacres, the New England squatter, and in the long debates concerning the ethics of this upstart and that of the heroic figures admired by Cooper. The tone of the first two books is judicial; only in *The Redskins* does the controversy dissolve in Cooper's incoherent rage at the impending defeat of what he held so dear.

With the beguiling confession of the Littlepage Manuscripts, really Cooper's own memories related in his late fifties, and with these adventures of the trilogy, it may be said that Cooper's career as writer of the creative imagination began its decline. His five remaining novels show little weariness; they include lightning flashes of his art, as in the careful symbolism of *The Crater* (1848) or the battle between the sloop-of-war and the brig in *Jack Tier* (1848). Yet toward the close of his life his disgust with the stupidities of civilization narrowed his literary horizon; his general underlying thesis concerning the blindness of mankind to his ideal of controlled liberty was not enough. Into *The Crater,* for example, our first important Utopian allegory, he poured his dismay about humanity's need for authority; into *The Oak Openings,* his fears concerning its insensibility to conversion; into *The Sea Lions,* his ideas on the Trinity; into *The Ways of the Hour,* his hatred of trial by jury; and into all that he wrote, the thousand little familiar petulances which we still associate with Cooper's temperament. Though he fled to the mysterious island in *The Crater* or to antarctic realms in *The Sea Lions,* yet he was still harassed and stung by these gnats of the mind. It is a strange, and in retrospect, almost a comic spectacle. His powers had not failed; the old narrative skill and the social idealism were still strong, but they were cluttered by the foibles of the society in which he lived so critically.

After all, as we look back on Cooper's career, we may well be lost in wonder at the magic which this American civilization, with all its follies and grandeurs, held for him, at once its enemy and its lover. He criticized it, satirized it, and abused it, but he never ceased to find it fascinating; for him its interest long outlived his intermittent experimentation with literary craftsmanship. All his writing after *The Deerslayer* indicates that he cared less and less for form and method and more and more for what he could say through the novel as a medium. To only one phase of art he remained loyal, to the talent which he could not have abandoned had he wished, the art of telling a story; this art he never quite fused with his devoted but often misguided patriotism. Thus, estimating Cooper, we should note again that in his writing America was first indeed and the novel for its own sake a bad second. Therefore in scope and in passion, it is barely possible that Cooper the social critic will outlive Cooper the novelist of the many novels, but never Cooper the romancer, Cooper the teller of the Leatherstocking tales. Yet even those tales could never have been so passionate, so profoundly and originally American, had he not probed relentlessly beneath the surface of facts to the principles of American society and of human conduct.

20. DIVERSITY AND INNOVATION IN THE MIDDLE STATES

BETWEEN the extremes of New England on the one hand and the South on the other, New York and Pennsylvania, as the leaders of the group of middle Atlantic states, were distinguished at this time by their "middleness," as Henry Adams put it—their practical and sagacious aptitudes for compromise and the blending of interests. Uniting now with New England, now with Virginia and her Southern neighbors, serving as a balance wheel, they provided the force that in politics made a nation and in intellectual and artistic activities was ultimately to fuse divergent elements into a national culture.

Cooper and Irving were, of course, the major literary figures, with Bryant joining them in 1825 after a New England youth, and Poe later, after struggling to make his career in Richmond. It is perhaps significant that these four writers, thus drawn to a center, became recognized, when they spoke for the region, as the first literary spokesmen for the whole Republic, both at home and abroad. A region that boasted the political and commercial capitals of the nation would have little incentive to develop a strong regional characteristic in its culture. Only in its minor writers, like Paulding, Willis, Barker, Halleck, or Bird, does the too insistent influence of a Dutch, a Quaker, or a patrician British ancestry, a naïve coffeehouse or greenroom sophistication, a patriotic fervor, act as a restraint on creative power. This was the hub of the national literary life—and a wheel is small but solid at the hub.

These minor writers created in the metropolitan centers of Philadelphia and New York—and to a lesser extent in the smaller cities of Albany, Baltimore, and Washington—something of the spirit of a provincial eighteenth century London. These were the men and women who gathered in salons and clubs for literary conversation; who supplied the magazines and the stage with acceptable offerings, patriotic in accent but usually British in form and tone. They were the logical inheritors of the earlier group (Freneau, Brown, Dennie, Hopkinson, Brackenridge, Tyler), but more numerous and more successful. Many of them managed, where the earlier group had failed, to make a substantial living by their pens. Poe caught their dominant characteristic when he called them the "Literati"; N. P. Willis, their tone when he

titled his essays *Pencillings by the Way*. There was scarcely an accepted literary form that escaped them, but they naturally ran to the short story, the essay, and the lyric poem because there was a market for such writings in the new magazines, or to the social comedy or the melodrama because there was a call for such plays in the new theaters.

2

James Kirke Paulding, throughout his life identified with New York State, was perhaps the most typical writer of his time and place—of the diversity and innovation so characteristic of the writings of these middle states. In his voluminous writings over several decades, he showed affinities with more literary movements and styles, even with more individual authors, than any other figure of the early nineteenth century. His virtues and his faults were those of a new nation just coming to self-awareness. He was a Cooper without Cooper's gusto, an Irving who stayed at home. His versatility, his impetuous enthusiasm for a wide variety of subject matter, his willingness to experiment with poetic epic, short story, novel, drama, literary criticism, humorous sketch, moral and social and political criticism of a Swiftian stamp—all these phases of his ever alert inclusiveness perhaps explain better than any lack of talent or perspicacity his failure to achieve the stature of a truly great writer. He was "middleness" personified, and "innovation" was his greatest virtue; he was as well a devout though sometimes noisy champion of democracy, but realistic, with his feet on the ground, and without metaphysical subtlety.

Except for minor contributions to Peter Irving's *Morning Chronicle* as early as 1802, Paulding's literary career properly began in 1807, with the publication of the first series of periodical essays entitled *Salmagundi; or the Whim-Whams and Opinions of Launcelot Langstaff, Esq., and Others,* jointly produced with William and Washington Irving, who had been his friends and literary cronies since his arrival in New York City from his native Dutchess County some ten years before. Though the collaboration of Irving and Paulding was so close as to make individual assignment problematical, Paulding is generally given credit for having first sketched the characters of the Cockloft family, modeling one of them on his own uncle. The second series of *Salmagundi,* issued in 1819, was entirely Paulding's work.

The Diverting History of John Bull and Brother Jonathan (1812), published as by one Hector Bull-us, set the tone and indeed to a large degree the pattern for a series of nationalistic political satires. This work, originally in sixteen chapters but later more than doubled in length, looked backward to Francis Hopkinson's *A Pretty Story* (1774) and forward to some of the later sections of Melville's *Mardi* (1849) in its intention and method. Bullock

Island, representing England, and the thirteen farms of Jonathan, representing the United States, are the chief locales of action, though activities are reported from the Manor of Frogmore of Lewis Baboon (Louis XVI) and Beau Napperty (Napoleon), "called Beau because he was no beau at all." The theme of the British traveler in America, which reappeared in Paulding's *John Bull in America; or the New Munchausen* (1825), is embodied here in Corporal Smellfungus. The sequel of this early work, though its inferior, *The History of Uncle Sam and His Boys* (1835), pictured Jonathan as now become Uncle Sam, with twenty-four sons (states), mostly large, though a few, "shrunk in the boiling," were "rather conceited and jealous, as most little people." Paulding's two plays—*The Bucktails; or Americans in England* (written about 1815) and *The Lion of the West* (which won a prize in 1830)—reflect this tendency of nationalistic caricature, though the major figures deserve more serious consideration as realistic character portrayals.

For most of Paulding's later serious work—whether epic poetry or fiction or drama—the keynote was sounded and the intention stated in his article on "National Literature," in the final issue of the second series of *Salmagundi*, August 19, 1820. Here, in discussing "rational fiction," Paulding attacked "servile imitation," "the ascendancy of foreign taste and opinions," "the aid of superstition, the agency of ghosts, fairies, goblins, and all . . . antiquated machinery," and advocated dependence on nature and "real life" where "events, however extraordinary, can always be traced to motives, actions, and passions, arising out of circumstances no way unnatural, and partaking of no impossible or supernatural agency." Though Paulding sometimes used foreign settings for his tales—rarely with much success—and occasionally introduced supernatural elements, for the most part he lived up to his creed. Some aspects of American life he saw through rose-colored glasses; he shared with his contemporaries an ill founded hope that pioneering and frontier life would develop only "doric simplicity" and strength of character, rarely noting that it might also develop crudity and cupidity.

Paulding's epic poem of some sixteen hundred lines, *The Backwoodsman* (1818), is less romantic than Crèvecœur's account of Andrew the Hebridean and foreshadows some of the ideas expressed in Frederick Jackson Turner's famous essay on the frontier three quarters of a century later. The story of Basil's westward trek from the banks of the Hudson to "the poor man's long-sought, new-found promis'd land" in the Ohio River valley, Paulding told "with homebred feeling, and with homebred fire," though the fire of the ruthlessly mechanical eighteenth century heroic couplets has dimmed. Indicating the success of Basil's Western career by sending him to Congress as reward is a fault more national than personal—merely another evidence of the common American belief that virtue and industry inevitably bring material

reward. The descriptions of natural scenery, the pictures of the Moravians in Pennsylvania, the interspersed accounts of the Wyoming Massacre and of various historical figures—Arnold, André, Greene, Marion, Franklin, Washington—as well as the central narrative, make the poem intrinsically American.

The tales or short stories and the novels are Paulding's most important work. His leisurely manner of writing, his inclination to introduce personal comment and opinion, and his variety of interests are best adapted to happy expression in prose fiction. Assuredly the Dutch stories are the best—and Sybrandt Westbrook of *The Dutchman's Fireside* (1831) is probably his most successful full-length characterization—but settings and characters other than Dutch are also effectively handled. Woodsmen and frontiersmen, whether Sir William Johnson in *The Dutchman's Fireside* or Ambrose Bushfield in *Westward Ho!* (1832), are drawn with veracity and compulsion. Paulding's first novel, *Koningsmarke* (1823), introduced the Long Finne as a character against a background of the Swedish colonies in Delaware; his fifth and last novel, *The Puritan and His Daughter* (1849), shifted from Cromwellian England to New England, portraying Puritanism in its two main environments. *The Old Continental, or the Price of Liberty* (1846) used the background of New York during the Revolution to tell a story of the vicissitudes of Whigs in a Tory community—a theme echoed in the account of the origin of the ancestral curse that haunted the melancholy Dudley Rainsford in *Westward Ho!*

In his zealous and often self-conscious efforts to build an indigenous literary tradition, Paulding took himself and his work seriously, emphasizing throughout accuracy and morality. As he took pains to point out, he frequently used original sources, such as Mrs. Grant's *Memoirs of an American Lady* (1808) for *The Dutchman's Fireside* and Timothy Flint's *Recollections of the Last Ten Years* (1826) for *Westward Ho!* He no doubt fully agreed with the publisher's (Harper's) preface to *The Dutchman's Fireside* setting forth the moral duty of the novelist to supply to his reader

> without the bitterness and danger of experience, that knowledge of his fellow-creatures which but for such aid could, in the majority of cases, be only acquired at a period of life when it would be too late to turn it to account.

By characterization, depiction of the mores of other times, dialogue, and direct auctorial comment, he inculcated the values of "doric simplicity" (a frequent phrase in *The Dutchman's Fireside*), rationality, common sense, and tolerance—the latter notably in his attack on the sadistic dogmatism of the itinerant preacher in *Westward Ho!* Sometimes he used broad satirical portraiture suggestive of Sheridan or Royall Tyler to reduce the qualities he abhorred to the absurd. The Obsoletes in *The Bucktails* are caricatures of this type, as also the suitors of Catalina Vancour in *The Dutchman's Fireside*: Barry Gillfillan, a "combustible gentleman," with "the truly Irish propensity for falling in love extempore," and Sir Thicknesse Throgmorton, the impecunious peer of "dignified stupidity." Less frequently, and most often less successfully, he embodied the admired virtues in a model character, like Sir William Johnson, also of *The Dutchman's Fireside,* or Virginia Dangerfield or Father Jacques, of *Westward Ho!*

In characterization and in handling of plot, Paulding was occasionally the equal of Simms and Cooper. Resemblances between *The Dutchman's Fireside* and Cooper's *Satanstoe* (1845), both dealing with the region near Albany during the French and Indian War, have often been pointed out. *Satanstoe* is a more compact and unified story, but Corny Littlepage's rescue of Anneke from the ice break in the Hudson was no more vividly described than Sybrandt Westbrook's saving Catalina Vancour when a violent storm flooded the island where the young people were picnicking. Cooper's hero had much in common with Paulding's: both represented the ideal fusion of Dutch and English blood; both saved the heroine's life on more than one occasion when she was threatened by a natural calamity or by Indians; both found their chief rivals in Britishers visiting the colonies. But Paulding's Sybrandt was less idealized, more bashful and lacking in assurance, less suave (indeed, even awkward), more credible thus in confronting the situations the plot involved him in, and withal more human and appealing. The author's understanding of his psychology was on occasion profound, particularly in the relations of Sybrandt and Sir William Johnson. Catalina, also, was in her womanly spirit and perversity more credible than Anneke. Paulding did not, however, produce any character so vividly compelling as Cooper's Guert Ten Eyck.

Though more fluently written, *Westward Ho!* which was published only a year later is less realistic, even less honest. Paulding did not know or understand the Virginia plantation owner type, which Colonel Cuthbert Dangerfield of Powhatan represented, as he knew and understood the New York Dutch. He was also less familiar with the topography and mores of Kentucky in the days when it deserved the name "dark and bloody ground." In his fascination for the psychological quirks of Dudley Rainsford, whose perverted guilt-consciousness is a major determinant of the plot, Paulding was on the track of profoundly dramatic material, but he was beyond his depth—unwilling to treat his character according to the superficial romanticism of Poe's practice and unable in realistic terms to understand and describe the aberrations of Rainsford's diseased mind. Thus he fell short of Charles Brockden Brown in picturing a situation reminiscent of *Wieland* (1798), when Rainsford feels religious compulsion to make a blood sacrifice of his fiancée, Virginia Dangerfield, though in a detailed transcription of the hell-fire sermon which immediately provokes the delusion, Paulding prepared the way for intense tragedy. In the character of Ambrose Bushfield he was more on his own ground. The burly and uncouth woodsman who is Colonel Dangerfield's executive officer in the conduct of the expedition down the Ohio to Kentucky and in the building of a new community is an inveterate Indian-hater, made so by the Indian massacre of all of his family in which he miraculously escaped. "Transcendent" is his favorite adjective, and he invariably desires to make the object of his wrath "smell brimstone through a nail hole." Woodsman's rodomontade—suggestive of the speeches of Nimrod Wildfire in *The Lion of the West,* which Paulding got ready for the stage about the same time—comes frequently from Bushfield's lips. Despite his eccentricities of dress, speech, and action, Bushfield is a well rounded, credible character exemplifying Crèvecœur's theories of the effects of life on the cutting edge of the frontier.

Of the Dutch short stories, "Cobus Yerks" and "Claas Schlaschenschlinger" —both included in *The Book of St. Nicholas* (1836)—are typical. The first, in mood and material suggestive of Irving's "Legend of Sleepy Hollow" though the situation described more nearly resembles that in Burns' "Tam O'Shanter," is the account of Cobus' return one night from a tavern presided over by a "bitter root of a woman." He is chased by a black dog turned "devil," and learns the fallacy of "the doctrine that spirit and courage, that is to say whiskey and valour were synonymous." In "Claas Schlaschenschlinger," the two main events are supernatural interventions by St. Nicholas; but the details of the plot and the characterizations are realistic. The psychological stories are best represented by "The Dumb Girl" and "The Ghost," though both might also be classified as stories of character or of plot. In the first, Phoebe Angevine, the title character, living a frustrated existence with her mother and idiot brother, Ellee, is attracted by the stranger, Walter Avery, allows herself to be seduced, and is deserted. Though some critics have made extravagant comparisons with Hawthorne and *The Scarlet Letter,* Paulding's tale lacks the fullness and depth to give conviction to the handicapped heroine's psychology or reality to the pathos of the story. "The Ghost," first published in both *The Atlantic Souvenir* and the New York *Mirror* in 1829, is the story of one William Morgan, who perversely delights in playing ghost, thereby occasioning trouble for others as well as himself. Paulding's characterization of Morgan and of Tom Brown—the chief victim of Morgan's pranks—and his handling of suspense and narrative are effective, direct, and convincing.

Restless like the young nation itself, Paulding was busy with political office as well as with writing—too busy ever to criticize and revise, too eager to be doing other things that also needed to be done ever to do anything quite to the best of his abilities. But he frequently did first what other writers—New Yorkers, or New Englanders, or Southerners, or Westerners—were later to do better and more memorably. Poe's comment, "Paulding owes *all* of his reputation as a novelist, to his early occupation of the field," is unjust. In his range of interest and materials, in his capacity for "innovation," in the breadth of his view of the resources out of which America could build her own literature, and in his formulation and practice of a literary creed, Paulding represents the catholicity and inclusiveness, the fusion of divergent strains, for which the whole body of literature produced in the middle states from 1810 to 1860 is most distinguished, and by which it is best characterized.

3

Closely allied with Paulding in the novel—and like him showing common traits with Cooper and Simms—was the Philadelphia physician Robert Montgomery Bird. After two novels with a Mexican background, *Calavar; or The Knight of Conquest* (1834) and *The Infidel; or The Fall of Mexico* (1835), as well as the earlier plays for Edwin Forrest which also used foreign settings, Bird turned to native material. *The Hawks of Hawk-Hollow* (1835), which Poe condemned as too much like Walter Scott, is the story of a Tory family in Pennsylvania in the year after Yorktown. *Sheppard Lee* (1836), to cite Poe's complimentary term, is a *jeu d'esprit* about a New Jersey farmer whose passage through numerous incarnations affords Bird opportunity to comment satirically on contemporary conditions ranging from fashionable life to plantation slavery. His most popular and best novel is *Nick of the Woods* (1837), the story of Nathan Slaughter, an uncompromising Indian-hater, like Paulding's Timothy Weasel and Ambrose Bushfield in many respects but a better realized character than either—or, for that matter, than any character Paulding or Simms or Cooper ever drew. Nathan the Quaker is called "Bloody Nathan" in derision for his refusal to join his fellow Kentuckians of 1782 to fight the Indians. In spite of his miraculous exploits and his weird dependence on his little dog Peter, who smells Indians and other danger afar off, he is a credible human being, the victim at times of a powerful monomania, but a consistent personality, whose actions and speech and personal appearance all fit into place. *Nick of the Woods* is a good novel, as good as any produced in America in the 1830's, with narrative directness and a skillfully handled complex plot. Bird's conception of the Indian is based on the belief that "in his natural barbaric state, he is a barbarian." Not believing the myth of the noble savage, as he affirmed in the preface to the 1853 revision of this novel, he "drew his Indian portraits with Indian ink."

Like *The Old Continental* by Paulding and *The Hawks of Hawk-Hollow* by Bird, *Greyslaer* (1840) by Charles Fenno Hoffman, a novel of the Mohawk valley during the Revolution, presented the favorite theme of the conflict between Whigs and Tories. This novel, which Hoffman based at least in a general way on the well known murder of Sharp, the Solicitor General of Kentucky, by Beauchamp, changing the locale and many other details, seemed to Poe less effective than Simms' treatment of the same event in *Beauchampe* (1842); and he thought both novels less impressive than the real events. Hoffman's talent lay chiefly in journalism. Thus one may understand the purposes and methods of the greater Fenimore Cooper by seeing his work as a part of a national movement in the novel.

4

In poetry, the field where Paulding was least successful, Fitz-Greene Halleck takes first place after Bryant. Poe in his *Literati* sketch so rated him a hundred years ago, with Nathaniel Parker Willis third. Griswold would perhaps have saved the third place for Charles Fenno Hoffman, best known for the martial lyric "Monterey" and occasional poetry like "The Mint Julep"; but Poe's ranking seems sounder. After Freneau's death in 1832, the middle states had no important poet until Whitman's emergence in 1855, except as New York could claim Bryant.

In 1819, the *Croaker* pieces, a series of humorous and satirical odes published pseudonymously in the New York *Evening Post,* launched Halleck and his friend Joseph Rodman Drake in popular poetry. Beside this joint production, Drake's fame must rest on "The Culprit Fay" (1819), a conscious attempt to utilize American scenery for poetic purposes, which though not altogether successful, hardly deserved Poe's label of "puerile abortion." The younger poet's death the following year occasioned the lines of Halleck "On the Death of Joseph Rodman Drake" (1820), by which Drake is now chiefly remembered.

Steeped in Thomas Campbell, Samuel Rogers, Byron, and Walter Scott, Halleck often seemed more a part of English literary romanticism than a native American product. True, the materials of *The Croaker* and of his own long poem "Fanny" (1821), also in the vein of social satire, were local. "The Field of Grounded Arms" (1831), about the Battle of Saratoga, "Red Jacket" (1828), eulogizing the Indian chief of the Tuscaroras, and "Wyoming" (1827), all used American settings, characters, or events, but are not distinctively American. Halleck's interest in the banks of the Susquehanna was derived from an appreciation of Thomas Campbell's *Gertrude of Wyoming* (1809); the eulogy of the Indian chief afforded opportunity to lament the good old days; the vanquished at Saratoga appealed more romantically to him than did the victors, because they represented an older tradition. His poem "Young America" (1865) was about a fourteen-year-old boy, but it was a "bonny" boy who dreamed of Titania and Diana—American, if at all, only in his desire

> to settle down in life
> By wooing—winning—wedding A RICH WIFE.

The unfinished "Connecticut," despite such intrusions as "the San Marino of the West," "delicate Ariels," and "the Rhine song," was in thought and feeling, as well as in material, the most native of Halleck's poems. Though identified in both business and literary career with New York, Halleck retained a nostalgic loyalty to his native state:

> Hers are not Tempe's nor Arcadia's spring,
> Nor the long summer of Cathayan vales,
> The vines, the flowers, the air, the skies, that fling
> Such wild enchantment o'er Boccaccio's tales
> Of Florence and the Arno; yet the wing
> Of life's best angel, Health, is on her gales
> Through sun and snow; and in the autumn time
> Earth has no purer and no lovelier clime.

His love for "Greece, the brave heart's Holy Land," could make a hero of the title figure of the justly celebrated "Marco Bozzaris" (1823); a "wild rose of Alloway" could inspire a masterful appreciation in "Burns" (1827) of the poet and the Scotland that gave him birth; a visit to the "home of the Percy's high-born race" could produce his masterpiece, "Alnwick Castle" (1822)—and these three poems were their author's selection as his best work—but it commonly took the far away in time and place to evoke the poetic muse in Halleck. Employed most of his life by John Jacob Astor, he found ample occasion to lament, as he did in "Alnwick Castle," that

> The power that bore my spirit up
> Above this bank-note world—is gone;
>
> . . . . .
>
> These are not the romantic times
> So beautiful in Spenser's rhymes,
> So dazzling to the dreaming boy:
> Ours are the days of fact, not fable,
> Of knights, but not of the Round Table.

Out of a "bank-note world" and "days of fact" Halleck was unable to make poetry. Though he lived past Emerson's pronouncement in "The Poet" (1844) and into the days of Whitman's fulfillment, his outlook and habits were fixed in an earlier period, and he could not agree with Emerson that

> banks and tariffs, the newspaper and the caucus, methodism and unitarianism, are flat and dull to dull people, but rest on the same foundations of wonder as the town of Troy, and the temple of Delphos, and are as swiftly passing away.

In Nathaniel Parker Willis, Poe's choice for the third most significant poet of the New York group of this period, there was generally the same failure to treat American materials with seriousness and poetic depth. Perhaps poetry is, by its nature, the last form of literature to become thoroughly indigenous; but one is tempted to agree with Lowell that

> For some one to be slightly shallow 's a duty,
> And Willis's shallowness makes half his beauty.

Willis was polished, urbane, sophisticated, but never—in poetry, plays, or prose—profound or great: a talented, versatile, and prolific writer.

As a poet, Willis seems today inferior to Bryant or even to Halleck. In bulk his poems on scriptural subjects loomed large; but a comparison of his "Absalom" with a masterpiece like Browning's "Saul" establishes the justice of Poe's verdict that though "quite 'correct,' as the French have it," they were "in general tame, or indebted for what force they possess to the Scriptural passages of which they are merely paraphrastic." In his poem "Parrhasius," the story of the Athenian painter who subjected his aged Olynthian captive to extreme torture that he might better from this living model paint the agony of Prometheus, the dramatic values somehow fall flat, and Willis shows himself unequal to the tragic theme. Of the serious poems, the "Dedication Hymn" (1829), sung at the consecration of the Hanover Street church in Boston, is simple and direct and owes its force to these qualities. "Unseen Spirits" (1843), Poe's choice as Willis' best poem, showed clearly that Willis' talent lay, not in picturing profound passion or tragedy, but in wistful sentiment. The contrast between the beauty who married for wealth and the woman who loved without marriage vows is effectively pointed by the final well known lines:

> But the sin forgiven by Christ in heaven
> By man is cursed alway.

"To M——, from Abroad" (1834) and "Birthday Verses," written to his mother, are charming examples of sentimental poetry, better suited to Willis' abilities, and, with his religious lyrics, account for much of his contemporary fame.

The bulk of Willis' prose writing was in a dozen volumes of letters of travel and personal reminiscence, beginning with *Pencillings by the Way* (1835) and extending to *The Convalescent* (1859), mainly collections of letters written for the New York *Mirror* and other periodicals of which Willis was at one time or another an editor. The earlier letters recorded excitement about Lady Blessington and her circle and the conventional tourist haunts and shrines of the Old World, but from *A l'Abri; or The Tent Pitched* (1839) onward, Willis' country estates, Glenmary and Idlewild, and his ramblings in the areas near by formed an important part of his subject matter. As he once said of an exploratory walk to the Chemung River, so it might be said of many a poem or letter or essay he wrote: "It was done *à l'improviste,* as most pleasant things are." For most of the results, in collected form, Lowell's opinion of the best known title still holds:

> Few volumes I know to read under a tree,
> More truly delightful than his A l'Abri.

At his best, Willis was, like many earlier pilgrims to the English literary scene, "a casual writer for dreamy readers." One is inclined to smile now at his more serious ideas, such as his pronouncement in 1839:

> *In literature we are no longer a nation.* The triumph of Atlantic steam navigation has driven the smaller drop into the larger, and London has become the centre. Farewell nationality! The English language now marks the limits of a new literary empire, and America is a suburb.

Willis' short stories often showed the "casual" quality of his other prose and the sentiment of his best verse. Most of them deal in a moral tone with highly artificial situations and characters. Only in "The Lunatic's Skate" from "Scenes of Fear" (1834) did he show real depth of feeling and sense of character. Though the story elicited from Willis' biographer, Henry A. Beers, a comparison with Poe, the treatment of the material here was more realistic than Poe would have given, and without stagy romanticism or generalized sentiment. Willis' approach to the psychotic skater was more like Paulding's in Dudley Rainsford of *Westward Ho!* though the story of Larry Wynn is more concise, better written.

Late in life, in *Paul Fane* (1857), Willis attempted a psychological novel about a young American artist who determined, after being shunned by a cold English girl, to make the noble and high-born women of England accept him on a basis of equality by whatever methods were available. Though several women fell in love with him, he spurned them. Since Willis proved unable here to sustain the keenness of insight of "The Lunatic's Skate," the novel failed to come off.

5

In keeping with the diversity and innovation of the middle states literature of this period, four writers well known for fiction or poetry were also leading playwrights: Paulding, Bird, Willis, and Mathews. The two main themes of the native drama produced in New York and Philadelphia during these years were the glorification of American nationality or distinctiveness, and a romantic escape into the far away or the long ago. The most successful plays often combined these two motifs, though the best of them, Mrs. Anna Cora Mowatt's *Fashion* (1845), was frankly an American comedy of manners much influenced by Sheridan, in which Adam Trueman was something of a cross between the Yankee type inaugurated by Jonathan in Royall Tyler's *The Contrast* (1787) and the serious-minded patriot represented by Colonel Manly in the same play. Mrs. Mowatt's villain, Count Jolimaitre, was also a variation on Tyler's Dimple, though more ingenious and more dramatically effective. There was considerable penetration in Poe's assessment in the *Broadway Journal,* March 29, 1845, that "*Fashion* is theatrical, but not dramatic," and in his elucidation, perhaps too tartly expressed:

> The drama has not declined as many suppose: it has only been left out of sight by everything else. We must discard all models. . . . compared with the generality of modern dramas, it is a good play—compared with most American dramas, it is a *very* good one—estimated by the natural principles of dramatic art, it is altogether unworthy of notice.

Notable among the plays with a foreign setting were N. P. Willis' *Bianca Visconti; or the Heart Overtasked* (1837 *), whose action took place in fourteenth century Milan, and his *Tortesa the Usurer* (1839), dealing with medieval Florence; Robert Montgomery Bird's *The Gladiator* (1831), a story of Rome in 73 B.C., and his *Broker of Bogota* (1834), which used a setting of the South American city in the early Spanish colonial days; and *Charles the Second; or The Merry Monarch* (1824), written by John Howard Payne with assistance from Washington Irving.

Plays on native themes which used material from the past included James Nelson Barker's *Superstition* (1824) and Cornelius Mathews' *Witchcraft* (1846), both set in late seventeenth century New England; a host of plays about Indians, by George Washington Parke Custis and John Augustus

* The dates of plays cited here are of production.

Stone; Mathews' *Jacob Leisler, or New York in 1690* (1848) and Elizabeth Oakes Smith's *Old New York, or Democracy in 1689* (1853), both of which made use of the same incident in the early history of Manhattan.

In *The Lion of the West* (1831), introducing a character suggestive of Davy Crockett, Paulding presented a salient aspect of contemporary American life not touched on in a play like Mrs. Mowatt's *Fashion*. Earlier, in *The Bucktails; or Americans in England* (not published until 1847), he had made an important contribution toward defining the American character by showing his countrymen against a European background. *The Bucktails* was a comedy of manners, often exaggerated into farce, designed to dispel the myth that all Americans were Wildfires or Crocketts. Among the few notable plays using contemporary American materials was Cornelius Mathews' *The Politicians* (1840).

Of the plays here named, only Payne's *Charles the Second* was without relevance to characteristic American themes and interests. It was an adaptation of a French play by Alexandre Duval and was originally produced on the London stage during Payne's long residence abroad (1813–1832), but was free enough of its original to be considered as part of American literature. Willis' *Tortesa, the Usurer* had a tenuous connection with the American theme of the rise of the underdog, in the success of the poor painter Angelo in winning not only the noble and beautiful Isabella de Falcone in marriage but also, through the sudden and largely inexplicable generosity of Tortesa, a sizable fortune along with her. But Willis' interest was less in American ideology than in the age-old theme of the triumph of true love over seemingly insurmountable obstacles, and more especially in effective theater.

In *Bianca Visconti,* the central character was Francesco Sforza, at the time of the action in high-pitched rebellion against the Italian dukes who were using him to fight their wars against each other while he himself was personally despised and trifled with. Sforza attracted Willis in part at least because of the dramatist's concern for democracy and the dignity of all men. Willis' interest in this character was similar to Bird's interest in Spartacus and his revolt against brutal Roman tyranny over conquered peoples, though Bird approached the subject of *The Gladiator* differently. Stone's sympathetic portrayal of the title character in *Metamora* (1829) was in the same vein, though here the dramatic impact was sharper since the oppressors of the chief of the Wampanoags, son of Massasoit, were the New England colonists of the seventeenth century, the ancestors of the audience now applauding the Indian's struggle for freedom. Jacob Leisler, in the plays by Cornelius Mathews and Elizabeth Oakes Smith, was another hero in revolt—the champion of an abortive democracy in New York of 1689–1690. The same theme appeared in Bird's *The Broker of Bogota* in the struggle of the bourgeois Baptista Febro to get his rights against people of noble birth.

It becomes apparent then that, like the essay and fiction and poetry of the day, the American drama prior to Boker's notable *Francesca da Rimini* (1855) reflects not a matured but an adolescent indigenous culture. The leading writers of the middle states between 1820 and 1850 were realistic at their best rather than merely picturesque, tolerant of variation and originality within the boundaries of intelligibility, well informed about European literary traditions and current vogues though disinclined to be swept away by passing fads, lacking in intellectual unity but thriving on diversity and innovation, catholic in interests though caring "but little for the metaphysical subtleties of Massachusetts and Virginia." In the middle of the road in opinions and tastes, the literature of this section during the decades preceding the Civil War became the unifying core of an American national culture.

21. IN NEW ENGLAND

DURING the years when Bryant, Irving, and Cooper were the major figures in American letters and the Concord-Cambridge galaxy were still schoolboys, authorship in New England was by no means confined to eastern Massachusetts. The editors of the *North American Review* and their chief contributors, it is true, were Boston men; but in that day the poets of Connecticut outranked the Bostonians and the most popular novelists lived in the Green Mountains, the Berkshires, and Maine. Thus literature in New England was shaped by the life not of any single community but of the entire region—the half cultivated, half primitive homeland of William Ellery Channing and Richard Henry Dana, Sr., of Daniel Pierce Thompson and William Cullen Bryant.

The literary tradition of Boston and its back country was overwhelmingly English, for New England at the opening of the century was closer in spirit as well as in fact to the British Isles than any other section of the United States. This is to say that the heritage of Pope was still strong, and that American romanticism was chiefly imitative. Where the great romantics in England wrote on English and Continental themes, early romantics in America copied, not American life, but English copies of English life. This literary colonialism focused the attention of New Englanders on decorum and sensibility, on the legends and history of Europe, on Old World religious and political concepts, and on both the substance and the style of the eighteenth century novelists and of the nineteenth century romantic poets. Thus the lesser New England authors were moved hither and yon by the backwash of classicism, the main current of derivative romanticism, and the ever increasing pull of indigenous American romanticism. In the poetry of William Cullen Bryant, New England found its authentic voice, not because Bryant was a rebel against the past and Europe, but because he absorbed tradition and made it his own. Other writers of his day were less successful either because they rebelled more violently or because they were swept too easily with the currents of foreign influence.

contribute to its pages. Eager for public recognition, he was hard hit by the cool reception of his essays and tales in *The Idle Man* (published in parts during 1821–1822), of his long poem, *The Buccaneer* (1827), and of his collected *Poems and Prose Writings* (1833, 1850). In middle life, he withdrew from the world which would not recognize his genius.

Dana's heart was not in this present "age of improvement" but in that golden day when, he fancied, "all was rustic and unforced" and "the relentless curiosity of modern times had not . . . soiled and torn asunder the flower." Past-minded in politics, he remained a Federalist long after the party had disappeared, and he even argued the superiority of monarchial to republican government. He was likewise an ardent Trinitarian and, during the twenties, an outspoken foe of the heterodoxy of Channing and Bryant. In his poetry and prose, as might be anticipated, he followed many masters: in *The Buccaneer,* eighteenth century sentimentalists, Coleridge, Wordsworth, and Byron; in his tales, especially "Paul Felton," the same Englishmen and Charles Brockden Brown. Dana expressed much sympathy for Brown's "loneliness of situation," his isolation as a man of sensibility in a mechanical age, and his ultimate success in escaping from "free thought" and becoming "a true believer." Didactic as Dana was at times, his extreme romanticism entitles him to a reprieve from Poe's sentence to death by hanging for all the *North American* men. The fact remains, however, that Dana was throughout his life an ardent exponent of the inverted provincialism which colored Edward Everett's earlier years. Except for Channing, this Boston group did little to break away from England or her literature and to discover the roots of American life.

3

Connecticut, according to Washington Irving, was populated by onion eaters, hog stealers, bundlers, improvers, and slab-sided schoolmasters. Such witticisms are an index not only to the complacency of New York, but to the dilemma of genteel men of letters in Connecticut during the early century. Cut off by distance from the intellectual stimulus of Boston, and by choice from the earthy stimulus of life among hog stealers and onion eaters, they too turned directly to Europe for precedents, as had the earlier Hartford wits. Thus it happened that the most enthusiastic medievalist of the period and the most complete romantic solitary were products of Yale—and the most shameless sentimentalist was a Hartford woman. The poets were no longer stirred by the old themes of religion and politics; the graces and amenities of life took their place.

The medievalist was James Abraham Hillhouse. In "A Discourse . . . on

Some of the Considerations Which Should Influence an Epic or a Tragic Writer in the Choice of an Era," he rejected the "heathen" world of the ancients for the glorious Christian era of chivalry ("Its spirit was pitched to enthusiasm, imagination was the ruling power, and the whole tenor of its actions was extraordinary"). America, he added, is an admirable residence, but it has no past and the American writer of tragedy or epic must therefore rely on our "indefeasible . . . portion in the fame of Arthur and Alfred." These principles he put into practice in three blank-verse dramas: *Percy's Masque* (1819), based on Thomas Percy's original ballad, "The Hermit of Warkworth"; *Hadad* (1825), a melodrama of the days when there was "intercourse between mankind, and good and evil beings from the Spiritual World"; and *Demetria* (1839), a "horrid" tragedy of Italian cavaliers and ladies. Always self-consistent, Hillhouse introduced nothing of the epic or the tragic into his American poem, *Sachem's Wood* (1836), but pictured his home in New Haven solely in terms of the sentimental and the comic.

The romantic solitary was James Gates Percival. Elegant steel engravings of distinguished authors, hanging on the parlor walls of America, honored him through the twenties as the nation's chief poet, and many reviewers gave him the same rank; but the public left him to starve. He met nothing except disappointment as a tutor, a lecturer on anatomy and later on botany, a physician, an editor, a surgeon in the Army, a professor of chemistry at West Point, a lexicographer, and the author of four volumes of poetry—all within the span of twelve years. Wounded, and too timid to mix with the herd, he next voluntarily secluded himself for a decade in three unswept rooms in the state hospital at New Haven. He spent his last years on the frontier in Wisconsin, where he died in solitude.

The world of poetry into which Percival escaped from New Haven was compounded of his own undisciplined emotions and his emulation of the English romantics. When a young maniac in "The Suicide" shouts, "Give me the knife, the dagger, or the ball," he echoes his creator Percival, who in youth attempted to destroy himself in a variety of ways; but the same maniac echoes Byron when he cries, "O, hell to me is nothing,—nothing's hell." When Percival generalizes windily in "Prometheus," he follows Shelley; but his condemnation of Prometheus for sacrilegiously rending "the veil Religion hung around us" voices his own pietism. Although the mountains which rise on many of his pages are dim copies of Wordsworth's first-hand observations, it should be added that Percival could write delightfully of the American scene when, on rare occasions, the charms of Seneca Lake or a landscape in New England caught his eye.

Percival's chief weakness was loquacity, but of it he made romantic virtue. "The highest interest of a poet," he declared, is "to write only, when he feels inspired, when his subject has gained full possession of him. . . . Then . . . his language will flow abroad without effort." It is too evident that his long poems and his flood of lyrics—there are more than four hundred of them—did indeed flow abroad, with all the ease of divine madness and little of the anguished effort which Bryant, for example, was putting into his best lines. Thus Percival, instead of expending his slender talent with caution and discretion, scattered it with a prodigal hand.

Sentimentalism came to a dead end in the verses of Lydia Huntley Sigourney. She offered the public neither the violence nor the abstractions which alarmed them in Percival; instead, she gave them literalness and propriety, convention and elegance. As her reward, she was editing an annual, contributing to a half-dozen more, and selling her work to a score of magazines while Percival was hiding himself in a hospital. She knew something of the humanitarian movements of the day, but all that she did for Negroes, Indians, the poor, and the insane was to embalm them in the amber of her tears. Until Longfellow came into his own in the fifties, the most widely read American poet (she published sixty-seven volumes) was "The Sweet Singer of Hartford."

4

Even the ruggedness of the hinterland could not wean New England writers from conventional European modes. The simple realities of contemporary life in Vermont, in the Berkshires, and in Maine helped bring national and international recognition to three novelists; but the hand of the past lay so heavily on all three that they capitulated to traditional melodrama or to traditional propriety and rejected, in varying degree, the region which made them famous. They too failed to achieve the nationality or the universality of an indigenous art.

Least original of the three and least appreciative of his resources was Daniel Pierce Thompson. In a day when native novels were few, *The Green Mountain Boys* (1839) was famous as a classic of Vermont life. But its author, a rural lawyer with no literary standards and no literary conscience, was less concerned with recording New England character than with imitating the blood-pudding school of romancers. Actually, the book is not a document in social history but a violent yarn of a villain who slinks, muttering, down the valleys and a hero who strides up the mountains with the heroine held high in one arm and her Indian maidservant in the other. *Locke Amsden* (1847), frequently praised for its account of education in early Vermont, is likewise so filled with clichés and stereotypes that it has little meaning as a record of local manners.

Catharine Maria Sedgwick, like Maria Edgeworth to whom she dedicated her first book, was at first keenly interested in the manners of her own region; and in her early novels she described those manners with naïve and convincing honesty. When she recorded the meanness of Yankee rustics and defended the Friends' religion in *A New-England Tale* (1822), her brother reported, "The orthodox do all they can to put it down, . . . and New Englanders feel miffed." Thin-skinned New Englanders were miffed again by the pungent, self-willed spinster, Miss Debbie, in *Redwood* (1824); Shakers protested that the novel treated them with "irreverence and derision"; the austere Dana in Boston charged Miss Sedgwick with lack of good taste; but her friend Bryant praised *Redwood* "as a conclusive argument, that the writers of works of fiction, of which the scene is laid in familiar and domestic life, have a rich and varied field before them in the United States." Thereafter she grew more interested in the chitchat of her ladies and gentlemen than in the homely ways of Berkshire countryfolk—she was now a distinguished authoress who wintered in New York and only summered in the Berkshires. She was also so infected by the vogue of historical romance that she deserted contemporary American life for seventeenth century Massachusetts (*Hope Leslie,* 1827) and Revolutionary New York (*The Linwoods,* 1835). Thus propriety and a new fashion in novels smothered Miss Sedgwick's innate realism and made her at last an apostate to her region and a purveyor of sentimental romance to genteel females.

The most colorful and original of the trio was John Neal of Portland, Maine, a Quaker and a tempestuous individualist, a shrewd down-Easter and a citizen of the world, and withal a strident prophet of Americanism in literature. With no education beyond elementary school, he went into trade with John Pierpont in Boston and was left penniless when their branch in Baltimore failed. For a few years he studied law, wrote for the Baltimore newspapers and the *Portico,* and dashed off one novel after another—now in six or seven weeks and again in twenty-seven days: *Logan* (1822), *Errata* (1823), *Seventy-six* (1823), and *Randolph* (1823). In his first novel, *Keep Cool* (1817), he attacked dueling; he enlivened *Randolph* by biting comments on American authors and public men, among them William Pinkney. Pinkney's son challenged Neal, who refused to fight. From 1824 to 1827 Neal lived in England, where he was the first American to write regularly for the great reviews. To *Blackwood's* he contributed a series of essays on American authors—sharply critical but no more severe than his comments written in the United States for *Randolph.* Eyed with suspicion in Portland after his return to America, Neal let it be known that he was a trained boxer and fencer (he had now been read out of meeting by the Friends for knocking a man down), founded the *Yankee,* a literary journal, and in due course was accepted as a leading citizen. In the thirties Neal was one of the first to praise Poe; in the sixties he wrote dime novels for Beadle.

The young law student who turned off a novel with one hand and a review with the other had no time to search for original characters or themes. He snatched high-minded villains from Godwin and low-minded heroes from Byron, then sent them roaring and murdering through the hackneyed routines of cheap melodrama: Logan, who sheds tears and blood with equal ease; and Harold, "whose very breath is poison." The public which supped deep and often on these horrors is well represented by an Englishwoman who, according to Neal, read his novels until "the high seasoning and wild flavor of these fierce and extravagant stories had rendered all other literary aliment unpalatable," and she "died with 'Seventy-Six' in her hand."

Unlike Miss Sedgwick wintering in New York, John Neal living in London developed new respect for our native character and speech. When he took stock of American books, he concluded: "Our best writers are English writers, not American writers. . . . Not so much as one true Yankee is to be found in any one of our native books: hardly so much as one true Yankee phrase." Adapting to his own ends the romantic doctrine of uniqueness, he declared: "It would not do for me to imitate anybody. Nor would it do for my country. Who would care for the *American* Addison where he could have the English?" Neal therefore proposed to abandon *"classical* English" ("It is no natural language—it never was") for common American speech, and to plow deep into American soil. American authors, he believed, would find "abundant and hidden sources of fertility in their own beautiful brave earth, waiting only to be broken up."

Although it remained for later generations to put these precepts into full execution, Neal at least attempted to observe them in his later novels. In the early chapters of *Brother Jonathan* (1825), he reported Yankee manners and diction with extraordinary fidelity, then relapsed into melodrama. In *Rachel Dyer* (1828) he dealt honestly with the witchcraft delusion and two of the unfortunate women sentenced to death by Judge Hathorne, then wandered off into polemics. In the opening pages of *The Down-Easters* (1833) he etched a striking series of Yankee portraits, then degenerated into bombast. Neal's most significant account of the resources of our "beautiful brave earth" is his lively autobiography, *Wandering Recollections of a Somewhat Busy Life* (1869)—his most distinctly American and, as a result, his most memorable book. Here was a romantic individualist who under more favorable circumstances might have exemplified Emerson's theory that any American who writes with full self-trust becomes a true voice of America. In him, as in Paulding and Cooper, belligerence served where art was inadequate to break the ties with the past and with Europe.

5

The interest in reform which had led Mrs. Sigourney into excessive sentimentalism was more vigorously pursued by another group of New England writers. During the two decades which followed 1820, they fought what Emerson described as "a war between intellect and affection." The war was won by affection, as exemplified by humanitarians who believed that "the nation existed for the individual, for the guardianship and education of every man." When a call went out in 1840 for a Convention of Friends of Universal Reform, all manner of men and women presented themselves at the Chardon Street Chapel in Boston. With as much approval as amusement, Emerson catalogued them as "madmen, madwomen, men with beards, Dunkers, Muggletonians, Come-outers, Groaners, Agrarians, Seventh-Day Baptists, Quakers, Abolitionists, Calvinists, Unitarians, and Philosophers." Among the members of the older generation who contributed to this reorientation of the New England mind were Channing, John Pierpont, and Lydia Maria Child. As reform was their ultimate concern, their lives speak more loudly than their books. And their books, lacking in literary distinction as they are, speak more loudly of America than do the more polished writings of their bookish contemporaries.

After Channing had analyzed the relationships between the members of the Trinity and between God and man, he turned to those between men and men. Translating into contemporary terms his "high estimate of human nature," his "reverence . . . for human rights," and his faith in "the essential equality of men," he warned his wealthy parishioners in Boston that "justice is a greater good than property, not greater in degree, but in kind." He told Southerners that a man cannot be held as property, because he is both a rational and a moral being—but he told Abolitionists that they were too violent. He attacked intemperance as "the *voluntary extinction of reason*"—but he rebuked temperance agitators for their irrational attempts at coercion. He lectured against war as incompatible with a proper recognition of "the worth of a human being" and helped organize the Massachusetts Peace Society. He declared that "it is a greater work to educate a child, in the true and larger sense of the word, than to rule a state" and gave his support to Horace Mann. He rejected Franklin's dictum that a man should improve himself to increase his earning power, and urged self-improvement as a means of self-perfection. And the perfection of society through the perfecting of each citizen was, of course, Channing's goal.

John Pierpont brought to the role of universal reformer less elevation but no less devotion than Channing. He sold dry goods and went bankrupt with his partner John Neal, wrote his widely popular *Airs of Palestine* (1816),

fifty copies were sold within three years. He had to undertake a great deal of miscellaneous hackwork for *Burton's Gentleman's Magazine* and other Philadelphia periodicals, but during the next half-decade, especially in 1841 and 1842, he displayed an access of energy in several directions. By 1845 he had more than doubled the number of his stories, and had added distinct new types. The most popular of these was the "tale of ratiocination," as inaugurated by "The Murders in the Rue Morgue." Poe, who was presently to make quite a stir as a solver of cryptograms, showed a lively enjoyment of analysis, and created in his detective Dupin a very different hero from Roderick Usher. In describing Dupin's extraordinary grip over the mind's processes of association, Poe again applied Coleridge to uses now entirely his own. For Dupin's "rich ideality" was a startling combination, both "resolvent" and "creative"; he held that "the ingenious are always fanciful, and the *truly* imaginative never otherwise than analytic." Poe had been a good student of mathematics at West Point, and in his further incarnations of Dupin, in "The Mystery of Marie Roget" and "The Purloined Letter," he attributed his hero's powers of reasoning and his ability to apprehend general truths to the fact that he was both mathematician *and* poet.

Another development of the tale of ratiocination, and Poe's most popular story in his own day, was "The Gold Bug" which, in contrast to the ten dollars he could usually expect for a story, won in 1843 the hundred-dollar prize offered by the Philadelphia *Dollar Newspaper*. "The Gold Bug" combined the fascination of cryptography with that of buried treasure. Its fresh description of Sullivan's Island near Charleston is a reminiscence of the days when Poe was stationed there in the Army, and in dealing with Captain Kidd he made use for once of an American legend.

Quite a different kind of development is apparent in such pieces as "The Philosophy of Furniture" and "The Landscape Garden," wherein he worked out his theories of taste and design. In considering the ideal interior he insisted that "an aristocracy of dollars" was far inferior to "an aristocracy of blood," that taste was ordinarily corrupted by wealth. He maintained that "keeping" was as important in a room as in any other work of art, and presented in detail such a room, the character of which was determined by a profusion of crimson and gold, wrought into "arabesque devices" in the pattern both of the wallpaper and of the carpet. Poe's longing for luxury and magnificence was in part that of a man who had been starved of them. Letting his fondness for the bizarre run riot in "The Masque of the Red Death," he devised those seven rooms of different colors, the last of which, with its tapestries of black velvet and its scarlet window panes, was a masterpiece of ballet décor for the dance of death. Taking hold of the contemporary interest in landscape gardening, he also designed his fabulous domain of Arnheim, an artificial paradise of fantastic vegetation, crowned by a mansion of "semi-Gothic, semi-Saracenic architecture." Such scenes vibrated for Baudelaire "d'un frisson surnaturel et galvanique."

Still another departure is found in his dialogues after death, such as "The Colloquy of Monos and Una," in which he first made open his scorn of the utilitarians and his rejection of the doctrine of progress, and ridiculed, "among other odd ideas," that of "universal equality." Here also he began the speculations, which were to culminate in *Eureka,* on identity after death, and conceived of a state in which the senses blended into one another and all man's perceptions became "purely sensual."

In "The Black Cat" and "The Imp of the Perverse" he enunciated the belief that sadistic cruelty "is one of the primitive impulses of the human heart," that we respond to the promptings of the perverse "for the reason that we should *not.*" In these stories, as in "The Pit and the Pendulum" and "The Case of M. Valdemar," he developed to the full his ability to convey hallucinated horror by making it immediately physical, as when rats crawl across the lips of the imprisoned man. In such stories he showed too what a thin line may separate a "grotesque" from an "arabesque." When the material treated in the two is the same, the difference depends solely on the shift in tone, whereby the ludicrous "Angel of the Odd" may become the deadly serious "Imp of the Perverse."

It is interesting also that after 1840 the proportion of "grotesques" declined to hardly one in four. He seems to have come to perceive more clearly the limitations of the genre. He stated that harmony predominates in the workings of the imagination, whereas novelty predominates in those of the fancy, novelty that may quickly turn from beauty to deformity and thus pass over into the realm of humor. In analyzing Thomas Hood's grim "struggles at mirth" he gave an unconscious definition of his own: "the result of vivid Fancy impelled by Hypochondriasis." The best of his later "grotesques" have a concrete object for satire, just as the plausibility of his balloon flight across the Atlantic hoaxed New York for a day. In "The Business Man" the quality of his mockery is obvious, but in "Diddling Considered as One of the Exact Sciences" his satire of knaves and fools has a sustained bitterness kindred to Melville's in *The Confidence-Man.* Yet to the last year of his life Poe would still be capable of the wasted ingenuity of "X-ing a Paragrab."

Another sphere of his energy during his Philadelphia years was an ambitious plan for a magazine of his own. He was among the first to discern the tendency of the age toward "the curt, the condensed, the pointed, the readily diffused," away from "the detailed, the voluminous, the inaccessible." Against those who deplored this trend as a sign of American superficiality, Poe urged that men might not think "more profoundly" than they had thought half a century ago, but that they must think "with more rapidity," since they had so many more facts at their disposal. For this reason they needed "to put the greatest amount of thought in the smallest compass": "Hence the journalism of the age." Poe often thought of himself as "essentially a Magazinist," and planned to make his journal an organ of "an absolutely independent criticism."

The money that he hoped to raise by subscription was not forthcoming, and during 1841–1842 he took the job of editor for *Graham's Magazine*. Here he reached his peak as a critic. He opened the volume for 1842 with an exordium on the proper method of reviewing. He repeated his attack on all forms of narrow nationalism, and stated that he would "limit literary criticism to comment upon art." With "the opinions" in a book, "considered otherwise than in their relation to the work itself, the critic has really nothing to do." He followed up this statement of principles with a series of masterly essays. He was the first to mark so clearly the inescapable limitations of the "pioneers," the generation of Bryant, Irving, and Cooper. He helped to establish the reputations of his own generation, while continuing to expose the mediocrity of most of our best sellers. In his resolvent analysis of the plot of *Barnaby Rudge,* in which he unraveled the mystery before the last installments had been printed, he also pointed out the common error of trying to separate practice "from the theory which includes it." "If the practice fail," Poe contended, as no one else in American criticism had done, "it is because the theory is imperfect." In his most balanced treatment of Longfellow, he objected to the "too obtrusive nature" of his didacticism, and went on to develop his own theory of poetry as the product of "supernal" longing, as "the rhythmical creation of beauty." In recognizing Hawthorne as one of our "few men of indisputable genius," he formulated his famous conception of the short story, which must be designed for "a single effect," and every word of which must be made to count.

Poe's imperfections as a critic have often been dwelt upon. Just as he was overimpressed by such pseudo sciences as phrenology and mesmerism, his tastes in literature were oppressively contemporary. When he had protested against being withdrawn from the University of Virginia, he had told Allan how far he still was from "a liberal education"; and gaps in his understanding of the past remained very apparent. Unfortunately he acted as he always did when he felt insecure. He made pretensions to erudition that he did not possess, and backed them up with quotations borrowed from some such source as D'Israeli's *Curiosities of Literature*. His critical temper was often unsteady. He was capable, as in his dealings with Lowell, of withdrawing his praise when Lowell ventured a few strictures upon his work. He exaggerated the conspiracy of New England to venerate only its own, he was vicious in his attack upon poor Ellery Channing, and his obsession with Longfellow's alleged plagiarism grew into a mania. Yet he also fought steadily to improve the conditions of American authorship, and his own near-starvation had taught him "the irreparable ill" that the absence of a copyright law wrought upon our native culture, even upon our writers' bare survival. His originality as a critic resulted from his refusal to rest upon any authority, from the way he considered *de novo* the capabilities of whatever art he examined. His greatest contribution was that he always insisted upon "the application of a rigorous *method* in all forms of thought."

5

After the plans for his magazine had failed for a second time in 1842, Poe underwent a period of hopeless depression. In that winter Virginia, who had now matured into womanhood—a fact usually overlooked by those who speak invariably of his "child-wife"—had ruptured a blood vessel while singing, and her condition from then on was always precarious in the extreme. Looking back to this period, Poe said that the continual uncertainty, her partial recovery followed by relapse, made the recurrence of his desperate anxiety more than his nerves could stand. "I became insane," he said, "with long intervals of horrible sanity." He also added that his enemies attributed the insanity to his drinking, "rather than the drink to the insanity." His relations with the proprietors of the magazines, with Burton and Graham, followed a variant of the pattern of those with the *Messenger*. During his editorship, the circulation of *Graham's* rose fabulously, from fifty-five hundred to forty thousand; but that brought no rise in Poe's fortunes. By 1844 he had become thoroughly dissatisfied with any further prospects in Philadelphia, and moved to New York, wandering, as Baudelaire conceived it, once again restlessly in the American desert. Poe himself had now come to believe that in America, "more than in any other region upon the face of the globe, to be poor is to be despised." But his New York years did not alleviate his condition. He became even less prosperous than he had been.

That remained true even after "The Raven" made an instant stir upon its appearance in the New York *Evening Mirror*. He wrote to a friend that for popularity his "bird" had beaten his "bug" "all hollow," and yet, "I am as poor now as ever I was in my life." It may be impossible any more for an adult American to have a fresh reaction to "The Raven," since it has become such a classic of declamation and its once original tones have been drowned out by parodies. Its repetitions and refrain, the impulse for which Poe may have received from Chivers, and which were so startling upon their first hearing, have long become so expected as to allow Aldous Huxley to take it for one of the showpieces of "vulgarity in literature." The suspicion of its being fabricated was given some color by Poe himself, who proceeded, in "The Philosophy of Composition," to deliver a cool account of every step in the process of designing the poem to "suit at once the popular and the critical taste." Poe spoke of this essay as being his "best specimen of analysis," but many readers have been bothered by its mechanical exactitude. Baudelaire, who delighted in Poe even as a *farceur,* detected a deliberate undertone of impertinence, whereby Poe wanted to scandalize again those who talked only of inspiration and refused to admit the necessary dependence of genius upon talent. It is possible that Poe wrote with his tongue in his cheek, since he had a fondness for what he called "funny criticism": but he also believed that an artist should possess the fullest consciousness of all the stages of composition, since "to originate, is carefully, patiently, and understandingly to combine."

As a result of his new fame Poe was able to issue, in the summer of 1845, a selection of a dozen of his tales, with a royalty of eight cents a copy on a small edition, and then a collection of his poetry for a flat payment of seventy-five dollars. This was the first time his earlier poems had any considerable audience. Griswold's widely circulated anthology, *The Poets and Poetry of America,* had included in 1842 three pieces by Poe, "The Coliseum," "The Haunted Palace," and "The Sleeper," as against seventeen poems by Lydia Sigourney and forty-five by Charles Fenno Hoffman. Poe dedicated his book to "the noblest of her sex," Miss Elizabeth Barrett Barrett, whose line, "With a murmurous stir uncertain, in the air the purple curtain," he had most certainly echoed. He said in the preface that there was "nothing in this volume of much value to the public, or very creditable to myself"; and, indeed, he had succeeded in composing scarcely ten new lyrics since 1831, the best of which, with the exception of "Dream-Land," had been incorporated into his tales. The only large addition lay in the scenes from his unfinished tragedy *Politian,* which dated from 1835 and were flatly undramatic. Yet the depth of Poe's concern over this book was apparent not only in the care with which he had revised many of his poems, but particularly when he said: "Events not to be controlled have prevented me from making, at any time, any serious effort in what, under happier circumstances, would have been the field of my choice. With me poetry has not been a purpose, but a passion." The reviews were prevailingly unsympathetic.

He was trying again to establish his magazine, and contrived for a few months to get control of the *Broadway Journal*; but the project blew up for want of funds, and because of his instability. From now on his ambition for a magazine seems to have become more overmastering as it grew less and less likely of realization; and he spoke of it in 1846 as "the one great purpose of my literary life." But in this year he had instead to undertake for *Godey's* his hack-work series dealing with thirty-eight of "the Literati of New York City." The announcement of this series fluttered the dovecotes because of Poe's reputation as "the tomahawk man," but the essays, as Poe himself knew, turned out to be hardly more than "critical gossip" of a prevailingly flattering kind.

Virginia was finally dying from tuberculosis, and sometimes there was not even enough money for a fire in their cottage at Fordham. After her death, in the winter of 1847, Poe went rapidly to pieces. One medical diagnosis at this time was that he had a "lesion on one side of the brain." He could not endure his loneliness, and threw himself into one emotional affair after another. He often behaved as though he hardly knew what he was doing, since at the very time he was trying to marry Mrs. Helen Whitman, he was torn also by his longing for the companionship of his "Annie," the wife of Charles Richmond. The only escape seemed to be suicide, and he swallowed an ounce of laudanum; but this acted as a violent emetic.

The Griswold legend was that Poe had now become diabolically possessed, and that he walked the streets with his lips moving "in the indistinct curses" of one who felt himself "already damned." Poe himself spoke of his "terrible agony." But the remarkable thing about these last years is the amount and variety of work he still managed to accomplish. Even in the midst of Virginia's final crisis, he had rallied himself and had written to Willis: "The truth is, I have a great deal to do; and I have made up my mind not to die till it is done."

Eureka was the fulfillment of prolonged meditation. In "Mesmeric Revelation" (1844) he had used the device of a trance to purvey his own doctrine of immortality, and had argued that matter is indivisible, that God "is but the perfection of matter." *Eureka,* upon which he was working through 1847, was advanced as "an Essay on the Material and Spiritual Universe." But he also called it "a Prose Poem." He was completely in earnest about the importance of his ideas, but he emphasized the beauty in their truth, and addressed himself "to the dreamers and those who put faith in dreams as in the only realities." He dedicated his book to Alexander von Humboldt, and showed himself well read in that naturalist's *Cosmos,* as well as in the nebular hypothesis of Laplace. Despite his rejection of progress, Poe shared with Emerson the contemporary concern with speculative science. He was finally giving, in *Eureka,* a full-length example of what he meant in saying that "the *highest* order of the imaginative intellect is always preeminently mathematical." Some critics have made much of the point that Poe's theories about the attraction and repulsion of atoms, and about "the stage of progressive collapse" of the universe, seem to anticipate twentieth century science. But at best these are lucky guesses of a mind untrained in physics and astronomy, and it would seem wiser to follow the course Poe urged in the last sentence of his preface: "It is as a Poem only that I wish this work to be judged after I am dead."

He started out by rejecting, in an oddly facetious passage, both deductive and inductive methods as too confined, and affirmed that for creative discovery "only Intuition can aid us." Poe's reliance upon the imagination as the discerner of truth, as the supreme faculty that brings man's soul to "a glimpse of things supernal and eternal," indicates again, despite his professed rejection of "immateriality," a belief curiously akin to Emerson's—as they both had adapted it from Coleridge. Poe once commented upon his tales of ratiocination that "people think them more ingenious than they are—on account of their method and *air* of method." The "air of method" is astonishingly sustained throughout *Eureka,* so that, whatever its originality or substance, it is a masterpiece of finesse, of intelligible and lucid exposition. At one climax, after expressing his awed admiration for the structure of the universe, he showed what kind of metaphor came most naturally to him when he added: "The plots of God are perfect. The Universe is a plot of God."

Poe ends on the note that was to become so prevalent in nineteenth century individualism, that he cannot believe "that anything exists greater than his own soul," that if God is to become "all in all," each man must recognize his own existence "as that of Jehovah." After such colossal egotism it is not surprising that Poe put an immense significance upon *Eureka,* and liked to talk of the metaphysical revolution that it would inaugurate. He had reached the stage where he was living a double identity, though not that of his William Wilson. It was as though the tortured and plunging chaos of his love letters were compensated by the way he proved that he could still conduct his intellectual processes with balance and decorum.

6

In his final years he also produced his *Marginalia,* that magnificently fertile series of suggestions on literary method. Here he condensed his leading principles of art. He gave recurrent attention to the similarities between music and mathematics, and found the basis of rhyme in our "appreciation of equality." He made his most original exploration of the unconscious by examining the images that well up at "the point of blending between wakefulness and sleep." These hypnagogic images are what surrealism has seized upon as its peculiar province; but Poe balanced his interest in them with a proposition that separated him also from most of the romantics of his day. He affirmed, "Man's chief idiosyncrasy being reason, it follows that his savage condition—his condition of action *without* reason—is his *un*natural state."

In "The Poetic Principle," which he delivered as a lecture during 1848–1849, he made a survey of contemporary poets and brought to its final stage his theory of "pure poetry," which we have already seen in formation. He betrayed again the limitations of his taste in speaking of Tennyson as "the noblest poet that ever lived," not on the grounds of depth or of intensity, but because he "is, at all times, the most ethereal—in other words, the most elevating and the most pure. No poet is so little of the earth, earthy." After such a passage one understands better why Poe thought the best conceivable subject for a poem was the death of a beautiful woman, and why both his poetry and his stories are so lacking in sensual body.

Other weaknesses in Poe's theory are manifest. The lyric, not the epic nor the dramatic poem, becomes the only norm. His occupation solely with supernal beauty risks turning even the lyric into a sustained tone, and nothing else. Atmosphere becomes not merely the envelope, but the content. The chief deficiency is owing to Poe's brittle terminology—in such contrast to Coleridge's resilience—which leads him into making mechanical and far too exclusive separations between the spheres of beauty and truth. He was so determined to root out "the didactic heresy" that he barred truth from poetry, and confined it to science and prose. In "The Philosophy of Composition" he had at least granted truth a subsidiary role in the total effect of poetic beauty, and in *Eureka* he had operated from a much broader basis and had held that "symmetry and consistency are convertible terms:—thus Poetry and Truth are one." But whatever its limitations and lapses, Poe's theory held firmly to his central conception about art, that it was not a spontaneous overflow of genius, but a designed effect. This separated it from all romantic theories of expression, and made it, in turn, the catalytic agent that quickened the French reaction from romantic disorder back to classic control of their forms.

Poe's production in fiction amounts to about seventy stories, only seven or eight of which were written after 1845. "The Cask of Amontillado" (1846) is one of the most compact illustrations of his belief that plot is not a "simple *complexity*," but "that in which no part can be displaced without ruin to the whole." "Hop-Frog" is one of the last of his "grotesques," the savage energy of which transforms it. Its story is that of a deformed dwarf who as court jester has been made drunk against his will and has watched a brutal injury to his girl. In the account of his revenge, by burning the king and his councilors to death, Poe's imagination became luridly destructive, as though in savage response to his own frustrations. In the winter of 1849 he devised the last of his hoaxes, "Von Kempelen and His Discovery," which purported to be a scientific description of how lead might be turned into gold. Poe's aim was to act as a sudden even if "temporary check to the gold-fever" of that year.

His growing bitterness to his times poured itself out most fully in "Mellonta Tauta," which looked back on that world from the vantage point of a thousand years. It defined a New York church as "a kind of pagoda" for the worship of the idols, Wealth and Fashion; but it reserved its harshest scorn for the notion that "the ancient Amriccans governed themselves." Poe traced their absurd course to its "abrupt issue" when "a fellow by the name of Mob took everything into his own hands and set up a despotism." In the latest installments of *Marginalia* he continued his attack on the pressures against the solitary thinker. He denounced "the modern reformist Philosophy which annihilates the individual by way of aiding the mass." He was still a Southerner looking at New England when he said:

> The fact is, that in efforts to soar above our nature, we invariably fall below it. Your reformist demigods are merely devils turned inside out.

After "The Raven" Poe composed about a dozen poems to bring the total number to scarcely fifty. "The Bells" is a case of onomatopoeia pushed to a point where it would hardly be possible or desirable to go again. "Ulalume," appearing in the year after the death of his wife, voices a strange collision of passions, and Poe is reported to have said that its ending "was scarcely clear to himself." This poem presents all the paradoxes that have so divided Poe's critics. It uses again the hypnotic repetitions that he inaugurated with "The Raven," and subordinates meaning to music. Mallarmé deemed it "perhaps the most original and the most strangely suggestive of all Poe's poems," but Huxley thinks that its "walloping" dactyls are "all too musical." Furthermore, those whose musical tastes are severer than Poe's declare that, despite his challenging analogies between music and mathematics, he showed little technical knowledge of the subject, since he so readily confused the musical with the vaguely indefinite. Again he professed to be a craftsman devoted to perfection, and was capable of rhyming "vista" with "sister." He was a super-rational analyst, the meaning of whose poems often eludes any analysis. The limitations of his terminology are apparent once more, for he declared that "a passionate poem is a contradiction in terms." He tried rigidly to restrict "passion" to "sexual desire" in contrast to "ideal love"; but those who respond to "Ulalume" are stirred by a deeply compulsive passion.

In "Eldorado" Poe voiced the pursuit of the ideal which should supplant "the gold-fever," and in revising now one of his earliest lyrics he added the lines,

> *All* that we see or seem
> Is but a dream within a dream.

But his latest poetry was by no means all escape. He became more directly personal in his sonnet for Mrs. Clemm, whom he called his "mother," in token of his dependence upon her after Virginia's death. His stanzas "For Annie" were torn out of his knowledge of tragedy. "Annabel Lee" raises the same issue that he raised in the preface to his *Tales*. For some readers it evokes merely an imitation Gothic "kingdom by the sea." But Poe knew that his longing for remote beauty could not be divorced from mortal sadness. His prevailing theme was ruin, and the intensity of his imagination could transform even the thinnest trappings of romance into the moving climax:

> And so, all the night-tide, I lie down by the side
> Of my darling, my darling, my life and my bride,
> In her sepulchre there by the sea—
> In her tomb by the side of the sea.

This poem did not appear until just after Poe's death. He had gone back to Richmond in the summer of 1849, still in the hope of founding his magazine, and turning away again from a harsh North to a South that was actually even more indifferent to his ambitions. He spoke for the first time of "an attack of *mania a potu*." But he found some happiness, and after a swift courtship became engaged to his boyhood sweetheart, Elmira Royster, now a widow. At the end of September he started North to attend to some literary hack work and to see Mrs. Clemm. Nothing is really known about what happened during the next week until he was picked up unconscious near a polling booth in Baltimore. When he regained consciousness, he passed into a violent delirium, and kept crying out for "Reynolds"—the man whose concern with the importance of exploring the South Seas had stimulated the composition of *Pym*. Perhaps Poe's fevered mind had returned to such details as he had conjured up in "MS Found in a Bottle," the first instance when he projected his inner world through the horror of his sensation that he was "hurrying onwards to some exciting knowledge—some never-to-be-imparted secret, whose attainment is destruction." He died of acute congestion of the brain, and was buried near his grandfather in the Presbyterian cemetery. He had recently written in *Marginalia*: "There are moments when, even to the sober eye of Reason, the world of our sad humanity must assume the aspect of Hell." He was one whom "unmerciful disaster" had "followed fast and followed faster" to the end.

7

Poe's final value may hardly be judged apart from the many traditions to which his work gave rise. French Symbolism, with its desire to attain the suggestiveness of music, began at the moment when Baudelaire recognized in Poe's logical formulas for a poem his own half-developed thoughts, "combined to perfection." But Baudelaire was indebted to Poe for more than form. He took the title for his intimate journal from a phrase in *Marginalia,* "my heart laid bare," and attributed to Poe's reaffirmation of evil the recovery of human dignity from the shallowness of the optimistic reformers. Another note in *Marginalia,* "The orange ray of the spectrum and the buzz of the gnat . . . affect me with nearly similar sensations," led to Baudelaire's epoch-making sonnet, "Correspondances," and in turn to Rimbaud's further development of this same doctrine of the interpenetration of the senses. Rimbaud's masterpiece, "Le Bateau ivre," also confirmed the degree to which Poe's image of man's destiny as a frail boat out of control on the flowing waters of life was to become a major symbol for the age. Meanwhile, Gautier and the Parnassian group had found in "The Philosophy of Composition" their conception that the form creates the idea. The relevance of all these complex developments to American poetry lies in the profound attraction that T. S. Eliot and Wallace Stevens were to discover in symbolism, and thence to bring Poe back to American art by way of France.

Poe's introspective heroes begat a long line of descendants. As Edmund Wilson demonstrated so brilliantly, the remote castle that Villiers de L'Isle-Adam's Axel inhabits was inherited from Roderick Usher; and when Huysmans voiced through his Des Esseintes the doctrines of decadence, almost every artificial detail of his shut-in paradise was borrowed from Poe's interiors, as was the disordered preoccupation with what Usher himself had called "a morbid acuteness of the senses." The furthest possible withdrawal of the hero from the responsibilities of a hostile world might seem to be that in Proust, and although nationalists in criticism now view with alarm any effect in America of such European influences, the feeling that the artist is at war with a business civilization was as much Hart Crane's as it was Poe's.

This may still seem to leave Poe remote from the main currents of American thought. And although Hawthorne admired the originality of his tales, and Lowell had been quick to recognize his double gift for imagination and analysis, the first generation of realists passed Poe by. Both Howells and Twain found his method as "mechanical" as Henry James did; and for the belated dedication of his tomb in 1875, Mallarmé wrote his great sonnet, but Whitman alone among important American writers attended—and Whitman judged Poe to belong finally "among the electric lights of imaginative literature, brilliant and dazzling, but with no heat." Yet his ultimate effect upon our most popular literature was enormous. As much as anyone ever invents a genre, Poe invented the detective story. He also inaugurated the vogue for the pseudoscientific romance and for that of adolescent adventure,

Jules Verne, Stevenson, and Conan Doyle are equally in his debt. "The Gold Bug," "The Pit and the Pendulum," and "The Murders in the Rue Morgue" have now been read by millions oblivious of their author's aesthetic theories.

The notion has sometimes been advanced that the materialism of so many of Poe's interests, his fondness for inventions and hoaxes, and his special flair for journalism made him more "representative" than Emerson or Whitman of ordinary Americans. His more serious importance was noted by the Goncourt brothers, who declared in their journal for 1856 that here was "the literature of the twentieth century," an analytic literature that would be more given to what passes in the brain than in the heart. That distinction may be as brittle as some of Poe's own, but the intense investigation of the roots of Gothic horror in morbid states of mind has been part of American fiction from Brockden Brown and Poe through Ambrose Bierce and William Faulkner.

Poe wrote at a time when America was producing more real and alleged transcendental geniuses than maturely wrought poems or stories. In opposition to the romantic stress on the expression of personality, he insisted on the importance, not of the artist, but of the created work of art. He stands as one of the very few great innovators in American literature. Like Henry James and T. S. Eliot, he took his place, almost from the start, in international culture as an original creative force in contrast to the more superficial international vogue of Cooper and Irving.

LITERARY FULFILLMENT

24. DEMOCRATIC VISTAS

In quality of style, and particularly in depth of philosophic insight, American literature has not yet surpassed the collective achievement of Emerson, Thoreau, Hawthorne, Melville, and Whitman. Having freed itself in these writers from its earlier tendencies either blindly to imitate or blindly to reject European models, American literature here for the first time sloughed off provincialism, and, by being itself—by saying only what it wanted to say and as it wanted to say it—attained, paradoxically, the rank and quality of world literature, a literature authentic not only in America but everywhere the English tongue is understood.

The release was both material and social. There was, to begin with, the increasing social fluidity of the mid-nineteenth century in the East, with its accompanying sense of unlimited cultural possibilities. While the West was expanding and experimenting, those parts of the country which had by now been settled for more than two hundred years began to lose their sharp social and regional contrasts and to settle into a cultural homogeneity more like that of the older civilizations of Europe, though built firmly on a democratic base.

The social stratification of the seaboard colonies, with their mercantile and landed aristocracies, their small farmers, their squatters, and their slaves, had begun to disintegrate during the Revolution, but was not yet reshaped into the industrial class structure of the future. Regionally, colonial distinctions had also broken down with the mounting pressure of populations to the eastward—from Europe to the Atlantic seaboard and from the seaboard to the frontier. The slow process of eroding these regional differences, so important in colonial assemblies, had already achieved, by the intermingling of ideas and of local customs, the national feeling which was to culminate later in a simpler, more inclusive, division of the country into the North, the South, and the West.

Moreover, this flux of institutions and people was marked not by a sense of loss or confusion but by a sense of potentiality and expectancy. The era of good feeling following the War of 1812—a war which at first seemed lost but was miraculously retrieved—had affected all levels of the national life and, blinding men to the risk of the American experiment, revealed only its adventure. And this spirit of self-confidence had been fed by other fires: by the material promise of timber, land, and waterway, convertible at a touch into ready wealth; and by the technological promise—already apparent—of American mechanical and social invention.

Yet neither the general confidence nor the manifold promises of the period can alone explain the peak reached by American literature at this time. For this we must turn to a third and more decisive factor: the reorientation of literature under the influence of New England transcendentalism. For, by reawakening—even among its critics—an interest in the great problems of human nature and destiny, transcendentalism conferred upon American literature a perspective far wider and deeper than that proposed by its own formulated doctrines, the perspective of humanity itself. This perspective it is which gives common purpose and meaning to the otherwise divergent achievements of Emerson, Thoreau, Hawthorne, Melville, and Whitman, and accounts in great part for their manifest superiority to precedessors like Irving and Bryant whose interests were less profound and more superficially literary.

2

Transcendentalism emerged as a full-fledged movement of New England thought between 1815 and 1836. The first date marks the maturing of the liberalizing ministry of William Ellery Channing; the second, the publication of Emerson's *Nature,* the original—and probably the best—systematic expression of the transcendentalist philosophy. Thereafter the movement continued to expand, first as a revolt against the sterile Unitarian orthodoxy, then as a protest against the continuing cultural dependence of America on Europe, and finally as a profound exploration of the spiritual foundations and moral implications of the new democracy. From the beginning it attracted eccentrics no less than men of genius, and after the Civil War it gave way to weaker forms of idealism. But at its zenith in the writings of Emerson, Thoreau, and Alcott—and by its challenge to fresh speculation in Hawthorne, Melville, and Whitman—its vitalizing effect upon American art and literature and, indeed, upon the development of American democracy as a whole, remains unrivaled.

The source of this vitality lies in the intellectual background of transcendentalism: in its appropriation of certain insights of Puritan, Quaker, and other colonial theologies as they had been refracted through the secular and equalitarian ideology of the Revolution; and in its reexpression of these insights in the vocabulary of contemporary European philosophy. For in spite of its oft proclaimed rejection of authority and its frankly nationalistic bias transcendentalism was rooted both in the American past and in the Europe of that day.

To Puritanism in the broadest sense, for example, it owed among other things its pervasive moralism. Like all those early pioneers who sought freedom of conscience in a new land, the transcendentalists were ever disposed to interpret life ethically, to subordinate the aesthetic, intellectual, and even political and economic aspects of human nature to man's significance as a moral agent. Once again, after two centuries and more, this conception was used as a means of dignifying all phases of human activity, even the most humble. Thus, just as the Mathers, Edwards, Penn, Woolman, and even Franklin had alike maintained that each man is "called" to perform as faithfully as he can the duties of his particular station in life, so Emerson argued that every act of the individual springs from his inner nature as a unique embodiment of humanity, and hence no occupation is inherently ignoble.

A similar affinity may be discovered between transcendental "intuition" and the doctrine of the "inner light." For each of these theories interpreted material nature mystically as a "veil" or symbol of the divine; and each maintained that every individual can penetrate the veil to discover divine truth for himself without the aid of traditional authority or even of logic.

But none of these doctrines had been transmitted in its original form. The Puritan orthodoxy of New England had from the earliest times been subject to the filtering process of dissent, and had finally succumbed as a rigid and dominant system to the less precise and more rationalized theology of the Unitarians. The tendencies thus manifest on the level of religious thinking were even stronger on that of secular radicalism during the Revolutionary epoch. The worldliness and "common sense" of a Franklin or a Jefferson had apparently made a clean break with earlier orthodoxies while retaining their zeal for moral enlightenment; and the same tendency had but recently moved even further from theological sanction in the equalitarian theory of Jacksonian democracy. These latter-day and transplanted expressions of the Reformation and the Enlightenment, which had coalesced in the preachings of William Ellery Channing and other predecessors of the transcendental movement in New England, had in some instances added to, but in all instances had transformed, the orthodox teachings of the early religious and secular leaders.

This is illustrated in the new meanings given to the old doctrine of the sovereignty of ethics. For one thing, the equalitarian implications of the doctrine were secularized and broadened to a degree hitherto unknown in this country. Whereas in the orthodox Puritan interpretation the doctrine of the equality of man with man was largely theoretical—being restricted to a mere hypothetical equality before God and the law—and, even in the political philosophy of the Revolution, had accepted social stratification, Jacksonian individualism demanded that it be applied as a practical principle of social reform calling for local autonomy, free public education, and universal suffrage on a scale undreamed of even by Jefferson. Coincidentally, the scope of the principle had been broadened. In place of the old invidious distinction between the elect and the damned which had suggested that only a chosen few were to be admitted to spiritual equality, the Unitarian and Universalist emphasis on the brotherhood of man proclaimed the perfectibility of all.

Still more subtly, this leveling process reoriented the very concept of ethics itself. For although it was still insisted that moral obligation is transcendent in origin—is determined by more than personal whim or habit—that obligation could no longer be construed in abstract universal terms or continue to be rooted in the will of an arbitrary God. Under the influence of Unitarianism, Deity was reduced to a kind of immanent principle implicit in man everywhere, and man himself thereby was made the true source of the moral law. Also, instead of continuing to conceive moral obligation legalistically—as a kind of ritualistic observance of a general code—it was now argued that no single code fits all situations adequately and that each individual must be left perfectly free to judge for himself what his actual duty on any given occasion is. Thus theology made its final effort to provide religious sanction for equalitarian tendencies inherent in the republic from the start.

Equally radical was the transformation of the doctrine of the inner light brought about by the acknowledgment of the autonomous power of secular reason, in part aided by the accelerating conquests of natural science. For this acknowledgment—validated anew by the role of reason in formulating the principles of the Revolution, and manifested concretely both in the rationalism of Unitarian theology and in the pragmatism of frontier thought—had undermined belief in the inner light at two points.

In the first place, it challenged the theoretical competence of the inner light. Although often authoritarian in spirit itself, the new emphasis on reason was wholly antiauthoritarian in implication. Holding with Locke that all knowledge is perceptual in origin, it demanded that every truth be held subject to the test of experiment and observation. And this was a test which, with its implicit mysticism, the doctrine of the inner light as the word of God could not hope to sustain.

In the second place, the new emphasis on reason challenged the doctrine of the inner light on the score of its immediate utility. For while the older doctrine could promise only the quietistic value of bringing man face to face with God, the reason, practically applied, promised a control of nature itself and thereby the immediate satisfaction of human needs.

Yet neither the period generally, nor Unitarianism and democracy in particular, was so pragmatically inclined as to deny the possibility of religious insight entirely. The hold of the Christian tradition upon belief and imagination was still too strong. Nevertheless, certain changes in the conception of the inner light were effected. One of these was to restrict the scope of the inner light to the moral and speculative sphere and to concede to observation priority in the understanding of nature. Another and more important change was the transformation of the inner light into a wholly natural organ. Instead of being dependent, as in the early orthodoxies, upon divine Grace—upon a kind of flooding of the mind by light from without—the power of the inner light was now grounded in the nature of the mind itself, becoming merely one mental faculty among others and subject, therefore, to the same degree of individual control. It was converted, in other words, from a "revelation," an act and agency of God, into an "intuition," an act and agency of man.

It is doubtful whether these transformations of the Puritan ethic and theory of knowledge ever could have become more than vague intellectual tendencies of the time or could have achieved the degree of articulate formulation they subsequently did without the stimulus of contemporary European philosophy. There had emerged in Germany an intellectually sophisticated movement elaborately embodied in the systems of Fichte, Schelling, Schleiermacher, and Hegel, and—at a further remove—in the thought of Coleridge, Carlyle, and Victor Cousin. This movement, idealistic in nature, had its specialized formulas and idioms, its accepted premises and methods. In literature it took the form of romanticism.

It was also a movement whose influence began to be felt in New England about 1820. New England interest in German thought generally goes back much further: to William Bentley who acted as cultural ambassador between the merchants of Hamburg and of Salem in the late years of the eighteenth and the early years of the nineteenth century; and, beyond Bentley, to the correspondence of Cotton Mather with the Pietistic theologians of Halle. The interest was not widespread until after the War of 1812, when it became intellectually fashionable for younger New England to make the grand tour or to enroll in German universities, and when particular notice began to be taken of German philosophy as reflected in the writings of its English and French disciples. Later, many of the transcendentalists were to make some pretense of studying German philosophy directly; but their initial—and probably most enduring—impression of the movement was derived from such secondary sources as Marsh's edition (1829) of Coleridge's *Aids to Reflection,* Linberg's translation (1832) of Cousin's *Introduction to the History of Philosophy,* and Carlyle's *Sartor Resartus* (1836).

What was important in this influence was the fact that it made available to the New England writers and through them to American writers generally an elaborate symbolic construction capable not only of expressing the general metaphysical hesitancy of the period—its inability either to retreat into frank supernaturalism or to advance to a bold materialism—but also of providing principles and distinctions whereby this midway position could be explored and defended.

Thus, the doctrine of human individuality as both self-transcending and self-asserting—as both acknowledging its oneness with and obligation to something higher than itself, and yet ever cherishing its uniqueness and independence as a distinct being—and the further conception that individual happiness depends upon the successful synthesis of these twin tendencies, provided an almost perfect theoretical framework for a new effort to discover supernatural sanction for the swift-moving and constantly changing panorama of American life.

Similarly, the distinction found in Coleridge and Emerson alike, between the reason and the understanding—which, by a curious distortion of terminology, identified the reason with intuition and imagination, and the understanding with logic and induction—could express and justify the transcendentalist's desire to retain both the mysticism of the past and the empiricism of the present, and to assign each a sphere in experience proper to its character.

Finally, the idealistic view of the universe as an embodiment of a single, cosmic psyche, now manifesting itself as man, now as nature, and achieving through the interaction of the two in history its own secret intent, permitted the self-asserting impulse of the individual—his determination to be himself at all costs—to be explained as the consciousness of his identity with the world-psyche, while his self-transcending or outgoing impulses could be attributed to the consciousness of his own finitude, to the fact of his awareness that he is only one fragmentary expression of the world-psyche among others. The theory could also account for and validate the distinction between the intuitive and the inductive, interpreting the first of these faculties as the necessary condition for conscious union with the world-psyche, and the second as the necessary condition for survival as a separate expression of that psyche.

The initial function of this movement was thus to act as a kind of model and repository of ideas from which American, and in particular New England, writers could borrow in their self-imposed task of creating a new metaphysic for democracy out of the theological and intellectual materials of the American past. Without slavishly imitating this model, but still inspired by it in various degrees, Emerson, Thoreau, Whitman, and even, by contraries, Hawthorne and Melville were able to achieve a curious blending of the alien and the native, a blending in which specific traditional conceptions were adjusted to specific American use. This fusion is apparent, for example, in Emerson's appeal to the Over-Soul as a sanction for Yankee self-reliance, in Thoreau's discovery that Walden recapitulated the universe in small, and—by its very failure—in Melville's ambiguities. It is also apparent in Whitman's *Democratic Vistas,* which preached a new brotherhood of man in terms of the mystic unity of creation, "the divine central idea of All."

But European idealism was to act as more than a mere model for New England transcendentalism. For, working in and through transcendentalism —and reinforced a little later by the influx of roughly similar teachings from the Orient—its influence leavened American literature as a whole, including even the writings of men like Hawthorne and Melville who were actively opposed to transcendentalism proper. The general leavening consisted not so much in the transmission and implanting of specific borrowings—although this also occurred—as it did in the setting of problems and perspectives like the nature of the universe, the origin of evil, and the meaning of experience, which were destined to give American literature a universal import and eventually swing it into the orbit of world literature.

3

At first sight, Emerson, Thoreau, Hawthorne, Melville, and Whitman seem to differ from one another more than they agree. For one thing, they are divergent in temperament. Thoreau, Whitman, and—above all—Emerson are prevailingly optimistic. Hawthorne, on the other hand, is at least fatalistic in point of view; while Melville seems to have run the entire emotional gamut from optimism through pessimism to final resignation. Again, all of them differ widely in their choice of subject matter and literary form. Primarily novelists, Hawthorne and Melville are concerned with the psychological and allegorical analysis of certain types of human personality and moral situations; primarily poets and essayists, Emerson, Thoreau, and Whitman focus, each in his own way, upon the underlying relation of man to nature.

Most widely of all, they differ in their interest and capacity for sustained philosophical thought. None of them could be described as interested in philosophical theory for its own sake—not even Emerson, who is less intolerant of abstract reasoning than the rest. But even within these limits their divergency is still great. For although we can find at least traces of a comprehensive philosophical system in Emerson, the traces become progressively more rudimentary in Thoreau, Melville, and Whitman, until at last in Hawthorne they almost disappear.

Yet this incommensurability is not absolute. Common to them, as to all great writers, is a profound sense of the human predicament, of the questions that beset man as man, and of the relation of these problems to man's defects and potentialities. Their common concern surmounts all differences, as may be seen in Emerson's and Hawthorne's treatment of the problem of evil. When Emerson proclaims the non-existence of evil in an ultimate form and Hawthorne rejects this conception as tragically blind, neither writer is proceeding on the assumption that the problem of evil itself is unreal or trivial. For Hawthorne, as we know, it is the most pressing of all problems, while for Emerson—as the haunting overtones of "Experience" intimate—it is a problem which can be optimistically resolved only after the most desperate of inward struggles and only after attaining a serenity almost stripped of emotion. In other words, the difference between the two lies not in their conception of the importance of the problem but only in their conception of its proper solution.

Common also to all these writers is the framework of ideas within which they seek to understand the problem of man. Even when it provides quite divergent solutions the framework or perspective is in all instances radically humanistic.

Its basic premise is that man is the spiritual center of the universe and that in man alone can we find the clue to nature, history, and ultimately the cosmos itself. Without denying outright the existence either of God or of brute matter, it nevertheless rejects them as exclusive principles of interpretation and prefers to explain man and his world so far as possible in terms of man himself. This is expressed most clearly in the transcendentalist principle that the structure of the universe literally duplicates the structure of the individual self, and that all knowledge therefore begins with self-knowledge. But it is no less evident in the moral earnestness of Hawthorne and Melville, which leads them to dwell ceaselessly upon the allegory of the human soul and to personalize impersonal nature itself as an allegory of human experience. It is because of this, for example, that few incidents in their plots ever turn out to be wholly fortuitous or to be without symbolic significance for the characters involved in them.

This common perspective is also, in all cases, radically universalized. Its emphasis is almost never upon man as particular—as European, say, or as American—but almost always upon man as universal, upon man as freed from the accidents of time and space as well as from those of birth and talent and reduced to his common humanity. It is apparent not only in Emerson and Thoreau but also in Hawthorne, Melville, and Whitman; none of them even in the most concrete and practical moments can ever quite forget that the drama of man is clothed with the aspect of eternity. Thus, for Emerson, the "American Scholar" turns out to be simply "Man Thinking"; while, for Whitman, the song of himself merges imperceptibly into a song of all the "children of Adam," where "every atom belonging to me as good belongs to you." Thus also, in spite of a frequently high degree of individualization, the characters and situations of Hawthorne and Melville are fundamentally impersonal, emerging at their best as a fusion of particular and type but at their worst as types only.

This turning away from the current scientific view of the world and regression under the impetus of European idealism to the Neo-Platonic conception of nature as a living mystery full of signs and portents, revives a conception with which some of the five were already familiar from their reading in the literature of the seventeenth century and of religious mysticism. At the same time, a principle of correspondence is evolved which promises the reconciliation rather than the rejection of science.

Nor can we overestimate the practical importance of this conception from either the literary or the social point of view. In terms of literature, for instance, its construing of nature as inherently symbolic invests the natural faculty of imagination with a new prestige, dissolving the older literary emphasis upon wit, sentiment, and rationality, and preparing the way for the symbolist literature to come. Even more far-reaching are the social implications of the conception. For by postulating, as it does, an identity between the categories of impersonal nature and the categories of human psychology—and thereby also the unity of creation—the conception provides a metaphysical basis for the belief in democratic equality to which the social philosophy of Emerson, Thoreau, and Whitman can and does appeal.

The second assumption common to all five writers is the belief that individual virtue and happiness depend upon self-realization, and that self-realization, in turn, depends upon the harmonious reconciliation of two universal psychological tendencies: first, the expansive or self-transcending impulse of the self, its desire to embrace the whole world in the experience of a single moment and to know and become one with that world; and second, the contracting or self-asserting impulse of the individual, his desire to withdraw, to remain unique and separate, and to be responsible only to himself.

The current theory of self as expounded by Coleridge and other Europeans was adaptable here, and its importance was more than theoretical because it stated in universal terms the central goal and problem of democracy itself. On the one hand, democracy as a moral and political doctrine implied an ethic of extreme individualism, one which preserved to the individual a maximum degree of freedom and self-expression. On the other hand, the democratic self was divided. There was, first, the conflict between its traditional sense of duty to God and its new-found sense of duty to man. There was, second, the conflict between the duty to self as implied by the concept of liberty and the duty to society as implied by the other two concepts of the revolutionary triad, equality and fraternity. Hence, a doctrine which recognizes the divisions in the self and insists that their reconciliation is necessary for true self-realization defines not only the democratic ethic in general but also the specific hope of democracy that the self can be realized without sacrificing any side of its nature, altruistic as well as egoistic.

There can be no doubt that all five of the writers define the ethical ideal in these terms, although, characteristically, they disagree both on *how* the ideal is to be actualized and on the degree to which it is actualizable. Thus Emerson, Thoreau, and Whitman, who accept its actualization as a real possibility because they have assumed to begin with that the self and the cosmos express one and the same spiritual force, disagree on what specific course of action will convert their inner harmony into an outward fact. For while Emerson and Thoreau believed the harmony can be fully realized by the simple, though paradoxical, expedient of forgetting the world and being true only to oneself, Whitman seems to hold that there is needed an unlimited love of creation as such, a love that will include the self and the world as one.

In contrast to these three stand Hawthorne and Melville, who doubt whether a genuine harmony between the individual and his cosmos is possible at all. For although both assume that the destiny of man is ever to seek such a harmony, they are also deeply convinced that the self and the cosmos are victim to tragic flaws which prevent their ever realizing it. Hawthorne discovers the flaws both in the spiritual pride and spiritual weakness of the individual and in the intractability of his social environment. And Melville identifies them with a defect in the universe at large, symbolized in the inscrutability of the white whale.

But both writers hold that the flaws, in all cases, effectively block a final rapport between the individual and the world. For although the conflict between these two protagonists is sometimes susceptible of an emotional resolution—either by a daemonic assertion of the will, as in Captain Ahab, or by the will's abnegation, as in Hester Prynne and Billy Budd—the resolution is only partial since it is at the cost of eliminating either the world or the self from final moral consideration. In other words, where Emerson, Thoreau, and Whitman discover in the romantic theory of self-realization grounds for ultimate hope, Hawthorne and Melville draw from it only tragic irresolution.

The third assumption common to the five writers is that intuition and imagination offer a surer road to truth than abstract logic or scientific method. It is a corollary to their belief that nature is organic, and corresponds to the technical distinction between the reason as intuition and the understanding as logical analysis. In the specific form of this distinction, the assumption appears frequently in Emerson. But as a general principle underlying both theory and practice it is present in all.

It is illustrated by their emphasis upon introspection—their belief that the clue to outer nature is always to be found in the inner world of individual psychology—and by their constant interpretation of experience as in essence symbolic. For both these stresses presume an organic relationship between the self and the cosmos of which only intuition and imagination can properly take account.

Finally, in terms of the third assumption, all five writers were able to deduce a consequence of immense practical importance not only for their own work but for the subsequent course of American literature as a whole. Not only could the belief in the primacy of imagination be used to justify their own tendency toward the concrete, the metaphorical, and the didactic; it also had the wider implication of attaching greater significance to the craft of literature generally. Once the faculty of imagination is placed on a par with the faculty of reason, the writer as the primary exponent of the imagination acquires an importance in society at least equal to that of the scientist, the philosopher, and the theologian. All equally can then claim to be engaged in the same pursuit: the search for truth.

It is undoubtedly their faith in the imagination and in themselves as practitioners of imagination that enabled Emerson, Thoreau, Hawthorne, Melville, and Whitman to achieve supreme confidence in their own moral and metaphysical insights. It is this also that led them to conceive of the writer as a seer, and thus to exemplify in their attitude toward literature the emphasis upon its responsibility to life which is characteristic of our own day.

4

The close affinity between the idealism of contemporary European philosophy and the romanticism of Emerson, Thoreau, Melville, Hawthorne, and Whitman must not be pressed to the point of identity or to the exclusion of other influences. The sharing between European and American thinkers of common concepts and a common idiom for their expression is merely one more evidence that the young nation was beginning to lose its provincialism and to take its place in the main flow of Western culture. American philosophical thinking had remained true to its own origins, which were of course European in the first instance, through the periods of settlement, early development, and now a first maturity. Once more it could look to Europe for a confirmation by parallel of its own conclusions.

There were, however, significant differences as well as similarities. Where the Europeans of the eighteenth and nineteenth centuries were predominantly intellectual and aesthetic in their interests, the Americans were predominantly moral; and where the Europeans often tended to underscore the role of hierarchy and institutional stability in human affairs, the Americans stressed the ideas of equality and freedom from state interference.

Nor was European philosophy the only such force to act as a catalyst on the nineteenth century American mind. Its importance was taken for granted even though it was not fully understood by the earlier critics of New England transcendentalism. Recently there has been a tendency to underestimate it in favor of the obvious influences of Neo-Platonic and Oriental kinds of idealism in giving new forms and a new vocabulary to American thinkers. Historians have demonstrated the catalytic effect of Plato and Plotinus on Emerson and of the Bhagavad-Gita and other Oriental tales and poems on Emerson and Thoreau. But more often than not such influences out of the past were shared by American writers with their European contemporaries, and the precise channels or directions of their flow can be distinguished only with the greatest difficulty. The minds of Emerson, Whitman, and Melville were characteristically American in their willingness to appropriate usable ideas wherever they might be found, without too much concern for logical consistency, and it is safer to assume that these men obtained many of their principal assumptions—or at least the language in which such ideas found expression—through their alert interest in the dominant intellectual movements of the time rather than from any single source in the past.

Whatever the sources or channels of their common feeling, the fact remains that there existed between these five Americans and their European contemporaries a community of interest based upon the use of a common philosophical idiom and upon the discovery, as a result of the common vocabulary, of a common set of problems approached in a common spirit. This community helps explain the promptness with which Emerson, Thoreau, and others of the group were "discovered" and acclaimed abroad. It also helps explain the almost proprietary sense these writers themselves had in European literary and philosophical movements.

Of even greater moment was the fact that contact with European philosophy and literature established a spiritual continuity not only with their contemporaries but with the great literary and philosophical traditions of the past. For in rediscovering such fundamental conceptions of Western culture as the correspondence between man and nature and the doctrine of the poet as seer, these writers acquired something more than a set of inert principles. Rather, by means of these ideas—by accident of the fact that the ideas had been perennial to Western thought—they acquired that spirit of universality which has characterized Western literature at its greatest moments, even making it capable of absorbing the best of the Orient. Thus the preoccupation with local customs, local legends, and local scenes characteristic of the earlier writers in the seaboard states, and again of those of the frontier, was generalized, at least for a moment of literary fulfillment, into a profound concern with human nature, while democracy itself instead of continuing to be construed as a mere experiment in government was now subjected to a more thorough examination of its fundamental moral and metaphysical meanings.

In other words, European philosophical theory, acting as a primary catalyst for forces already deeply indigenous to the American mind, had effected and accelerated a reorientation of literature which was tantamount to raising it to a new plane. Having revealed the American character and experience as identical in form and substance with the character and experience of man everywhere, it had created the conditions whereby American literature without ceasing to be national could become a part of world literature. And it is one measure of the genius of Emerson, Thoreau, Hawthorne, Melville, and Whitman that they were able to transmute this possibility into an opportunity.

25. RALPH WALDO EMERSON

From these currents of thought and feeling Emerson emerged as the delegated intellect—his own "Man Thinking." "There are periods fruitful of great men," he wrote, "others barren . . . periods when the heat is latent,—others when it is given out." A half-century had passed since the United States had been baptized in political independence; the time had now come for confirmation in freedom of the soul. Ralph Waldo Emerson, of Concord, Massachusetts, declared the ceremony performed and became spokesman for his time and country.

His preeminence has caused our literary historians some embarrassment. America was ready for a Shakespeare, a Dante, or a Dostoevski to give literary voice to her achieved majority. She was given an apologist—an Aristotle, a Paul, a Bacon. In the wise and temperate Emerson, the heat became radiant light. It was he who brought into its first sharp focus the full meaning of two centuries of life on the Atlantic seaboard of this continent; of the economic and spiritual revolutions which had unsettled the Old World and settled the New; of the experiment in democracy which was to make a Holy Commonwealth into a world power.

He did this in two ways: by carrying to its ultimate statement the individual's revolt from authority, which marked the transition from the medieval world to the modern; and by formulating the dichotomy between the vision of a Jonathan Edwards and the common sense of a Benjamin Franklin, a conflict and a balance which has always provided the creative tension in American life. But he translated these discoveries neither into formal philosophy nor into fully formed art. His logic and his metaphysics remained without system; his art, like that of all great American romantics, retained its organic freedom.

As Emerson had no Boswell, he must speak for himself, and he spent his life in doing so. Upon an audience he played with the sure hands of a master organist; but the oft shuffled manuscripts in his study were cold. "We do not go to hear what Emerson says," wrote Lowell, "so much as to hear Emerson." A tall blond figure in black, he leaned forward across the reading desk in shy

Yankee awkwardness and searched the hearts of his hearers with sincere blue eyes and controlled voice.

"Where do we find ourselves?" he asks in his essay on "Experience," and he gives his answer: "On its own level, or in view of nature, temperament is final." The inner wholeness of the man is his true self; his life "is a train of moods like a string of beads"; temperament, the iron wire on which the beads are strung. Striving to give expression only and always to this central self, Emerson has left a handful of essays and poems which are to many an essential part of their religious literature; but the man himself evades discovery. "So much of our time is preparation," he explains, "so much is routine, and so much retrospect, that the pith of each man's genius contracts itself to a very few hours."

Preparation—routine—retrospect; these are the entries on the calendar, the frame of life for a reticent New England man who is Emerson the seer. He devoted thirty-three years to what he thought of later as "preparation" before he published his first book in 1836; some two decades provided the "very few hours" when his genius was at high pitch and all of his great work was produced from the essential stability and calm of "routine"; and finally there were almost thirty years of "retrospect" before his death in 1882. The central twenty years have left us our impression of a man who always stood firm on moral ground and admonished his fellows to turn their eyes from evil, to have faith in themselves and in one another, and to seek God through Nature. But the Emersonian confidence and calm were not achieved, nor were they maintained, without struggle, doubt, and self-examination.

2

The chronicle of Emerson's preparation may be reconstructed from letters and journals; it would have been alien to his temperament to leave an autobiography of the soul such as *Sartor Resartus, Dichtung und Wahrheit,* or the *Confessions* of Rousseau. But the romantic pattern of introspection, doubt, and psychological crisis found in a Carlyle or a Goethe was his as well, marked by the familiar circumstances of poverty, loneliness, illness, idealized love, and the discovery of death.

Poverty was the lot of his youth. The second of four boys, he was only eight years old when his father died in 1811 and the congregation of the "Old Brick" Church in Boston granted the "pious and amiable" widow home and subsistence for a few years, while the boys shared one winter overcoat and the housework, studied their grammar, and ended the "toils of the day," as Ralph reports to his Aunt Mary, with their private devotions.

During Ralph's school and college days this diminutive aunt, appearing suddenly out of her private wandering for visits at the Emerson home or writing admonitory letters to her adopted spiritual orphans, became the substitute for both father and conscience. Her life, writes her nephew, "marked the precise time when the power of the old creed yielded to the influence of modern science and humanity." The zeal and consecration of Puritan ancestors was mingled in the latter-day sibyl with shrewd common sense and an insatiable intellectual curiosity. Mary Moody Emerson lived this life in preparation for the next, but she lived it with gusto. The correspondence between her and her nephew charts his course as his mind and spirit grew. There is solemn thought and wiry humor in the letters of both, even though the boy's sophistication is sophomoric, that of the little old lady crisp and intricate. For Aunt Mary was both mystic and critic, Calvinist and skeptic; Ralph could laugh at her because he profoundly respected her. To her he took both his doubts and his discoveries. She sharpened his wit and deepened his perceptions. Here is at least one source for that mixture of insight and common sense which characterized his thought, that aphoristic directness which sharpened his style.

During these early years, Emerson learned the habit of introspection. His intimate experience with people seems hardly to have extended beyond the family. "The friends that occupy my thoughts," he wrote at Harvard, "are not men, but certain phantoms clothed in the form and face and apparel of men by whom they were suggested and to whom they bear a resemblance." But his intimacy with his brothers, William, Edward, and Charles, was close. The journals which he, and apparently Charles as well, kept from an early age have not all survived, for the first is now dated 1819 from Harvard; but even in these we can see the somewhat affected litterateur gradually recede and the true man emerge. By 1824, the journals have ceased to be a "motley diary" and have become a "soliloquy," a "savings bank" where he can deposit his earnings. Here is the workshop, with saw, hammer, and plane, where the raw lumber of thought, reading, and experience is stored and worked. There is a vast difference between the early and late volumes. The first four or five constitute a moving autobiography of the spirit, but the others may be read in almost any order and are most enjoyable when dipped into. Between 1820 and 1836, when his inner life was growing steadily, the record of his progress has dramatic conflict and movement. Thereafter the journals gradually become to the reader what they were to him, a mine to be worked rather than a journey to be taken.

To poverty and introspection was added a struggle with sickness and adversity sufficient to supply a romantic hero with all the sorrows he might need. For the shadow of the white plague lay across the Emerson household, and Ralph barely escaped its doom. It carried off his two younger brothers,